T0337998

DIGITAL
GOVERNMENT
EXCELLENCE

DIGITAL GOVERNMENT EXCELLENCE

LESSONS FROM EFFECTIVE DIGITAL LEADERS

Siim Sikkut

WILEY

Published by John Wiley & Sons, Inc., Hoboken, New Jersey.
Published simultaneously in Canada.

For general information on our other products and services or for technical support, please contact our Customer Care Department within the United States at (800) 762-2974, outside the United States at (317) 572-3993 or fax (317) 572-4002.

Wiley also publishes its books in a variety of electronic formats. Some content that appears in print may not be available in electronic formats. For more information about Wiley products, visit our web site at www.wiley.com.

Library of Congress Cataloging-in-Publication Data

Names: Sikkut, Siim, author. | John Wiley & Sons, publisher.
Title: Digital government excellence : lessons from effective digital
  leaders / Siim Sikkut.
Description: Hoboken, New Jersey : Wiley, [2022] | Includes index.
Identifiers: LCCN 2022000945 (print) | LCCN 2022000946 (ebook) | ISBN
  9781119858874 (cloth) | ISBN 9781119858898 (adobe pdf) | ISBN
  9781119858881 (epub)
Subjects: LCSH: Internet in public administration.
Classification: LCC JF1525.A8 S58 2022 (print) | LCC JF1525.A8 (ebook) |
  DDC 352.3/802854678—dc23/eng/20220304
LC record available at https://lccn.loc.gov/2022000945
LC ebook record available at https://lccn.loc.gov/2022000946

Cover Design: Wiley
Cover Image: © phototechno/Getty Images

SKY10034175_042222

To all the digital government doers—
wherever and whoever you are

CONTENTS

PREFACE   IX

ACKNOWLEDGMENTS   XI

LIST OF ABBREVIATIONS   XIII

INTRODUCTION   XV

1.   Aisha Bin Bishr, Dubai, United Arab Emirates (UAE)   1

2.   Alex Benay, Canada   15

3.   Anna-Maija Karjalainen, Finland   31

4.   Barry Lowry, Ireland   45

5.   Bolor-Erdene Battsengel, Mongolia   59

6.   Cheow Hoe Chan, Singapore   71

7.   Daniel Abadie, Argentina   83

8.   Diego Piacentini, Italy   97

9.   Hillary Hartley, Ontario, Canada   109

10.   Innocent Bagamba Muhizi, Rwanda   123

11.   José Clastornik, Uruguay   135

12.   Lars Frelle-Petersen, Denmark   147

13.   Luis Felipe Monteiro, Brazil   159

14.   Mike Bracken, United Kingdom   173

15.   Pedro Silva Dias, Portugal   189

16.   Randall Brugeaud, Australia   203

17.   Shai-Lee Spiegelman, Israel   219

18.   Taavi Kotka, Estonia   233

19.   Tim Occleshaw, New Zealand   245

20.   Yolanda Martínez, Mexico   261

Epilogue: How to Lead a Government to Digital Excellence   279

ABOUT THE AUTHOR   287

INDEX   289

PREFACE

Digital government is an increasingly hot topic around the world. That is why there is a growing body of knowledge and a growing circle of consultants helping governments to develop their digital strategies as well as put in place the governance mechanisms for its delivery.

As we have seen so many times in so many places around the world, good plans and even right institutions alone do not cut it—if the right teams and, especially, the right leaders are not there to make the most of them. Still, surprisingly little know-how has been available about the good practices and insights on how to practically lead governments to next levels of digital transformation successfully.

I have had the luck and privilege of meeting many excellent digital government leaders as colleagues and peers along my own professional journey of leading this field in Estonia, a country with more than twenty years of digital government track record to show. Each time we have had a chance to properly sit down and talk eye-to-eye, we eagerly pick each other's brains and ask for advice or for each other's practical methods on how to lead our government's digital change the best way.

This book was born from the desire to bring such candid, peer-to-peer conversations to a wider audience. There simply are many, many more of us, the digital government doers who could hopefully benefit from these insights. If it helps to advance the digital services and governance anywhere in the world a tiny bit, it already has served its purpose.

In this book you have conversations with twenty remarkable digital government leaders from around the world, each sharing their journey and lessons in their own words. It was a pure delight to have these chats with them; I myself learned from each one even if I have known the person for a long time.

I hope you will find their lessons valuable, too. If you even get only one idea for your work from each chapter, you will have at least twenty tried-and-tested good ideas to add to your own practice or suggest to your clients by the time you finish this book.

ACKNOWLEDGMENTS

This book would not have been possible without the twenty remarkable digital government leaders who are featured here with interviews. They all agreed to be included as soon as I asked, which is a great honor. They all contributed exactly what I knew they would: their leadership wisdom through practical insights, their hard lessons, and their happy learnings. They also patiently went through the pains of reviewing the transcripts. Thank you for being my peers, and my friends! I keep learning from you, even if you may not be in government anymore.

Barbara Ubaldi from OECD, David Eaves from Harvard Kennedy School, Linnar Viik, and my brother-in-arms Kristo Vaher, Estonian government's Chief Technology Officer, were instrumental in encouraging me to move the book from idea to proposal by sparring with me on the concept and content plan at inception of the idea.

More than thirty experts and practitioners from the field of digital government from all over the world were helpful contributors to the small early snowballing exercise I conducted before the book proposal submission, helping to shape the substance for the interviews and the list of interviewees. There are so many of you to name but you know who you are! Your encouraging answers also confirmed that this book would be a good idea.

Sheck Cho, executive editor at Wiley, was brave and kind to pick up my initial LinkedIn ping, had faith to sign me on, and in the most effective manner guided me through to the initial book preparation. Susan Cerra, managing editor, was most kind in steering me until the end and allowing for some pushback of deadlines beyond the initial schedule. Thanks also to everyone else at Wiley, who put time and effort for this title to come together in the most professional and easiest way through editing, proofing, typesetting, publishing, promotion, and beyond.

I have been lucky to have an extraordinary team come to work with me at the Government CIO Office of Estonia and allow me to be your lead. You have helped me grow and educated me on-the-job; you have made all our successes happen. The chance of working with you and the challenges we have jointly addressed were exactly what pushed me to wonder what the good practices are out there, and how some of the best in our game have dealt with the same issues.

Finally, I do have to thank my wife, Riina, for making it possible for me to take the time and space to get this book together even as we have three kids running around at home and there are day jobs to be done, too. Love you and our girls!

LIST OF ABBREVIATIONS

AI	artificial intelligence
API	application programming interface
CEO	chief executive officer
CIO	chief information officer
CTO	chief technology officer
GCIO	government chief information officer
ICT	information and communications technology
IT	information technology
KPI	key performance indicator
OECD	Organisation for Economic Co-operation and Development
UX	user experience

INTRODUCTION

Whenever government CIOs or colleagues with similar titles and responsibilities meet, be it within a country or at an international level, it is like a support group meeting of sorts. We listen to each other's challenges and trials; we bounce ideas off each other about how to solve them and share practical insights on what we have tried ourselves for it. We lean on each other to hear if anything has worked well or not—and then perhaps copy that practice.

This is natural, because peer-to-peer sharing and learning are one of the most valuable ways to learn. At the end of the day, our jobs and, therefore, the joys and troubles are very similar country to country or organization to organization.

There is a growing number of international and other groupings, annual events, and chat channels for peer learning in the digital government space. One of the reasons is that the good practices and country examples are still too seldom codified and mostly spread through word-of-mouth only. Too often, these conversations and learnings stay just between people and closed doors, or direct chat channels.

However, digital government is a growing phenomenon and movement all over the world, in latest part because of COVID-19 pandemic's (one good) impact. There is a growing eagerness around the world to digitally transform governments—to take the public services and governance to a digital era, finally. Yet, actual success and achievement in building out a digital government greatly varies among countries as well as within them, with many failed or stalled attempts.

Thus, there is a growing demand to learn how to *really* build a digital government that works well. That is why there should be value and interest for the sharing of the relevant leadership or management lessons more widely.

And that is why the idea for this book was born. As a digital government leader myself until recently, I always yearned to hear from peers how they did what they did, how were they solving some strategy or management or other issue that I encountered in my work.

In my ten years in this business, I have had the good fortune to meet literally hundreds of digital leaders from all kinds of geographic, sectoral, and digital maturity backgrounds. Each time I picked their brains and their practical experience drawers for tips and tricks. That is what got me thinking—could we somehow make these nuts of insights available more widely?

In a way, there already exists a lot of research and writing on how governments have, can, and should build up a digital government. You can easily find cases and guidelines on what should be the strategy and the policies to make the most of digital technology for improving public services and policy delivery. Such literature covers either or both the theoretical models as well as practical case study angles. A range of international institutions and all kinds of consultancies work daily to compile and disseminate these kinds of findings and know-how.

Attention has also been paid to how to build relevant institutional conditions and mechanisms for digital government progress. Similarly, a body of literature and online advice is growing for practitioners on how to build up public sector teams to really deliver on the digital efforts: why and how to start digital (transformation) agencies or ministries, or even digital teams within various departments, borrowing bits of practice and know-how from private sector companies.

In this existing pool of very useful knowledge, surprisingly, only very little attention has been paid so far to leaders and leadership as one core component of achieving digital government excellence.

If you study history or management, you learn that great achievement and changes always are the sum of factors combined: a good plan, a good set-up and institutions, good leaders with effective practices. In other words, it takes great individual leaders to make things happen in a great way in great groups in right context.

Hence, this book. It is an attempt to provide a tour guide or playbook on how to achieve digital government excellence in terms of how to best lead such efforts and the relevant teams. Perhaps *tour guide* or *playbook* are not the best terms, because I do not even pretend to provide comprehensive models and a full checklist.

However, you do find in this book a range of tried-and-proven leadership practices and learnings from seasoned practitioners on how to make digital government reforms a success. They come in the form of firsthand accounts of leadership stories and tips from twenty globally renowned digital government leaders—from governments in all parts of the globe.

It is a collection of interviews with remarkable people who have led their governments to digital government excellence. These are their stories, in their own words, about some of the core dilemmas that practitioners are dealing with the most in digital government leadership jobs. I opted for the story or interview form because stories (case studies) have been proven to be one of the most effective methods to really learn from others.

Similar-style books have been compiled about private sector digital transformation leaders, but these are not entirely relevant to public sector specifics—although many insights can be surely transferred, too.

So, this long story finally short now. This book was written because the topic of digital government is increasingly hot, and governments and practitioners yearn for learning the best practices on how to make it all work. No one has assembled the lessons of relevant best leaders so far. The book presents shining examples of what good looks like in digital government leadership and management sense.

Choice of Twenty Remarkable Leaders

The professionals featured in the book have not been chosen because they happen to be known on the digital government circuit. They were chosen because they have been remarkable as leaders in this field and because they have shown a remarkable track record of leading digital government to progress in their countries. Another criterion was that the person would be insightful as an individual and as a leader, and effective as a manager. Somebody we could really learn from.

Some of these professionals had to start their government's digital journey from scratch. Some of them had to restart it or make a turnaround in strategy and delivery. Some of them had the hard job of continuing the track of excellence and bringing it to a whole next level. They represent a mix of backgrounds in terms of their government's digital maturity.

These leaders have not been chosen because their country is necessarily high-ranking in some digital government benchmark or another. Instead, they were chosen for the relative change they managed to make in their leadership term—the countries represented have been the fastest-improving ones in the global digital government space during their time in the role.

Some of them have been called government chief information officer; some have been chief digital officers. Some have been deputy ministers at the same time; some have been CEOs or directors general of digital agencies. The titles do not matter. They all have had the same kind of job—to lead the digital transformation and *across* the relevant government, not just in a department. Thus, all of them have had large-scale coordination challenges as part of their problem set. Their experience in this area should be particularly valuable, because coordination issues and how to best tackle them are among the biggest questions in each digital transformation leader's mind anywhere.

All of the twenty have inspiring stories to tell and real-life experiences to share. Each has a unique story, but there are many recurring themes.

None of the interviewees achieved excellent outcomes alone, and they are the first ones to acknowledge it. We could make another book on digital government excellence about the stories of remarkable number-twos or most-valuable experts. Or ministers and country leaders, without whom sometimes also nothing can really happen. Yet, this book is about the actual digital leaders only. Let us start with them, because they have had the ultimate leading duty despite ministers and teams around them.

The interviewees have been largely selected from national governments, given my own background as a government CIO in central government and bias of interest in this level. There are just a few very notable exceptions of people who were simply too remarkable to leave out.

It so happens that most of the professionals featured here have left their governments now—but their insights are just as relevant today. By the way, it so happens that several of them left during 2021, the year of preparing this book—I had started with about half the interviewees on-the-job, half already past that. Most of those already outside of government work as advisors globally, sharing their practical experience and thinking with next governments and organizations. Thus, they can be available also for you!

There could surely be many more digital government leaders to include. These twenty are by far not the only remarkable digital government leaders with lots to share. Yet, they are some of the most remarkable ones for sure—given their results and given their insights that you can read right now.

Who Can Benefit from This Book?

This book and its stories are of most value to other digital government leaders out there. You could be a chief information officer, chief digital officer, chief technology officer, or head of a digital and technology agency. Titles do not matter, as long as your job is to lead digital change in the whole of your government.

The book might resonate most powerfully for those just starting in such roles because you can immediately set sights and get tips to make a step change on how your organization delivers. However, mid-role leaders also can get a much-sought-after new inspiration on how to tweak and improve their team's and their own work further.

I think—and hope—that this collection of practically implementable, effective practices and thinking models is widely useful for any digital government practitioner, managers, and specialists who want to do their job in the best manner possible. Anyone can adopt the practices from here and make their team more effective in digital government delivery or suggest these practices to their leadership after reading the book.

That is why the book is for digital government policymakers and builders from around the world. From all levels of government. Whether in policy or technical delivery role, whatever the title. Whether in ministries or agencies, although especially in digital coordination units and digital service or govtech teams. Whether in a whole-of-government or policy domain responsibility—digital transformation as a challenge and as a practice is in some ways the same everywhere.

I would hope that even politicians, especially ministers in charge of digital government area in their jurisdiction, and parliamentarians could also find this book useful. If they want to up their government's digital game, here they can get a glimpse on what kinds of leaders to select and how to best empower them or work with them.

In addition, the book could be useful for anyone studying the field, whether in academic circles, where there is a growing number of professors teaching digital government courses around the world, or to their students (especially graduate level). Or to a growing number of researchers studying and doing reports as analysts in the field of digital government lessons and success. I hope that you can include the leadership and management aspects more now.

For the same reason, I do see that consultants and experts who increasingly work on advising digital government initiatives and teams around the world, from national to local levels (including in international organizations), should also find the book to be of great use. If you do not include leadership aspects in your advice, you are doing your clients and their countries a disservice!

Last but not least: some bits and parts, the book can be useful beyond the public sector sphere. I believe that practitioners, consultants, academics working on and studying digital transformation and digital leadership in any sectors, especially in big corporate settings, can find several insights relevant to their work. The lessons learned and practices shown are often not government-specific at all; they are universally applicable to any digital change team or leadership role. In exactly the same way, the practice of digital strategy and delivery in government has benefited from learning from private sector examples.

Structure of the Chapters

All twenty stories, or interview chapters, are largely structured similarly, with some questions common for each person and some specially catered to their background or depending on how the conversation went.

Each story covers the following themes:

- **The person's background:** what led them to taking the digital government leader's job? What was their past experience and motivation for it?
- **Context:** what was the digital government situation and setup at the time? What were the challenges and political issues that needed tackling?
- **Starting the job:** first hundred days and sequencing of steps
- **Vision and strategy:** their ambition, the key initiatives that they set out to do—what were their mandate and levers for it?
- **Leadership style and practices:** routines with the team or building a team and its culture, the values or practices they tried to instill
- **Successes and failures:** lessons learned from them and from the time in office
- **Transition:** leaving and how to make changes stick
- **Key recommendations:** for all peers doing the same job—what does it take to be an effective digital government leader?

Most of the interviews were done between August and September 2021, so COVID-19 was a theme we touched on as a special focus with leaders who had been most recently or still were in the job, sharing how they coped with it in their role and strategy.

Each chapter is accompanied by a short background story on why I chose this person for the book. My attempt with these sections is to try to pass on what is special about that particular leader and what to look for in the chapter that follows.

You will find a short epilogue in way of a summary, where I have tried to distill a few of the biggest common learnings and takeaways from the twenty stories. This epilogue aims to provide the shorthand playbook on key themes of how to be or become an effective leader to drive a government (or any organization) to digital excellence.

CHAPTER 1

Aisha Bin Bishr

Dubai, United Arab Emirates (UAE)

Her Excellency Dr. Aisha Bint Buti Bin Bishr has been the vice chairman of Emaar Development Board since December 2020. She was the founding Director General of the Smart Dubai Department, UAE between 2015 and 2020, the government entity entrusted with Dubai's citywide smart digital transformation.

During that time, Aisha was a member of various boards, including the Dubai Future Council for Blockchain as its chairperson, World Happiness Council, World Economic Forum's Global Future Council, and many more.

Prior to her Smart Dubai role, Aisha served as the Assistant Director General of Dubai Executive Office and Assistant Undersecretary of the UAE Ministry of Labour. Throughout her twenty-seven-year experience in ICT development, Aisha committed herself to humanizing digital transformation, from developing technologies to transforming human experiences.

She is considered among the world's most acclaimed digital transformation and smart cities thought leaders. Forbes Middle East ranked her among the Middle East's top ten most powerful businesswomen in 2020. She has received numerous accolades and awards, especially for her leadership as the first woman to lead the transformation of a smart city globally.

Aisha stands out in this book, because she is the only one among the twenty people featured here who was a digital government leader on a city level. There are also many other great city digital leaders, of course, but Aisha has been the most exceptional of those I have encountered.

One reason is to simply take a look at what Dubai has achieved on the smart city front during her time. These have not just been flashy showcase works, but systemic change and at breakneck speed.

Aisha really has been at the helm there, (re)defining in the process globally what a smart city is and should be about—the widespread application of digital tools in government for real advancement of peoples' lives in a city. She managed all this with zero initial budget, the context of top-down governance, and as a strong woman in a classically very male environment.

In addition to all that leadership courage and acumen, she is also the most caring leader you can imagine. It manifests even in the slightest of encounters with her, including in this chapter.

—SIIM

How Did You Rise to the Digital Government Leadership Role in Dubai?

I am a curious person by nature, and this characteristic fed my interest in technology as early as my school years. I remember that day when my brother brought an early-generation PC home: I immediately fell in love with the machine. This is a simple example of the accumulating passion to technology discovery that I had and still have. I did not like technology for itself but what technology can do, and the solutions built with it and around it. I believe this was the flame igniting where I have reached today.

My major at university was business information technology: how we can apply ICT to help businesses to fulfill their targets and objectives. I was attracted to how we can utilize such innovative ideas and tools for advancing government and its services.

This was the concrete area for my PhD, after which I was appointed to work with the Executive Office under His Highness Sheikh Mohammed bin Rashid Al Maktoum, UAE Vice President, Prime Minister, and the Ruler of Dubai. The office is a think tank with responsibility to bring ideas to implement in Dubai to take the emirate ten years ahead. Many bold ideas, such as the Internet City or the Dubai International Financial Center, came out of that office before.[1] I worked in different projects, none of which was an ICT project per se.

About 2014 or so smart city ideas became trendy across global conferences. It was attractive to us in Dubai, and we started looking at how a smart government or a smart city would be different from having an e-Government. Because I had the background, His Highness Sheikh Mohammed bin Rashid Al Maktoum appointed me to lead the Smart Dubai project, which was called initially Smart Dubai Office. I was the first woman globally to be commissioned with such a mandate.

To be honest, I thought I would lead it only in the first initial stage and put the high-level strategy together, then hand it over to one of the other bodies in the government. The usual role of the Executive Office was to design a strategy or design a direction and a high-level road map, after which the implementation was done by someone else.

I was thrilled that His Highness chose me to run the smart city strategy we had designed with my team. Part of that strategy is to build an office with responsibility to orchestrate all the activities happening in the city, whether it be from public and private sector—in order to convert Dubai into a smart city. From there my story really started.

What Was the Concrete Expectation Laid Out for You?

It was exactly to execute the strategy of converting Dubai to a smart city. Connecting all those dots that were already happening in this direction to make sure that we had a unified fabric across all the sectors in Dubai. For example, we focused on the high-achieving sectors in Dubai because the city is a known tourist hub, and also a trade and a logistics hub. We looked for smart opportunities in these areas. But we also looked a lot from the perspective of infrastructure for the whole city—from Wi-Fi everywhere up to a common decision-making platform. This was the direction given by His Highness.

The main challenge His Highness commissioned me to resolve was to allow His Highness to know that everyone in our city is happy and satisfied with whatever service has been provided. Not only from government, but from the whole city in a holistic approach. Our main mission and key performance indicator (KPI) were to make sure that our people are happy, as part of the overall Happiness Agenda that His Highness had started.

Yet, no one was measuring happiness well at the time. To measure happiness, you need to measure everything in the city. I was puzzled about it at the beginning, because happiness is far-far away from my major in IT. How can I map such an objective to make sure that we have a proper setup to measure such kind of goals?

How Did You Go about Devising the Strategy and the Metrics Then?

There was some initial work done before I got a call to join the team. Some team members had put together three to four pages of very high-level ideas on how to be the smartest city: provide free Wi-Fi for everyone, have an online trading platform or online system for logistics, and other such things. I was called by the chairman of the Executive Office that His Highness wanted to start a smart city project, and to come in the next day to take it over and lead to a proper plan.

His Highness had the vision to make Dubai the number one smart city globally. But there was no unified definition in the world for what a smart city was. I started with some desktop research first: I looked into different frameworks of smart cities. All of them were very rigid as a set of KPIs for certain cities. For Dubai, we needed to revisit the KPIs that were often used and come up with a blend of our own.

Then I sat back and looked—do we have these things here at all that we might measure? How can we make sure these different metrics and sectors are visible to everyone, connected with each other? We needed to run the city and make decisions about the city as a whole. So far, every manager and agency looked at their own perspective only. Transport would just look at the transport perspective, municipality would look at theirs. We did not see the same image of our city.

It meant that we needed to build a digital urban planning platform for all of us. This was different from the KPIs that all the existing frameworks talked about. So, we moved from a set of KPIs into knowing that we wanted to redesign the city experiences and to give everyone managing the city a tool that would allow them to talk to each other and revisit the full city experience to enhance it. Instead of KPIs, we started to rethink the city from design thinking perspective to make sure the experiences would be happy ones.

Later, I pushed a lot to share our thinking and learnings and data widely, too. The data we came up with can be a tool for city managers from around the world to better understand how to uplift their cities to the desired level.

You Already Hinted a Bit about It, but Did You Hesitate at All When Taking the Job of Leading the SDO?

There were some challenges; sure.

It is not easy when you work with an existing infrastructure. In Dubai and in UAE, we have a young infrastructure and do not really have legacies. But it is still not a greenfield context. There was and is a brownfield context also with existing executives and leaders who were leading their sectors, such as mobility or transportation, business or health or education.

It is not an easy job for a woman like me to go knocking on the door of each organization responsible for their sector, telling them to open their infrastructure, to plug their infrastructure in with our infrastructure. Each one of them has their own CEO, and they think they have a solution. Yes, it may be the best solution for their own sector, but not necessarily the best solution for the whole city. This was one of the challenges.

The other was how to put up a budget for such a project. His Highness the Ruler said that Dubai had invested so much in our infrastructure, and he was sure that we had enough. He was sure about what was already there in our city, and he was right. The additional funds came later when we started the uptake of the next, fourth industrial revolution technologies like artificial intelligence and blockchain. At the beginning, we had to instead connect the existing systems in our city and that did not need that much of a budget. His Highness also said that we first needed to make sure we understood what we requested. That is why we spent the first months on a real exploration finding out what we had here in our city and what the next steps could be.

Maybe it is part of my character to love challenges, so I did not hesitate much after all. This also part of what we have learned from our leadership here in Dubai: any day that does not have a challenge, we do not count it as a day.

Given These Challenges, Did You Have Any Requests Going In?

It was not a condition per se, but part of what I presented to His Highness the Ruler and to the Executive Committee was that we needed to have champions in all the government, semi-government, and private sector entities to work directly with us and have dual reporting lines. If we wanted to reach our goals, we needed to run in a very high-speed mode, different from the existing government mode.

Although Dubai has been known as the Dubai Inc. government for the way we operate as almost like a private sector, what we needed for smart city building was a very fast decision-making process and a very fast access to the infrastructure in different government organizations. We needed all the CEOs of the government and city on the same page, in one platform and organization.

The idea behind this request was also to integrate efforts and to make the agendas clear in front of each other. The benefit of one organization would mean the benefits for everyone. We needed to become close to them to be able to deliver at speed, and that is what we achieved later thanks to everyone's cooperation.

What Was Your Own Motivation in Taking Up the Call by His Highness?

First of all, if His Highness asks you to join his team, you do not hesitate for a moment, because it is His Highness Sheikh Mohammed bin Rashid Al Maktoum, the UAE Vice President, Prime Minister, and the Ruler of Dubai's team. The leader who has disrupted how governments work and plan forever.

But it also was a dream come true for me to be part of the decision-making process in the government. What would be a better role than running the digital backbone and platform for the whole city? Knowing that the digitization had become a very necessary tool for any organization, whether it be in private or public sector.

My motivation also was that I would be the first woman there. This way, I would support my other female colleagues in the government to also grow and their career to advance.

To be honest, I also like to be challenged! I had just submitted the final draft of the strategy to His Highness and took a few days of break. My plan was to leave government to look after my mother and my daughter, as I had been away for a long time. I had even written my resignation letter already.

Then I received the call on my trip that His Highness had signed the strategy into effect and even signed the decree I had written to establish the Smart Dubai Office (SDO). I said it was great news and asked whom had he chosen to be the director general. I had suggested some names, but not my own.

That is when I heard that His Highness had said I should be the best person to lead it because I had led the strategy from the beginning. He saw how I was eager to bring the best of global knowledge to the table. I was blessed that His Highness had faith in me.

What Was the State of Digital Development in Dubai at the Time, and What Led You to Suggest Creating the SDO?

In 2003, the Dubai government issued a decree that we were to have a unified enterprise resource planning solution for the government to manage human resources and so on. No government entity could go and invest in its own separate solution. Similarly, in the same period, the e-Government Office was launched on the idea to unify all of government services. It ended up having only a unified website after the first eighteen months. It took them almost thirteen years to try and push organizations to move from offline to online and from informative services to transactional services, but not fully online.

Why did it take thirteen years? Because here in Dubai, we have both a centralized and decentralized government at once. We have centralized budget funds, but decentralized execution in different bodies with their own directions and strategies. They come and meet at the center only for funds. It had been difficult to maneuver and bring everyone on the same page.

This had been the main point of my PhD thesis—such kinds of change in any organization should be top-down with strong leadership that supports the change across the organization. This huge change will change the lifestyle of an organization, a city, or a government or a country. You cannot expect that to happen by agencies themselves. Transformation had not been given such a momentum in Dubai before; that is why SDO was necessary.

I knew that SDO and we needed to work in several layers and not only in technology. The technology part is the easiest part: you can bring in any vendor and they will build it for you. The main issue is people, processes, and decision-making. The challenge was in all these layers and to link each layer to the other.

What Was the Mandate for SDO and the Tools at Your Disposal to Make Change Happen?

The mandate really was to use technologies to enhance city experiences, to make our people happy—whether they are residents or visitors. It is very easy to state that but difficult to implement because of the layers explained.

The challenge first continued to be the same as it had been during the e-Government time. Each governmental organization was going ahead with its own plans to digitize their systems or enhance their tools or attract experts. We could not just go knocking on their doors. We had to show that we in SDO, we were experts in smart city topics. We also needed to be very humble and down-to-earth to show others that we were there to learn from them and see how we can benefit from their experience to help us in this new government body.

It helped us a lot that Smart Dubai project was very dear to His Highness and the Crown Prince. In any organization, if you want to be a successful leader and have a successful transformation project, you need to have a sponsor. A good sponsor is one of the main driving people of the organization or a city and someone who believes in you, who sees that you are the one who can succeed in that role, and gives you all the power and space to develop and to deliver the desired output.

That is how we got the champions across the government whom we selected. With sponsorship from the rulers, we had each of the leaders of each governmental body sign off that their nominated champion would be the person who could access anything, anytime just to fulfill the Smart Dubai strategy.

What Were the Very First Steps You Took When You Started Leading the SDO?

The first thing was to recruit. I did get an initial team of different consultants who worked with us; they were all outsourced. I needed to recruit a team of nationals, also grow them and have gender balance in the organization.

One of the main early activities was to sign all those agreements with other government entities and champions to make sure that they understood what we do. I was in daily meetings with the decision-makers in all these organizations, sometimes covering three layers of executives to make sure we became very close to them and that they embraced our vision.

I wanted them to talk the same language and to breathe the same air that we did in Smart Dubai. Because later, when we would start to implement the real projects, I wanted everyone to run at the same speed. We were going to have very tight deadlines and I did not want anyone to lag behind due to any miscommunication. That is why I was touring daily from one organization to another.

It was also important to rent us a space for an office that could reflect our identity. A space to show that the smart city is not only technology; it is a new lifestyle, whether in business or in leisure. We needed to embrace that new lifestyle in our office space. A new district was coming out in Dubai, called the Design District. I had suggested to a friend leading its development that the district could be the first green and smart one in Dubai, with sensors and data collection everywhere to see everything happening in the district. SDO became an early mover to this area. Our idea was to be a showcase to anyone visiting our office to help them feel and touch how could technology help us on a daily basis.

We paid a lot of attention to the design of the office itself. We did a huge search among global organizations to see how they had managed to build a successful atmosphere in their organization. At the end of the day, it is not the colorful Google offices but the fabric of the environment and culture inside Google that makes it successful. The culture is within people who will be working in that space as an office, so who can be better than them to design their own offices? Many of our recruits were young and that affected the design of walls, doors, desks, even toilets—everything. We made it 100 percent different from the way offices were designed previously.

What Was the Focus or Core of the Strategy You Had Laid Out and Started Delivering—What Were the Steps for Building Up a Smart City for Happiness?

We designed the strategy for two phases. First was to be three years, from 2015 to 2017, and focused on making sure that all the infrastructure and regulation was going to be up and ready. Second phase then, from 2017 to the end of 2021, was to build on these, to really transform the city, the society, the economy from services, transactions, and data perspective.

In infrastructure, we aimed to create a digital backbone for the city—to have a full stack of new infrastructure designed from blueprint to enable Dubai to grow without any limitations and on open standards so that any kind of new technologies could be plugged into it. We made sure not to be tied to any specific technology or big vendors as such.

We also designed a new business model and a law for government and the private sector to join in public-private partnerships, or PPP. We also had to get in place the previously lacking proper regulation about data: from understanding what we meant by data to classifying data, making sure that data storage and dissemination was to be well documented, and so on. We then had to train government on that new regulation; we even got some degree courses out there. We made some regulations concerning open source, cloud, the internet-of-things.

How Did You Embrace New Things That Must Have Emerged along the Way? Did You Ever Adjust the Strategy?

New things did emerge along the way, such as blockchain and AI, that came from nowhere to the picture. We needed to make sure to plug them with the other stack we were building up. It was easier because we had different teams running different projects, so focus and delivery of overall strategy did not suffer. For example, we had a special team looking at next technologies and scanning the horizon—next to the backbone team, the data team, the strategy team.

Blockchain is a good example of how we adjusted our strategies. We first took it to testing in the Future Accelerator that the Executive Office had set up to embrace new technologies and have Dubai as a hub to implement all these new ideas. We took a small project to see if blockchain could actually help us. The project was about converting all the settlement and reconciliation of the government accounts into the blockchain platform. Citizens pay all public bills to one unified count; the government distributes it in the back end. We got a small start-up from Dubai to help us, and they took a previous forty-five-day process down to a zero-time settlement. A great gain in efficiency.

We took that example and started mapping all the use cases across the government that blockchain could be applicable for, plus we did desktop research and study visits to see how other countries had done it. We mapped some forty use cases and ended up putting a deadline of two years to implement everything in our government with blockchain. Then we found through the implementation that not everything can be applicable for blockchain. So, we changed the direction of our strategy and focused on applicable services only. In this work, we also saw we needed to design procedures, policies, and regulation—for example, for operating a unified blockchain platform for the government.

You see how new directions started from having a team scanning the horizon. They had to suggest a proper strategy, a plan of execution for experimentation. Based on this we could plug it into the existing strategy or road map on a yearly basis.

At the end of every year, we would sit with SDO management team and revisit our strategy to reflect the changing realities. Such reauthorization of strategy was also important because our understanding of what a smart city is would evolve. Every year, we would start to understand more and become more mindful about what can be successful and what cannot be done. This openness and transparency to be able to reshape made the strategy all the more applicable to be implemented—rather than having a very nice, shiny strategic document only.

Many organizations shy away from revisiting their strategy, because they think it might imply that they did not understand what they put in the strategy before. Instead, the revisiting means we understand better now because of our experience! That is why we made the revisiting mandatory.

It was done as a three-day retreat with all the directors in the organization. The one condition to be there was to remove your heart from the department you were in. I did not want any emotional attachment to any projects when entering that room. Otherwise, if we decided to pause some projects, the people leading would feel we did not want them—which was not the case.

You Spent the First Months on Daily Tour to Build Relationship with Other Agencies. How Did You Sustain These Relationships Later?

At the beginning, when I was doing those tours across the government, we spoke to the CEOs plus the CIOs. I wanted to make sure the CEO himself believes in our mission, so that his CIO who already believed in us could support us. That opened a new door for me personally to be able to be very close with those CEOs.

Whenever we later wanted anything to be implemented in our city, it often took just a phone call with the CEOs to get to implement a thing. We did not need any of those protocols or procedures to convince anyone or send letters.

By the way, this helped us a lot once when the COVID-19 pandemic hit our country in 2020. We had three days to test all the systems and make sure that during the weekend everything was ready to convert the government from physical to online work. This was possible only with the support of all the CEOs.

We did not work with the CEOs as a group too officially, more from a casual perspective. This was on purpose, as I wanted to show that when we would implement smart systems, our lives become easier and our communication should be much easier. If we wanted changes in our communities and environment, we also had to change how we related and worked as CEOs.

Every year, we did an international visit together with government entity CIOs. It was like a retreat, but for learning. Every year we chose a different topic and a different destination—depending on the topics we had at hand in our journey. Or we went to an event like the Smart City Expo in Barcelona, where we could sit down with all the cities attending the summit. These trips were a way to bring CIOs onboard, uplift them from a knowledge perspective to see the new technologies the way we saw it, and also enable them to share their knowledge from their sector—be it health or mobility.

How Did You Attract Talent to Join You in SDO?

I surely utilized my brand, my personal brand, to attract young stars to our teams. We shared our activities and day-to-day SDO life through social media, showcasing everything we did—also on my personal accounts. I do have a lot of followers from our country, but not only from there. I had been one of the early adopters of social media in our community, when Twitter and Facebook were just starting back in the day.

This way people started to know what I was doing and what were the positive changes we were doing. A lot of junior and also some senior directors came through such social media interactions.

The main philosophy in this area was to walk the talk. We wanted to show people that when government said that we want the future to be implemented today, that we in SDO were living it today.

I had gathered some following already before—as I am from Dubai and the business community—and they keep talking to each other closely. They had noticed that there was this lady doing things, had high values, and was brave. This combined with our being very transparent in SDO started to grow our name and to change the perspective of people on how public servants can work different. We made our image to be close to the simple people in the street, aimed at changing the image among young people at schools and universities on the perspective about working in government.

We also got people to join the mission from largest consultancy companies and from Facebook and Google to help us redesign a city experience. Several of the people who joined us were from the Middle East but living in the US or Europe. They got to know us through conferences, liked the mission, and they just sent their CVs to be with us.

What Qualities Were You Looking for in Your Hiring?

I always told people that we need to be human first. People in the ICT sector tend to forget sometimes that they are human at the end of the day, that we are not robots. We are requested to digitize systems, but we are also the people who will benefit from this digitization. Thus, we need to see these systems from the perspective of human eyes first rather than from IT analyst or strategist eyes.

I also had to make sure that the team members saw the vision and mission of our organization when selecting them. When I recruited senior team members, I did not care about their specialty degrees. The most important part was if they believed that we could change things through ICT. The main thing was if they were enthusiastic about using these tools to make positive changes in our communities.

Who Was Your Most Valuable Hire?

One of them was Zeina El Kaissi, who joined as the Chief Digital Director. She had worked with me in my previous role in the Dubai Executive Office, then started her own IT solutions company. Once I had been assigned to run Smart Dubai, I called her to tell we had a new challenge and mission and to see if she wanted to join. Immediately, she jumped onboard and was one of the main members in the decision-making layer in Smart Dubai. She handled our strategy, and she was like a joker in the playing cards that you can throw anywhere, given the way she thought with her consultancy experience. She could always read the reality and then suggest where to go forward.

Another key team member was a younger guy named Hamad Alawadhi. He handled the network platform and was responsible for our communication and connecting to all the government entities. He had a civic engineer background, a master's degree from Imperial College in London. But he was so fond of the happiness agenda and how we could spread positiveness and happiness with proper communication with people. I immediately recruited him for it and handed him a special project on championing the platform, building human relations with others.

Can You Tell Some More on What Was the Culture You Were Trying to Create in SDO?

There are some very integral values that are close to my heart. I personally do believe in transparency and openness between the teams, and especially in the same organization. I do think that there is no shame in copying and pasting, as long as we know where we are pasting it and understand what we are copying in the context of adopting successful examples. I also do believe that there is no shame when you work yourself to the ground, because if you work you will make mistakes. Better to say that we did a mistake, and this is the way how we rectified these mistakes, than not to try.

To have a healthy organization, you need to have trust with your people, or your system, and with other agencies and members. So, trust is another value that I emphasize. I cannot work with teams that I do not trust, and if they do not trust me—if I want to run with them in this race and win the race. Our race was to reach our deadlines. That is why trust was a very essential part of our philosophy.

In addition to these values, we needed to bring the change mindset to the front. Of course, His Highness Sheikh Mohammed bin Rashid al Maktoum had started in the mid-1990s to revamp the Dubai government and have an enterprise or Dubai Inc. mindset—so that everyone in the government should have that entrepreneurial spirit. I wanted to change Dubai to be in continuous change: that we would always continue to change how we did things for the benefit of our people, the citizens and residents.

What Were Your Mantras That You Kept Repeating to Your Team?

I often said: be human! When you are in your organization, do not forget that at the end of the day, we are all human. We need to take care of our people in this organization. I have grown up the ladder myself; I was very junior in the organization when I joined the government in 1994. I have seen how people can be treated as juniors, and that is why I made sure that every single senior person in our organization had a proper human relationship with colleagues and teams.

Another aspect about being human is that, as a public servant, we need to put ourselves in the shoes of citizens or residents. Public servants tend to forget at the end of the day that they will receive the same services that they provided during the day. Think about how you want to be treated if you are not part of the service organization. That is why each time we designed a system or a service, we brought in employees from across the organization to shape the design of the service, in addition to going out of the organization to the ground and listening to people.

"Listen with an open mind and heart," we said. Normally as a public servant, we are so attached to our services, we fight when the client says the service is bad. Just listen to them and go to the ground and test! I find that many of the government leaders, the CEOs themselves, they have never tested their own services. Their office will handle everything for them. Leading the organization, you need to know your kitchen, you need to draw the process maps and know exactly how things are cooked and what is going on. That is why I made sure that everyone in our organization, in SDO, they had less ego and were very down-to-earth when it came to the services that they provided. That they would be very open-minded to listen and hear others to be ready to revisit our services and processes.

What Were Your Regular Practices or Routines to Act on These Values or Make Delivery Happen?

It was important to be there myself with the team as necessary. One of the things in our office was that the walls were made of glass so that everyone could see each other. The team could always reach me; I was always there: whether in the office or WhatsApp or any of my social media accounts. This enabled me to put more pressure on them to deliver. Because they knew I would always be there if needed.

Speed was our pressure. I needed the team who could run with me. They needed to believe in me under the pressure. They needed to see that I was there 24/7, so I did reply to their requests, emails, calls immediately as soon as I could.

We had a policy in the meetings that anyone could attend any meeting. Register at least half an hour before, and we would make sure you have a seat. If it is with external members, listen in during the meeting—if you have anything to ask, ask at the end. This opened more doors for the people to understand what happened around them. Imagine you are in this organization and working very hard, then suddenly there is a new project or success, and you hear about in the newspaper or radio only. This will kill the enthusiasm in your heart that made you every early morning come to work and join this organization. So I made sure that everyone in the organization believed and felt that they were an important part of the of the organization.

We also needed to be happy employees to make the lives of people happier. That is why we took leisure trips together or went to events, also outside the country. Or we would go biking or sailing. Some of these things were going on every weekend, also with families. Happy employees could present this vision to the others, and they would believe it more if they saw it in us.

In the last years, we implemented the tribe and holacracy models.[2] That changed the mood for later-stage deliverables. People who used to punch in at 7 am and punch out 3 pm, they started working as if they were new people—as soon as they saw that each one of them was valued and could contribute. I had to send people dinner to their office or ask them to go home!

We went for the tribe approach to have a very fast way to deliver even small deliverables all the time. It was also a way to make sure that management needed to interfere only if necessary. No need to interfere if things were going right anyway. This was also a way to allow for experimentation, to have teams go and have a space to implement and test what works.

What Were Your Biggest Achievements as the Director General, in Your Own View?

Building a livable digitalization and our Smart City blueprint.

I am proud of having had and built this strong team in Smart Dubai that was a team like never seen before in Dubai. They came from different nationalities, from different entities, but believed in the same goal. They were like fire, every day and night, just to make sure they implemented things. They were really building things for themselves. Like one of the teams that worked on registering the buying and selling of cars in the city. They tested it with their own cars: one sold his car to the other guy through the system. I saw how powerful and happy these tiny teams of enthusiasts were when they achieved a change, even if small.

We surely also achieved for Dubai making a mark on the global digital transformation agenda. It was a huge achievement to become one of the cities that has managed to transform its own systems and experiences in this way.

My third accomplishment is a very personal one—understanding and believing in myself that I can change my own skin to grow this organization and at such a speed.

What Prompted You to Move Ahead from Smart Dubai after Five Years in 2021?

I had been working and in government mostly for the last twenty-eight years; I never had a break. Even for summer vacations, I took one week at best. My mom had started to need me more as she was getting older, and I did not want to lose the chance to be close to her. My daughter is grown now; she is twenty-two and started her own business. I also wanted to start a new journey with myself, therefore.

I learned from Smart Dubai that I need to be open-minded and transparent also with myself to see where are the nodes that I need to expand in my own way of thinking and my own body. I started on a personal growth journey—with meditation, lots of yoga, learning new things about my own self. Started a new hobby of tennis; I had never held a racket before! I am still a member in many areas of the city management, but my main time is for me now.

How Did You Prepare for the Handover and Making Sure Your Initiatives Would Live On?

New management groups surely come and have their own agendas; they will change the work at the end of the day. But I made sure that the teams themselves were mature enough to deal with such change so that the systems could adapt.

What Were—or Are—Going to Be Next Challenges for the Team and Smart Dubai?

There still is delivery to be done to meet the initially set deadlines.

Also, I tried to push in the last five years that IT is not just IT. Normally IT is seen as a support function, right? In Smart Dubai, IT is a digital platform that can change the whole perspective of the business—it can push you up or kill you. Either satisfy your client or lose your client.

In my role, I was not just paying attention to the deliverables per se, but the philosophy and way of life across government about how to see IT people. That they are not there to provide you cables and Wi-Fi and troubleshoot—they are the masters of reshaping the business. This idea of IT still needs cultivating to last.

What Do You Wish You Had Known When You Started the Job? What Do You Think You Learned the Most?

I learned to be more open-minded and not to judge things upfront, especially when new technologies or ideas or systems are being presented to me. Before, I used to shut down often in these cases. In Smart Dubai, I learned to listen, to allow others to elaborate more, to showcase and to convince others. If they are convinced, then the issue is with me and not with the technology or idea itself.

So, I pushed myself more into practicing this new way of thinking or seeing things in a more open-minded and in less judgmental way. I also see it more in my own life now, as my daughter has grown up from being a teenager to an adult and starting her own business now. I have learned to let her go by supporting her and trusting her.

What Do You Think Are the Key Skills One Needs to Do Your Kind of Role Well?

To be passionate, first of all. Passionate about the sector or area that you want to grow in.

Be open-minded.

When they say that we need to have new skills such as coding or understanding of data, these you can learn in any school or training. One of the major issues that we will face is how to work in teams and to let go your own perspective. We—and especially our kids—they need to understand the need to work in collaboration with others. We cannot work in isolation from others. The moment you say, "I want to work in collaboration with others" you need to have this kind of setup in the brain to accept the others, their ideas, or their ways. Even if it conflicts with your own ideas, you need to reach to a point wherein we can both survive or live or work in the same space.

What Are Your Three Recommendations from Your Experience—What Does It Take to Do a Digital Government Leader's Job Well?

Have the project or program close to the main decision-maker in that city or government—have a proper sponsor or a champion, have it in his or her daily dashboard.

Have champions all over the organization who do believe in the vision. This will expedite change.

Revisit the road map and the strategy. Not every three years, but every year. The speed and the momentum of changes that are happening today are much faster than they used to be. Do not feel shy and embarrassed to do changes, even if you change the direction from east to west.

Notes

1. Dubai Internet City is a free economic zone targeted for IT companies. Dubai International Financial Center is a special economic zone for financial industry in Dubai.
2. The tribe model management is product development approach popularized by Spotify (and others) to scale agile development whereby teams working on products are separated to autonomous units working on specific parts of a product. Holacracy is a model for decentralized organizational governance and management, focused on spreading decision-making to self-organizing teams rather than arranging it through a management hierarchy.

CHAPTER 2

Alex Benay

Canada

Alex currently serves as Global Lead, Government Azure Strategy at Microsoft, where he helps governments around the world adopt cloud technologies. Prior to this, he was a partner with KPMG, where he led the national digital transformation practice.

In 2017–2019, Alex was a Deputy Minister at the Treasury Board of Canada Secretariat and the Chief Information Officer of Canada, and before that the President and CEO of the Canada Science and Technology Museums Corporation. From 2009 to 2014, Alex was a Vice President at OpenText, Canada's largest software company.

In 2018, Alex was named to Apolitical's international list of the one hundred most influential people in digital government. He serves on the board of the World Wide Web Foundation and is cofounder of CIO Strategy Council of Canada.

He is also the author of books *Canadian Failures*, an anthology of essays from prominent Canadians openly talking about failure, and *Government Digital*, an in-depth look at how modern governments are tackling digital change.

With Alex, we just hit right off somehow. He became one of the closest friends in the international digital government gang. We both are straight-talking, too-much-talking, and fast-talking; both appreciate deadpan and satire.

We both are eager to not just kick the can down the road in our work but take on the machinery of government as widely and deeply (and in case of Alex as loudly) as we can.

Alex is very impatient; that is why doing the GCIO gig must have been hard. But he came to the role with experience and wits to employ this impatience as a strength. Although he may not have managed to turn the Government of Canada fully around (it is huge, too!) in his short term, his bold attempts and bold ideas led to quite a few lasting changes in how digital is done there.

We copied quite a bit off from each other on what works—to me, the Canadian architecture governance mechanisms is world class, for example. He was taken to Estonian digital ways to the extent that he has covered our practices in his talks on so many occasions that it would be hard for me to even attempt to match it. Sorry about that, eh.

—*Siim*

How Did You End Up in a Digital Government Leader Role for the Government of Canada (GC)?

I probably have a very eclectic route and background. I started in government, moved over to the private sector for four or five years in a Canadian tech company. Then I came back because I needed a break from traveling and ran some of our national museums. Knowing tech and getting to know some of the senior leadership in Canada through my work, people started asking if I would be interested in taking the government CIO job.

I said "no" at first, like every sane person should. Then after talking about it a little bit, I realized that maybe it would be a good thing for me to take a stab at it, having always been around the tech scene and around the public sector in Ottawa. I had a commitment in my head that I would do it for about three years.

Why Did You Say "No" at First?

In Canada, some of the policies had not been updated in over a decade. Digital considerations were not integrated with policy decision-makers as much as it seemed to be in other countries. Doing a new service digitally, properly, is not at the forefront of decision-making. Digital economy or infrastructure, like digital identity, require accelerating the digital economy and is not integrated with policy view.

That is why the government CIO is a very challenging role, because you are not privy to all the decisions—but you are privy to "Oh, well, we tried to do it this way, and it did not work. Can you please fix it?" You always get the garbage at the tail end of the stream.

Also, the role was not at a deputy minister level at first, and I did not have all the right tools needed to do the job. Also, they had just launched in Canada about a year before I took over the job of an upgrade of our government-wide human resources and pay system called Phoenix. A little lesson here—you should never, never, never call a tech project Phoenix because you are just tempting fate that something is going to go wrong! You are just tempting the tech gods to really blow something up.

So, Phoenix had just failed to launch and it got worse and worse over time, too. Everything you could do wrong was done wrong with it. It just highlighted the fact that the profession of technology in government had been neglected for a long time. It had not been seen as a priority because in government here in Canada the policy and communications are the drivers for senior leaders through their careers. You do not become the top person in government in the public service through tech. But often technology failures are what make governments turn.

I was also having super fun in the museum work. We were about to launch a new museum, had a great team, a great mandate, a great budget. But in civil service you learn that sometimes you are needed elsewhere and so you do it.

Given This Context, Did You Have Conditions or Requests to Take the Role?

We had a really good head of Treasury Board Secretariat, the agency where my position sat—Yaprak Baltacioglu. She, her deputy, and I sat down, also Minister Scott Brison and I sat down to talk about what the scope of work was going to be. We talked about the need to do a lot of cultural change, and we could not do cultural change from behind the desk—we would have to be very public about this change. This meant getting public servants onto social media giving their opinions, which was a new thing. We needed to change the culture in the mind of public servants through the media, because the Phoenix failure had become all-consuming for the GC at that time. As soon as people said the word *tech*, they cringed because of Phoenix.

We had to come to an agreement on how we would work together in this different way, and then we figured out how the traditional ways that government worked would cause friction. So, there were a lot of those kinds of discussions for the first month or two before everybody thought that my joining was going to be the right idea. Honestly, it worked super well from there, because that pre-stage created a communication with the elected side for most of my term.

What Was Your Own Motivation for the Role?

I fundamentally believe that digital government can change the nature of the interaction between a citizen and his government forever. I told everyone that we had the opportunity to do that, right now. That we were not talking about adding new programs; we were talking about changing the nature of the relationship.

For example, it means that a citizen can choose to get a government service from its bank. We should make it so seamless and transparent, automated, and ethical. This means decisions quite high up—because the plumbing of the government needs to change. It means that the government has to accept that they are no longer going to be the sole provider of a service. That they could actually give that right to other groups.

In all fairness, we were doing some of it in Canada already. Third-party companies can fill out your taxes, for example. We have shown then that we can do an omnichannel approach if we want to. I fundamentally believe that I was waking up to do some of that work every day. It is the government-as-a-platform approach and on steroids.

What Was the Concrete Mission Set to You through These Conversations by Your Bosses?

We set these targets through our conversations together.

Step one: fix the boring governance stuff. At least half of the job of a national CIO is going to end up being about governance and policy. The broad stroke of mission was to update all of our digital government policies, because nobody had done it in a decade. Our IT policy, our information management policy, our security policies—all of it had never been done right.

Then we had to create new legislation and new policies that would permit the government to steer the ship to where it wants to go digitally. It meant that we should create legal levers in order to be able to go into a department that was rolling out something like a Phoenix and stop it. It was not clear before that we could do it, but we needed to react to this perhaps biggest failure or debacle in the history of the public service in Canada. Unfortunately, governments tend to be reactive as an institution. We were able to create new authorities, new policies, and direction in government because we had Phoenix, a big failure. That kind of trigger was necessary.

We needed to create the right governance in order to review all of the budgets, review all of this spend, have the legal right to create a national architecture, and have the departments and the ministries execute against that architecture.

We also decided that we would do a lot of work on artificial intelligence, a lot of work on people to get the right kind of succession planning in place, and so on. It was to be a complete overhaul really.

Besides Phoenix and Outdated Policies, What Was the State of Digital Government and Strategy in GC?

Probably, if you look at the level of digital government maturity from on-premise to transactional to service-centered to intelligent, Canada had been somewhere near the transactional level at the most. There was not a lot done about putting users first digitally or what you could do with digital service delivery; there was not an appetite to do a "digital first" service delivery. Lots of fax machines, lots of counters were still there around the country.

We had—and still have—departments as groups that do not talk to each other. Citizens, or customers, if we can call them that, have to know which department to go to in order to get a service. We impose that on them. The other thing you have to understand is the legislation in Canada is very vertical. Every department has its own set of legislation and its own authorities, which means it can execute certain things and it creates a great confusion.

It is a system that is designed so that one person cannot make a quick decision. You should make the decisions together for the better of the citizens, but this does not really work that quickly as it should in the digital area. As opposed to measuring twice and cutting once, you could actually cut a thousand times digitally, and you could do it faster, too. Some departments out of the forty-three were doing quite well in this regard, but others were not.

Because the policies had not been centrally updated then nobody used the cloud, as an example. That is why we had to come in with new policies and new ways of doing things, forcing a little bit of modernization on a system that was not really service-centered.

What Were Your Levers besides the Legislative Powers You Asked For?

It was mostly governance and steering. The government CIO role sits at the Treasury Board Secretariat, where all the funds are decided. Departments do not get new funds if they do not follow the policies. So, we had the stick and the carrot right there. There was a whole mechanism for reviewing technology projects along the other spending requests coming in, which we could tap into.

However, we started also delivering some things ourselves as a central agency to show change. We started having a heavier hand in building some AI products so that we could do more than just "that is the policy, and you should follow it." Instead, it was going to be "here is the policy on AI, here is the framework to use it that we are developing." For example, we did an Access to Information Portal for all departments that was AI-based.

For me, it was important that I just not preach on a soapbox and the team to get used to not being in an ivory tower, but actually delivering some stuff itself. In a similar way, when we started talking about doing agile procurement and an open procurement for the first time, we did the very first open procurement process in the history of the Government of Canada ourselves. So, we would get our hands dirty, and do policy and architecture at the same time.

Given Your Overall Mission, Did You Set Yourself Any Concrete Goals or Deliverables to Reach?

We do need to consider the stresses of the CIO kind of job on people because these are not easy jobs. I did not think I could survive more than three years because in a town like Ottawa you have interests and lobbying. When you come in and shake the trees, being disruptive, you upset many people. That is the reason why some of the policy things had not been updated for a while because it had not been a priority politically, and on a civil service level, you avoided putting off influential groups. Like if you pushed for using the cloud, someone supplying hardware would not be happy.

That is why the goal number one for me was that I needed to survive and needed to be comfortable in making some decisions that were not going to be crowd-pleasers. I set the aim of making them anyway because I had been around the tech space in Ottawa long enough and I knew that the decisions might not be popular, but I knew they were going to be the right ones to make for the Canadian citizens. So, number one goal was to survive.

Survival would mean that I was going to do my job in the most transparent way that any senior civil servant had ever done in history. In a way that would make everybody know what we were doing.

Second goal was that I knew what we had to do, and these things I wanted to accomplish. I knew that AI was important, that we needed the cloud, that we needed to start looking at changing procurement.

My goal was that I will change what I can control. People often ask, "How do you change the culture of government?" The answer is you do not do it by waking up in the morning as an individual, and saying, "I am going to change the culture of government today." Your job will become depressing as all hell very quickly because it is an impossible task. A lot of policies and the legislation are designed for people who are quite comfortable in the old model. So, you cannot change the whole of the government culture at once. But you can change what you are in charge of and radiate it out.

With All This Load Ahead of You, What Did You Start With? What Was the Focus for Your First Months?

I always start in a position with the people I have in front of me. The first thing was holding all staff meetings regularly, and then booking one-on-one meetings with staff members and especially with a mixture of people I had heard to be "problematic" on the team. Usually, those are the people that are the most frustrated because they want to make the biggest difference. So, I purposely sat down with them first to find out the history, what was going on and not going on, and what they would change.

I also sat down with all divisions and units within the CIO office; I sat down with other CIOs of other departments. It was basically just a lot of listening because I had certain assumptions coming in. You need to talk to people because they are probably the most important leg in this "stool" with three "legs" to digital government and any change: the governance, the tech, the people. People compose the one "leg" that will make it all fall apart if they do not do the work or want to follow—even if you have the best tech stuff and the best governance. I wanted to understand how the people on the team and around us did technology and what were the existing governance processes.

Another thing was to leverage the political support that we had when I came in. For the first time ever, we had in Scott a minister at the Treasury Board who was willing to say "no" to IT projects submitted if the right technology architecture was not being deployed. That veto power had been there before, but the problem was that pulling this lever is the last step. The preferable option is to engage with the department before you get to that point and try to fix it.

Pulling the minister veto and sending them back to the drawing board is a very nuclear option. It means that you are delaying programs, delaying services to Canadians.

What we then could do instead is to set direction; for example, departments would have to do things in the cloud. Then six months later we would make sure they were using the cloud. So, we wanted to start with precision direction from a central agency quickly. This took a lot of political leadership at first, as the mandate of policy did not exist at first. So, we quickly started with the longer-term policy renewal and legislative renewal.

I also launched a series of Skunkworks projects—stuff that was close to my chest and that I managed with the staff directly. Things like doing open procurement really quickly, or I wanted an AI policy in place really quickly, or restart having a big govtech conference (which became the FWD50 series). Things like Talent Cloud to change how government hired by taking it down from a year-long process to thirty days and breaking a lifelong career model into six-month bursts where people could come in and out of the civil service more easily.

I kept those close because I wanted to show that we were going to set the tone and how we were going to work differently. I did not want to leave that to anybody else, to have a series of quick wins and special projects that we could start announcing to the world.

How Hard or Easy Was It to Maintain Your Focus on the Skunkworks as Time Went On?

I managed to do it with the help of a very strong chief of staff and my inner core team. People asked why I was meeting staff six levels below in the organization about this little project and I said that it was important. I had my chief of staff and my administrative support make sure we had recurring meetings with these people, that we would always find me time. Even if I had to be called into parliament for something, we would reschedule these meets as top priorities for me. I just had a really good set of people around me who knew that those things were important to me and understood why.

I made sure to also find the time to do "follow-through" because too many times leadership just does not follow through on stuff. Those projects needed my support, they needed an umbrella so that the white blood cells of government would not come in and kill the innovation that they were driving.

Usually, as you get to the top of a pyramid in an organization, you have to delegate; otherwise, you cannot survive. So, you delegate to your second in command, they can do the same, then someone will execute the task, and then everybody is happy. But in the digital world the products need to move faster, the decisions need to move faster, the collaboration needs to be broader.

If you are not directly involved as a leader in two or three or four key initiatives that target your organizational culture or your country's future, and you are not personally following through by meeting with these teams weekly or monthly, I think you are not executing your leadership duties properly in this day and age. You just run out of time. So, it is up to you to be super-disciplined to make time for those priorities.

It also helped to retain the focus that we were speaking about those things publicly. This made us kind of stuck to deliver them—you cannot let it die, because people would ask. Doing something in public adds another coat of Teflon to pushing change through because nobody could say you did not warn them. In addition, if you involve more stakeholders by being public, nobody can say they were not involved. Plus, it keeps you accountable. That is why we made those priorities very public and very important, so that we were able to follow through on them.

You Spoke about the Need to Work Very Openly and Transparently—How Did You Do That Really?

We had had the Phoenix conundrum that put the spotlight on government tech in a way that it had never had. However, this was not good media coverage; the media was all over how that system was mishandled.

Our strategy was that media was not going to be our friends, and if we do not talk on social media about the good things that the civil service is doing, nobody will. So, we needed to get out there on newer platforms and start talking about our own messages.

I encouraged every single employee in the CIO Office to talk about the projects that they were working on. Not because I wanted media attention, but because I wanted real-time collaboration with other sectors. Often in government, we see policy consultation with a beginning date and an end date. This way you are just limiting collaboration opportunities by not engaging continuously. With LinkedIn, Twitter, or other social media platforms, we could collaborate 24/7 now. The government way of doing business had not changed so far with the tools we had at our disposal.

Our way of being open by default meant saying continuously, "Hey, this is what I am working on." I wanted the vendors to know, I wanted the provinces and regional governments to know, I wanted other departments to know. People just had to start talking about the work they were doing. It was great, even if it is a double-edged sword because it adds more attention to your work.

It also meant that we had to start talking about the failures better because some of these projects did not work well. Government does not like to talk about failure, right? Like I keep joking, *fail* is four-letter word that starts with the letter *f* and that you are not allowed to utter in government. We had to make it known that failing fast and small is better than failing slow and massive, like Phoenix.

You Did End Up Taking the Work of Saving Phoenix into Your Own Portfolio. How Did You Go about Fixing It?

The more you start to demand that the system of government or a large corporation change, the more you are preaching about it, the more people will say, "Well, do something."

We were never charged with fixing the existing Phoenix; I still do not think that was doable anyway. Nothing worked in it: government staff were getting overpaid, underpaid, not paid. There was no architecture done, no data, no testing, no backup plan, you name it. There was no way to get out of that mess in any other way than starting a new system.

In parallel, we had been telling all the procurement officers in the GC doing digital procurement to please stop giving specifications out and instead give out the problems for procurement instead. Then the really smart people that do tech outside of government can come up with a whole bunch of different solutions. And we might use them all, why use just one? So, we gave ourselves the task to run the country's most important open procurement up to that point to replace Phoenix. We started putting our policies to work to execute, pulling all the tools we had brought in and out.

We went to the market and said, "We want a cloud-based software-as-a-service human resources and pay solution; who is interested? We got about a dozen interested parties in a room. Then we said that the process is going to be like the Hunger Games, with gates to go through where we would up the requirements as they passed through the gates. We did not want any paper response; we wanted to see the actual software change and work against our requirements at each gate.

The procurement people at first thought we would have to pay the suppliers as they were going through the process. I said no to that. So, we did three gates, five months, the last gate was with real anonymized user data and suppliers had to show that they could pay the people properly. We ended up with three final suppliers—not by prescribing a solution, but by working with suppliers at each gate and working from the problems up. In less than six months, the government had three viable options, whereas nothing had been achieved for years before.

We put our money where our mouth was, and we showed what can be done with a different approach. It shows that you have to get your hands dirty on some of this stuff.

How Did You Build or Rebuild the GCIO Setup to Achieve the Changes?

Just for context's sake, Government of Canada has up to 25,000 people who work in Information Management and IT professions in forty-three departments. The Office of the CIO is about two hundred to two-hundred fifty people to coordinate privacy, access to information, AI, data, service delivery, architecture, project oversight for major projects, open government, people hiring policies, you name it.

I had a whole bunch of silos within my own team. I could not ask the rest of GC to integrate digital with everything if in my own team, say, privacy people did not even talk to architecture people. Or if tech people were creating products without the privacy and policy people along. We had to get our functions working together before expecting the rest of government to do it.

I also remade the immediate team around me. We went from eight to ten direct reports to three as I built my team on the three legs of any kind of change in a modern organization: people, governance, and technology. I consolidated all the policy work together, all the people work together, all the tech stuff under a government CTO to oversee architecture and project oversight. Over time, as we continued influencing the system and got more money to do more things, those roles became more senior.

Also, I wanted to make sure I did not become the single point of failure myself. If you have eight to ten divisions with silos and you are not around to coordinate and orchestrate, like if you get hit by a bus, there will not be a lot of integration left. My three reports had to work together so that if I was hit by a bus, the next day the organization would continue delivering in an integrated way.

I also needed to change the culture in the office. I needed to have my direct reports comfortable with the fact that I would not go to them for updates but would have the team come into my office for an update—like we did with Skunkworks. It takes a lot of trust to work that way. They needed to trust their teams to brief properly. So, I did on purpose create a different flow of conversation within my office, leading to everybody able to replace everybody or at least understand everybody's job.

Getting past silos and getting the conversation flows going took a lot of informal effort. You know, people want to have fun when they work hard. If they have fun together, they are increasingly working better together as well. The office had never even had a Christmas party. We did an offsite party and against all doubts a whole bunch from our team showed up. We started doing Winddown Fridays, basically once a month sitting together and going for a beer or glass of wine. Winddown Fridays even started attracting people from other departments to join. All of a sudden, we were running out of room.

It meant that we got people talking and it reduced the government hierarchy and silo structure. It was sort of our attempt of attacking the Industrial Age organizational structure of the government bit by bit all the time. Unless you do it relentlessly with a series of micro adjustments, like our Winddown Fridays, the system will win because it has been there longer than you.

I Know That You Also Made a Big Push for the Team to Work in the Open. How Did That Work?

We would have our GCIO office all-staffs quarterly and have them mandatory. We also started recording these meetings, because we were the policy center, and I wanted the operational departments to know what we were talking about. We would livestream the meeting or just send the record out to all other departments. The direction setting to me is always about open and transparent communications, plus letting people challenge the direction.

With my own team, we would also do periodical "ask me anything" hours so that people could air out some of the issues there.

Openness and transparency are huge because they mean that we are also forced to deliver. Enabling the staff members to talk themselves about their projects and their programs was a small thing that turned into a big deal. They made themselves accountable by talking about their work online. The effect of open-by-default working on self-discipline at the staff level became apparent through the work we were doing.

We also very openly sang praises about the successes, including to other departments, which had done a great digital project. We started using for it the online platforms we had created for ourselves. That was a way to publicly show the change that was going on, and it became a carrot on its own to other departments and our own team, frankly.

In an era of global digital collaboration, it does not really compute if public servants are anonymous and hide behind their desks. Governments need to be way more transparent, open-by-default on everything they do as long as it is not a national security matter. Why are policies developed behind closed doors? Why cannot every Canadian citizen whom the government serves have access to the draft of the policy before it is signed off and comment on it? The world would be a better place if governments went even a bit further down the road of being open and transparent and collaborative. It is better for the economy and better for the democracy if people participate. That is why we started doing all in the open.

My open-door policy worked great in other ways, too. There are twenty to twenty-five thousand people in GC. I basically said to them, "If you have a great idea, contact me," and some did. Most people did not because they thought you cannot talk to a deputy minister if you are a technician. Yet, this is where the good ideas usually come from. They are not going to come from me. A great example is our Talent Cloud, which had the aim of bringing a "gig economy" approach to allow GC to hire short-term employment more easily and faster. There was a person with a vision on how to do it; she only needed some air cover and support. She came to me with the idea, we brought her in, and she got it done. Others had called her crazy before for what she wanted to do and how bold her vision was.

Tell a Bit More on the Skunkworks Approach—How Did That Working Method Really Work?

To get these projects off the ground, we usually did one or two meetings a week for the first month. My chief of staff was always amazing at keeping action items, at keeping people's feet to the fire on them, and keeping people honest about them. Once proper cadence and routine emerged with the concrete Skunkworks project lead, we would maybe meet weekly, then maybe once every two weeks. If I felt that the work was falling off the rails, then we would get back into twice-weekly mode.

The meetings were stand-up, half an hour each time, rapid fire or blitzing it, going very specific. The people who were working these projects were delighted that the CIO was giving them all the attention. It also kept them on their toes: we just talked, another meet was coming, you have to be ready and bring in your new work. So, the need for follow-through was not just from me, it had to be from everybody. My direct reports also worked hard to get their teams ready for these briefings, but they also watched out to not to get in the way for them.

In the meetings, I asked mainly, "What is in the way right now?" Meaning, what prevented the team from moving ahead? We might bring then someone in for the next meeting to get it fixed or decided. Like if the issue was privacy, we would have a privacy analyst along for the next meet and make a decision there and then to move things forward. I think a lot of civil servants are not necessarily used to making decisions on the spot. We did it; the team then told the deadline for the next step and had to update me by that time. With the hierarchy gone, delivery was that much faster.

Of course, as the CIO you cannot work this way for everything because you will lose your mind. That is why you got to be pretty astute about what you pick to be your Skunkworks to make a difference.

What Sort of Competence Did You Seek to Add to the Team?

I needed people who knew how to get policy signed off by ministers. That was our weakest point from the three legs of tech, people, and governance—which includes policy.

I would always say that policy is useless if you do not execute and do not make it executable. Policy often is a too abstract thing. Take privacy as an example. There were always privacy people on the policy side saying we should not do this or that for some reason. I often asked, "Did you talk to a technical person because probably we could fix all those problems?"

We clearly needed the good policy, too, because just doing tech without policy gets you in trouble. Policy coverage also gets the funding you need and gets the projects off the ground. I needed policy people who got it and who understood the process of policy to steer us through it. In the GC, any policy must go through Treasury Board Secretariat, a bunch of ministers, and so on. It is quite a process.

Who Was Your Most Valuable Addition to the Team?

Bringing Olivia Neal from Government Digital Service (GDS) in the UK early on as our Executive Director for Digital Change to lead the people side of our work and a bunch of special initiatives. She had run the digital service standard work in GDS. She had no staff when she started, and she ended up having a team of fifty to sixty people running a lot of government programs when she was done. She added so much in a number of ways.

First, I find that Canadians are often insular, only looking at ourselves and not liking to compare ourselves internationally. It means that we are not always in tune with what is going on in digital government or technology around the world. Olivia brought that view with her instantly. She also was not part of the group thinking going on, coming from outside and even from another culture. I cannot imagine the challenge she must have faced with pushback. The way she handled it; I learned a lot from her. Bringing her on early also showed that we could attract the best talent from around the world, as she came from GDS.

I got her onboard because Olivia had been looking to come to Canada, and I heard through the grapevine she was talking to a whole bunch of different groups in GC. I told her that she could have the most impact with us. Also, the other groups were kind of dithering, as the typical government hiring takes time. I made it my number one priority to get her letter of offer done fast. In office, people were wondering why was the deputy minister focusing on her so much? Well, because she can unlock ten things for us. These things will unlock the next ten more macro things. That is why it was worth my time. Also, I believe in managing people with respect and did not want to leave her hanging or stuck in the government hiring land.

In addition, there were the managers or directors in the team who helped to take the vision forward and execute. Let us face it: the day-to-day work was down to them and not me.

What Do You Consider as Your Biggest Achievements in the GCIO Role?

I think we set up a policy framework and a legislative framework that gives this role the teeth and an ability to avoid another Phoenix if the right leadership and courage is in place. It brings hope that users would not have to suffer the way they have suffered in not getting paid and so on because of Phoenix.

As the result, the role became a deputy minister one during my term. We got it authority to execute and push the otherwise traditional town—the government in Ottawa—to fit the digital age better. These are the preconditions for success for the next CIO, who can now focus less on policy and legislation and more on getting actual change done.

Second, I think that people who bought into the program of doing things differently felt that the work they were doing was meaningful and that they were not bureaucratic robots, even if it was just for a moment of time. I could see it in their eyes; they would also tell me that it felt good to do some real things, because sometimes in a central agency, you do not feel like you are doing real stuff.

Last, I am glad that I am still in touch with a lot of people who worked there. Even if I did make some mistakes, like I became too deadline focused at times, and might then forget the people working for us. That is why it still feels great that we are still talking to one another.

What Was Surprising for You in the Job, Looking Back Now?

I think I went into the job thinking I knew how to manage stakeholders. Boy, was I wrong! The stakeholders I knew about were not a problem because I am very direct, and I want honest feedback back. This way we can have a conversation.

The stakeholders I did not know about are used to engaging with government through lobby arms and through letters to the minister or the prime minister. That is how the government had conditioned the dialogue in the past. So, when I came in saying that "I want to talk to you on LinkedIn, if you have got a problem with what we are doing"—not everybody was comfortable with that. A lot of people would still take the old traditional route and send letters to ministers, and that was where the disconnect happened.

For me it meant that I had to go to brief higher-ups instead of just doing the thing and putting it in front of people for codeveloping. If you end up writing briefing notes more than doing anything else, the project starts to slow down in this briefing nightmare.

I went in thinking I was a digital lead and everybody in my world knows and does things digitally. Well, it turned out even technology companies did not really do digital. It required that Scott (the minister) and I talk all the time, for example, to manage the outside relations. It required a lot of conversations outside the formal governance arrangements we had anyway, like the weekly department board or spending request meetings. It required also to build trust with other ministers and deputy ministers in the system.

Is There Anything Else You Wish You Had Known When You Started?

I would never take another position like that without giving myself a little bit of time to do some retrospect—or forward look—on what would be the things or interference that would cause me walk away from the job or be ready to take a big hit for it. I did not have that figured out when I started, and that caused me a lot of stress. For example, with the AI work.

We pushed for the policy that citizens cannot be serviced by an AI black box forever. If you are going to do AI in the Government of Canada, we need to have access to your code and be able to trace the decision from the machine. We were asking to have a dialogue on this, and it brought on heavy lobby toward senior government. Obviously, the vendors did not like the policy, because the code is proprietary.

In the end, we did change the tune and the position. We only did that because we got pushed back openly. But it made me realize that not everybody in this game of government is out there for the better good of serving citizens. That is why I think anybody taking a national CIO or any CIO job needs to be very comfortable with themselves about where they are going to draw the line on ethical matters. I was ready to jump on the grenade for our AI policy, so to speak, because the work our team was doing and how they were doing it—because I fundamentally believed in it. Even if lobbyists got some politicians to not like it.

The question to ask yourself—and myself next time—is what is the line that you will draw in the sand? What are your convictions? What are you willing to take a stand for, if asked to do something or not do something that you fundamentally disagree with?

What Do You Think Were Your Biggest Failures in the Job?

As I said, there was a period of some months when I became too focused on deadlines and too focused on managing up. It was a time when we had to find an alternative to Phoenix. I became too blunt with people in the team who were just trying their hardest. Someone had to call me out to make me realize it. To avoid it happening in the future, I would try next time to find more people who are not afraid to speak. I would also ask them for feedback more often. We were delivering home runs and home runs, but it was killing people in the process.

I had been conscious about my own mental health from the start, but the job still had an effect. I gained a lot of weight, and my state was not always the best during the job. I was open about it and a deputy minister told me that I should not be showing cracks like that. It did not sit true with who I am as a person. I am very honest, am emotional and transparent as a person. I believe it is OK for people to see the leadership struggle because it is not easy all the time and nobody wants to work for robots anymore. They will not believe you then when you speak because you are not genuine. It would be like senior officials having people write their social media for them. Other people will know it and not buy it.

So, I should have made sure that my health and mental health came first. I did prioritize longer days over family at times, and that is no good. An evening eight o'clock call could have frankly just been a meeting the next morning, not happen immediately. The thing is that once you leave office at the end of your run, you are just a person. I should have realized that I was always first a person, while also in the position.

Was This the Reason You Moved On or What Was behind Your Decision to Leave Office?

It was a few things together.

I did not want to go over my three-year limit that I had set for myself at the beginning. Either the government could move me to another job, or I would just find my own job. I do not think that governments are used to people taking their future in their own hands and asking to be moved or to leave on their own timing. I got questions and comments back from people like, "You cannot leave, what are you doing?"

We had done so much change in three years, it was going to be more operational now. I was not interested in that. So, even if nobody wanted to move to another portfolio and thought I was doing a good job, I was ready to move on. Elections were coming, too. Scott and Yaprak had left, new people were coming in. Even if they were great, it was not the same relationship anymore that we had had with the minister or the secretary before.

It was also a time for me for reasons of health and family. My then wife was working in tech and some doors were closed to her because of who I was and where I worked. So, I had to put myself and my family first. I find that people who have not worked inside the machine and have scars to prove it do not understand the level of stress and damage that it does to your body and to everything else.

What Are the Remaining Challenges on the Table for GC and Your Former Team?

First, it is still necessary to do a better job of integrating all the new policies into the department. Also, to the other departments. I think it is necessary to move digital conversations all the way up to cabinet decisions more regularly and with more discipline.

The GCIO unit also needs to coordinate better with other departments that are involved in the digital economy. I have always been a believer that most governments around the world are still applying Industrial Age thinking to the digital world. But looking at places like Estonia and its e-Residency program triggered a thought that in the digital world it does not apply that government has a monopoly over the citizens' lives. What if Canadians could choose whom they get their services from because they could choose to launch a business in Estonia now and even never set foot in the country? This has impact beyond the government, on the whole economy, and we could intentionally work on that.

These would have been *my* next steps, at least.

How Did You Ensure Your Initiatives and Changes Would Be Sustained?

As changing policy and legislation in the Government of Canada is so darn hard, and I knew this, then I knew these things were not going to change any time soon. Because of our legislation and policy, GC now is doing AI, is using the cloud, all these things. The boring stuff and the stuff you do not announce publicly because nobody cares are the stuff that will stay the longest. The governance stuff.

The GCIO team also has got levers now. Say, another Phoenix happens—they cannot blame the fact that they did not have the authority to stop it. It could still happen because of a lack of leadership, but not because there is a lack of technical tools or legislation or policy or architecture or direction.

The strength of the machinery can be seen from the fact that it took so long to find a formal replacement for me—the new GCIO started in the fall of 2021. Two of my former deputies had a shot at acting government CIO for a year, and everything continued to work. Even despite COVID-19; it is unreal the work they did to adjust to the pandemic. They had the governance and the right technology and their own leadership to keep things going.

Would You Do the Same Job Ever Again, Being Wiser Now, Too?

I have talked to a number of CIOs for other countries, including G7 and more. At the end of the day, the jobs are the same. I would definitely consider a job on the business side and citizen service side, not the technical side, and do it the way I think it should be done. So, I am never going to say that I will never take another public sector job. But I have done the government CIO job already.

What Are the Core Necessary Skills to Do This Kind of Job Well?

I think you need to definitely be able to have a public presence. Whether it is presentations, social media, media interviews, parliamentary committees—you need to be able to articulate your vision and the reasons why you are doing the things you are doing.

Listening is another big skill. I should have listened even more.

You have to be able to break things down into micro adjustments and keep at doing them. You need to do it this way in order not to fail big and to have a shot at changing the system.

You absolutely need to understand work-life balance in these jobs. These jobs can be all-encompassing. So, you definitely need some internal discipline on how to manage the balance in these cases.

What Are Your Bottom-Line Takeaways or Recommendations on How to Do the GCIO Type of Job Well?

My number one rule would be: remember that it is about the people, not the deliverables. It is about the memories you are going to have with those people, not what you will have delivered necessarily.

Number two: it is still just a job. A job like any other job. Do not lose sight of who you are, your hobbies, your family, whatever makes you really you.

Third thing: make sure you leave things in a better place than you when you inherited it. I think that you have to take a job like ours with the *intention* of leaving the place a better place than you started off with. If you do not do it, or if you cannot afterwards look back and say it, you should try harder or leave.

CHAPTER 3
Anna-Maija Karjalainen
Finland

Anna-Maija Karjalainen was the Director General in the Ministry of Finance of Finland for over seven years. Her responsibility area was the public sector ICT and digitalization, including the digital security.

Before joining the Ministry of Finance, she worked for five years as the divisional director in the State Treasury of Finland, leading the shared service center for state ICT services.

Prior to these governmental tasks she worked more than twenty years in the private sector leading ICT in international companies in the metal and paper industries.

She holds a master of science degree in engineering.

Maija was by far the closest colleague I had in the global digital government leaders' circuit. Part of it is because of the special relationship between our governments, which extended to the digital government sphere and took us to lead some internationally novel efforts. This included cofounding NIIS, the world's first intergovernmental govtech infrastructure consortium, to jointly develop the core technology of X-Road.

But we got close also because of our styles match. Maija is always very pragmatic, straight-shooting, no time wasting—but also always happy to have a good laugh and some fun, when the occasion is right.

Whichever international meeting she took part in, she always spoke out actively to share what they were doing in Finland, and she made her country noticed for the progress going on. She must be one of the most outspoken Finns there is, knowing the national stereotype of Finns as the most reserved folks on this earth!

It was not just talk that got others' attention, as you see from this chapter. Maija steered the Finnish public sector to a real turnaround in how it was delivering on digital government.

—SIIM

How Did You Become a Digital Government Leader in Finland?

I was working in IT in the private sector, and there was an opening to lead the consolidation of state IT services in the State Treasury of Finland. They wanted to build up a department to centrally provide to the public sector infrastructure-level services like network, email, collaboration, data center services.

So, I applied for that role, and I got it. I worked there for five years.

By 2014, there was a situation building up in the Ministry of Finance that the government CIO, my predecessor, was offered some new responsibilities. The heads of the ministry wanted to make a change, and I was asked if I could come in to cover the GCIO role for half a year, because so long appointment could be done just by the decision of the minister. Once I accepted, I was not sure I would not be in this position necessarily for longer.

What Was Your Motivation in Taking Up the Offer, Especially Given the Short Time?

I had seen that goals were not achieved. I had seen there was a sort of mistrust on how the GCIO team was able to deliver and do things. I saw the mistrust in if and how we could digitalize Finland. I wanted to build back the trust and belief that our government, and our ministry, would be able to deliver on digital government.

Of course, I was also very flattered to be offered the position. The Ministry in Finance is called the "super-ministry" in Finland, because they have power to see things through. A job with them was not something I had ever even dreamed about doing.

Did You Have Any Hesitations at All?

When I got the call, I asked how much time I would have to decide. They said ten minutes! I did not hesitate then at all and said "yes" because I thought it was worth a try. I did not even have time to talk to my husband at all. I was actually on holiday and jogging at the time of the call!

I surely did not know exactly what the work would be like. Of course, I had seen and been following from the agency side what was happening. But I did not know what the daily work was like. I was still anyways hoping that I could make some kind of change because of the mistrust in the atmosphere.

What Was the Expectation Laid Out to You or What Were You Called In to Do?

That was also the expectation from the boss when we met the first time. He told me three times: deliver, deliver, deliver.

If You Only Had Ten Minutes to Think, What Gave You the Confidence That You Were the Woman for the Job?

Because of my background from before: I had done tough work and handled responsibility in both the private and public sectors already. Also, the people at the ministry were confident that I could handle a situation that was not so good at the time.

I had been taking care of ICT in the second biggest pulp and paper company in Finland. It was also a multinational company and I had had responsibility over multiple countries all the way to China. The next five years at the State Treasury had given me an understanding on how the government works: what the processes are, how you get money, these sorts of things. I had shown good delivery there; my boss there was very happy with me.

What Is the Institutional Background of the Digital Government Setup in Finland? Why Is the Ministry of Finance in Charge of the Area?

The Ministry of Finance has been taking care of shared or common services in Finland: from financials and human resources to purchasing and real estate. In 2008 or so, the responsibility to steer the municipalities was moved from the Ministry of Interior to the Ministry of Finance. Then they also combined the public sector ICT guidance responsibility there in 2011.

My political boss was the minister in charge of the public administration side in the ministry. We always had two ministers in the house in my time. One handled the state financials, budget, taxation, and such; the other oversaw all the public sector steering, the municipalities, and the common service areas. I did have a civil servant boss as well in the permanent secretary who supported me in how to work with the minister or with the parliament. My own or the government CIO role was officially titled the Director-General of Public Sector ICT Department.

The role is meant for coordination: to get everyone to work together and onboard, to show the direction of where to go. To show what is digitalization and what we want to achieve, what are the benefits. It is a person who needs to put things together, to gather the ideas and persons together, and organize them so that we are able to meet the outcomes. One important part of the role is to negotiate the financials. My staff praised me when I left office that I had gotten all the money we needed!

What Was Going on in the Area of Digital Government in Finland at the Time You Joined?

There had been the first government-wide digitalization or e-services program called SADe from 2009 to 2015. The program had brought money and a strong coordination mandate to the Ministry of Finance for digital government, and the ministry was giving the money to different ministers for making digital service projects.

The Public Sector ICT Department had been there for three years already but not yet combining the whole of public sector steering together at both the state level and for municipalities. A new agency called Valtori had been created, and a law had been adopted to consolidate the state ICT infrastructure together from all agencies to move their relevant personnel and equipment to Valtori. There was also another law in parliament, giving public sector security services responsibility to our ministry.

In Finland, the government program of the current government sets the agenda for work.[1] Before I joined the Ministry of Finance in 2014, an external study had come out and influenced the government to start work on a nationwide digital government architecture.[2] It included initiatives such as taking over the X-Road from Estonia and implementing it in Finland.[3]

We had been given more than a hundred million euros to deliver this program. But it was unclear what to do with the money, although the department had their own public sector ICT strategy before. When I went to the first meeting with all the big bosses, they were asking about what we were delivering with the money and with the X-Road. So, we had to figure out the best way to actually use the money, to figure out what we would want to build. A big part of the money was to be used by the agencies to join the X-Road, but we needed to build central solutions, too, such as the suomi.fi services.

Tell a Bit More—What Are the Suomi.Fi Services?

We have three hundred municipalities and about eighty agencies in Finland. The plan was to create common base digital services for the public sector so that none of these institutions would have to create the same things themselves. Instead, there are common services that everybody can find, reuse, and be more cost-effective this way. This included electronic identity to connect people to services securely and a digital mailbox for secure communication between people and public sector agencies. There is a service catalog, where all people can find information about all public sector services, and there is a one-stop-shop for citizens to access the digital service and see all their state-held information in one place. All these are part of suomi.fi package.

Our achievement was that we got those common services built and available. Then we got the agencies to use them with money as a support to start using the services and with a law that told them that everybody also had to do it this way. In the end we would not have common services that nobody would use.

What Was Your Own Strategy: What Did You Set Yourself as Concrete Objectives to Achieve?

I wanted to digitalize Finland. But because my initial period was so short, I was really just looking into what were we really supposed to do and what had we promised to do. Things like X-Road implementation and suomi.fi delivery was one of the only high-level priorities handed to us.

In addition, we came up with a set of proposals that were the big reforms or projects that could make a big change for digitalizing Finland. It included things such as making a push for open data. I have always been trying to see the big picture and what creates benefit for Finland. I always said I was working for company Oy Suomi Ab—the country.[4] The government was very focused on increasing employment in Finland at the time, so our proposals played into that. For example, doing an income register could allow people to take up more short-term work without upending their unemployment benefits like before.

We actually wanted to make a new full digital government strategy, but then we got a new government with 2015 elections, and digitalization was made a cross-cutting theme in the whole of the government program. We were not allowed to do a strategy of our own, because it was felt that this would duplicate the government program. We made an internal strategy for the department, nevertheless. The government program gave us the concrete overall direction for it.

How Did the Strategy or Your Proposals Emerge?

Of course, you first work with your own department. But we also worked nicely together with CIOs from all ministries to collect ideas and see what the things were that we would like to do together. We did a series of deep workshops to cocreate the strategy.

We also had an advisory board, where we had some ministries but also CIOs from municipalities represented. Politicians also had their coordination group, with some agency heads to talk about what needed to be done or moved forward.

I felt that if I would get everybody behind the strategy, then people do it themselves and I do not need to push. The strategy needs to be created together.

I always say that in an expert organization, if everybody knows where to go and if the target is clear, then people will deliver even if times are a little bit shaky sometimes. You also have to be honest and tell if things are not so good sometimes. But the key is in setting and explaining the goals.

A really useful thing was to go outside Finland to learn. Once I started, I soon went to the meeting of Nordic Government CIOs and then the European Union CIO network meeting. I also went to see some countries' colleagues directly just to understand what they were doing or what was going on in the world. I had worked in public sector only on consolidation of IT services in Finland; I did not know what was happening at the state level in other countries. I wanted to know what others were doing and pick up from them the good things. You also start to learn from good colleagues the things you should not do!

When I went to these international meetings, there was initially a mistrust in the team that I was doing it just for travels and wondering why was I not in Finland. I tried to show the value to the team by always going through in our monthly meetings what I had learned abroad: what were the other countries doing and how. It was a way to create trust that I was really trying to figure out what we were supposed to do and what are the good things to get done.

What Mechanisms Did You Have for Coordination and Leading across the Public Sector?

First of all, we had a governance structure with different government bodies where we were able to express what we wanted or to jointly agree on which steps we needed to take. What worked best was doing workshops together with all other CIOs from ministries and local governments to create a path together. Then everybody already had bought into the idea because they had been creating the decisions themselves. Our method often was that we split into different groups, each working on the same problem, and then we voted in the end within the whole group on which solution was the best to put to work.

The tool has also been the legislation. We know that when people think that their own solution is the best solution, they do not want to change or give it up—legislation can force them to do that. There also can be a carrot with money, of course. For X-Road implementation, 60 percent of the funding we spent went to agencies and municipalities to use the suomi.fi tools. Even if legislation is in place and an obligation is set, money still helps to really get them to do the work they need to do.

We did get more legislation done in my time. When I left, we already had ten laws in place. One of my learnings is that if you create a project of wider change, such as bringing in digital identity, you should start with the legislation at the same time as you start with the ideas. Then the legislation supports the implementation of the change.

A very important piece was the information management law that was adopted in 2019, which is the law about how government needs to handle and manage information in a qualified, secure, and trustworthy way. But it also has clauses that give a role and mandate to the Ministry of Finance in the digital government steering role. For example, new software projects now need to pass our team's quality check. The team can check them for financials, interoperability, security, the use of common tools, how information management is done. We can use it to push for better and more digitalization, but also to ensure that information gets shared more between the agencies for better services.

We got more levers once we started to deliver, and once we were taken seriously. When we delivered suomi.fi services in time, within scope, and actually for less money than planned—that gave the confidence that what we tell and we promise, we deliver.

Doing Workshops Is a Fine Idea, but It Does Not Have to Lead to Buy-In—How Did You Achieve That?

It depends on how you structure these discussions. When we discussed strategy work in the meetings, we sometimes used outsiders for facilitation, but mainly we ran the sessions ourselves. It was either me or some of our team's experts. We worked out beforehand how we wanted to run the workshop, what we wanted to have as the outcome, the time lines, and methods. So, these discussions were very well prepared.

That is also why those who joined the workshops loved them. Whenever we got the feedback, it showed that participants thought the strategy sessions were the best ones. People got straight to work because everything was prepared beforehand. There was no general discussion only, but working on boards, getting to results, voting on the best ideas, moving on to work on those best ideas.

That is how I have always worked. My earlier boss in the private sector always said: "We do not take or get any consultants; we have Maija!" I am not a consultant but have gotten a lot of practice on cocreation, looking, and understanding together with others the pitfalls or possibilities.

How Did You Choose Your Priority or Where to Focus?

I did not follow any concrete criteria. It more comes back to what I believed was best for Finland. From that perspective, I always tried to see how we can influence Finland more.

I also tried to look how to get things done more effectively moneywise. I was always saying that I would rather save money and put it to grandma's daycare than putting it somewhere where it does not deliver anything. We tried to do cost-effective things to deliver what was sensible with the money we had. In my department, I also said that let us have money unspent or leftover at the end of the year, and hope that it would be used wisely elsewhere in the state, rather than use it for something we do not really need.

It comes from my private sector background where I had to cut costs every year some 10 or 15 percent, and that was a tough job. At home, you also do not waste money at the end of the year. So, it is common sense not to waste money.

Besides Trying to Figure Out the Strategy, What Other Steps Did You Start With in Your First Hundred Days?

I went to all kinds of meetings and other stakeholders, to know the persons there, hear their expectations and if any kind of targets had been given to us. That was a conscious step to start building a network but also to figure out our strategy.

I knew that primarily I had to look into what changes to do in the organization, because it was not delivering. I started in mid-March and made the proposal on how to change the setup at the beginning of June. I had the changes in place by the beginning of the next year.

My first task was to see what we did, what skills we had. I had an interview with everyone in the team, asking them for their opinion on what we should do differently and what was good. What he or she would do in my job. During those three months, I had the discussion for thirty minutes with each person working for me, going through structured questions that they had gotten beforehand so that they were able to prepare.

I reformed our team into three units or areas. This way people knew better what they were supposed to do and deliver. One part was digitalization, another part was policy and data and law, third was delivering services by supporting Valtori, security, and so on.

I had first only the six-month period in office, which ended at the end of August. I had to wait to be appointed to the actual term in the office in order to fully implement the team changes. This period was quite horrible, in fact. Some people did not want me to be their boss; they did not like my proposal for the new organization. Some of them even went around trying to lobby against me. But in order to deliver I needed to change the organizational structure.

How Did You See That Change Through Then with Your Team?

It helped that I came in with new ways of working. For example, I heard that my direct reports were telling their units partially different stories compared to what had been agreed on or discussed in the management team of the department. I then started doing and sharing out management meeting overviews after these meetings. Basically, the whole department was invited for a short overview meeting where I told what we had decided so that everybody heard the same story.

There had been all-department meetings that had been optional, and I made them mandatory. You could only miss if you were ill. I did not allow the use of laptops in these meetings anymore, because I had heard that previously they used the laptops during the meeting to joke on what was being told and to not take part. I also started doing Maija's morning coffees: a regular meet where anybody was allowed to come in and ask whatever questions they wanted.

Were the Meetings Popular and Did You Keep Them as a Routine? What Were the Other Ways You Kept the Team Onboard?

The morning meetings were popular at first, but less so later because I was telling everything already in other meetings—so there was no need to ask again. The two-hour monthly meetings that were mandatory for everyone worked really well. I wanted everybody there to hear the same message from me or from my unit heads, or we had somebody visit. I wanted everybody to be informed. Some people disliked that I made these meetings mandatory, but I had learned from my previous working places that there is no other way. I have had people who worked for me in the past and then left come up later to say that my monthly meetings were the best.

For some people, this all was still not enough. So, I started to write a message to the whole team every now and then. About every three weeks I would send a note on how things looked to me, what things were on my agenda, what things were going on. Some people liked to read more than to listen, and it was important to reach everyone, especially as the team grew twofold in size. I always tried to figure out three main points I wanted to say out in the note: informing them about some progress or change and that they should be prepared for it, giving thanks to somebody, and some intro and outro on the side, and that was the note.

How Did You Keep Things in Focus for Delivery?

We used the Kanban tools. We had targets on the board at all times, and weekly we looked through them in the management group as well as in the unit meetings. We focused on how things were moving forward, what the schedules were, were we meeting the targets, and if we needed to make critical changes. This way I had very clear targets in my mind all the time, once we had agreed what we wanted to take forward.

We had one common Kanban board for the whole department. It was important because then everybody was able to see where we were heading and how things were going. At a monthly meeting after every quarter, we went through all the big programs or targets we had for the department and highlighted in traffic light mode of red-yellow-green how things stood. If anything was in red, meaning late or not doing well, there was explanation also in the notes on the board. When we had success and big things were green, we celebrated. I took quarterly review practice with me from the private sector.

Of course, politicians do come and say that something needs to be done additionally. Then you do have a prioritization issue because if you do not have enough persons, you do have to see what formerly planned things you will just have to do later. Well, it can also happen that you deprioritize and then two months later the minister comes and asks where is the thing that was promised earlier? I did then honestly always say that we had to prioritize. I usually had taken such cases to the political level before, giving them options and asking what we should prioritize if we had to choose. Kanban was also a useful tool to talk prioritization and resourcing through on a management team level within the department, such as when borrowing and moving people from unit to unit.

The Kanban board had a column for proposals that we had not decided yet if we would move forward or not. The proposals were on the level of initiatives that had already had some work in them, but we also included raw ideas as well.

What Were the Principles or Values You Tried to Push Forward to the Team?

I tried to bring in the "yes, we can" culture. I wanted people to think that we could achieve all that we wanted to achieve.

Also, I wanted us to have the customer focus. I started to talk about customers, and the team told me that we did not have customers, because we were the Ministry of Finance! It took some hard talks with the team, but then the 2015 Prime Minister Sipilä's government came in and talked the same way. And nobody spoke against it anymore.

It was important to me that everybody in the team would have their opinion, and that everyone could challenge each other for delivery—until you are not arguing against the person, but on the substance. That was something that the team was not used to. They were even a bit afraid of me or thinking that everything the boss said had to be the truth. I told my team that I expected them to challenge me, too. I dislike if people just say "yes" and "yes" and do not really think so. People did pick it up nicely. I even received some emails that started by the line "Since you asked us to challenge you. . . ."

I also always said that it was important to have fun at work. We started doing the team's own strategy meetings as overnight stays or retreats so that we would also have fun and dance or party a bit. Because people had so much fun after a day of hard working, they were always waiting for the next time.

How Did You Rebuild Your Team? What Were the Competences You Were Looking For?

I had initially about thirty persons, mostly long-term civil servants. They were often more used to making studies than delivering things. The expectation from outside was that even with the X-Road money, there would be no outcome. We were not seen as an influencer or deliverers.

For X-Road delivery, we recruited about ten more persons temporarily, and we looked for a little bit new type of staff member with good delivery skills. Then ten more persons with new competences came to deliver the 2019 government program, to work on AI, and so on. When I joined, I had in my department only one lawyer and we had already two or three laws to take care of. So that needed to change. When I left, we had about ten lawyers. We also got in some people who were looking at new things such as AI, the information policy, and so on.

We changed our way of working so that we reorganized the agencies under the ministry to deliver things. We at the ministry focused on strategy, political work, money, laws. However, if you are starting new initiatives such as mobile ID, you also have to be able to figure out the high-level technical solutions to understand how it combines together with other things in the architecture. These sorts of things we kept in our own hands, so some sort of technical understanding we also still had to have, even with agencies taking care of delivery.

How Did You Find People for the Team?

I have been always good at finding good people. We got on the team people who were knowledgeable, able to deliver, saw the big picture. People wanted to join our department, even temporarily—because they had a feeling that this way, they would be able to influence and make a change in Finland.

That is because the word gets around. You work on the culture and atmosphere of the department, and if it changes, people start to notice and talk about it. Like the word went around that not only did we deliver, but it was also fun to work there on the team with our strategy sessions and other social events.

What I have always done is to have the last interview. I call it more a discussion even because it is not formal. I meet everybody before they join or before we sign them on, so I can understand what sort of person we would get. I am trying to see for myself how they fit on the team. We need people of different types; they are not supposed to be like me. I am also trying to understand where we could use the new person in the future. What are his or her intentions: to remain an expert or also become a manager? Things like this.

I also started using personal tests in recruiting. The interview times are so short that it is difficult to be sure of the person fitting the task. The tests supported the final decision-making.

Who Was Your Most Impactful Hire?

The three heads of unit, or team heads who were my direct reports and managed people in the team directly. A big part of my initial department reorganization was opening the management team positions. I got in people that were willing to cooperate, with whom we were able to create a trust relationship, with whom we were on the same page so that we could also easily substitute for each other. Each person was also of a different type. This made us work well as a team because there was always good, necessary discussion about the best way forward.

What Do You Consider Your Biggest Achievement in the GCIO Role?

I had been asked to deliver, and we delivered: the X-Road implementation, suomi.fi services, information management law, and so on.

We also created a Digitalization Agency to drive true digitalization in the government and its services.[5] Its trial some years earlier had not succeeded. With people and mindsets changing, we managed to get the idea adopted. The agency is meant to aid and boost digitalization efforts of ministries.

I am happy that I was also able to create good and trustworthy relationships. This includes with all my four ministers. We built up personal good relations with them even though they were from different parties. I have always told my opinion, and always looked out for Finland as a whole, and that was the premise of our collaboration.

I also built up a wide network in the whole state, including municipalities and especially ministries, but also on international level. Our customers are our agencies, we need to deliver for them and keep in touch. But the network meant I was able to always connect and ask for advice or help. If you have good contacts, you always find where to ask for help or support. Networking takes work. That is why I started to work on it in the beginning already.

Are There Things You Would Have Done Differently or Things You Even Failed At?

I did not manage so well to get some politicians to understand what digitalization means and why we needed to invest in it. I wanted them to look into the future more, when factories are not the only working places, and what sort of opportunities this creates for doing work in Finland. Getting them to understand that world is changing around us.

We were told that public sector ICT was very expensive and spending too much money. We even had some ministers who did not understand that everything in the government needed ICT to work, or staff such as police officers would have to go back to using paper and pencil. This meant that money had to be put into ICT for it to work.

I think I did not find the right channels for this message. Looking back, we could have perhaps early on done more benchmarking or showcasing on how much money other countries were committing to digital government. Looking at it now, I do not blame the politicians but myself—that I was not able to provide the right material or background for them to understand what needed to be the way forward.

The thing is that I am not the person who wants to be in the public spotlight. All my predecessors had been in IT news and other professional media continuously. I told to my bosses already in our first call that this was my handicap. Perhaps a publicly more-visible leading role would have also helped to make my case with politicians, too.

What Made You Leave Office in 2021?

Well, I had been in the position seven years in total by that time. The last of my terms was ending and I had to decide if I would apply again for next years. I felt that I had given what I could, for Finland and for these tasks. It was time for a new person to come in with bright ideas, also time for the department and the network to get in someone new with fresh ideas and ways of doing. I believe in change.

How Did You Work to Make Your Changes Last or Stick?

During my last year, we worked on a new strategy and an action plan with the whole department, looking out to year 2025. I thought this would make it easier for the next government CIO to take over, because the strategy and work plan would be laid out. He or she should make adjustments, of course. But as the team was involved in working it out, then the whole organization would be already behind it and ready to take this way forward. The department team actually had demanded or suggested to make the strategy.

Some of our ongoing initiatives also are supported and prioritized by the minister, especially those based on the government program. This adds to the platform that my successor can take up. But the platform of plans is still open enough so that its own changes can be made. I also went through the strategy with my successor when he came in, and I hope he finds it a bridge forward and worth building on.

When I actually left, I told my department that I admired their work and believed that they would support my successor by taking our achievements forward to the next level. I hope that this helps everything to go forward, too.

What Is the State of Finnish Digital Government Today? What Are the Remaining Challenges?

When I started, I went abroad to see how other countries had digitalized and learn about what to do. The same countries I went to visit have been now coming to visit us in return. It shows that we have achieved something by digitalizing Finland if others are coming to see our results.

The remaining challenges are to develop and implement a mobile identity, which is a big change in the short term because it is not just improving the current electronic identity and how it operates. We were looking at a whole new way for identity. Also, the Digitalization Agency is now a couple of years old and still needs work to stabilize its services for delivery and customer satisfaction as well.

COVID-19 has supported people seeing and understanding the big value in consolidated common services. Otherwise, government staff would not have been able to move to work at home in such a way so that everything continued working. This would not have been possible earlier when every agency had its own services. Now it is better understood that shared services can really give you a benefit.

What Do You Wish You Had Known When You Started in the Job, If You Look Back Now?

I guess it would have helped me if I would have understood better the expectations on substance. I remember that when I joined the ministry and the department, people were already talking about digitalization more than ICT—but the department still had (and has) ICT in its title. So, for half a year I had to learn to understand that my work is not actually ICT, but digitalization! The thing is that nobody really explained what they expected from me.

What Are the Key Skills Necessary to Do the Government CIO Job Well?

As the CIO, you need to understand digitalization and the possibilities on a general level of what you can do. On the state level, you need to know how the government operates, the decision-making, the financial processes. Or you need to learn it. The faster you learn it, the better.

My boss at State Treasury told me that social know-how is the skill set you need nowadays, and this relates to networking. You need to be able to create the network. This includes that you should be willing to learn from others and not create your own bicycle—instead, copy from the best.

Finally, you should be able to build the culture that works.

Would You Actually Recommend This Job to Anyone? What Makes It Special?

I would definitely recommend it. There is one and only government CIO. There is no other position like that in Finland or any country. Because ICT and digitalization are cross-cutting themes, you are then able to see so much. You can see all the ministries and how they work, all the municipalities. You also see the private sector, if you work with them in your network—and you should. In Finland, working in the Ministry of Finance as the "super ministry" is especially worth it as you see how it works and operates.

What Are the Key Recommendations You Would Have for a Peer on How to Do the GCIO Work the Most Effectively?

First of all, you have to create the strategy and to have the big picture about where to go. This is necessary for yourself, for your team, for your network or for your state. As I said, the team of experts will move in the direction you show by themselves. If the goal is clear and they see the big picture, they are then able to deliver it and you do not need any management at the level of details.

Second—and it is related—you really need the network. You need the people and to know the people. You need to create this network, and not only in your own country but other countries as well. That makes you able to see the big picture better. If you do not have the network, then you do not hear, you do not learn, and you do not see when you need to revise your direction.

Finally, deliver what you have promised!

Notes

1. The government program in Finland is the political work plan for the Cabinet of Ministers for the duration of the government term, agreed by the parties upon forming the coalition government. It essentially contains the political goals and promises of the current government.
2. It was the report called "21 Paths to a Frictionless Finland: Report of the ICT 2015 Working Group," published in 2013.
3. X-Road is the data exchange and interoperability platform used for government-wide secure data sharing in Estonia first, implemented then under the name *Palveluväylä* in Finland and now in other countries, too.
4. Oy Suomi AB could be translated as Finland Inc., or Finland Ltd.—denoting the concept of state as "one enterprise."
5. Maija is referring to the Digital and Population Data Services Agency, titled Digi- ja Väestötietovaristo (DVV) in Finnish.

CHAPTER 4

Barry Lowry

Ireland

B arry Lowry has been the CIO for the Irish Government since April 2016 with the primary task of taking forward the government's digital agenda. He is also the chief advisor to the government on all digital matters affecting the state and its citizens.

Barry was previously the Director for IT Shared Services and Strategy and head of the IT Profession within the Northern Ireland Civil Service.

Barry is a Fellow of the Irish and British Computer Societies and is a former winner of the BCS Northern Ireland IT Professional of the Year. He was awarded an OBE. for services to the Northern Ireland government and the Northern Ireland computer industry in 2017.

Barry is a public servant at heart, the best of the breed. Deeply driven to the mission of serving, he blends this calling nicely together with social intelligence and with the technologist's training and a manager's thinking.

It must be this blend that has seen him take the digital work of government to a whole new level on several occasions, first in Northern Ireland and now in the Republic of Ireland. The challenge in the latter was to put the house in order, basically, and Barry surely has managed that. Through careful planning and relentless work on delivering the strategy, the Office of GCIO has also lifted Ireland to the ranks of digital government role models—including with their COVID-19 pandemic response.

Barry is very structured and methodical in his thinking and in the way he approaches his work. That does not imply he is theoretical—oh, he is as practical as can be. But the next pages will reveal how much systematic thought he gives to how to be effective in whatever he does, and then puts these thoughts to practice in building up his team and his work every day.

Barry has built himself to be a true people's person. If you are to meet him, opt for a meeting with a pint in the pub (he will not decline!). You will then have a grand craic, I promise.

—SIIM

How Did You Become Involved in the Digital Government Work?

I have been working in the area for over thirty years. I started at the very bottom. At the time when I had left school and had been accepted by university, I found teaching interesting. But in Ireland, there were just no jobs for teachers at that time. I had successfully applied for a temporary position in the civil service over the summer and it was full of unemployed teachers!

Then civil service offered me a permanent job. I planned to take a year for this job and then go back to the university track. They put me in a clerical role in the pensions branch. There I learned that I really liked the idea of public service and the difference you can make to people's lives.

One day my mentor came to me with this form and said I should complete it. I read it and it was to do an exam to go train in IT. I said I did not even like computers! He encouraged me, I applied, and was one of eight people selected. After six months of training, I was a programmer and suddenly realized this is what I was born to do.

After a couple of years, I was promoted into the analyst stream and worked on several major projects. As I was starting to get offers for jobs in the private sector, every time I thought of taking one, an opportunity came up with the civil service. So, I sort of felt I was meant to stay there. I ended up becoming a team lead, then I became a manager in my late twenties. I was the senior technical lead on the (very successful) Animal and Public Health Information System project in Northern Ireland and got a real taste for what being a program director was like, with all the aspects of change and transformation.

What Was Your Road Then to the GCIO Role in Ireland?

I first became the head of technology at the Department of Health in Northern Ireland, then moved to become head of technology for the whole Northern Ireland government. I was then asked to deliver IT shared services, ended up being the head there. I did all of that for four years and then started to think, what will be the next big challenge?

I was invited to have a conversation about possibly going over to London to take a role at the Cabinet Office, and was also offered the role of head of IT at a major London Borough Council, because Northern Ireland is a region in the UK. At the same time, I was not sure if I actually wanted to uproot the family for London. I had joked that I was going to wait until they approached me from Dublin. Out of the blue one day, I got a phone call that the GCIO job had come available and had I thought of it?

The Office of the Government CIO (OGCIO) was created in 2013 and the first GCIO was Bill McCluggage. Unfortunately, Bill had to leave the role after several months for personal matters, and Michael McGrath temporarily came in to deliver the public service ICT strategy. Apparently, both Bill and Michael had suggested that the next government CIO should have a strong focus for program delivery and mentioned my name as a good possible fit.

When I got the call from Bill, the applications closed that night. I literally had a few hours to decide, to talk to my wife and apply. The candidacy was a two-interview process with aptitude tests and such thrown in. Once I was offered the job, the Northern Irish civil service agreed to put me on a career break for up to three years. If I decided I wanted to stay, I could make it permanent with the Irish civil service. This was generous on both sides.

So, in some respects, I never had a grand plan. I just saw opportunities for growth and for increased challenge. The universe lined up in a way.

Do You Still Miss a Chance to Get Your Hands into Code?

What I actually loved the most was dealing with the people around my job. I really enjoyed that I could take a conversation with customers and turn that into an output. The purity of the code was not what interested me; it was what you could do with it, what you could do with technology.

Jenny Johnston, my first boss and a terrific mentor, saw in me someone who was really comfortable talking to the users. What started to emerge was that my real skill set was to translate the customer vision into technical conversations that technical people could use. I could talk to customers; I could work out ways of doing things.

I did love to code, because I like the idea of sitting in a room and writing stuff, seeing its output was quite thrilling. But when I got to see the first electronic driver's licenses being produced in Northern Ireland, and to be able to say that night to my mom and dad that it was my system—that bit really started to rock my boat. So, the design and leading the delivery of the project became the bits that excited me the most.

A large part of my current job still is dealing with the more senior people to work out how to deliver things. Having conversations with politicians and bouncing ideas off them, taking their ideas and translating them into possible ways in which we can resolve the issue. You start to ask the right questions and start to almost crystallize their thinking into something that would be achievable, that could be a project.

How Is the Digital Government Work Led in Ireland and What Was Your Motivation to Join That Effort?

OGCIO is under the Department of Public Expenditure and Reform. The department itself was formed in response to the national financial crash of the late 2000s. It was created in 2011 from splitting the Department of Finance in two to keep things that were missed precrash more in focus and steer the recovery in public administration. It is focused on making sure that taxpayers' money was spent as well as possible and to evolve the civil service through reform.

The creation of OGCIO was very much in line with the UK's Cabinet Office's Government Digital Service model, a unit responsible for strategic direction but also the sanction of major spend: stopping things from happening if they were not aligned with the strategy or enabling them if they were.

This really appealed to me. In Northern Ireland, there I was in the chief advisory role. But the idea of being responsible in a national role, including for health service, welfare, policing, so on—that really appealed to me. I had seen what Mike Bracken and Liam Maxwell had done (in the UK) and when you watch other people doing their jobs, you do think what would you do in their position. When you are then offered the same chance or a chance to compete for that, it becomes very appealing.

I currently report to two ministers. One is Michael McGrath, the minister for the whole department. The other is minister of State for eGovernment—we really do need to change that awful old title! Ossian Smyth is the current minister there and he has background in technology himself, and is very passionate and keen for change.

What Did the Bosses Expect You to Deliver; What Was the Goal They Gave You?

I think there was a sense that they wanted an acceleration of e-government but very much with a reform focus. They also wanted this to be done in a "safe" way. Ireland really has had only two bad experiences with IT at the national level. One of them was called Reach. A brilliant idea but not that well executed. It was the idea of a single relationship with the customer, way ahead of its time. The other was PPARS. Again, a good initiative but one that failed as a transformation program. No one wanted another major IT disaster in government, and plenty were being reported from other parts of Europe.

I am not sure many politicians fully understood the new public sector ICT strategy, but it just felt to them like it was the right thing to do. So, the expectations for me were very much to bring stability and to start to show a forward momentum.

What Was the State of Digital Government When You Came into the Job?

Ireland was seen, also in international studies, to be a country that had progressed well in the past but was in stagnation in public sector ICT. It was probably a fair assessment. In the early days of e-government we had done extremely well, but then there was the financial crash and Irish government had to get financial rescue packages in place. Similar to all other infrastructure development, technology spend had been more or less curtailed because there were other priorities.

I joined at a brilliant time really because the country was coming out of the worst of the recession. There was an appetite to reinvest again. My predecessor had done the public service ICT strategy and I thought it was an extremely good document. In fact, in my second interview one of the questions was that if I accepted the job, would I want to rewrite the strategy? I thought it was a perfect strategy, exactly what was needed. My ambition would be to implement it as much as possible, as quickly as possible.

Where Did You Start with It? What Was Your Focus in the First Hundred Days?

There had been previously a very bad relationship between the center and the departments. That needed to be repaired because we had to get national solutions in place. I had to bring in the departments and try to get them to feel part of an overall solution and a plan to go forward.

The first thing I did when I came into the post in April 2016 was to meet all the secretary generals. I got a real sense that some of them felt very "unloved" by the center; there had not been a lot of attention given to them by our department. My priority was to rebuild those relations and get together a really strong cross-departmental team, all committed to change.

I used for this a tool set I had used before, called reference design and governance. This tool gets a really good conversation going and can help facilitate an action plan for the achievement of a shared vision. One of my traits is that I always manage to absorb information from really, really clever people. One of my best friends is Dr. Joe McDonagh; he is an expert in change and transformation in Trinity College, Dublin. He taught me two critical components of successful change: always honor the past and invite people to cocreate the future. That is what I used.

I never criticized where the departments were at the time—I said they were doing the best they could in a difficult context. But here was an opportunity for us to accelerate if we all worked together. I made it very clear to them that I wanted us all to work together and be part of the leadership of ICT-enabled change and development. I think the way these relationships started and have strengthened over the last five years has really paid dividends to government.

The other thing was to create a concrete plan for going forward. We took the five pillars of the strategy, which were a better digital experience, more joined-up data, and the three enablers of more talented staff across government, shared infrastructure, and better govern-ance. We took a look at these five pillars using this reference design and governance method, and we created what was called the "18-step plan." I presented the plan as my priorities for my first three years.

Once accepted, we broke those eighteen major deliverables to projects and also grouped some of them. We then got CIOs from the departments to cochair their delivery boards with someone from my department. It created a real sense that we were all in this together and we were going to build something better together.

What Was Your Time Horizon with the Plan?

I had set out for three years on the job initially because your planning has to be very much linked to the longevity of the government in place. They need to achieve things; they need to show the public that they—and you—are achieving things. In 2016, we had a strong govern-ment in place; it was going to be in place for three or more years and so my three-year view felt like aligning to that window. In this period, you can also make sure that you already have some wins as well. So, we articulated where we needed to be in three years.

What Were Your Levers to Make It All Happen?

The least sexy part of technology and transformation is the most important—good governance, good project, and program management. That was one of the things that we did rigidly intro-duce, and it made a huge difference. I think it really increased the government's confidence that we knew what we were doing, and that we were going to deliver.

As I said, we started to bring the departments into governance and gave them more influ-ence in and understanding of what was happening. That worked. Also, it is important to have a program support office driving the change, demonstrating the progress, putting out good communication about what you are achieving and saying.

One key lever has been that I can stop a project in the government. I used to say to people that it was a perfect tool to have; it was a bit like having a powerful missile. You want everybody to know you have one, but you never want to fire it. There was only one occasion with one department where they were really being difficult about something that we wanted to do, and I threatened to sanction the project. The department followed in the end, and it actually went well for them.

It was a powerful demonstration that you need two things. You need to work with the other parts of the public service so that you get a common vision. But they also need to understand that in the end it is you as GCIO responsible for all the bits working, and they have to play their part. That is why sanction is a really important tool. It has really increased cooperation.

In OGCIO, we have worked really hard to be helpful, too. We have been suggesting solu-tions, helping departments develop things, and so on. If you approach it the right way, with the right governance, are open to reuse, and are open to principles such as the "once only,"[1] and so on, then we will support what you do. We will help you in every way. But if you are not going to follow and you are not delivering what the public needs, we will not let you do that. These are the rules of engagement. It is a bit like with your parents. Once you know the boundaries and do not cross them, you have a pretty good relationship with your parents when you are growing up.

Besides Setting up the New Governance Model, What Were Your Major Priorities in the 18-Step Plan?

On digital experience, there were two big plays: to grow MyGovID and to build a government portal (gov.ie). These gave us the platform to do amazing things next.

One of the things that I really wanted to do was build out a national electronic identity system. There already was one called MyGovID. It had only 8,675 verified accounts. I saw an opportunity to give a priority to growing the use of this system. We introduced it as a log-in capacity next to the proprietary log-in capability with the Department of Revenue, our most influential department, and then onwards in others. Today MyGovID is one of the fastest growing digital identities in the world at the moment in terms of actual use, according to Gartner consultancy.

In addition to the discussions on MyGovID was the idea of a single portal to access all government services because it was not easy to find the right government service in the first place. We had done one in Northern Ireland, but trying to sell that idea was hard initially. The Taoiseach's, meaning prime minister's department, liked the idea, though. This gave us the political mandate and interest to push it ahead. The portal proved invaluable during the management of the COVID-19 pandemic.

On the data side, the work was very much about building the foundations: legislation, the data sharing and governance act, and a data strategy itself. By the way, the data strategy was largely developed by departments with our facilitation, which was really powerful. We have a new Data Governance Board model, data catalog, and so on.

On the infrastructure, we wanted to move to a single data center for the government and the hybrid cloud computing model. We now have most departments using the exact same service and the same network.

On people, we developed an ICT professionalization strategy. We got an ICT apprenticeship scheme up and running with graduates, and we have a government-wide shared approach to recruitment.

Once the three years were done and I decided to stay onboard for longer, we have been growing from there in all these directions.

How Has COVID-19 Changed the Way You Operate and What You Are Working On?

I have had to effectively lead some of the national response to COVID-19. Remember that it was one of my attractions to the role at start—to be able to take such a lead.

When COVID-19 broke and started to get really serious in 2020, I was involved in a governance group that included the Department of Health, Health Service Executive, and An Garda, meaning the national police service. We started to plot out how could we use technology to help in the battle against COVID.

One of those tools we identified was the contact tracking app. That appealed to the politicians, so we designed it out and implemented. It actually was a huge success. It was not just optics, because the bigger it began to be, the more we were approached by other governments to use it. The most recent one was New Zealand, and this was a huge motivator to the staff, because we admire New Zealand so much in terms of what they are doing in the tech space.

The other big area of COVID-19 response was people flipping to work from home. Several departments would have struggled to do this had they not signed up for our "Build to Share" desktop solution. We have a very good team on shared services who were able to very quickly enable thousands of civil servants to work from home. This really helped the senior people and the civil servants to understand what the shared services model is about—the value of being on the same network, easier to protect, and so on.

I was then approached to take the lead developing the digital COVID-19 certificate, and that has been a huge success.

OGCIO has always had two arms to it: a policy arm and a delivery arm. We learned from the UK that sustained delivery is very hard when you have people coming and going through a revolving door. The one strength we have in Ireland is that a lot of really good people have wanted to stay. The contractors have been loyal to us as well because they love the work. So, when it came to COVID-19 response, this all gave us an element of confidence that we could deliver things and quick.

COVID-19 also demonstrated the strength of the relationships built way back. We realized that a big number of people were vaccinated by general practitioners, and we did not have email addresses for these people, because GPs tend to record only physical addresses. As we were going to push out the vaccination certificates, we were going to have to use post and OGCIO had no way to do it. Then it occurred to me that revenue service has a world-class postal capability. I phoned the CIO and he said, "We will not let you down." They printed and posted about 1.2 million certificates that could not be emailed and they did it all for us, for government.

How Have You Managed to Keep the Political Backing Necessary for Delivery and for Keeping a Focus?

You have your long-term objectives of what you believe you need to do, and sometimes that may not be particularly exciting for a politician or a minister. A classic case was our data center. I wanted to build a hybrid cloud model, wanted to use more of a public cloud. There were many barriers to it, all the way from people who had their databases on their work computers and their own computer rooms. It meant physical barriers, cultural barriers, and so on. Breaking that was harder because government ministers are not particularly interested in back office stuff. At the start of 2021, we finally convinced the new minister that it was the right thing to do—also for green agenda reasons, because we will be shutting down inefficient computer rooms—and procurement is starting now. So, sometimes you have to just keep trying.

You also have to give politicians opportunities to show that they are having an impact as well. You have to always be alive during the conversations with them, to try and pick things that might interest them. Then you try and deliver those, especially if you have the tools ready for it. A good example was with a previous minister of state who had the idea to take the budget and present it graphically to enable the public to see how their taxes were spent. So, we built the website to show where people's money goes. We knew we could make it work, because we actually hosted all the budget data and had lot of analytics capabilities. A year later we even got awarded a prize for the contribution to fiscal studies! The teachers were using it in schools.

The learning for me is that you have got to be alert to what politicians pick up from talking to their constituents, to other ministers, and so on. You then have to be flexible enough to take this sort of political work in, and it might be actually a good idea they bring.

What Was the Team Like When You Joined and How Did You Build It Further?

I started with fifty-two staff members, four direct reports. This year, I have six direct reports and sixty-six staff members, plus a lot of contractors.

When I joined in 2016, I came down to Dublin for two induction days and met the team. I was incredibly impressed at the talent that was within the OGCIO. They just needed the opportunity to use that talent. They needed top-level support to get the political support to get money and set the direction, the narrative, all that stuff a CIO does.

In terms of setting up a program and then the support office for its delivery, it needed someone with a natural skill set for that. But that was always my strength, my bread and butter: to develop programs, allocate resource, balance the team, move a project forward. We were also able to recruit someone for it and we built up momentum quickly.

Even though people have left, I have been lucky to replace them with people of equivalent talent.

What Has Been Your Trick to Attracting Them to Come and Work for You?

I think you get a reputation.

The best thing that ever happened to me was that I decided to get an additional degree in my mid-twenties once I was in the IT stream in government. I ended up doing a modular degree, including subjects on occupational psychology, industrial relations, advertising, marketing, public relations, finance, and so on. In other words, all the components of a CIO role, and that was invaluable.

I started managing staff using the principles I studied: empowerment, trust, continuous learning. I always loved the McGregor Theory X and Theory Y approach. It suggests that if you trust your staff members and they are able to give their best, they will. If you are watching like a hawk thinking they are not working enough otherwise, this will happen, too. It is all about trust. I was doing it in some very conservative departments and all of a sudden people could see that my area was performing way above expectations.

These tools have never let me down in my entire career. People have wanted to come and work with me, because they know that is how I manage. They know that they will be given the space to make their own decisions and do their thing. I have managed to develop every team of mine to where we use the strengths of the individuals to make them the strengths of the team. We do deliver things in unison, and that works.

What Have Been Your Values or Mottos to Steer the Team With? What Culture Did You Want in the Team?

One of my mottos to the team has been that you have to earn the right to ask for more. In other words, let us deliver with what we have got, then we will go and have the conversation about what we could deliver, if we had an increase in resources.

Also, because we are the strategy unit, we have got to invite people to cocreate the future. It takes respect; it takes empowerment.

I have wanted us to be an organization that is good to work with. I constantly have said to the team that we do not turn people away with any requests for help; we take the time, and we answer them. I have always done it myself, too. Just as an example—got an email from a guy who was doing a team project for his master's degree. He needed to interview a CIO and was there any chance he could interview me? I said, sure, come and have a cup of coffee. And then I got him another interview with a private sector CIO who was a friend of mine.

I am a great believer that you always get more back. Help is the best investment you can make. If your organization reflects that culture, then people trust it and want to work it. The reputation of OGCIO in this respect is beyond our wildest dreams from when we started in 2016.

What Have You Used to Sustain the Relationships with Other Departments and Stakeholders?

We started and have kept going a forum of heads of technology from all the departments. What we often do is bring in somebody to do a presentation, and we will have a chat about it afterwards. People networking and thinking together can be really productive because it sustains relationships, or you pick up information. We do not always have a clear agenda, where we tick the boxes in the style of a commission. At the same time, our relationship becomes stronger.

We only sometimes talk about the strategy program because delivery is mainly going forward through one-on-one relationships. So, I also meet the CIOs directly on a regular basis. As a national CIO, you want to make sure that you are seen by the department CIOs as someone of their own, that you are representing their views, and sharing the same opinions when possible.

I also sit in a number of governance boards, which are all important for different reasons. For example, one of them looks at offline services, which is a big part of inclusivity. I have always said that the success of government is in how it looks after the needs of all its people. So if there is 10 percent that will never go online, we need to give that 10 percent the best experience possible as well.

Besides the Routines with External Stakeholders, What Routines or Style Have Been Effective with Your Own Team?

I have six deputies or direct reports, responsible for different areas.

We do have a formal process of meeting twice a year, but we speak at least once a week to catch up. They look at my diary and put something in, although I am available to them also on need in the meantime. Some of them want a regular slot, some of them take ten minutes, some want an hour—that is all fine. I want to be moving at their pace. At the end of the day, my success will be gauged through what they achieve more than what I achieve.

I always have a great sense of the rhythm of the organization because I am getting the weekly updates. I do not need to be in the minutiae of every project, though occasionally, things will come up that the team will want to discuss with me. When somebody comes to you with a problem, just by letting them speak, they can often resolve it themselves. They are almost performing an extra layer of analysis as they speak. When you ask them questions, you are driving them to tell you what the answer to the problem is and you are not telling them. That is how it works out nine times out of ten. Only occasionally, I will have an idea and want them to think about or work on it.

Given All You Have Achieved, What Has Been the Hardest Part in Your Job and What Have You Also Perhaps Failed With?

The hardest part has been getting the whole of government to an understanding of the importance of technology. I think that has changed. Whether because of COVID-19 or it would have happened anyway, is another question.

There is a different attitude toward technology in the Irish government; it is not seen as a peripheral topic anymore. They have seen that the whole government policy of reopening the economy, the travel, enabling dining in, and the reopening of hospitality would not have been possible in COVID times without the technology. But there were times over the last few years where I was a bit disappointed that there was not one minister responsible for all things digital, that I had to work with different ones. Yet, I tend to be a person that sees a positive in everything. Having five ministers with some responsibility for wider digital policy has helped me build relationships with five ministers rather than just one. This strengthens our work in another ways.

One of the things I would change, if had to start again, would maybe be to push for a specific piece of digital legislation to enable MyGovID. The value and safety of MyGovID is only now being understood—previously there was misunderstanding about the process. Recently, a report recognized that it was a huge success both financially and in terms of delivering digital government. So, it is clear we are getting there—and the public uptake has continued to grow.

Although there is only a small group of people against data sharing, they are very vociferous and will not acknowledge the other side of the argument. Most people think that the "once-only" principle is the most obvious thing. Yet, there are people who say that they want to choose that one government department would not have their real home address while another one does. I am not certain how can you address these people. Do you stop investing your energies to persuade them and just move around them? I was shocked by the first newspaper vitriolic narrative about the Public Services Card and the MyGovID back in 2016. I could not understand the logic behind the fears of reusing identity data to serve people better when many actually wanted to be served better. I guess you have to accept that you cannot be loved by everybody, or you are going to be very disappointed. And I know now of course there are pockets of opposition in most countries.

What pleases me, though, is that MyGovID has seen such a growth in use. People see it is a good thing! For example, MyGovID made it easy for people to apply to the new national childcare scheme recently. It really helped the people understand the benefit of data sharing and a single ID. You get the public support if they clearly see the benefits.

What Do You Consider Your Biggest Achievement in the Office?

All the eighteen steps in the plan have been achieved, even if some took longer. However, I am most proud of what OGCIO has achieved as an organization.

Around the time of COVID-19 certificate delivery, I was doing twice-daily standups with our tech team. I saw how many hours the team was working and how proud they were of the changes they were making. They are so motivated and driven if they see what their work is going to achieve. I have seen it a few times over the last few years. That fantastic experience of seeing what we can put out as a team, the potential we have, is better than any single one achievement.

How Long Do You Think You Will Still Be in Office and What Might Be Next for You?

What the Irish government needed was sustainability and longevity. I have wanted to give the organization real confidence that I would not ask them to do stuff that is risky and then next minute I would be joining an IT company or something. I promised my team already the first time I met them that I would be there until the job was finished. And I am still there! As a government CIO, you have got to play a short and a long game. It is very, very hard on a national level to make a sustained impact in two years. We need to commit and that was the contribution I made.

I personally wanted from Ireland the experience of running national programs, as I said. I have learned so much about it: about developing laws, the parliamentary process, working with the most senior ministers to understand their agenda. All that has been challenging but really enjoyable as well.

I was approached last Christmas to sign a new contract for the GCIO role. I did sign it, so I will be here until 2026—I feel there is a lot more to do. I will not sign another contract after that; it will be time for somebody else to take over and I think the next GCIO will be an internal candidate reflecting the growing talent that we have.

What Will Irish Digital Government Look Like in Five Years Once You Hand Over? What Are the Next Things or Even the Next Strategy in the Works?

We have got a draft of a new public service ICT strategy coming together now; I am hoping to get it out in the next couple of months. The theme of that is very much to build on the strong foundations we have laid.

The next big thing we want to do is around life events and have all the related things in gov.ie. Once you will register the birth, we will do everything for you, the whole package of services, because we know who you are. Or same thing with bereavement, when you are setting up a company or when you are returning to Ireland. This one is a big thing for us with diaspora coming back. We are going to make all these services more proactive.

On the identity front, the big development would be to have it on the phone like all of Europe is going to. We are already putting out some of the next generation technology for it. Also, we want to extend MyGovID into personal private sector use. Government owns the process but allows others to use it. We are in discussions with the central bank, for example, about how your government credential can be used to open up a bank account.

There will be single infrastructure, also for home and blended working within public sector. With that, the government will be an even more attractive place to work.

Getting cohesive and joined-up European systems would be something I would like to see us achieve in the next five years. We have had an awful lot of good ideas about how we could use ID across Europe but have not delivered too much. We did not manage to deliver a single COVID-19 certificate or tracing system for Europe.

The area I really want to see improved nationally is health care. I think there is so much potential that we really need to give this a push. What I want to do is set up an ecosystem, where any Irish company that has a big idea has to be given a chance of an approach by the public service. In other words, we have got to tell them why we will not use it, rather than ignore their calls. I want to make it a rigid process where the government is obliged to do something.

At the end of the day, if we are going to keep talent in this country, we have got to give them an opportunity to test the ideas and refine them, and then show other countries that it will work. By accident, what we did with contact tracing in Ireland was a perfect example of how our govtech industry can grow. Under emergency provisions, we were able to do a very quick procurement, engage an Irish company who were experts in a particular area, and give them the testing bed to show what they were able to achieve. Their solution ended up being used in other countries around the world and creating employment in Ireland out of that.

In Northern Ireland, too, we completely changed the procurement framework, and suddenly all these start-ups and SMEs started to grow. That is what I want to achieve in Ireland. Our relationship with multinationals is terrific, but I want our indigenous sector to be as good as anywhere in the world.

Overall, I believe we are at the cusp of technology pervading everything and I want Ireland to be the best in it.

How Are You Building Things to Last so That the Journey You Started Will Continue?

Well, the big things from our strategy are here to stay now. Gov.ie, MyGovID, infrastructure, data work. They will evolve and might be replaced with newer versions, but their value has been demonstrated and their vision will remain. It is them changing that gives the initiatives sustainability, also—like we are now changing what MyGovID is or how it works with mobile phones.

It pays to be open to new technology developments. There are loads of people in Ireland that are constantly trying to push the boundaries with research. What I need to do is have the conversations with them and give them the opening to test out ideas. Then they might change how we do things in government.

The biggest thing for sustainability is the culture and practice of people development in your organization. I have never been afraid to recruit people and develop those people to take my job. I have never been interested in this cult of the supreme being that some CIOs fall into. I have been more interested in building an organization that is really strong, really respected, and has several people that can do my job extremely well. It worked well in Northern Ireland just the same. So, do not be afraid of developing people.

What Are Your Nuggets of Advice for Any Peer about How to Do the National CIO or Similar Role Most Effectively?

It is all about the people. That is the first thing. If you do not build relationships and foster relationships, you will not succeed. It is as simple as that.

As I said, one of my great heroes is Douglas McGregor for his Theory X and Theory Y concept. It is the idea that if you trust people to give of their best, they will not let you down. If you do not trust them, then they will let not you down on that front either. Understanding of how you trust your staff members and empower them is really important.

The second thing is that you have to invite people to cocreate the future in the transformation projects. That means everybody, from lowest level onwards. When I started the shared service center in Northern Ireland, I sat with the first-level staff members and listened to their ideas because I wanted their support to the change.

Third, do not be afraid of your limitations. Joe McDonagh has this four-quadrant model. In order for transformation to happen, you need four skill sets. First one is architecture—the big picture thinking. Second one is engineering, turning that big picture into projects and deliverables. Third one is humanist dimension, bringing the staff along. Fourth one is broker skills, which is about building the support you need.

In any transformation project, the first thing is that you have to assess your skill set against those four quadrants and then bring in the people with skill sets you do not have. I was good at architecture; I was good at the humanist and brokering part. I needed good engineers to work with me and so that became the focus of my enhancement of my team. If one of those four quadrants is missing, transformation is unlikely to succeed.

If you look at major project failures, the vast majority of them fail because they did not have a long-term champion who would support it through any tricky moments. That is the broker stuff. Next biggest reason for failure is because the staff at the front end did not get it. It is a humanist-quadrant failure.

CIOs tend to be focused on the two of architecture or engineering, but the reason that projects fail are the other two. Focus on people and brokering issues, getting the political mandate, the senior mandate—because you are the leader. The only way you are going to lead a change is to engage all the stakeholders and bring along the critical ones, especially.

Note

1. "Once only" denotes the principle for designing government services in a way that the users would not have to submit data to the government more than only once, and the government agencies should reuse and share that data for service delivery from there onwards.

CHAPTER 5

Bolor-Erdene Battsengel

Mongolia

Bolor-Erdene Battsengel is the State Secretary of the newly established Ministry of Digital Development of Mongolia, effective starting January 2022. She was previously the chairwoman of Mongolia's Communication and Information Technology Authority, the youngest and first female to hold this position since July 2020.

Raised in the countryside, Bolor-Erdene has started the "Girls for Coding" program, which trains girls from vulnerable families in remote areas who do not have computer or internet access. Until end of 2021, fifty girls received training in the program and were offered jobs at companies.

Bolor-Erdene graduated from the University of Oxford with a master's degree in public policy in 2017. She previously worked at the World Bank, United Nations, Asian Development Bank, and Cabinet Office of the United Kingdom.

She has been selected into the *Forbes* Asia "30 Under 30" list of outstanding young leaders.

There had been several attempts to get a digital government going in Mongolia, but it took Bolor-Erdene to make it happen. As always, there have been important supporting factors, too: strong political support and push, plus COVID-19. As she has said herself, in a way it has been the right time and about time.

But her story is to me a good example of the premise of this book: the right strategy and right conditions do not cut it by themselves; you also need to a right leader to make the magic happen. That is why I was keen to have Bolor-Erdene in this book, even if her journey as a digital government leader has been a short one so far.

She does have the results to show, no doubt. The e-Mongolia introduction in 2020–2021 has been perhaps among the most shining recent digital government progress stories globally in terms of the speed, width of services, as well as public appreciation. Which all translates into impact.

Her youth should offer encouragement that you do not always need long experience to make stuff happen. Rather, the right attitude (look at what she says about importance of bravery!) and approach can help just as much. It will be fascinating to see in the next years how the changes that this power-woman and the Mongolian government started will continue and last.

—*Siim*

What Was Your Journey to the Government in Mongolia and to Digital Government Leadership Like?

I did my master's in public policy from Oxford University, although I was not focusing on digital topics then. I got an opportunity to work within the UK Cabinet Office on an internship, in the team that worked on the International Civil Service Effectiveness Index. That led to me to digital governance issues, as we were doing surveys and learning about relevant experience of countries from around the world. It was very interesting to see the different mechanisms and different systems how governments had been digitizing and how they received the benefits from it.

After the studies, I worked some time as a consultant and also went to work for the World Bank in Sydney, overseeing some of the agricultural projects in the Pacific Islands countries. My parents kind of pressured me to come back to Mongolia; plus, I found that University of Oxford was working with the Bill and Melinda Gates Foundation on a project called Digital Pathways. It is about analyzing the digital development readiness of countries, and then developing relevant strategy proposals for these governments on how to transition to a digital economy.

They chose a few countries; I lobbied to include Mongolia. Their requirement was that the government had to have ownership of the work. We managed to get that from the current president, Uhnaagijn Hürelsüh, who was prime minister at the time, and the current prime minister, Luvsannamsrain Oyun-Erdene, who was chief cabinet secretary at the time. We got the funding, got the project going, and I led this work in Mongolia.

It was an important initiative to convince the leaders on the importance of digital development and digital economy; it was before COVID-19. Politicians did not care much about it before. The strategy we ended up proposing entailed six steps for the transition to a digital economy in Mongolia. The assessment basically concluded that the government itself was a bottleneck to digital development as digital services were not there, and the government was very bureaucratic and corrupt. I suggested a strong move toward digitizing the public services and building up a digital government; I was trying to convince the Cabinet Secretariat to take it on.[1] I was planning to go back to Sydney after handing over the proposal.

It so happened that then the chief cabinet secretary and several parliament members went to Estonia, saw what the digital government could be about and how it saved money. They came back and established a digital development committee under the Cabinet Secretariat, asking me to lead it. It was a policy coordination body; I had some five people working under my supervision. We were trying to pressure Communication and Information Technology Authority (CITA) to start work on e-Mongolia, a digital government program. We had everything prepared for it but CITA chairman was not having it.

After the 2020 election, the new prime minister offered the CITA chair job to me saying that if I really wanted to do the digital government, I had to do it myself. There was no way I could convince others to do it for me. It was a big decision for me because I had a lucrative job waiting, and I always wanted to be far away from politics. But I had a motivation to try and make e-Mongolia work.

So, on the 22nd of July 2020, I was appointed as the first chairwoman of CITA. It was still a civil service role, even if I do have to deal with politics by working with the cabinet and parliamentarians to get things approved—like laws in parliament.

Where Does Your Motivation for Improving the Government Come From?

My grandfather was a public servant; my parents were public servants. Even though I wanted to be away from the politics, I was always interested in civil service, and how it works. I also got a chance to work with a lot of governments around the world and see their approaches, including when I was working for the World Bank.

There is also a cultural thing for Mongolians, perhaps because we have a small population. We always want to come back to Mongolia and do something good for the country. I always had this thing in my mind that I should go back to Mongolia and do something, to help the country to do something.

When I was given a choice to work as the leader of the CITA, I thought it was a good chance for me to change the country in my own way. E-Mongolia could help a lot of people because corruption had been a very, very big issue for a long time. Also, I had had myself the experience with bureaucracy. I remember spending like three days at the registration agency to get my passport; it was so terrible. So, I thought it was a good chance to do something about it!

The only thing I asked for from the prime minister was political support. He has been very supportive. If we would not have had that, we would not have succeeded with our tasks. It is very important to have faith in whomever you are working for. One reason I joined the government is because I thought there were good leaders, and they could help me do these things.

As the Prime Minister Asked You to Join, Did He or Anyone Lay Out a Concrete Expectation for You in Terms of What to Deliver?

It was about putting to action the six steps proposed in the digital economy report, which include a lot of different things: digital governance, cybersecurity, digital signatures, and so on. CITA works on all of these and with a wide digital development mission, including skills and connectivity infrastructure, even space topics.

The political leaders paid the most attention to getting the government services digitized and getting our government services available on the phone. That was what moved them. So, the biggest expectation for me, from the people who offered me the job, was to bring e-Mongolia out as a platform with services in it. My purpose within the first hundred days was to launch e-Mongolia. And we did it with exactly the first hundred days, on October 1, 2020. That was when the new digital service platform launched, with 181 first digital services available there.

What Was the Digital Government Scene and Situation in Mongolia before That?

Some countries do not have too many public services perhaps. In Mongolia, we have thousands of government services at every step of the way. You have to get some signatures; you have to get some approvals for whatever you do.

Some infrastructure for digital government had been built up. We had data centers, we had government data collected and kept. We had an authentication system to register the citizens and allow them to use online services. But there were not many actual government services using these options.

We had lacked a lot in leadership, to be honest. In civil service, certain ways of work had been in place for thirty years; public servants were not supportive of new ideas and new projects.

What Have Been the Levers and Mandate of CITA to Bring Change to the Scene?

What I wanted to do from the beginning was to build services for the agencies, because there have been a lot of projects implemented and failed in terms of actually digitalizing the different sectors, like health, for example. As CITA is an agency, we could not take over the delivery and leadership of different sectors—there are different ministries for that. We have to work with them.

I got a lot of support from the current prime minister, because when he came into the office, he announced that leaders or ministers who are not digitalizing their services will be considered as pro-corruption. That was a big political move. It was a big help, because when we started digitalizing with e-Mongolia, I got a lot of backlash from the government, from different agencies. People were against because, first of all, they did not understand the importance of it as they had not seen it before. Second, there have been corruption issues in some organizations but thanks to digital governance, corruption options are reduced. The prime minister saw the importance of e-Mongolia in this sense; also e-Mongolia became instantly a very appreciated government project by the public. So, he and other leaders paid more attention.

As CITA has been under the Cabinet Secretariat, we can bring backlash and challenges to the highest level. The prime minister has also set up a mechanism whereby citizens can send complaints, and these become priorities for government to solve—also priorities for our digitalization work. So, if there is a complaint for specific service, we will digitalize that service first. This structure and the political weight behind have given a lot of leverage to the work.

Starting from January 2022, CITA is actually becoming a Ministry for Digital Development. We will have a minister; we will be working at the same level of and directly with all other ministries. Previously it was a challenge to go directly to other ministries and tell them what to do; now such coordination will be stronger. We can also start reducing the overlapping digital investments, for example.

If e-Mongolia Was the Deliverable, What Is Your Wider Mission? What Is the Objective You Have Set for Yourself and the Country in Digital Government?

My vision has always been to develop the digital economy more broadly, just like in our studies under the Digital Pathways work and in the recommendations we made. Digital governance is important, but in the end, it is a very small part of digital development. We want the Mongolian economy to grow, to make the country very inclusive, want to support companies and encourage people to use digital services more widely, to have a well-developed digital infrastructure for it. Then we can create a digital economy. This matters especially because Mongolia has been heavily relying on the mining industry.

In a digital government, the aim is to digitalize *all* the government services, excluding perhaps only the ones where you will have to make emotional decisions, like getting married. By end of 2021, we have made 610 services digitally available on e-Mongolia. In 2022, we will focus on services that help special groups of people like those living oversees or who are left out of digital development for age or disabilities. Most important, we are looking at services for herder communities, as we are still a nomadic country in Mongolia.

My own goal would be accomplished if a herder from middle-of-nowhere can use his or her phone and get the government service right there—and not need to drive to for five hours to the nearest province center or to the city to get a simple government service done. A lot of combined work has to go into reaching this objective: from governance and digitalization of services to infrastructure and digital literacy, for example. But that is the mission I have.

The time line we are operating with is 2024. All services have to be online before the next elections that year. We are halfway there, I would say, in terms of digital services reaching all the people and communities.

With All the Government Services to Digitalize, How Do You Prioritize and Sequence Them? What Are the Criteria for Selection?

There are two types of ways we set up the priorities and the work plan.

First, we do regular surveys, assessments. We conduct this research to see how many services people are getting from each agency, what are the most commonly used ones. This way we see the effect of potential digitalization. For example, a state registration agency is one of the most common places citizens go or need to go—so we started with them quite a bit.

Second, it is the complaint mechanism that the prime minister has set up. There have been complaints coming in about health services, like hospital appointments, and army registrations, which we have digitalized just recently.

Given the Tough Context You Started From, How Did You Start in the Role and Gear CITA to Start Delivering from Your First Hundred Days?

I had a lot of challenge in the beginning for people to accept me as a chairwoman, to accept my leadership and to follow my leadership. A lot of people in government widely and in CITA, too—they have seen many leaders come and go. They thought that I would leave soon anyways. I also caught a lot of attention from the public, being the first woman on the job and being the youngest. There have been suspicions about me coming from a political family, from a rich family.

I worked very hard. I did not have weekends off that first summer. I was a harsh boss also to the team, pushing them to work long and a lot. A lot of people were against it at first, but then they started seeing the results and they started seeing the recognition. They are now very supportive, and do not mind working weekends even.

The results of our work brought public support. I wanted to come out and announce e-Mongolia very publicly on purpose, in an Apple or TED-talk kind of way. We did a big event and launch. Except for elections, it was the first case when a civil servant came out and introduced the product to the public. That got notice. Still, when people saw me or my video of making presentation about e-Mongolia launch, they did not trust immediately. Once they tried out the services on the site, then we got the support.

We did not stop there with the outreach. One of the most important things we have done to ensure the support is to try and have more citizen involvement and participation in the digitalization process. If there is a service you do not like or you are experiencing bureaucracy or corruption, you can inform us, and we will solve it. We have done a lot of public communications to publicly say these things. We got a lot of citizens involved, and they see that it actually works this way.

Training and communications have been a big part of getting agencies onboard. When you digitalize a service, the whole process has to become digital, and you are changing how work gets done. You have to change the internal processes and that takes different skills. We also highlight and praise other agencies' good work in the media a lot, in press conferences. This has helped to win them over.

Still, How Did You Start Working with the CITA Team and Perhaps Changing Things There to Get the Speedy Delivery and New Approach from Them?

When I was working at the Cabinet Secretariat, at the digital development committee, I got to know the people in CITA and the government. I knew whom to talk to, how they work, whom we could work with.

I also had the plan ready from before. I had myself a list of services to start with, from different government agencies—things that people use regularly. We started on them from the first day.

I hired some companies to help us with the actual tech development. I established a project unit immediately with ten people. So, we had then a technical team from outside working on code and solutions, and we had a new project unit working on digitizing the government processes. Convincing people and training people. I started bringing in younger people to join us.

It obviously was a bit lonely at the beginning, but then I had some people join the team. The previous team leaders left their jobs, as their previous boss left. I promoted some specialists to become team leaders, once I worked with them in these first months and got to know who was who. They are now my main partners on e-Mongolia. It was a good thing because they already knew how government worked, but they are young and ambitious—and now given an opportunity.

Once you got e-Mongolia Up and Running, What Have Been Your Key Initiatives and Milestones since Then?

We have done work to promote technology and make people in the country understand the importance of technology. We continue actively with communications work. We have organized a big ICT Expo each year. In 2021 we named it "Digital Nation Expo" and had more than one hundred companies joining. It had the biggest stage ever built in Mongolia, we had two hundred thousand people come to the event in three days.

We have done a lot of legislative and policy work, in addition to continuing the fast-paced digitalization of services and to support these efforts. There was a lack of proper legal environment before. We have been creating a regulation framework to promote and to encourage digital development not only within the government, but to support the digital economy in general. It has meant five new laws within the last year, which has been possible due to the wider public's strong support, again.

The laws have included a personal data protection law; cybersecurity law, which was discussed for almost eighteen years but not passed; a data sharing law; a digital signatures law.

Building CITA has been another important part of work. We now have about eighteen people working in e-Mongolia unit, a third of them are in customer service. They take calls and messages from citizens about e-Mongolia, offer instructions or guidance, solve complaints. I have started using an expert team or group structure, where we involve specialists from various units. So, there is a horizontal e-Mongolia team, a public relations team like that, so on.

How Have You Been Building the Team? How Do You Find People and Whom Do You Look For?

One of the biggest challenges I have had is to find people, to find good people. It is a very small community here, in Mongolia. There are obviously some qualified people out there, but they prefer to work for the private sector, because the pay is much higher and there is less stress.

I have done a lot of headhunting. I have tried to convince young people, talking to them about the importance of the work itself. This way some ambitious guys joined my team: not because of the salary, but because the ambition itself. We have gotten some people who are educated in Australia, the UK, or the US to join. They have been good additions because they have seen how other countries work and they are relatively open-minded.

I have been seeking team members who think differently from the usual government. The culture of government is very boxed, in a way. I want people who can be innovative, who can be creative.

How Do You Work with Your Team? What Are Your Methods and Style?

I work directly with my team; I talk directly to the specialists. Often in government, you have to work through the directors or that is how people do work, at least. I work with people at front desk, the junior staff. I do not have a problem talking to them directly. I like working with people without having to spend time to translate things through the team leaders. In CITA, we are still a small enough team to be able to do it like that.

Before there were a lot of delays in government projects in Mongolia. I did not want to have that. One thing I always believe is that if you give people ten days, they will finish the task in ten days. If you give them three days to finish and really, really push it, you can still have the same result—in three days. I have been aggressive with my team in this way.

I am the one that sets the goals. When we launched e-Mongolia with the first 181 services, I set the next goal right after. I had dinner with the team after finishing the first task, appreciating them, and recognizing them for their work. And then gave the next very strict deadlines for the next few months.

We have very productive short meetings. I do not like long, extensive, inefficient meetings. These are issue or substance meetings. I plan ahead the things to talk about. Once a week, we do a meeting where people can report what they have done. However, if there is an issue or an idea, we will talk about it right away. Even after 7 pm, we can do it over the phone, does not matter.

We do have a very dynamic team in this way. The team has a hunger to do something. I myself do not give interviews that much anymore. I want to have more recognition for my team. That is why I have them talk to the media more: so that they get recognition for what they are doing and working on.

I am involved in my style, I would say. I do not just give the assignment and disappear; I follow up. I think I make people feel like I am their partner, more than their boss. And that they are my partner as well. One aspect of it is that we do not have much hierarchy within the teams.

What Type of Culture Have You Tried to Build into CITA?

I want to have the team as a very dynamic, very active one. I want it to be a power team.

The best way to build a culture is to show and be part of that culture yourself. So, I try a lot myself to be very dynamic and active, to be qualified, to be hard-working, to be friendly. In a way, I create more stress on myself. But if people like it, they kind of tend to follow it.

A big part has been to induce people to be creative. The way I give tasks is aimed at this. If there are ideas or issues on the table, I want to see three options or solutions or suggestions. If I give an assignment to somebody, I want to see the options so that people do not just bring the simplest solution. I want them to think harder, be more innovative, more creative. That is why

I ask for three options that are different from each other. It gives them an opportunity to really understand the issue and think more widely.

Looking back, we achieved the things we have achieved with the team because we—and I—have been very brave. You need this kind of bravery, even if some might call it stupidity, in face of risks and political issues.

Where Does This Sort of Bravery Come From?

It comes from the vision you have—that I have. The feeling that it has to be done, that we have to do it.

What Have Been the Mantras You Have Kept Repeating to the Team?

I do tell them to be more creative and innovative. To be persistent. These are the things I say in every meeting.

And the three options! Always have and bring three options.

Especially at the beginning, I used to say often that we are re-creating government services. We are changing and re-creating the culture, the standards for government. I often say this just to make people understand and realize how important it is what we are doing.

What Do You Think Have Been Your Biggest Achievements in the Role So Far?

I am most proud that e-Mongolia is pretty safe now, even if I were to leave the job. That is because we have introduced service standards to the public and have the public's support.

I am also proud that people now understand the importance of digital transformation more widely, within the shortest amount of time. That there is wide support for digital development itself. This comes from the capacity building, from the public relations work we have done. But it also comes from the fact that we created the e-Mongolia platform and people have been able to use services there, even during the COVID-19 lockdowns. Even in this time, people could order passports, renew driver's licenses.

COVID-19 had a useful impact as well in that it helped people, especially the public and older generations, understand the technology and the benefits of it. If we would not have used the COVID-19 opportunity to deliver services during the lockdown, we would not have the two million users on e-Mongolia that we have now. It stands for 90 percent of the adult population. We grasped the opportunity during the lockdown by preparing a lot of video content, instructions, TV programs, a lot of articles, and experience sharing and feedbacks. So that more people can understand digital more.

What Do You Think You Could Have Done Better? What Have You Learned the Most?

I was rather inexperienced in handling the political stuff. I have made some mistakes in dealing with politicians, not always calculating the political factors in. I would be more careful with some steps of building up e-Mongolia if given second chances.

I also wish I had known more on how to deal with civil servants. That could have saved some time. You have got to give them praise, recognize them for what they have done. Listen to them very carefully, to what they are doing and trying to achieve. I was fairly stubborn: I would come out and fight in the big meetings. That is the bravery part; I get very aggressive when people are not supporting whatever I am doing, especially within the government.

Now I have learned to use soft power more, being friends, being supportive. Still, I do not think it would have been beneficial for us to be very soft and understanding when we started. In the beginning, it was a good approach for me to be very aggressive, even though it was very stressful to me. We needed to shake things up.

What Are the Next Challenges Ahead for You, for CITA, for e-Mongolia?

We have now a very big historical responsibility by turning into a ministry. We have seen a lot of ministries succeed, and a lot of ministries fail as well. I will be spending a lot of time creating a culture that is dynamic and proactive. I will also work very hard to do good team building as well, because we will not have many people. As a ministry, there are government protocols we have to follow, more hierarchy. That is why I need to make sure to create very good fundamental infrastructure for the ministry itself, including the culture and how work happens.

For e-Mongolia, the challenges are in cybersecurity area and in user-friendliness. As we will digitalize all—or at least 95 precent—of government services, it becomes very challenging for people to find whatever they need on e-Mongolia. Especially so because government official names of services and how people learn to name the service is often different. For example, the COVID-19 vaccination certificate has an official title that is very different from what it actually is about. People do not know this and as they are searching for services, these can be hard to find. So, we want to offer citizens more services based on their data. For example, we want to include voice helpers like Siri on e-Mongolia: then people could explain to the app whatever they need, and we can then bring this thing out.

How Have You Managed to Make Sure That on Your Departure the Work Would Last—You Mentioned Standards, for Example?

I have given quite a lot of thought to it, because we have a very high level of political instability in Mongolia. The risk is that if the government is overturned, it would be hard for us to continue what we are doing. That is why we have indeed focused on creating standards for services. Then anybody coming after me, they will only have to do improvements. This way whatever happens in the future, it will also still keep getting better.

In order to create the standards, we have not been following the existing ones, because we are re-creating government services, government cultures. We have defined certain experience, even feelings of people as a standard. When we introduce a service, it is important how it is going to be perceived and experienced by the citizens. We do a lot of tests, research, even neuroscientific tests for this purpose. Does the service feel bureaucratic or friendly, for example? These sorts of standards have public support behind them, too. It helps to make sure that people themselves would be asking for improvements.

In addition, I am more confident that things could last because of the culture we have created and the team. At some point, I want to have my team working without me. That is why I have been training them to be more independent, more innovative. In the beginning of my leadership, I was very involved in everything, every small details. Now, I want to see what the team comes up with and then I promote it.

What Is Your Advice to Young Students on What Skills to Develop to Do This Kind of Job Well?

The first thing I always say is to work hard. I think people look for shortcuts. When you see all the success stories, they do not talk about how they were stressed or how vulnerable they were in fighting the hardships. That is why the first thing is to work hard and to be able to last.

Second, people should have negotiation skills and be very good listeners. Especially in politics, there is always a message hidden in people's conversation and whatever they are saying. There is a motive in some hidden meanings as well. That is why it matters to develop good listening skills.

I also think people should have coding skills. Soon enough, it will be a basic requirement. I would say: learn how to code just to understand how technology is built.

What Are Your Key Recommendations on How to Reach Digital Government Progress?

The first recommendation is to understand your customer and know what they are going through. What is the challenge? What is the problem? How do they feel? Do really understand the experience of existing digital service or non-digital government services before making it digital.

Second, you always will have problems and you kind of deal with them one problem at a time. This way you lose the bigger picture and vision; you get lost in the system and stuck on issues. Do draw back to bigger picture. Envision to yourself the bigger picture and reassess yourself, your team, the situation. See where you are in the bigger picture.

Third, be very good at planning!

Note

1. Cabinet Secretariat is the office supporting the prime minister in Mongolia; chief cabinet secretary is its head.

CHAPTER 6

Cheow Hoe Chan

Singapore

Chan Cheow Hoe has been the government chief digital technology officer (GCDTO) of the Smart Nation and Digital Government Office (SNDGO) since 2014. He is also concurrently the deputy chief executive of the Government Technology Agency of Singapore (GovTech).

Cheow Hoe has more than two decades of extensive experience in the public and private sectors, with a strong track record in leading digital transformation changes in organizations and the government.

Prior to joining GovTech, Cheow Hoe held senior appointments at international banks and consulting companies in the areas of technology, operations, finance, and business.

Cheow Hoe graduated from the National University of Singapore and obtained his master's degree from Wharton School of the University of Pennsylvania.

Cheow Hoe is surely a technologist first and foremost and tasked with a more technological role compared to many other peers in this book. However, his contribution and leadership in digital government area has been way beyond technology or govtech only. He has pushed the way the government works to transform in Singapore at large. That is why Cheow How was honored in 2021 by the prime minister of Singapore with the Public Administration Gold Medal for his service.

He was brought into government there several years ago with a deliberate attempt to bring in experience from transforming large organizations and building up in-house digital teams, also to have someone with a different thinking take the lead of digital government. This could have easily failed, because coming from a strong private sector background is rarely easy. Yet, Cheow Hoe has led full revamping of how digital tech is done in the Singapore public sector, which was a leading government in that regard globally already before. The more impressive is that he continues going strong at it, with no signs of tiring!

Cheow Hoe has helped to build the GovTech agency into a world-class tech organization compared to any industry or standard. While their digital governance model may be more centralized or in-house than would be doable in many other countries, his practices of building up digital teams and culture should (and better) resonate widely.

—Sim

You Have a Double Position: Government CDTO and the Deputy Chief Executive for GovTech Agency. What Is at the Core of What You Do?

If you want to bring out the core, then I basically run technology for the Singapore government and am responsible for technology products in it. I am also responsible for the entire development of technology capabilities and talent within government, and for the overall implementation of our digital government strategy in Singapore.

How Did You End Up in This Role—and in Government?

I have spent most of my time in the private sector; most of my career has been in banking. I never thought I would end up in government. In fact, it was probably the last thing in the world that I thought would happen.

But over time I started to want to do something different, to do something that I thought was more meaningful for affecting citizens and helping them out rather than just trying to help a company make more money. So, my coming to government was very much purpose driven as I wanted to really move into a job where I could have more social impact and economic impact for the country.

A few people had called me up as the government started looking for the role someone from outside, someone who would think rather differently. Who would have no legacy, no history to (re)start things up from scratch and basically truly rethink how government should deploy technology. This conversation went on for eight or nine months with several people before I finally joined.

At the time, digital government responsibility was with the Infocomm Development Authority (IDA), which later became Government Technology Agency of Singapore (GovTech). On IDA's board of directors was one of my colleagues from Citibank, and he had recommended me as the guy to talk to if the aim was to have someone thinking different and transforming the government digitally.

If the Conversation Lasted Many Months, You Were Then Hesitating Quite a Bit at First?

I have had an allergy to bureaucracy and was actually scared in that sense. I have spent most of my life executing and making things happen. If I would have to be embroiled in bureaucracy, I was just afraid that we would end up talking for a few years and nothing was going to happen. In fact, when I took this job, all my friends thought I was crazy. They were making bets on how long I would stay: three months, six months, nine months, one year. It was very funny.

I was actually prepared that if I could not make it work, I would leave. So, not only did I surprise my friends—I surprised myself and that is the best thing!

What Was the State of Digital Government in Singapore at the Time—Why Were the Leaders Seeking a Different Approach and Someone New?

There was no real govtech approach at the time. It was a time when the government as a whole realized that the existing way of doing technology was not very useful. A couple of big projects were starting to blow up. Essentially the government outsourced almost everything and because of it, several things were blowing up quite badly. My first year was a lot about cleaning up bad projects, actually.

There was a realization that government could not wait, that citizens were expecting a lot more from the government. The citizens were getting a great experience from the tech giants and similar services—from the likes of Google or Apple—but when they dealt with government, it was very painful. So, government had a very important task to catch up or at least maintain a certain level so that we would be able to serve.

Such realizations led to the notion that we needed to transform, needed to do things differently. There was a compelling need to digitalize as we moved forward.

If This Was the Background, Were You Given Any Concrete Mission to Fulfill or a Deliverable to Reach?

I was not, and, in fact, I do not think anyone had a clue what the outcomes were going to be. Including myself. All that everybody knew was that that we needed to change, and that the way government was using technology could not remain the same as before. If we looked across the horizon, we saw what all the tech giants were doing, and thought that government should at least do some of that.

Everybody was talking about Smart Nation, about digital government, but these words were very high-level. Nobody actually knew what these things meant, or how to actually make these happen.

How Did You Then Carve Out a Plan or a Road to Follow?

When I first joined, I joined what was called the Government Chief Information Officer or GCIO branch of IDA. I inherited a group of people who were supporting most of other agencies, probably some sixty government agencies in technology. Supporting meant essentially that our people were helping to outsource the work. They were good at writing tenders. If lights went out, they would call vendors to repair it.

I came from a place that was quite different in that sense. For example, at Citibank, I actually ran the development team; we had product teams in development track. I had created it because I found that many of the vendors were not doing a good job.

So, a couple of things were obvious to me. I came from very much a product organization, and there were four things that I say are necessary to turn government into this direction.

First, talent and capabilities—we needed people who could build products and understand technology enough to build it. The worst thing was that the government was not a smart buyer. They were buying things but had become nothing much more than contract managers. When I came in and saw that, I said that we needed to build real capabilities in our team.

Second, products themselves—we needed to start building horizontal products, not vertical ones.

Third, we needed ability to look at government from outside in. For the longest time, every agency had been doing their own stuff. Nobody ever looked at the customer.

Fourth, I thought it was very important that we needed to really move to new technology, have the democratization of technology.

Were These Directions Easy to Start With?

It was difficult because these things were very alien to the government, not what or how the government was used to doing. It meant that I had to start very small and show results. When we first started, we started with a small group of maybe seven people. I had to carve that team out of a thousand-people organization that was doing project management, contract management, program management.

I had to find people who actually believed in a new journey. I told them that we were going to do very, very small but impactful things. To really rethink what problem were we trying to solve and how we get benefit from it if we are lucky.

We took a few first projects, built them in a really different way and in a couple of months as opposed to years, and with small budget as opposed to large sums. The beauty of it is that people appreciated it: the citizens, the businesses. When we launched, people said that was the right thing to do. That was a great start.

What Could Be an Example of an Early Small Project with Great Outcomes Like That, and How It Was Different?

A good example is the project we did with Singapore Civil Defence Force that runs emergency ambulances and had the issue of how to get to patients much faster. Especially as people are getting older, there are more cases of heart attacks or cardiac arrests. In this case, the person has about ten to fifteen minutes to live. This means that help needs to arrive very fast. The initial approach of localizing ambulance deployments would not work, because you would need thousands of crews; it would take billions of dollars.

Then one of our developers suggested crowdsourcing for first responder support—using a bunch of trained volunteers from our population, who could be notified to go help nearby during an emergency. We built an app for it in a few months, called myResponder. We were very disappointed initially because we got only about a hundred volunteers to sign up. But then something interesting happened: a first life was saved by one of the volunteers and it ended up in newspapers. Then volunteering went up and now we have over a hundred thousand Singaporeans walking around as volunteers at any one time and able to respond in emergency situations.

It was a good case because the traditional way of doing things was not possible. But there are other ways! We were trying to solve a difficult problem in a very non-traditional way, and it is not about technology. It is about solving problems, using technology. It told the government that the way to solve citizens' problems is not always throwing money at something and getting a system integrator that would build a bespoke system that costs $50 million. A lot of times a small group of good people with the right mindset can change the way we help citizens or business in much better ways.

Once people see that there is a better way of doing things, they start believing in you. Very few people believe until they see something, just like in the Bible story of the doubting Thomas.[1] Our challenge as leaders in technology is that we need to show a better way of doing things, and then people will start believing in the journey. If not, nothing is going to change.

If Starting the Journey with Small Steps Was the Strategy, Did You Ever Set Yourself Any Time Frame for Longer Term?

The time frame part is hard, partly because we are doing things that people in government have not done before. The whole thing can fail miserably if you are not careful. If you are a Star Wars fan, you know that Episode V is about the Empire striking back. When you do massive changes, you are going to have a reaction because there are people afraid of you destroying the status quo. It is scary for them, if it means that someone in government could lose jobs or lose traction or relevance.

I have always been afraid we might have to be taking some steps forward and then more back. That is why my focus and horizon has been on inflection points—where things can go further up, or crash and burn.[2]

What Has Been Effective to Manage for or through These Inflection Points?

There were two things I realized in my career, and that we have done in GovTech, too.

First, we spent time identifying partners: people who are more forward thinking and that we could work with to help them succeed. Exactly: helping *them* succeed, not helping *us* succeed. It is great if they can take credit, because then they will become our best friends. We did not clash with people or tell them they were a bunch of clowns, that only we knew everything. We were sincerely going out there to help the agencies really succeed.

The other thing we got right was spending a lot of time trying to educate our leaders to get the support. You should not underestimate that in the public sector. We were very lucky because we managed to convince the most important person, our Prime Minister Lee Hsien Loong to be fully behind us. When this happens, like it or not, people will have to pay attention. If he speaks about Smart Nation and digitalizing, people will start to move in this direction.

But first you have to start from your own bosses. They have read about digital transformation, they have had presentations about it, but they are not necessarily affective about it—they are cognitive about it. Transformation is not about the head; it is about the heart. You need to appeal to their heart and say how doing digital could make a difference here or there. If people support you from the head, things will happen but very slowly and probably not be sustained. If they believe truly in their hearts that it is the right thing to do and not for you but for them—then things will change.

What convinces leaders the most is showing them the results. Then it becomes an irrefutable fact, as opposed to a PowerPoint presentation. That is why we do not like to do too many presentations; we rather should have the prototype to show. When they see the real thing, it resonates, and things can go on.

Once You Had Started on Your Journey of Small but Impactful Projects, What Became the Core of Your Journey Thereafter?

One of the most difficult things of a digital transformation is building the infrastructure—not the data centers, but the core infrastructure of digitalization.

It includes the people. If you do not have talented people, if you do not have capabilities, nothing is going to happen. Second important infrastructure part is culture. You do not need people just running around or writing tender documents. We had to build a "build culture"—allowing them to experiment, to try to innovate.

And then there is the tech stack. We have been able to do the things we do because we have very strong technological infrastructure that we built in the last six or seven years. This includes our ability to leverage the commercial cloud, our ability to do full stack development within the government, our ability to build reusable services, our ability to have a proper data architecture or a cybersecurity framework. All these things are tremendous because if you do not have them, nothing is going to happen in the end.

These things are hard to build because it takes a lot of effort and money. Whenever we build something, in every project we build, we try to build as part of the project some new infrastructure that will be reusable later and add to overall stack, whether it is an API gateway, DevOps environment, authentication, and so on. That is why when we do something today, it is much easier as we do not reinvent the wheels.

The infrastructure parts have become our products. That was my aim to raise the level, or what we call the line of innovation. I want my developers to focus on building a product that matters, rather than dealing with plumbing every day. The plumbing should not be done by them! That is how it is done in most government projects and where most money or time is spent. Why do we use cloud in our team? Because to me compute, storage, and so on are utilities, just like electricity. I buy my storage like I buy electricity: we do not need to know how to produce power or where the power station is.

Besides Strongly Moving to Cloud, What Other Parts of Infrastructure Stack Did You Choose to Focus on and Why? What Have Been Your Priorities in This Sense?

When we started, we were trying to move the pure infrastructure to an infrastructure-as-a-service model. We committed to moving 70 percent of workloads to commercial cloud, because this solves a lot of problems, takes costs down, quality and resilience up. This was the first step.

The next thing was to start building up the stack. The next level of stack is what we call the base layer. It includes things like API gateway for sharing information.

Then the next important thing is the proper CI/CD[3] and DevSecOps[4] processes because we really want people to be able to push code in a very, very quality, safe, and fast way. This way we ensure that quality is maintained through the entire work. We do not do things from scratch; we buy things and are almost like a Git Lab in some ways. What we do is make sure compliance, security, and so forth are built into things we launch. So that whenever you push code, you do not have to worry too much. For example, if it is not secure enough, it does not go through and out. This has also allowed us to focus very much on finding the problems in the beginning, as opposed to finding out in the end. Most tech projects are traditionally about endless fixing of bugs, whereas we clean things up in the beginning.

Then the next layer we built is what we call the service layer, where we have common services used over and over again. For example, authentication with SingPass or payment services from commercial providers. We started this line of work by crystallizing what are the core components of an application that can be used over and over again, rather than rebuilding. Building an app then becomes more like putting together the Lego blocks.

What Have Been Your Effective Routines or Methods to Evolve and Deliver Such a Strategy?

I do spend a lot of time with my team, writing our core strategy items out—both from a technical point of view as well as from a user point of view. This way we identify the anchors we need to put in place as we move forward, but it is always a moving target. We focus on the next one or two years.

Overall, I find that most people in government do not do one thing well—they are not on the ground enough. I am on the ground a lot. Involved in architectural discussion, in product discussion, am involved in laying out a strategy most of the time. I do not just sit in my office and clear papers. Most government people are used to that only. I spend most of my time in discussions, whereby we sit down with a whiteboard, and we draw what needs to be done. Then agree to get it done.

I think it is a culture thing that government struggles with. Most government organizations are very formal: their formal meetings have a chairman, someone will be presenting, and they will be then approving the papers. I think that culture is not good enough. Leaders on the ground, working with the teams, getting them to do what makes sense, and motivating them. That is what delivery is all about.

I write most of the strategy documents personally, which is a surprise to many. I write them from scratch. Why? Because I really want to expose my thinking to the group so that they understand where I am coming from and that it is not put together by somebody else. In the government, there usually is a team that puts all these things together for you. I do not believe in that. Even today, most of my presentations I do actually prepare myself. The reason is that I believe that you need to be on the ground enough to understand what the real problems are that we are trying to solve and what are the things that matter. Then you can prioritize, then you are able to focus on what matters.

How Much Has Your Strategy and Focus Pivoted or Changed through Your Term?

All the time. Because we are very agile in our setup and work mode, also because I am very involved in everything. So that when we do need to pivot, it does not take twenty-five different approvals, we just do it. Like we did when COVID-19 emerged.

COVID-19 was a real challenge to us in governments. In digital government circles, we keep selling that we are agile. Now, all of a sudden, a change comes, and you are told to do things quick, too. Or your bluff is called. In GovTech, we had organized and equipped in such a way whereby things could be done in weeks and months and good things, not trivial things. We were lucky to be able to pass the test.

In this way, GovTech has been very much like a company and not a typical government organization. I am very glad that a lot of our bosses have given us a lot of freedom. They are more interested in the high-level strategy and delivery, but they leave the actual day-to-day to me. That allows us to pivot quickly, and the team also appreciates it.

How Have You Been Building Your Team Out? What Has Proven to Be Effective in This Area?

When I started to build out the capability, everybody was looking if we would be able to actually do it. Who would want to join government if they could do the work from outside?

The funny thing is that people work for people, people do not work for organizations. That is why the key thing was how do I attract good people to work for *me*? Once I could build that level of leadership, then it would become easier to find people.

You also need to understand that when you go out there and hire people for the government, you know that money cannot attract them. You can never pay as much as the private sector.

The key is in purpose. You need to hire people who have a very strong sense of purpose. There are a lot of such people out there, especially among the tech people. They want to solve difficult problems, big problems, and many of them have great empathy. They want to solve real problems, things that affect them. Then they are ready to work like hell.

I say that I am a chief recruitment officer most of my time. I spend most of my time talking to people, telling them stories, and many of them are quite touched by it. Then they come and join.

We also started a technology associate program whereby we hire very good young people who are graduating from universities, and we train them. Many of them remain in government for longer.

You Said Yourself That Culture Determines the Delivery as Much as Talent, and You Have Wanted to Build a "Build Culture" in GovTech. How Have You Gone about It?

The real key thing is to allow people to do things rather than putting them in an Excel sheet somewhere.

Most of our team are working more like engineers in a tech company. We wear jeans and T-shirts all the time. We keep the organization very flat. We have a very open culture, where it is really about who has the best ideas and not about seniority. All these things have to be built into the organization. A lot of bureaucracy, a lot of rank, a lot of hierarchies would not work.

We also enable people to build more by something called a Whitespace Fund. If someone has good ideas, we empower them to try it out with some money and time. We managed to convince the Ministry of Finance to give us funding for such a trialing fund. If the person comes to me with an idea, we will evaluate it quick. If it makes sense, we might give them a small amount of $30 thousand to $50 thousand and three months of time. They need to come back in three months with something that they can show us and how it makes sense. If it is something good, we will give more money and another three to six months. Or in next stage we could fund them trying it out in a pilot in an actual agency, or then a rollout to multiple agencies. This way we support the culture of people innovating—by moving also funding toward a start-up style funding process more.

You Were Afraid of Bureaucracy Yourself at First. How Have You Managed to Avoid Culture Getting Caught in It?

I do spend a lot of my time insulating the real people from that, the engineers from that. So that they can actually do their job. If I do not insulate them, they will die—or leave. Having things like the Whitespace Fund is an example of that. It is a funding mechanism to work around the usual government funding bureaucracy that otherwise exists.

I myself have been lucky, too. I have had a lot of support from many people and for many years. Especially once we have been proving that things can be done differently and better.

What Have Been Your Mantras to Instill a Culture You Have Wanted to See in GovTech? What Have You Kept Saying to Your Team Over and Over?

Our mantra is, "Start small, think big, act fast."

There also is the overall mission of GovTech: agile, bold, collaborative. ABC. We have to be nimble; we have to have courage; we need to work together.

These things we put in place quite far back and they have really helped us.

What Have Been Your Biggest Achievements in the Role? What Are You Most Happy With?

GovTech has become much more than I expected, especially given where we used to be. Both as an agency and as a practice of doing things.

Today, we have more than a thousand engineers. We have grown that much from the initial seven people we started with. We are building very good projects and products, which benefit the civil service and citizens. We have managed to produce very good people, who are now hunted and hired by the Googles of the world. This speaks to me about the fact that they have done a good job with us.

There was a recent survey among fresh university graduates on where they might want to join. GovTech ranked number seven in Singapore, right after the tech giants. I feel proud about that. It is a tremendous achievement on the part of many people.

What Are the Things You Think You Could Have Done Better or Differently?

In this technology area of ours, there is never an end to the journey. I think we are still so far behind the tech giants in many ways. The beauty of them is the scale that we will never have. We do not have hundred thousand engineers building state-of-the-art stuff. We will never get there, we know our limitations, but it does not stop us from doing good things.

I do not believe in regrets. I believe that everything is a learning opportunity that we move forward with and do better with, and we have had many such lessons. In building up our stack, we took a lot of calculated risks. For example, when we started building platform-as-a-service out, we were among the first, and the underlying technology was not ready really. Our initial API gateway ended up pretty much hosted on-premise because of it and we redesigned almost everything when we moved it to the cloud. It shows that sometimes it really is a journey we must go through, if we want to evolve.

What Have You Learned the Most in This Job?

I have never stopped learning. I am so glad that in our case everybody in the industry wants to work with us, all the tech giants, because it is not competitive. We are not competing with them. I have learned so much about how to build technology in the last couple of years by working with them.

More important, I have learned how to navigate highly complex and large organizations like the government. In the end, our delivery is not about money or technology but about convincing people that it is something worth doing. Navigating the government is important for that, and finding ways how to make people successful, as I said before.

With that mindset, people will start listening to you. Everybody wants to be successful, in some ways. People are going to be welcoming if you are trying to make them successful. If you say that they are idiots and you want to do things for them, then things are going to fall apart. Humility is very important.

What Are the Next Challenges or Milestones on the Horizon for You and Your Team?

The big challenge going forward is how to keep pushing the platforms as a concept rather than systems. I do not believe that governments should have so many systems. I believe in a horizontal approach, whereby we need to build platforms that become infinitely reusable. Yet, it is difficult to convince people as they want to keep their systems.

We need to ask ourselves, does the government need fifty licensing systems, for example? Or one? Even if the domains are different, which is just an excuse not to think carefully enough about it. We need to go back to the function of what is licensing and what are the processes or requirements for it. The rules will be different for each license, but functionally they are not different. Why can we not build one or two platforms that everybody can use in their different domains for licensing?

We take it as a leap of faith, but, really, we are talking about taking a public transport as opposed to having your own car. Still, people like their own cars, especially the big agencies. It is not technology that is difficult in this area; it is always the people. We need to get people involved and committed to this next direction.

What Might Make You Move from Your Role One Day?

I am one of those guys who will spend my life figuring out interesting things to do. I am not driven by money. I am driven more by doing something interesting and challenging; I like solving problems. I will only do things if I think it is worth the while. The moment this stops with GovTech, I will look for something else.

What Steps Have You Taken to Make What You Have Started Last?

For succession planning, building a team of good people is everything. It is about building a team that can take the work on as you go forward. I am glad that I got some very good people in my team. I am confident that they can take this over from me one day.

What Are the Core Skills for Doing This Sort of Job Well, in Your View?

Intellectual humility. You must always learn, be trying to learn. The moment you stop learning, you are dead. Whatever we do today will be irrelevant next year. It is not important to talk about what you know but understand what you do not know and learn from it. I have followed this in my whole career.

Also, the ability to try. Many people like to hypothesize, but there is nothing like trying or implementing something, trying different things. If it does not work, it is OK. You try again.

What Would Be Your Three Core Recommendations to a Peer on How to Build an Excellent Digital Government as Its Leader?

Start small. Many people come up with a huge master plan, spend time studying for it, years talking about it, trying to implement it then. Ability to start matters, and small steps make it easier.

It does not mean that you have to keep it small. The "think big" part is very important, too. You have to have vision on what is going to happen. You have to have guts to say, "I want to change this,"

And then start quickly doing it. Get moving! In governments, we talk about things too much. If you do not get it moving, you do not get it done. You end up in endless meetings and presentations only.

Notes

1. Doubting Thomas is a reference to Apostle Thomas from the New Testament of the Bible, who refused to believe the resurrection of Jesus and his emergence in front of the apostles until he could see Jesus's wounds with own eyes.
2. Inflection points are points on mathematical curves where the curvature changes, or points where the graph of the function changes "concavity."
3. *CI/CD* refers to the software engineering practices of continuous integration and continuous deployment.
4. *DevSecOps* stands for development, security, and operations, an approach to IT development and delivery that combines software development, information security, and IT operations practices in an integrated way.

CHAPTER 7

Daniel Abadie

Argentina

Daniel Abadie helps public and private organizations to adapt to the internet era.

With twelve years of experience in the public sector, Daniel was the director of Electronic Government of the City of Buenos Aires (2007–2015) and appointed Undersecretary of Digital Government of Argentina (2015–2019), developing and transforming digital services for citizens.

Dan now works with organizations on the development of their digital strategies and the delivery of products (mobile applications, virtual assistants or chatbots, websites) aimed to improve services, increase customers, and make processes more efficient. In January 2020, he joined Public Digital, a London-based consultancy specialized in digital transformation, to lead the work in Latin America and the Caribbean region.

In 2019, Daniel was chosen by Apolitical as one of the twenty most influential people in digital government in the world and won a Webby Award in the health category.

Daniel is one of the most thoughtful colleagues I ever met. He is deeply self-aware and introspective on how to do and how to be better all the time. Especially on how to be a better leader, a bit better every day. You can get a sense of his candidness about himself and his learnings clearly in the next pages.

His digital government leadership journey was clearly a personal growth journey. However, it was also a journey of excellence in taking a country in just a few years from a low digital level to a state of whizzing change.

Daniel stands out among digital government leaders for his careful thinking and thorough steps on how to make the work last knowing that it might end abruptly. His exit time from office greatly inspired how I approached my own departure from the CIO role in Estonia by storming to deliver until the last days in office and making the entry of a successor as frictionless as possible.

—Siim

How Did You Rise to the Role of a Digital Government Leader in Argentina?

I used to work in the internet industry back in the day. In 2007, a new mayor was taking office in Buenos Aires—Mauricio Macri, who later became the president of Argentina. As his administration was taking over, they were looking for someone "who works on the internet." Some people I knew from the telecom industry suggested my name to mayor's chief of staff and his team, so I met them. I had never met a politician in my life, I told them I hate politicians and did not trust them! But at the same time, I was sick and tired of things that were not working. So, I was willing to get into the government to try to do things and not live in some lousy country forever—to complain without doing anything about it myself.

My job in the first six months was basically to support all the city administration with IT services. When I went to my city office the first day, the previous administration had taken the hard drives and memory sticks of every computer in government to not to leave any trace of information! We started from zero. I then centralized twenty-eight call centers into a single one, took over the websites, and built the single website buenosaires.gob.ar for citizens. I ended up spending eight years as city's head of digital.

When the mayor started running for national president, I became his chief of technology for the campaign. When he won, President Macri appointed me as the Undersecretary of Digital Government.

What Was Your Motivation to Take the National Job? Did You Hesitate to Take the Role?

I did not hesitate; I wanted to make things work more widely. I had experience from the city level, where I had been extremely lucky to test and to learn, to fail a lot. My thinking was that if I go on to national level, I can fail in other things, but at least I had some previous experience of how government works.

I was also lucky, because I was given on both city and national level unlimited freedom to do things and to make any decision.

Politicians do not get into building things. My responsibility with my team was to ship products that were working, to build things that people used. As we did so, it gave us the credibility to do whatever we wanted. Such a freedom was the basic precondition for me to go on to the national level with the president.

However, I truly believed that I had the opportunity to build at least something that would be useful for the country.

What Was the Expectation for You? Were You Given Any Concrete Task or Objective?

They never told me what to do. I told them later on the day I left the office that I was truly thankful for the freedom to basically set the whole agenda. In general, the expectation was to do the same thing I had done in the city of Buenos Aires—to build a single-domain website, a platform where citizens can have all their requests and services handled in an integrated manner by all the city offices. To me that was a bit boring because we had done that in the city before. So, I ended up building MyArgentina instead: a single dashboard for citizens with verification to provide them personalized experiences and access to their digital documents.[1]

What Was the Institutional and Governance Setting Like for Public Sector Digitization in Argentina When You Started?

The new administration brought in the setup they used in the City of Buenos Aires before. I was the undersecretary in charge of digital government, reporting to the secretary, and then the minister of modernization, who in turn were directly under the president's office. Effectively, I had a direct line to the president and his chief of staff, even if formal lines were more hierarchical.

Essentially, the undersecretary role has a lot of power in its institution. The president was there on need—"Just send me a text." But the model was that I was given the freedom and I could solve things myself. Surely, this created some friction with other people in government at times.

How Did the Transition from City to National Level Then Work Out Still, Was It Similar after All as You Had Thought?

I had thought it would be just the next level, but I was extremely wrong. First, we wrote a strategy before coming to office after elections, during the transition time. Once we actually started, I realized that we did not have any money to hire anyone; the budget was ridiculous. The structure of government was huge, full of silos, and people were not motivated. There had been no real strategy or coordination; we had to start working from scratch, with very few resources.

Second, I was at first "drunk with power"—jumping at every opportunity and saying yes to everything. My chief of staff used to call me the Pac-Man as I was going through the office grabbing tasks or projects. The day job was to build a single-domain citizen platform, services, mobile apps. But I also ended up in meetings discussing some software platform in some ministry. We ended up with a wall full of projects. That took my focus away from what I should have been doing. After a year, I realized that is not the way I should be working and decided to rethink everything and focus. With the freedom I had requested, trust also came, and we needed to deliver. But if there was anything happening with the word *digital* in it, it was thrown my way still. I had to start changing the expectation of what we were trying to do.

What Were the Things You Could Not Say No To?

One of the things I learned in government is that in a way it is like the space race. There is always someone competing with you, trying to do the same thing you do. I tried to own as many projects as I could just to prevent another government area from building something that would have competed with our strategy. I saw it as a bit of a chess game. For example, at some meetings we talked about chatbots with another unit who was planning to develop them. With my senior staff, we decided to simply build one during a Friday afternoon. So, in twenty-four hours we had an alpha delivered that later became the root of the governmental virtual assistant program. If others had done it—if others try to do the same, at some point they are going to compete with your strategy. But ours was meant to be a whole-of-government solution.

What Was the State of Digital Government in Argentina When You Started as Undersecretary?

There really was no state of digital government. There were like two thousand websites; every agency had their own approach to digital. Ninety-nine percent of the websites basically advertised what the politicians were doing and did not provide institutional information. There was no focus on the citizens.

The main agencies handling social aid, pensions, or taxes had resources to build transactional services. Yet, these agencies also had the worst solutions, as evaluated by the citizens. Agencies bought things always from the same vendors and never had an idea how to sustain them.

Nowhere was there any dedicated team that cared about the citizens and followed a strategy.

How Did You Start Changing That Picture? What Were the First Steps?

I spent my first two months in office basically doing archaeology of what had been there before and what had been left: interviewing people, trying to meet with a lot of vendors, and basically picking up the bills that had not been paid. Too many people in too many places had ordered things that were never delivered.

A key step was to write up and get a mandate for our team. In Argentina, the president issues executive orders to define roles of institutions, including for undersecretaries. You basically need to do it in the first ten days.

We made it our mandate that every website in the administration should be centralized into argentina.gob.ar and any citizen login or dashboard should be centralized into MyArgentina. Any mobile app that anyone wants to build or publish should be published in the government's central official stores in Google Play and Apple Store. We also got the mandate to intervene and to transform how people are being served in the physical offices. Finally, any digital system built had to be approved by my office. This mandate is currently still in place in the current administration, with some minor changes.

We set the deadline that in the first two years of this administration, 100 percent of websites should get migrated to the central platform. In fact, migration ended up not being the right word; we decided to rebuild 80 percent of content from scratch, because it was not focused on citizens before.

The Mandate Essentially Featured Your Strategy for the Next Years Then. What Were the Key Stages or Milestones for Delivering It?

The main goal was to make things similar and simple for citizens when they interact with authorities.

Government asked too much information from citizens. The idea behind MyArgentina was that let us build a website where we request the citizens to create an account only once and use that to verify their identity from there on. With that information provided just one time, we would solve everything behind the scenes—that one time should be enough for us to afterwards bring data to the citizen instead.

Delivering it took all of my four years. As I said, in the first year and with me saying yes to everything, I lost focus on building MyArgentina. The single-domain direction was well on track; I never lost sight of that. That was the thing that the president and others measured our progress by, and we achieved every goal in the first one hundred days, in two hundred days, and so on. We had to do it because my freedom to set the agenda was based on me achieving what I had said I was going to do. That was the base of my power: the moment I would have stopped delivering what was good enough to be used by citizens, my power would have evaporated.

This started to happen a bit when in the next stage we were not delivering MyArgentina as intended—given the resources and the team we had. Luckily, I had accumulated enough credibility through the first year of delivery on the single domain to then have space to bring MyArgentina back on track in the next twelve months.

What Were Your Key Steps for the Quick Delivery of Single-Domain Efforts?

We split the website efforts into two tracks. All the government transactional services were going to be gob.ar, a bit like gov.uk. But for the political ones, we were going to build something similar to the whitehouse.gov site. That had to launch fast, as soon as the president was taking office, and this was also a way to get credibility with his chief of staff.

We did launch that website on inauguration day, then three days later we launched the first version of argentina.gob.ar. When I was on the city level, during in my last year we had created a Drupal distribution for governments and released it into GitHub. Any government could reuse it. We then deployed it in our infrastructure on a national level, and that is how we had a website working in three days.

How Did You Regain the Strategic Focus after the First Year?

My second year was awful. MyArgentina was not coming along, and then there was pressure from minister's level and above.

I know I had to stop being all over the place. My middle management was not calling the shots, I had to stay in office more and steer myself more. The team thought that with the resources and talent we had, we could not build anything—even if we only had to build a website. I found out that as I was so much outside the office doing institutional relationships, traveling and other things, that the agreed work was not happening. Things were not going to production line; my team changed the plan agreed after the meetings we had held. It was a bit of a rebellion in that sense, also slack perhaps.

The problem was that they were trying to build everything perfect, and the view was that if the outcome is not perfect, we should not do it. My view was that I do not care if it is perfect, only if it works; let us keep it simple. We had already set the goals and we needed to deliver.

There is a lot of risk involved in being bold. I cannot judge the team for not trying to take that risk because I had never achieved to give them the resources they wanted to build the things the way they wanted to. Also, my team at that time did not have enough maturity yet. When the team is too young and not used to working your way—say, having deadlines and you start setting a lot of deadlines—you are asking too much. My second and third year, I adjusted my approach and said, "Let us do it your way, because you are my team, and I trust you." I tried to contain myself and my anxiety and not try to lower my expectations and assume we cannot win the World Cup every year.

Did the Resourcing or Financial Situation Ever Get Better?

The budget was less than a million dollars a year. Once politicians discovered that we could achieve things by coding ourselves and not hiring vendors, they thought, "Why allocate a lot of resources if the team can deliver things that are so cool anyway? Let us keep it that way." In a country with a lot of needs, like Argentina, you compete for your budget with other senior ministries.

The second year the pressure was always, "When is MyArgentina coming?" The team was building it, but taking things slow, building a lot of smaller components, and so on. There was a huge backlog of things to build.

But as I had accepted my team's course, my role was to keep going to the meetings with the minister and say that we did not have a product yet. I used the power I had gained to defend my team, but I was losing that earned power at the same time. Other agencies started to compete more, saying that they would not migrate their web or give API access to their service. My team got frustrated; they hated bad news. I accepted that, took the villain's role, and I weighed in more on agencies to fall in line and to keep my team working better.

How Did You Break That Cycle?

I changed my deputy director, brought in someone who agreed with my view on how to do things. Twenty days later, we were releasing MyArgentina. Sixty days later, we released digital driver's licenses. And then we started releasing services sometimes twice a week.

I needed a good chief operations officer, or COO, who could get the team in order. Somebody who kept the team on mark at what had been agreed and said, "Yes, we can do this."

From that point on, my third year all through the end we delivered as much as we could.

It Seems That through All of This You Had to Work with Your Team and People Management a Lot Hands-On.

My team at the city level were like the Navy Seals: super senior, a smaller team, but top experts in the country. As this was not the case on a national level, I had to learn how to get that team to perform its best. Each person in the team was different, so I had to approach them differently.

Someone never spoke at the meeting, but I told them just to email or WhatsApp me at the end of the day and we got things done this way. With the product design team, my approach was different: we talked every day. We had an open floor setup in the office, and every morning I went to where they were sitting, took a chair, got a cup of coffee, sat between them for an hour and listened. They showed me mock-ups and so on. Then there was the developers' team with whom we talked coding. It was all about building confidence so that they can trust me on the things I asked them to do.

How Did You Build and Empower Your Team?

Seventy percent of my team used to work in other parts of government before, because hiring people from the outside was not an option. We could not afford them. Some we brought in from outside using the little money we had. Some of them used to work with me in the city.

I started recruiting people from inside the government, seeing if they wanted to work on the digital track or our team. I was going around in offices, talking to people and, if what I was hearing them say was OK, inviting them to come to work with us. As for the roles, it was really crucial to get a head of user experience, a head of product design, a head of engineering, and DevOps on the team.

The idea was to be horizontal as much as we could, with everyone responsible for their job. We had leaders of the teams, as managers or directors. I always said that my role as undersecretary was there for ten minutes a day, to make the final decision. So that if we screw things up, it is my decision, it is my responsibility. But otherwise, I was a peer.

It was the same with the managerial team. The UX director sets up the strategy, but in the discussion he or she becomes the senior advisor steering the conversation so that the team can grow. If the team does not grow, I or the manager cannot grow either. We were then going to be limited in our delivery, because our team was just so small.

A lot of my approach comes from sports. As a kid, I played a lot of basketball. I guess I got a lot of that coaching mindset from that.

What Was Your Selling Argument to Get Someone to Join the Team?

"We will give you a chance to build things that people are going to use." They would have a sandbox of forty-four million people, building things that your mum is going to talk about over lunch. The scale is huge and there is no company with a similar opportunity.

But it was always hard because money talks. Industry was paying good salaries, but the government did not. The higher your role and your expertise, the tougher the gap. You do not get ten years of experience with Django or a PhD in software engineering to join the government on small pay.

One thing that worked was to scout out developers, designers, researchers, roles from other agencies, as well as to tune in during the meetings we had with agencies. If we saw that someone got what it takes to do digital, we offered them a relocation inside government.

Who Was Your Most Valuable Hire?

We got a medical doctor, a cardiologist who oversaw everything in the health and social area. She was a game changer, because she gave us a completely different approach to build out health infrastructures. It later even became the foundation for the COVID-19 digital vaccine certificate.

I also hired a new deputy for me, one of those whom we scouted from other agencies. She used to run Access of Information Agency's technology and changed how we developed and delivered services in MyArgentina.

How Did You Motivate the Team to Keep Going, Even If There Were Never Enough Resources?

First, trust. Giving them a voice and letting them speak and decide. "This is my ship, but we can discuss the strategy as much as you want." That is the way to make it richer and better.

Second, we had to make our place and team great to work in so that people would feel comfortable spending a lot of hours in it. Helping them with anything we can to allow them to think or work. If you do not have anywhere to leave the kids, bring them along. Work cannot be the bad part of your day.

Or can we support your learning? There are some training programs, degree school support, and such within government. How can we invest in you? To upgrade you from junior to senior level, to build confidence in you.

With my managerial team, we tried also to use what little extra budget we had to go around the world and learn from others to be better at home. For example, to take the team to Singapore on a study trip.

Some people also left, of course. Companies were eagerly recruiting from our team, so that we were a bit like organ or talent donors for the industry.

What Sort of Culture Were You Trying to Build within the Team and How?

The main culture we wanted to build was that no matter what we were doing, we needed to always improve. We were not building services for citizens only; we were building services for us. Everyone went around and tried the services when we were building them—staying in a queue for hours, trying to understand what it was that we had to change.

A key part was that we needed to be doing a bit of everything. Our single role was to build and deliver services, not to have discussions about how the theory should be. Every time we had a problem, my take was that we were going to deliver and that was going to solve any issues. Once you build something out, once you have accomplished something, there is no more discussion—especially if there is a competing agency somewhere.

Another benefit was that our office was extremely open, no separate office rooms. I did not have an office myself. I had a meeting room with a single large table where we worked and discussed as a team.

What Were Some of the Things You Always Told Your Team, Your Mottos?

I never gave huge spiritual or motivational talks to my entire team. I tried to get them into a state of mind where they could solve a single problem at a time, in a way they wanted it. That gave them confidence that whether we succeeded or failed in solving the problem, I would still be behind them.

I did emphasize to make things simple, make them easy. But really the only true slogan was that "doing beats everything else."

What Was a Common Day Like on the Job?

On the one hand, being an undersecretary is a political role. You have to replace the minister at events, talk to other politicians, shake hands, take pictures.

On the other hand, there were meetings to show PowerPoints to people or meetings to get agencies to share access to service or APIs or migrate websites.

Then there were a lot of meetings for discussing things through with the team. Product meetings. Topics like how we get health records around the country to be interoperable because it had never been done before. My team hated it, but I like discussing things. I believe that I do not have all the ideas. That is why I love listening to people or challenging people and asking why. I am super comfortable listening to better ideas than mine and adopting them or discarding mine during the process. I pushed my team a lot into discussing things through—to talk about why we were doing what we were doing.

A lot of my days were about products to learn where we were on delivery and to plan for the new services. Each day I tried to also consume as many ideas, products, or content not related to digital government as I could to see if anything could be an inspiration to our domain from outside. For example, when we built Poncho—a bootstrap design system—I brought in the idea to build something similar to McDonald's. I can go to a different McDonald's joint each time and buy the same product. Even though there are different restaurants, they are built on exactly the same components, and they are preparing to burger exactly the same way. I thought how could we commoditize our design system so that anyone could build on it following our guidelines? We took a page from the fast-food industry and its franchise model to build a design system that anyone could apply.

During the day, I would write down the things I had in my mind and then do the same once more before going to bed. And the first thing I did every day when I woke up, was to watch analytics on my phone: how our stuff was running.

How Did You Ensure the Support of the President during Your Term?

The former president of Argentina, Mister Macri, is an engineer himself.

We had monthly meetings; he took that routine along from city level. The meeting was to review and showcase things. I never showed mock-ups, always products he could "touch." So that when he would go to the media, we could talk about the products and explain them in the best way. My role was to help him learn how to use the things we built. With technology, you are otherwise going to get into a mess if you do not know what you are explaining. It was not about "do you like it?" Instead, it was "two million users are using the same thing right now."

When we launched the digital driving licenses, we made the president enroll on the app, create an account, verify identity, access the documents. We made videos and photos of him doing all that, especially of him showing his digital driver's license on the phone.

It was also his preference: "Do not show me the PowerPoint; give me a phone or a computer." So, I exploited his curiosity in this way. We had two hours every month to show things, show our progress, discuss strategies, discuss new things.

How Did You Build Relations with the Other Agencies?

I took the approach that we cannot be just asking things; we need to give things away so that others can trust us. Building trust is exhausting in that sense. When you centralize technology, someone is losing power and that creates resistance. Despite the president's executive order, we had to build relationships to actually get websites, apps, access to infrastructure or databases of agencies.

I made clear that I was not going to own their services. I basically only asked for API access. That is the way to build trust on a daily basis.

I was able to have a somewhat informal approach because I had already met all the ministers in the past. Some of them used to work in the city administration, some in other parts of government. In the political ecosystem, being so close to the office of the president allowed me just to pick up the phone and call a minister without a problem.

Once we got the president to talk in public about MyArgentina and got a picture of him showing his digital driver's license to everywhere in the media, then everyone wanted to be with us. The license was our blockbuster moment because it meant so much for the citizens. Now every minister wanted the same things in order to be in line with the president.

What Were Your Biggest Failures and What Did You Learn from Them?

Losing focus within the first year was a failure because I could not recover in any way the time I lost. I lost a year out of a four-year term. That is too much. Even if you trust your team, you need to be there. You cannot lead a team without being with them.

I had to also learn how to ask for things. As opposed to the city team of experts with whom we were on the same page, I discovered that I had to learn to explain better to the new team. In my mind, things may have sounded awesome, but I needed to translate them better with examples or requests. I could not at first explain the MyArgentina idea, not until our third year. Or explain to the director of services the role that I expected from her. "What do you mean by a service end-to-end?" she asked. I could not assume anymore that the team had skills or experience to immediately understand what I was requesting. I had to become more specific, more obvious in detail because the team also never challenged me and otherwise simply guessed.

What Were Your Biggest Achievements during Your Term?

By far the biggest achievement was the digital driver's license, because after it the rest was easier with MyArgentina. The driver's license had to look exactly the same as a physical card but was in fact a digital image with a QR code. There was no need to make it more complicated or cooler, just to have it meet the rules for compliance and such. Basically, we pulled images of the card through APIs, and added a signature time stamp. The same approach could then be replicated for other things, such as documents or certificates. Based on the example, it became so easy to explain the recipe to the rest of government but also to my own team, who now knew what to ask, what to build, and that they could do it.

This was the biggest achievement—to finally simplify what I wanted for MyArgentina. We could then go on to have a drug license or national ID or online passport or vaccine record on the app the same way—replicating the approach real fast. In a nutshell, we managed to flesh out the common digital infrastructure approach for the country. It became also very handy later, once the COVID-19 pandemic started and quick delivery was necessary for related documents, for example.

What Made You Move on from the Role?

The president did not get reelected at the next elections in 2019 and the administration changed. In Argentina, it means that every political appointee changes.

However, even when we started our job, I could not think about a second term anyway. Everything I built, I built thinking, "Let us do our best effort in four years and build as much as we can."

How Did You Ensure That What You Started Would Last?

In developing countries, at least in Latin America, it is often that the incoming administration erases everything that their administration has done. Just like my predecessors did in the city. It means that you are starting from scratch all over again and it means throwing away people's money. Also, often the egos of the new government make them think they are better than the previous and they do not want to reuse things on purpose.

I acknowledged that there is a past, present, and future for digital and technology in governments. I was building in the present on something that someone from past had left and one day someone was going to replace me. Then that person will build in the future on what I had been doing in present. That made me see that every decision I made should be simple and common sense. Anyone coming into the office for the first time after me would have to be able to look at what has been done and say, "Yes, this is the way." That is why we made things so modular, easy to grasp for anyone.

We also left behind solutions that were easy to build or manage, even without a budget. Plus, once I left in December 2019, the knowledge remained because most of the team and managers remained. Surely some have left since then, but many remained. That is the core of sustainability: the team, the culture, the practices.

And the platforms themselves—the users were there on our infrastructure and solutions. Most often used government documents were in MyArgentina, the vaccine and health records, car insurance, and so on. We had built the quick-to-apply backend of API and connectors, and we had gotten every government agency on our website. Agencies were using our tools and standards, reusing our modules that we had built up. To make sure this happens, we invested a lot of time into building communities of practice across agencies, be it developers or designers or UX research. This all made it harder to change course and also made it unnecessary.

Finally, I also left a huge playbook or report for the new administration. It outlined what we had done in the four years and what we would have wanted to do in the next four. There was a job description of everyone in the team, including my own role. I outlined the key roles to sustain or needs for hiring. There was an overview of what our budget looked like, the latest budget requests, and so on. This way it was easier to pick up for the next person.

What Would Have You Done in the Next Four Years, If You Had a Chance? What Were the Outlying Challenges?

For example, we had built an appointment system for meetings at government offices into MyArgentina. We wanted to roll it out widely, and the next government did so, especially in the COVID-19 context. There also were more digital certificates to be brought onto the platform and this has happened, too.

What has not been picked up—and that is a fundamental challenge in my view—is that I think websites are going to be replaced by digital assistants. Once we solve search engine optimization into the assistants, there is no reason to keep websites with content. Thus, my next fight for MyArgentina would have been to build a governmental virtual assistant with all information to replace websites.

This would help to get rid of middle persons who help people to get things done with government, and charge money for that. We should not have poor people paying someone to get appointments made, for example. Why not build a virtual system that assists you to navigate the government bureaucracy for free? We can train artificial intelligence to read structured information, to comprehend the government rules, which are basically binary (you can do something or not), and then to give assistance to the citizens. Virtual assistants could be the next stage of government.

Is There Anything You Wish You Had Known When You Started the Job?

I wish I had known better what to expect or how to manage my expectations. At first, I changed offices by two hundred meters, from city to national office, and expected the change just to be to a bigger scale. But it was not just bigger, it was more diverse, more complex work. I should not have expected to solve things in two days and should have known that the clock was running to manage my time.

Also, what I said before—I wish I had known from the start to translate what is in my mind to my mouth better to my team so that they could act on what I wanted them to do.

If Someone Were to Offer, Would You Take the Job Again?

I would not do the same job in Argentina again, because I truly believe you need new leadership with new ideas. Then it would not be the same people doing the same things from government to government.

What Do You Think Are the Necessary Skills to Do This Kind of Job Well?

Clarity—you have to be able to be clear on what you want.

Trust—know how to trust and to build trust. You have to enable your team to trust you.

Empathy—understanding what is that you are affecting when you are trying to make people's lives better. It is complex, not a simple fix usually. People often reach government at a stage of life when they need help. It is not the place where they come to have fun. When you are trying to transform social services, for example: if you do it the wrong way, you make someone's day or even life miserable. Creating a service is a huge power; you have to watch out for inequality and pay attention to the quality of service in all aspects. This starts from empathy.

What Are Your Three Main Recommendations to Someone Starting on a Similar Job? What Are Your Key Bottom-Line Takeaways on How to Be Effective in This Role?

First, the digital government universe has its own rules. Too often, we only see the usual rules about technology and digital. Yet, there are also political rules that you need to see and play with to achieve more things in government. The digital government leadership role is not just an operational role; you also have a leadership and a political role.

Technical people like myself sometimes learn the hard way the political rules of this job's universe. Like when you try to reduce friction of bureaucracy, you are taking things away from someone and that means taking away power. You need to manage the people's friction in that sense, and that is a lot more emotional terrain than technology issues. The resistance for initiatives will not come because others think you are wrong in your ideas but because they feel they are losing things. Once you understand this, you can approach the situation differently.

You can reassure others that the path you offer is better and build out a path that allows them to not lose out. Leadership does not have to be a fight; it is about convincing people that there is a better way.

Second, "doing beats everything" at the end of the day. It is the only way to get things done.

Third, make things visible and understandable. Digital government is not something you can touch by itself, and it is too abstract for most people. However, government is something you can really see in its services. The only way to make an ancient organization change the way it has worked for two hundred years is to show them how it can be different—not by words, but by something they can use and then say, "Oh yeah, OK." The driver's license was a game changer with MyArgentina.

And finally—at the end of the day, the job is not about tech. It is about how you solve people's problems by using technology, or not using technology. So, all the talk on blockchain or AI or whatever new emerging technology does not matter—we have to help people deliver services whatever way we can. That is what matters.

Note

1. MiArgentina in Spanish.

CHAPTER 8

Diego Piacentini

Italy

Diego Piacentini served two years—from August 2016 to November 2018—as Italian Government Commissioner for Digital Transformation, reporting to the prime minister. In this role, he founded and scaled the government's Digital Transformation Team.

Prior to the civil servant role, Diego worked at Amazon.com for sixteen years as Senior Vice President of the international consumer business and a member of the senior executive team (S-team). Early in his career, Diego joined Apple Computer in Italy in his home city, Milan. Ten years later, he was appointed General Manager and Vice President of Apple EMEA based in Paris, before joining Amazon in Seattle.

After the civil servant experience, Diego finally started his own endeavor: a venture capital fund—View Different—that invests in and mentors entrepreneurs who use tech to reshape traditional sectors. In addition, he is a director on several boards, including Apolitical, The Economist Group, Bocconi University, Endeavor Italy, and IHME, and he has formal advisory roles with KKR, Exor Seeds, and Endeavor.

He holds a degree in economics from Bocconi University in Milan.

It is hard not to be impressed by Diego. Here is a man who left a top job in one of the global top companies to go serve his native country. And he did not even ask for or get any pay.

Given the context and complexity of governance in Italy and the messy state of digital government before his tenure, I guess only a person with the strategic and operational leadership acumen at Diego's level could stand any chance of generating some change there.

Diego did this and even more—in just two to three years he put in place the fundamentals to carry the digital government forward in Italy beyond his time there. His story speaks lengths on how bringing onboard the necessary type of deep experience shortens the transformation cycles and increases likelihood of lasting impact.

His story is also a much-needed assurance that with the right skills and mode of thinking, the right powers and some resource folks from the private sector still can succeed and excel in changing the public sector surroundings they get thrown into.

—Siim

How Did You Enter the Digital Government Role—and the Italian Government Overall?

The story is super simple, actually. I was contacted directly in 2016 by the then Italian prime minister Matteo Renzi. He was a young incoming politician, one of the few government people I know who actually understands the value of digital transformation. He was coming to Silicon Valley to see the Italians there and said that he would like to talk to me.

I met him for breakfast, and he told me his vision to accelerate the digital transformation of Italy. He had no idea how to do it, which is fine—I mean, he was a prime minister, not a CTO. He had this idea to go outside of Italy and try to target Italian diaspora from Silicon Valley or Seattle to relocate and start changing things.

I was very skeptical at first, but then realized that I had been working at Amazon for sixteen years, done Apple for thirteen years. What was I going to do next? I was happy. The company kept growing and doing different things and I was not bored. But I did think that at this point I wanted to stop being one of those Italians that keep criticizing that things do not work, and go and do something about it. I told Jeff Bezos way back in a job interview that I wanted to do something for my original country at some point, although did not know what it could be.

I used this sort of regret minimization approach. Would I regret two years from now not trying to work for the government or would I regret leaving Amazon? For me, the answer was very easy. I would have regretted not to try this.

I agreed on a two-year term. In two years, you can build many things. Especially, you can build a continuous set of processes, which is very unknown in politics as a concept.

What Was the Prime Minister's Motivation behind Wanting This Sort of Change? What Task Did He Give You Concretely?

The ultimate mission became to simplify the bureaucracy of the public administration. He also had a long-term vision of bringing Italy to a more technological ecosystem. So, his vision was much bigger than just the digital transformation of government.

My point to him was that "I see your big vision, but we have two years. We need to build the backbones to make it happen." Good thing is that he really understood that.

A criticism I received later was that I made a choice to focus my role in just one area. Initially, my role could have been for thinking about digital on a general level—how to regulate social media, how to tax the multinational tech companies, all this stuff. My choice was to focus on digitizing the public administration, not all those other issues—to actually get something done. If this was a mistake or not, I do not know.

I still remember a conversation we had with Prime Minister Renzi four or five days into my job. There was this big conference where he wanted to bring me and have me tell the audience everything that needs to be done. I said I was not ready. I said I did not want to be one of the many slogan tellers because I wanted to have a very clear plan and a clear set of processes. Then maybe two or three months later, I would be happy to speak to those conferences. He was disappointed, he was not used to such an answer—people would die to go to a conference with him. But he accepted it.

Did You Still Hesitate at All about the Role While Deciding?

My hesitation was that there have been so many examples of people coming from the private sector to government and being ineffective. Most of the time, it is because their role was to be an advisor or something not defined. Therefore, they would get lost in this chaos that government is. I was thinking, "What should I do differently to avoid that kind of failure?" That is why I designed the role and hired people the way I did.

What Was the Role You Created?

The role was very unclear at the start. That is where many people coming from a different sector fail—they do not realize that they need to tailor and design the role based on what the needs are. They do not expect that the people within the government do not know exactly what to do. Actually, that they may not know at all.

I went to Rome in August, and nobody works in Italy in August, even less in Rome. I started recruiting and found an amazing lawyer, Guido Scorza, who found us the role of a commissioner. For example, there was a commissioner for earthquake reconstruction and one for spending reform. The commissioner role had never been used for my type of job. It has powers for emergency situations. Being a commissioner gave me the opportunity to hire people without going through the never-ending process of public administration hiring. This was the thing I was really looking for.

So, the role of Government Commissioner for the Digital Agenda was a role we invented. One of its upsides, in hindsight especially, was that I did not have to change if the government were to change. You can resign when you want to, but it is one of the very few positions that is not required to change when a new government comes in.

What Was the Institutional Setup Before or Who Had the Responsibility for Digital Government?

The responsibility had been in the hands of the minister of public administration, Marianna Madia. She was very receptive to me. She told me she was not going to be in my way and would actually help to remove the blockers. She called us the "dream team."

There also was the Digital Agency, AgID. It had been created ten or fifteen years previously. I had a two-hour meeting with the head of the agency and the management team. It was easy to realize that they were the problem and not the solution. It is a digital agency full of lawyers and very few digital experts. All they did was design laws, bills, regulations. Very confusing ones and always for someone else to execute. They were not an agency; they were not executing. They just issued regulations and directives. The few technology people who were on that team were, with all due respect, just speaking mainframe and UNIX.

Now, politics is politics. I started in August and Renzi resigned in December after he lost a referendum. Because he left, everybody was expecting me to leave because I was seen as Renzi's protege. After a sleepless night, I decided that I was there to do something, and that something was absolutely independent from any political color. Why would digital transformation belong to the right or the left or to the center if this is something that everybody needs? So, I decided to stay with my team, which was forty people strong by then. Not one person decided to leave.

The new prime minister, Paolo Gentiloni, was from the same party and he was super helpful. However, he had only one year left until the elections and with one year, you do not push for big structural change. I had wanted to close the Digital Agency and maybe keep the best people, but that is the kind of thing that you need to have enough time ahead of you to execute.

What Were Your Levers or Tools in the Commissioner Role to Push for Change?

We had three macro-level goals: writing a plan, building the infrastructure, and coordinating activities.

One was building a three-year digital transformation plan, as detailed as possible. By the way, this had been one of the main objectives of the digital agency that they never accomplished.

For coordination, I hired a few software developers with very technical know-how to make sure we were in a very strong position to assess the teams in local centers and agencies. These guys were not used to talking to a counterpart. I was told at our first meeting that "this is too technical; we are not going to cover this." I said, "Oh no, stop right there—we absolutely want to cover this *because* it is technical." The architecture and the quality of code is important.

As commissioner, I had the power to impose a directive on the administration and to replace people who were not doing it. I never used the latter, although I was tempted a couple of times. It was just as important and good for people to know that I could do it. But I kept working on nudging them and developing the tools for them.

We created a forum for all the administration to exchange opinions and ideas. This is the way we got digital identity implemented in the services. The City of Milan was doing it at home and then the City of Genoa saw that and asked what tools they used, and then they took it on. The forum had a couple of thousand discussions every day—the users were all civil servants and vendors.

As for tools, we asked the vendors to put code on GitHub. We created a set of tools and guidelines for designers, which was always evolving.

Where Did You Devote Your Time and Focus on at the Start?

The first three or four months, I was hiring people. I received a couple of thousand applications, ended up having 120 people. I was also going around looking, picked the best possible existing great processes and ideas.

To create a great end-user service, you need to start building the basics. That is why we chose as the four big projects to work on: the digital payment platform PagoPA, the digital identity platform, the national resident population register, and an analytics and reporting platform. Activities had been going on for all of them for four or five years; I did not invent any of these four.

We chose these four because these were going to be most useful. If you make payment transactions between citizens and government easy, you can simplify a lot of the services. Identification is another constant in many services. Also, agencies would send information or documents to citizens—we needed to archive them. These all turned into the core of a citizen app called IO later.

We selected a few departments, starting from the City of Milan, and began by working on building out the services for the government app. You can build any technology, but if it is not perfectly integrated to services offered by administrations, it is completely useless. There were twelve thousand public administration units, from schools and hospitals to central government to cities, regions, and provinces. The work on integrating all of them is impossible.

We decided to select ten or fifteen administrations at different levels, right from small towns to large towns to different ministries. They were the ones who were enthusiastic about our role, and they saw a need for a big change. Our point was to work with those who really wanted to work with us, not waste any time convincing others. Hopefully over time, through emulation, the other ministries and the other cities would see how much better the others were becoming. Previously, the digital agency had spent a lot of time trying to create a bill to punish the administrations that were not using their digital laws. I was spending time on nudging the administrations that wanted to work. Two completely different approaches.

You Said at the Beginning of Our Chat That You Set Out to Build a Continuous Set of Processes—How Did You Do It?

The main thing was to build the practices, guides, and tools that could last and keep supporting change. You would be astonished that we had to do one piece to introduce the concept of project management, because there were no people with a background in it. We had to do really basic stuff.

The existing processes I found were just about the regulators writing a rule, sending it through some archaic government communication tools (often through registered mail) to administrations and giving them six months to read and ask questions. We moved everything onto a central platform and published immediately, using existing tools like GitHub.

By the way, everything we did is still available on the web. I did something that had never been done before in Italy. Everything we published was immediately bilingual. I knew that we wanted to get other countries to help us in giving suggestions and to also tell the other countries what we were doing. So, it had to be available in English, too, from the start.

Honestly, I fought hard against the written rules that were describing the technology because every such rule will be obsolete before the law is adopted. I completely stayed away from that. That is why I transformed the concept from rules to guidelines. We separated the concepts—what should be part of the law—from details that should be part of the guidelines, and the guidelines would keep evolving.

In fact, in my plan, the guidelines were to be updated once a year, to make sure that everything was lasting a generation.

You Emphasized That Your Main Work Was to Build Out a Different Team—How Did You Go about Doing It?

Team Digitale, as we called it, started from a blogpost on Medium. I wrote about my mission, my plan, and the kind of people I wanted to hire. I decided to publish it on Medium, because the people I wanted to read it and hear about it were on Medium. This post became the main source of receiving applications. Later I also did regular newspaper interviews, and these did get some good coverage.

We received a few thousand applications and bought a license for a hiring or recruiting software. With the first three people I had, we spent literally hours and hours looking through all those applications. By the way, to find time for that, I had to say no to 90 percent of conferences I was invited to. I do not know if it is true in other countries, but Italy is a republic founded on conferences. Everybody wants to have a conference!

I did not hire people only from the private sector. Ten to 15 percent came from within the public administration, because you do not want to show yourself as this new, total alien that comes from outside and does things that people do not understand at all.

In addition, I was looking for people like me who wanted to give back to their country and they wanted to spend some time actually doing it.

As for technical people, you need to go to a level of granularity about what those people need to do and hire accordingly. For example, one of my best hires was at the time the chairman of Python Software Foundation in Europe. He had great experience in developer relations, he knew exactly how to manage the relationship with technical people, and had all the things that were needed for setting those processes up in government.

As You Were Bringing These People Together, How Did You Mold Them into a Team?

I think that with very few exceptions, the people who were applying for our jobs already had existing in them a fundamental type of culture or traits of what I was looking for. Even the public sector people were the hidden gems from the government who saw our mission and saw it as an opportunity that would never again come in their life. Most of the people were super with IQ, incredibly well-structured at work.

I also did a lot of what I do not like to call team building. I really spent a lot of time in making sure that our people understood my modus operandi and what I was expecting from people. Most of the evenings, I would go out for dinner with one or two team members. In fact, I gained six kilos in those two years!

What Were the Things You Always Used to Say to the Team, Your Mottos, or the Values You Wanted Them to Follow?

First of all, the concept of starting from the citizen and working backwards. I copied this from Amazon. We need to remember that everything we do is not because there is a law that has been written. The endpoint is to simplify the lives of citizens and companies. And guess what—we are all citizens. We all are suffering from the pain, so we should really work at solving it.

The second one I did not have at first, but I had to introduce it pretty quickly. Every time I was proposing something, there would always be someone saying it was not possible. Like: "It has never been done." But why? So, I educated my team to the five whys method—keep asking why until you are happy with the answer. Turns out most of the time you cannot do things for privacy reasons—tell me why? You can go deeper and deeper and deeper until you realize there was really no obstacle. Most of the nay-sayers did it because they did not really want to change things or because they hated the fact that someone else was doing it. So, the principle was "Never take a no for a no—implement the five whys."

In addition, I did not want to have an approach that *nothing* had worked before. You need to do your homework, and you do not want to kill everything. Identify existing projects or processes that have promise but were mismanaged, poorly managed, or not managed at all. Focus on building something really transformational out of them for future use. We were not the only good guys, and we did not want to be perceived as arrogant. No one would work with us if they would perceive us as coming in and wanting to destroy everything.

We also had to create this culture of being really data-driven. People would sometimes see a number and then say, "We achieved it." But the number would look strange. Then I had to say, "Does the number not look strange to you?" Then they would dig deeper, and the number was wrong. Over time, your empirical experience must tell you that if a number looks wrong, it probably is wrong. Oftentimes, when people show you numbers, it is because someone gave them the numbers. They are happy because "numbers are numbers." You need to create a culture where everyone dives deeper.

There also is this principle of "disagree and commit." You often find yourself in situations where people disagree on things and never agree, and it takes days to get things done. My point was that after a good debate, we may agree or disagree on something—but, even if you are disagreeing, I want total commitment in the implementation. Not that you disagree and say you will do it and then do not. Disagree and commit.

What Routines Worked to Keep People Delivering?

I introduced the weekly business reviews. Every week we looked at the major metrics and reviewed them. The team needed to explain why this or that metric was not working in the desired way. At the very beginning, people were coming to the meetings not prepared—not knowing the answers to why delivery was not happening. Next time, they had to come knowing. It was about educating people to that level of attention that they did not expect from a top leader. They do not expect the boss of your boss to ask you a detailed question that educates everybody. If they see the boss doing it this way, they do the same way and you have raised the bar. It does not mean micromanagement; it means that I want you to take notice.

As we were forty people and not an army in size, I first involved everybody in the weekly reviews. You want to educate everybody. You also want to start interacting with two or three levels down, because it is the best way to have intuition about who is the next star or successor in your team. But, you also need to be careful because you do not want to have meetings that become too much of a burden. So, when I felt some processes were well run, I took the risk of stopping to monitor them.

To keep the focus on the citizen experience, we would start the meetings with a ten-minute description of some bad experience. We were receiving citizen complaints, anything from serious to small issues. We knew we could not solve each single issue that day, because that would be like emptying the ocean with a spoon. Still, I wanted to educate the team to the fact that you are a citizen and need to be sensitive to citizens' problems.

How Much of Your Work and Team Practices Came from Amazon Experience? What New Things Did You Learn on the Job?

In a way, it was hard to replicate Amazon because the quality of the people was different—not everyone was at the same level. But I honestly did try to bring what was applicable and a large part of it was.

For example, I took along the approach of writing things simple. Every piece should have a summary of it in a comprehensive language. Small detail, but it mattered a lot. See, each time a new regulation was issued by the government, it was all written in legal terms. Many pages, primes of paragraphs, written in a formal language that sometimes reads like a different Italian that nobody uses anymore. The real content is in two paragraphs somewhere inside.

The thing I learned was not to get frustrated. If you are easily getting frustrated, do not work in or around politics and just stay away from it!

The funny thing I used to say to journalists was that I learned to negotiate with irrational people. What is unique about the psychology of those people is that they are not driven by delivering a result, but by different factors.

The thing I had to unlearn from Amazon is the culture of innovation and invention, the focus on coming up with the new all the time. In some way we were doing it as far as Italian context is viewed. But in another way, we were copying others. Looking around internationally, and also within the administration, at best practices to get the basics right, get platforms working, get the guidelines in.

How Did You Build and Develop Relationships with Stakeholders While in Office?

This is very important, I totally underassessed at first the need to find the right stakeholders who would help us in implementing our projects. I thought that a good project should sell itself.

I realized soon that I always had to have with me two or three stakeholders, the first one being the Ministry of Finance. It took me six to nine months to understand to build a special relationship with the minister of finance and his team, because then they would see digital transformation as a money saver—but I had already lost one year. I was in this one meeting with some department's executive who asked, "What does the minister of finance think?" when I realized that I had not consulted with them.

Another one was the Data Protection Authority. In all my projects, there were privacy risks and privacy implications. It would have helped to build that relationship sooner.

This relationship building can often be confused as being political, while I was trying to be practical and not political. I was seeing things as black and white but should have been managing a little bit more with tones of gray.

Also, it took me a while to build trust into relationships. With a few exceptions, everyone was seeing me with a little bit of skepticism like, "Who is this guy?" "He comes from Amazon; does he have a second agenda?"

Also, the prime ministers were changing and so did governments. When government changed a few months into my time, everybody expected me to resign or be kicked out. As a commissioner, I did not have to resign. So, I started meeting with some of the most vocal critics of mine from the new government, one-on-one. I had to move from running a team to running a communication process. It was successful because those people realized that we were building stuff and the same stuff was going to be useful for them. One of my most successful moments was when one of my fiercest critics transformed to be my strongest ally in the Five Star Movement party that had gotten into government.

How Much Did the Relationship with Prime Ministers Work Out?

I went to the prime ministers when I needed to accelerate a few decisions, to remove the blockers. I used it only three times, I think. You do not want to overuse it because then you lose credibility.

Once every quarter or five to six months, we would have our whole team meet with the prime minister, especially with a new government. I wanted them to get an understanding of who we are and what we can do. Never undervalue or underassess the power of showing who the people are behind the scenes.

What Was the Hardest Part of Your Job?

My kind of work was less controversial than the average work of politics when you must talk about migrants or universal income or retirement age. These huge political issues are at an amazing level of controversy. Mine was nothing compared to that.

Most of my blockers were created by human nature: the rational or irrational sense of making it their job to disagree. Whether they say it has not been done before or something else. Blocker number two was the not-invented-here syndrome. "We have the competence' let us do it completely differently."

At the end of the day, public procurement in the way it works is probably the biggest blocker of digital transformation, and we did not get a solution to that.

I still remember when Jeff Bezos was giving a talk a few years ago about Blue Origin.[1] One of the people in the audience asked why he thought that Blue Origin could do better than NASA? Jeff was very humble, but his main point was—because it was a private company and did not have to go through all the procurement rules that NASA had. That is why NASA was sometimes three or four years behind the newest technology, because by the time you do a procurement process, by the time that the losers do appeal (because every time there is an appeal), it takes three years to get anything done.

In Italy, the procurement regulations are affected by several crime control mechanisms to prevent bribery and against possible infiltration of the mafia. It is a consequence of how powerful mafia was in some historical times, and when local and central governments were affected by several episodes of bribery and corruption. To be able to counter this, a huge amount of regulation has been created to make sure vendors were not linked to criminal organizations. But guess what—there were many unintended consequences. Occasionally the bad guys went through the process anyway and gamed the system, while for everyone else, selling to the government was a very hard and cumbersome process.

Procurement is also a blocker because of a feature intrinsic in the nature of governance. When you issue rules, laws, guidelines, then they are meant to be universal and work for everybody. That is why they are adjusted to the minimum common denominator, which in the end result is something completely useless because you cannot make everybody happy.

For example, all of the Team Digitale website content was written by several contributors from the team. We needed it also in English immediately and as there are a lot of AI-automated translators, we went to buy the service. We had to go the central procurement website, managed by an agency that does procurement for the entire federal government. Our team was looking for a solution and some five hundred results came in with no differentiation. The procurement agency told us that they would not allow the translation vendors to list the features of the product because in this way it would favor the best products while they want to give everybody equal opportunities. Now, that was a new one to me. In some situations, you want to give full equal opportunity to serve everybody. But, in other contexts you want to give better opportunity to the best.

What Made You Move on after the Two Years?

I can honestly say that I did not want to continue to work in the government, and I considered my job done. When I first approached the newly elected prime minister, Giuseppe Conte, the government asked me to stay three to four months to ensure succession. I built the plan for it,[2] and I chose my successor.

As I said, the role of commissioner is meant for managing urgency and extraordinary situations. But you cannot have a long-lasting emergency. Plus, with two years you slowly become part of the system. I realized I was starting to give up in some situations. I was losing that level of energy to get things done.

How Did You Make Sure What You Had Started Would Last?

Six months into my job, I was already looking for my successor, which is another unknown concept in politics. That is one of the things that you do as a leader of a company, one of your best moves. Your good team is your succession plan.

I did not want to build things into a "Diego-centric" way. So, one of the proposals in the last paper to government was that it was probably time to move away from the extraordinary commissioner approach and build a much more permanent organism, a much more permanent body—by reforming AgID and have a seat at the cabinet for digital topics.

The most important thing is that we moved from building rules to building services. Let us take, for example, this last summer of 2021 when a COVID-19 pass became mandatory in Italy. As soon as people got their second vaccination shot and the vaccine office put their information in the central database, people who had downloaded our IO app received the green pass immediately and had to do nothing more. These sort of concrete changes we managed to make for better services, and they are here to stay. The pandemic accelerated it, but if we had not built the basis, we would be in a different situation.

What Do You Think You Managed to Achieve and What Are You Most Proud Of, Looking Back?

It is the culture change. The fact that the digital way and how we did it are now considered more normal, not exceptional. It is because we built—and it is because of the COVID-19 pandemic, which stopped the talk of digital divide, which is often an abstract excuse.

The cultural change is evident in the fact I could choose a successor and now there is a full ministry for technological innovation, leading the work from the cabinet level. We managed to build the continuous set of processes that were not interrupted when governments changed.

There are now a bunch of agencies that are following the path. There are a few administrations that we did not even start with, though. For example, I did not go into departments that had regional management. The Ministry of Health in Italy has twenty regional offices and every one of them operates on their separate set of codes, hardly integrating. I thought it was going to take me ten years to get anywhere so I said, "Do not even start." We also did not go into ministries that had been with specific vendors for ten to fifteen years—as the drivers of making things work, they were not under my control. Even though we told everyone that "here is the plan, here are the guidelines, use them."

So, we focused and worked with six to seven departments that did very well. Plus, several cities. I am very proud of the City of Milan and Roberta Cocco[3] there—they did an amazing job building enabling platforms, enabling tools.

At the end of the day, we were climbing Mount Everest, and I do not think we reached the basecamp yet or perhaps just around there. But my job was done, things were in motion.

Is There Anything You Regret Not Doing or Wish You Had Done Differently?

Most of the regrets were at the technical level, such as some of the choices in building tools for big data analysis that were wrong. Two nontechnical mistakes were impactful, though.

I should have been building a deeper relationship with the stakeholders, like I said.

I would have also needed to communicate a little more on what could be achieved—the potential. I was a little bit shy because I come from this culture where you should communicate when you have something to communicate, as opposed to doing it while still being on the way. We probably could have had a more comprehensive communication process.

Would You Ever Consider Doing Such a Job Again?

I have no regrets about taking the role, even though these were very tough twenty-seven months. But I understand better now the life of policymakers and politicians; it is a tough life.

If I were to do something like this again, it would have to be a very visible top job. Not because it is cool to have a top job, but because it is the only way to get things done. And I would not do it for another country!

What Are Your Three Bottom-Line Recommendations to a Colleague on What Does It Take to Do This Sort of Job Well?

First one is not just a recommendation, but a necessity. Any transformational project needs to come from the top. Being competent is necessary, but it is not enough. Picking the right team is necessary, but it is not enough. Finding the right other stakeholders is necessary, but it is not enough. Building a plan, as detailed as it may be, is necessary, but it is not enough.

What you need for all of this is the blessing and the support of the highest possible role in government. In my case, it was the prime minister. Otherwise, you will never be taken seriously. Otherwise, things are never going to happen because there is too much discussion, too many diverging interests. If the transformational project does not come from the top, there is no success.

Second, try to build the mechanisms that would allow for continuity and not be interrupted when the new government comes onboard. That requires a combination of strategic communication, very clear plans, and the management of the succession plan in the transition.

Third, keep the citizen-centricity in mind. Keep in mind that you are here not to comply with laws, but to make life easier for the citizens.

Notes

1. Blue Origin is a company founded by Amazon's founder Jeff Bezos to start offering spaceflight services commercially.
2. The paper was called "Strategy for the Future of Digital Transformation," and consisted of recommendations based on the experience gained over the twenty-four months of operating—this was published in September 2018. The paper is available at https://teamdigitale.governo.it/.
3. Roberta Cocco was Deputy Mayor for Digital Transformation and Citizens Services in the City of Milan, Italy, in 2016–2021.

CHAPTER 9

Hillary Hartley

Ontario, Canada

Hillary Hartley is Chief Digital and Data Officer (CDDO) in the province of Ontario, Canada, and Deputy Minister of the Ontario Digital Service. As the CDDO, Hillary is responsible for leading the government's digital and data transformation efforts to deliver simpler, more easily accessible services for the people, communities, and businesses of Ontario.

Hillary joined the Ontario government in April 2017. Before moving to Canada, she spent nearly twenty years working with state, local, and the federal government in the US. While working NIC Inc. as a sales and marketing director, Hillary collaborated with many state and local governments on their digital transformation strategies.

In 2013, she was one of the Presidential Innovation Fellows during President Obama's second term. After her fellowship, she cofounded and helped build 18F, the first digital services team in the US federal government, and served as 18F's deputy executive director.

With Hillary, you get a bit of a bargain: two-for-one. She brings to the table her the insights from two governments: the federal one in the US from her 18F gig and the state (or provincial) one in Ontario, Canada. In both roles she was right there at the lead in kick-starting a whole new team and a whole new way of doing digital in that government.

Hillary is the only regional-level digital government leader featured in this book. This is not because of the lack of excellent people working at that level. On the contrary, we could compile a whole book or a few just from such folks alone. It was simply my choice and the bias of my own interest to focus on national level digital government excellence. However, I did have to make an exception for Hillary, as the book would not be complete without her in here.

This chapter focuses on her time in Ontario. Hillary has built up culturally and manageri-ally perhaps one of the most fascinating digital government teams anywhere, and because of who she is herself. She is very humane, really breathes and radiates empathy, true to the servant leadership approach she has adopted to practice. Her story shows that excellence can come from many different styles.

—SIIM

What Brought You to Work in Digital Government, in the US and in 18F at First?

I came from outside, from fifteen years of working with governments as a consultant or strategic advisor. I worked for a company called NIC and my last stint with them was working for their corporate office. They work with some thirty states in the US, becoming a digital service team for the state on fee-for-service kind of model. So, I got to work with a bunch of different state and local governments over the years.

I was also actively part of the emerging civic tech scene as I was living in San Francisco. Code for America started right around that same time, and I got engaged with them on mentoring and supporting. When the Presidential Innovation Fellowship started in 2012,[1] I told my boss that we should put someone forward to apply. We convinced one of my colleagues to apply and he got accepted. We stayed in touch and tried to figure out any way that NIC could be helpful in some of the things that they were thinking about like platform pieces and API connectivity to state data.

Someone then said that I should apply for the second-year batch, and after a first laugh about it, I did at the eleventh hour. I got accepted and so in 2013 I was a Presidential Innovation Fellow. That was the first time that I was a bureaucrat inside government. And I loved it!

It was just really different. It was challenging, but it was refreshing. It was so exciting to be on the inside, trying to make change, instead of just giving my best advice and pushing from the outside. It changed my perspective and was a pivot for me in my life and career.

At the end of our fellowship, I was part of a group of fellows who formed 18F—the first digital services unit for the US federal government.[2] My fellowship program was already in the agency that became home to 18F, so the executives asked a few of us to spend a couple of years building that up—with me as the deputy executive director. The mandate from President Obama at the time was that he wanted five hundred digital folks inside the government. Between 18F and the US Digital Service, we actually did achieve that by the time he left.

What Made You Jump to Ontario Government from There?

The founding Ontario digital government team was ten to twelve folks sort of pulled together, working with the government minister to figure out where it could go and what shape it should take. A couple of them and the minister came to Washington, DC, and met with 18F. We chatted with them about our model, how it was set up, and some of our priorities. Not too long after that they put the job description for the chief digital officer (CDO) out.

I remember tweeting it and sending it around and saying this was a great job for somebody. I did not really anticipate going anywhere myself, but the folks in Ontario were working with Public Digital and Tom Loosemore was helping them shape the role.[3] He reached out to me a bit later and said, "Hey, have you ever considered moving to Toronto?" There had just been the 2016 presidential election in the US, and my four-year term contract was almost up. I started talking to the folks, went up for an interview, and things went from there.

What Appealed to You about the Job in Ontario Once You Learned More?

I was definitely interested to learn more knowing that the folks at Public Digital were involved with the program and the leadership. Ontario had invested in bringing in the folks who had helped create and shape the Government Digital Service in UK. They had now been involved in laying the groundwork, doing the early work on the political side and the bureaucratic side to shape and to help folks understand what the digital service team could do.

I also liked that they were explicitly looking for a CDO—a role that I understood and had advocated for in other jurisdictions. It was not necessarily about technology, it was not trying to replace the CIO. It was going to be to be a different kind of leader and to a different kind of team. It was also a chance to start something, to really shape something even if it had lived in a kind of embryo phase for about a year. It was still a start-up. They were trying to become part of the machinery in a way that I do not think 18F really was ever able to do. That was exciting to me.

What Was the Minister Saying That They Expected for You? What Was the Mission Set for You to Do?

It was clear that there was enough room to have a vision of my own and that was exciting to me. They knew that they wanted a leader with a vision to take this sort of fledgling team and figure out what to do with it, so it could become an agent of change. Also, to put a few lighthouse projects on the hill to start showing a different way to do things.

Did You Hesitate at All in Making the Move?

I definitely hesitated. It was a big move. It was a cross-country and an international move for me and my family physically, too.

At the time, the job scared me a little bit. I remember that I had coffee with a colleague, one of our managers at 18F, and just talked about it. She said, "Sounds like it scares you a little bit. Well, then you have to do it!"

I knew what a CDO was, and I had a vision for growing the kind of team that could make a difference. However, I did not know very much about what being a deputy minister meant—which was the other institutional part of the role. I have joked several times that I do not think I wore that hat very effectively for the first six to twelve months of the job, at least. I led my team and was proud to be the leader of my team, felt lucky to be at various tables that I recognized were important in terms of conversations and relationships. But I really did not fully grasp the hierarchy and some of the Westminster pieces for the first several months.

Did You Set Any Conditions or Prerequisites for Joining In?

As I was thinking about what the team components would be, I said that we could not even begin on the mission that we were being given if I could not have a proper starting team in place.

Initially, the digital service team was mostly a combination of communications and policy, with some technological folks that were obviously very good at hacking the bureaucracy. They had partnered with the IT team that ran ontario.ca. But there was no real product capability.

What I was able to negotiate was essentially a team for ontario.ca because it was going to be the heart of the whole effort at first. I needed a team of forty to fifty people. I was very lucky to walk into a situation where the budget had landed, and I actually started that very week. This new budget gave us the positions for people and the money, and it officially created the Ontario

Digital Service (ODS). We had a team running ontario.ca, and this is what we could build from; we had room to grow.

Where Was ODS Placed Institutionally?

My role and the ODS has moved around the government every June since I started!

We started as part of the Cabinet Office, and that is where we incubated for the first year. Then there was an election, which also brought a change in government. They moved the ODS into the Ministry of Government and Consumer Services. They made me the deputy minister of consumer services, which also included our service organization—Service Ontario—which has the physical service locations along with online services.

The next year they moved the ODS back into the Cabinet Office because we had a lot of big things going on and they wanted the team and the CDO role closer to the premier.

Then we were moved into the Treasury Board a year later because of alignment there with the minister, Peter Bethlenfalvy. He was becoming the chief champion for digital transformation, and he really understands the mission. Then he moved and became the minister of finance and so we moved with him. So now we are in the Ministry of Finance.

The constant has been that I have been the Deputy Minister of the Ontario Digital Service all this time. As such, I report to the head of the public service, which in Ontario is the secretary of the cabinet. And then, in addition, I also report to a minister.

What Was the State of Digital Government in Ontario, and What Prompted the Creation of ODS?

It is not that the services were lousy. Ontario had been an e-government leader. In those early days, the thought was that if you just get the service online then people will use it. But governments learned that simply having an online presence was not enough.

To me that marks the transition to "digital," which is not just about technology but how you make things easy and simple. If people—especially the digital natives, who live on their phones or their laptops—are not using your online services because they are not usable, then what is the point?

The nascent digital team in Ontario was seeing what was happening in other jurisdictions and knew that Ontario could do that, too. The leaders knew ontario.ca could be a world-class website and that they had the talent, the resources, and the ability to do it. They had watched many services come online, but not always using modern best practices for design and application development.

Ontario is the biggest province in Canada, the most populous, and it certainly sees itself as a leader—in Canada but also proudly always wants to be an international leader. So, there was enough momentum to set up a team that could spearhead this change, really this culture change.

What Was the Concrete Objective You Set for Yourself to Achieve?

It had appealed to me that they were trying to hire a leader who would start "turning the Titanic" on a lot of different fronts like agility, funding, procurement, really bringing a user-focused perspective to everything that we do. This really got baked into my goals from the beginning.

When I say I knew what a CDO was supposed to be, it meant to me the opportunity to build a world-class team, at the time centered on making a world-class product out of ontario .ca that could evolve into the basis for lots of different changes. These were my goals.

It was not necessarily a five-year vision. Even with the new budget, we knew we had a pretty short runway to get hiring done up to the number we had been given.

What Was Your Focus in the First Hundred Days or Three Months?

As we are a Westminster government, we receive mandate letters from the premier and were essentially given our first set of lighthouse projects with the first letter.

The most immediate work was building the team up and working on ontario.ca. But we also had a few other early projects. One of them was building something called Ontario Student Assistance Program calculator, an online estimator for the amount of money you could get to go to college. This project was the first call to action as to how can we create something very, very quickly and was simple to get the necessary job done. Our team helped the program team pivot from an online application that was several pages with many questions to a simple JavaScript-based tool that was four questions long. It was a game changer because suddenly there was a very easy thing for the minister and the government to demonstrate the change in approach. Users also had a great experience: 90 percent of completion rate as opposed to almost no one bothering to check before.

This project was something that the team continued to come back to for a long time, because it was one of the first times that we got to work with a ministry partner in a way that fundamentally changed how they approached their problem. They now saw the value of starting small, they saw the value of the service design process, they saw the value of sitting with users as they click through something and watching them and seeing where they failed.

In those first hundred days, we put together and published a list of ten key priorities for our work. It was really ten different missions to deliver.

What Were Your Initial Tools and Levers in the Mandate to Ensure Delivery Across the Government?

The ten missions were carved out as the core mandate of the ODS and the CDO and there were some levers already planned among the ten.

For example, we were specifically tasked to work with three departments on some high-priority projects, then move on to high-impact transactions. The mandate letter approach was effective in our early days because it was a call to action for other ministries to partner with us.

One of our key priorities was to help Ontario deliver a consistent high-quality user experience. In addition to partnering on delivery, the ODS established a digital service standard and introduced an assessment process to bring these principles and patterns into practice across ministries. We also developed performance benchmarks to begin to understand our digital maturity across the enterprise.

A lot of our mandate was about helping the public service be better. For example, at fostering digital talent or doing procurement in new ways or embedding service design into policy and program development. On the people side, I was tasked to give strategic advice in recruiting key positions at a senior level.

In addition to defining our priorities and focus, a key lever from the beginning was the fact that we had a champion from the top. Our minister was the deputy premier. We were in a

Cabinet Office at first, and the secretary of the cabinet published the initial ten priorities for us. This made it clear that it was government priority.

Another influence lever—but also something we have had to overcome—is the "cool kids" factor. When we first started, it helped as well as hindered to be seen that way. It helped internally because we got some priority around our early projects. It also helped us recruit, because there is a growing community of tech folks who want to help the government modernize. However, of course, there are always pockets of any institution that are resistant to change, and for better or worse the ODS was the face of that transformation.

If These Were the Initial Tools at Your Disposal, Have You Added Some More or How Have They Changed?

In 2019, we worked with the government to pass some legislation—a law called the Simpler, Faster, Better Services Act. It did a few things.

First, it created a statutory role called the Chief Digital and Data Officer (CDDO)—so, we added data to the title and expanded my role. It essentially established my role as setting standards and expectations. It put in place some stronger hammers to be able to compel certain things like reports or data.

Second, we elevated the digital service and data standards. The data standard is about principles concerning open data, mostly. We did not put the actual digital service standard into the legislation, but the high-level principles are there. It made the CDDO responsible and able to set those standards.

It was an important milestone because it meant that we could finally get off and running with the digital service standard and the assessment process. Assessments had been in place for a while, but now we could take the principles and write directives to compel agencies to comply with them.

How Did the Law Come About Politically? What Set Things Rolling in This Direction?

We had a government and a premier's office that understood where we were headed. The phrase that has taken hold here is "digital first"—and the goal to become a world-leading digital jurisdiction. The political champions understood it is not just about technology, but about the way we work, the way we think, the way that we approach our problems. They understood that to get results across the public service, we have to both enable and compel.

I do not remember exactly what sort of meeting or moment it was when we turned that corner and said, "Let us put this into legislation." It was a way for government to show that they were prioritizing our digital transformation, similar to privacy or other topics. There was a statutory role for the chief privacy officer. Now there was going to be a statutory role responsible for helping the province deliver great online services.

I think I was lucky in that this step came about pretty naturally. Our team just never failed to deliver. Whatever questions the political level had, whatever we set out to do, whenever we were asked to report back—we delivered. So, there has not been a hesitation about anything that our team has pitched. Which is crazy! We are seen as a team that gives our best advice, and we will fiercely advocate for the direction we believe we need to go.

It has also been my style (and possibly a bit of naivete) to be very honest with our political partners and give my best advice. I have tried to put myself in their shoes, think in terms of their accountability, and be brutally honest to hopefully be a voice they can trust.

Besides Having Champions to Have Your Back Politically, How Did You Ensure Buy-in from Other Departments—for the Wider Role and Power?

We started the Deputy Ministers' Committee on Technology and Transformation very close to our beginning. We had been building relations and champions one-by-one and delivering great products—kind of turning the lights on. But it is slow this way, and it does not always trickle up the chain to the deputy minister level. The committee has been a way to surface some of those conversations, to surface projects and to shine a light on teams across the public service. I think it has helped folks understand what we were thinking about, and what we mean by digital. We have had a conversation many times on understanding what it means to be digital. Kind of keep going back to that, and we have been able to reiterate our North Star this way over and over again. I feel this is my main job: to constantly be reminding all the various actors and my peers on what our North Star really is and has to be.

Being able to shine light on ministry teams has helped a bit with that "cool kids" factor—showing that ODS has really become an enabler as opposed to just doing cool projects.

I also have one-on-ones with lots of my peers each month. I try to stay in very close contact. Some of them are close collaborators, just other pieces of the same bigger machine. So, I have constant touch points with our delivery partners or the comptroller general about risk, for example.

How Did You Build a Team That Excels in Delivery?

At the end of the day, I think it has been possible because of setting a tone from the top that ODS is not a top-down organization. It is a bottom-up organization. We are in government and, of course, there is hierarchy and bureaucracy. We do have executives and managers, but our teams feel empowered to understand the goal in front of them and run at it as fast and as hard as they can, without having to constantly check up the ladder. I think that is the difference, and it is a tone set from the top. My executive team fully believes in that, buys into it, does not micromanage.

I have spoken a lot about servant leadership, and I believe in it. My job is to sit at the bottom of the virtual hierarchy, not at the top. I can support, and I can get things out of the way. I can also make tough decisions when other folks need me to, but I try to leave it to them mostly. This concept of servant leadership and the concept of pushing decisions down as far as possible in our organization. Those two things really lead to a team culture in which they are constantly trying to do their best work and know that we have got their back.

We do have a code of conduct for ODS. It has been created by our team for our team. The code talks about some of those practices, and some of those things that we feel help us be a high-functioning team.

What Are Some of the Things You Have Been Telling Your Team as Your Mottos, Your Philosophy?

I sent an email to the team a few years ago about servant leadership and about what it meant to me. Folks kind of started quoting pieces of it back to me from time to time, and it has become a part of our onboarding now. As new team members get on boarded to the team, they get a handbook, and this email is part of what everybody who joins ODS reads now.

So, all or most of the two-hundred-person team know that I am not a micromanager. That I am there to ask tough questions about strategy, help them clarify a path forward, or get stuff out of the way for them. I do not want decisions showing up on my desk unless they are truly executive-level decisions.

We do not have "The strategy is delivery" painted on our walls, but that certainly has been a guiding mantra we stole from Mike Bracken. It has been a nice guiding light for teams like ours to just get started, to deliver and let that guide us.

"Focus on the user." I think my peers would say, "Oh, there she goes again!" when they hear it. I keep saying it over and over again. Designing for users, designing with users, have you talked to a user? It is worth repeating, so that eventually everyone is asking the same questions, and it would become the way everyone works.

"Working out loud" and "working in the open" are big things for us as a team. When you work in the open, sharing the lessons you learn along the way, you not only document good team practices but you also help future teams avoid the same experience. "Make new mistakes"—do not repeat someone else's mistake. We use chat tools like a lot of other digital teams do. We have to constantly remind ourselves to get out of our direct messages and private channels, onto open channels. This way someone can see something and weigh in or add to the conversation, or search for it later and reuse it.

"Use data." Sounds straightforward, but as leaders and teams we have to rely on evidence and data for our decision-making.

Another one that I love is the idea of "embracing the chaos." This has been central to our success and survival at ODS, having been moved every year or working from home these last 18 months. Even before COVID-19, it was an idea to recognize that everybody has a different style of work, everybody thinks differently. How do we come together as a team to embrace all these different pieces of the puzzle and work together to get things done? Throughout last year I have tried to be very open about the chaos in my own life with COVID-19 around us and kids jumping into meetings, so that everybody else feels comfortable showing the chaos in theirs.

What Have Been Your Regular Routines or Practices with Your Team?

We try to behave like a product team, from actual staff members in product teams all the way up to the executive team. Our management team does daily standup via chat, which helps us make connections across the files. Additionally, at the start of the COVID-19 pandemic we did an executive standup at the end of every day for fifteen to thirty minutes to review what happened that day and to connect. In the chaos those early months brought to our work, it was a way to create transparency and connection. We have dialed it back to meeting two or three times per week, but it is still an important touch point for our senior executives.

At the full team level, we meet each week and have an all-hands every Monday. It probably averages about half of the team each time, depending on who can attend. This is our team touch point and an opportunity to check in to show new faces to people, to make announcements, and to do show and tell. Each quarter one of these turns into a kind of "Ask me anything" meeting with the executive team. It is a great opportunity to hear from the team and communicate where things are at right now.

How Have You Managed to Attract Folks to Join the Team?

Often state capitals, especially in the US, are not the most exciting cities in the state. We are in Toronto, and this definitely is a plus for recruiting because there are lots of companies here and in nearby universities. There is a natural talent pipeline here. We tend to recruit folks from consulting firms, tech companies, and other civic tech organizations.

We also make generous use of co-op placements. For example, there is the Kitchener-Waterloo corridor area an hour and half drive from Toronto. It is like a mini Silicon Valley, with innovation hubs and start-ups coming from the universities there. We have some office space at a local innovation space there for talent to reach us better this way.

Who Have Been Your Most Valuable Hires?

Choosing the right organizational model made a big impact, as said.

We built the teams not based on their daily work but on their skill sets as chapters, taking example from the likes of Spotify. That is why in the first years, as we were growing, the hiring of the chapter managers was crucial. They have been the heart and soul of the organization responsible for supporting our people through periods of growth and stress. Without people we would get nothing done. We found five incredible managers, and they have enabled us to know how to build the right teams with the right tools using the right practices.

If You Look Back to the Journey So Far, What Have Been Your Biggest Achievements That You Are Most Proud Of?

One certainly was the 2019 legislative act. It was a watershed moment because it showed that the Ontario government understood our North Star and that they wanted to make it a reality by putting the expectations, standards, and indeed statutory responsibility in place. It was a huge moment for the team, and especially for the folks, this little team, who were there before me and started down the path with the digital service standard.

Second, thanks to the championship of my minister who really wanted to learn some lessons from the pandemic, we created a cabinet committee. It is a committee of cabinet ministers called the Future State Modernization Committee. It has been meeting over the past year to help us identify priorities, set expectations, and get some funding in place. We managed to help the government set up a fund similar to New South Wales in Australia or other jurisdictions—a modernization fund called Ontario Onward Acceleration Fund. It has CA $500 million for three years to push forward on big modernization initiatives. With that fund we have managed to start an attempt for more agile funding. It will have funding for small projects that can get off the ground quickly, then the next round for growing them, then the next round for scaling.

Another achievement is sort of on the machinery side. It has been the most satisfying thing, honestly, to see the magic of our team and the ODS foundations we have put in place for the last few years to really come to life when COVID-19 hit. Having a team that is product focused and is organized as a matrix, as opposed to a business or single product only, has helped us to be able to pull teams together quickly to meet ongoing priorities. We have a foundation that enables us to be flexible. We also have the team culture in place where the second we change priority, the team knows they are empowered to get at it.

That is really what has driven our success over the last eighteen months. We were able to pretty much overnight get the team working very quickly and efficiently on COVID-19 priorities. Our matrix model and chapter setup enabled quick pivots and the necessary support from people managers.

One of our first COVID-related products showed the value of working in the open and with open source. In Canada, the province of Alberta put out the first COVID-19 self-assessment tool. Someone from our team saw it, we approached them for the code, got it, and built from it our own solution in three days. That tool has now evolved into a mini-platform with life of its own, because it has been many times iterated with changing guidelines and has become the basis for several other health self-assessment tools, like for going to school or entering businesses or workplaces. That shows the promise of our work: we build this small thing in three days, and it turns into several tools that people can rely on and use millions of times a week.

Is There Something You Have Failed at or Regret Not Having Achieved Yet?

Improving procurement was there in the initial ten key priorities but we always knew it was too big. In 18F in the US government, we were able to do quite a bit of hacking around innovative procurement. I thought we would have done more of this in Ontario by this point than we have managed to do.

The task to build stronger partnerships with digital suppliers was part of our initial mandate and priorities. It involved testing flexible approaches for procurement. We created a new procurement vehicle, using what is called the vendor of record mechanism in Ontario. For various types of work, there exist lists of vendors of record that ministries can use for easy access to certain types of services. It is like a preselected pool of vendors. We created a new pool of service design, user experience, and user research. We worked hard to streamline the application process for bidders, with five-page bids as opposed to hundreds of pages of request-for-proposal requirements. We ended up getting about thirty to forty businesses in, available to help ministries meet the digital service standard and digital-first assessment process. But the adoption of this particular pool has not been as high as we assumed.

In a way, it has been a classic case of "if you build it, they will come" type of fail—the program agencies did not come. We are still figuring out how to create those pathways. We have been able to move a few programs forward with it, but how to incentivize ministries to bake it into their process? We have to somehow get the necessities of user research and service design baked into the inception phase, at the idea phase.

This is where probably our digital maturity work has to come in. Change will come only when program leaders and program owners are thinking this way. We have just recently completed a digital maturity survey across the public service and are working with ministries on their individual digital strategies about building out all-around capacity.

And then there is the issue of funding. Governments are not necessarily agile with how they plan budgets or forecast funds. I have said it a few times that if I could wave a magic wand and suddenly make the entire public service think and work like we do in on digital teams, in an agile way and with a product focus, I think we would still fail—because government funding does not know what to do with those projects. Funding is the next hairy thing to try and solve. Ontario Onward Acceleration Fund is a baby step forward in this.

What Would Make You Move on from the CDDO Role at Some Point?

If I get to a point where I feel like I am the blocker for the team on their way to get things done quickly or not getting the support we need from political level—say, I do not click there or am pushing the wrong buttons. If I am not having value.

What Have You Done to Make Sure the Change You Initiated Is Sustained?

The way we built the team, both the model and the people, have made it possible. I have excellent buy-in, same style of leadership from the executive team. We have champions, we now have good buy-in from rest of government. This gives me great comfort to understand that whatever happens, the team will keep going and thriving.

Is There Anything You Wish You Had Known at the Start?

I did not know much about being a deputy minister. I perceived the opportunity to come in and lead this team, to do our thing. To be the kind of leader that I wanted to be. I did not understand how my role fit into the bigger picture, the "lay of the land" on a political level. I did not use the hat effectively to push earlier to get some more leverage and hammers for the team. We could have likely used the "machine" to our advantage to change certain practices and standards sooner.

It has definitely also been four years of learning how to be a different kind of executive in an institution where titles convey power and importance. I will take accountability; I will be the person that can get blamed. But I want to encourage other folks to make the day-to-day decisions and figure out how to make things work, because they have more knowledge than I do and are closer to the work.

What Kind of Skills Are Necessary to Do Your Job Well?

I think there is some natural competency that can be learned, about realizing what good service delivery looks like and then being able to advocate for it. Then to figure out what are the levers for it, what components will help to get us there.

If I were to move along from CDDO role and another person come in, I would be most nervous about whether that person has a good sense of what "good" looks like, is that person able to push back on peers and push teams in the right direction. It is a subjective understanding that comes from experience of delivering—which is why no matter the role, we hire product-minded folks.

From my bias, I would also say that it is necessary to know how product teams work. You would have to have been on product teams or a product manager or owner in the ecosystem somehow. You need to have experience with what it means to work with users, to ask the right questions, to bring something to life and see it through end-to-end.

What Are Your Key Recommendations about How to Be Excellent in the CDDO Job?

The first thing is to figure out what levers you have. If you discover that you do not have any, go to work on figuring out how to get them. I think that the list David Eaves from Harvard Kennedy School and Public Digital have put together about levers for digital service groups really nails it.[4]

It depends also on what your goal is. Do you want to be a client-centered product factory? Or do you want to be an organization that is working itself into the machine the way I have described? That will determine what type of a team you need to build. ODS started as a product factory, and hopefully we are moving toward becoming a team factory—building the digital maturity of our partner programs and ministries.

Second, figure out how you prioritize people above everything else at the end of the day, with your own style and whatever it means to you. For me, it manifests in user-centered design, in servant leadership and team empowerment.

The reason why digital government teams feel so magical to me is that they are a confluence of folks that are super smart and capable, but also super empathetic. Focused on what good looks like, on people, and on doing the right thing. Not everybody will have the same leadership style, but you have to recognize that in the digital government world, we have to stay focused on people.

Notes

1. Presidential Innovation Fellows is a program started by the Obama administration in the United States to bring in top innovators from private sector, nonprofits, and academia and pair them with government agencies to deliver better and quicker results.
2. 18F is a digital services agency within the General Services Administration in the US government, helping other agencies build and buy technology within the federal government.
3. Public Digital is a consultancy set up by the founding team members of United Kingdom's Government Digital Service after their departure from Her Majesty's Government.
4. See Eaves, D., Loosemore, T., & L. Lombardo. (2020). Introduction to levers for digital service groups. In D. Eaves & L. Lombardo (Eds.), *2020 state of digital transformation*. Harvard Kennedy School Ash Center.

CHAPTER 10

Innocent Bagamba Muhizi

Rwanda

Innocent Bagamba Muhizi is a senior technology and business executive with more than fifteen years of industry experience in the public and private sector. He was appointed in April 2017 as the first CEO for Rwanda Information Society Authority (RISA)—a position he still holds to date.

Prior to that, Innocent served as the regional CIO for AccessHolding, including leading the digital transformation for three banks across Africa. He has also led digital transformation works in the rest of the telecom and banking sector in Rwanda, including deploying the first e-tax services in partnership with the Rwanda Revenue Authority.

He started his career in the Office of the President of the Republic of Rwanda as the director of IT back in 2001.

Innocent's job goes far beyond the digital government only, and many of the accomplishments of Rwanda and RISA reach far into the digital society and digital economy at large. Rwanda is often hailed as the tech star of all Africa, and for good reasons.

This all has been the result of a long-term effort launched by the Rwandan president Paul Kagame, who had a bold vision already many years ago that his country's future has to be carried by digital and tech.

During Innocent's tenure and under his watch as the first CEO of RISA, Rwanda has reached into deeper transformation of public services in the digital government realm. In his very humble manner and steady effort, he has built up an agency and government-wide mechanisms to be able to meet the country's high ambitions. Yet, he says surely that it all is still only a work in progress, with so much more to learn!

Indeed, do notice in the next pages how heavily the notion of the need and desire for constant learning features in Innocent's thinking and practices, starting from the way he has built it into RISA work and setup.

—Siim

How Did You Become a Digital Government Leader in Rwanda?

When I finished my undergraduate at the university back in 2001, I was honored at this very young age to be invited to work in the Office of the President of the Republic of Rwanda as the director of IT. At that time, we were really at the infancy stages of Vision 2020, the national development plan that has steered our government's work since.

I worked there for about three years, then went for my graduate training. When I finished my graduate studies, I came back and worked in government for about one more year. Thereafter, I went to the private sector, into the banking industry.

In 2017, I was very lucky to be appointed by the president (which I am forever grateful) as the CEO of Rwanda Information Society Authority (RISA). I was lucky in a sense that there are many other competent Rwandans who could have done the job, but I think the experience from both the government and from the private sector might have added to inviting me to the role.

What Was Your Motivation to Take Up the Calling and Join RISA?

My first motivation is and was my love for my country. Anytime, anywhere I am called to serve my country, it is an honor for me to serve. There are so many people who would love to serve as well. But if *you* are given that chance, it is always an honor.

Second, I looked at what the vision was, where the country was heading, and looked at what the roles entailed in terms of the digital transformation requirements. For me, it could not get any better. If you are a true digital enthusiast, and passionate about how to use technology for the good of the people in the country, this was the place to be.

There Was a Massive Challenge Ahead—Did You Hesitate at All?

Frankly, I do not think there can be any hesitation if you are called to serve.

Hesitation was the last thing that really came to mind because the opportunities were (and are) immense. When I looked at what was on the table, at the opportunities that were before me, and when I understood that I could contribute to the development of economy, the people, and the whole country—I do not think there could be any more or any other motivation there.

What Were You Called in For? What Were You Expected to Deliver?

We are lucky to have a head of state in President Kagame who is very visionary and passionate about technology. He has had a very clear vision about technology and ICT as part of Rwanda's future. He has also communicated it very effectively; he sells it in a contagious way.

He understood that ICT was not a matter of choice for us. We are a very small country that was coming from literally the ashes. Our only critical resource is people. Looking at the global trends, the only thing that would enable us to grow at the pace or develop the way we wanted was to employ technology. It has been clear from the vision 2020 that ICT or digital tools are not stand-alone things but enablers for many other sectors. I would actually say that it has become an existential aspect for any other sector to grow and we have to make sure that they will be embedded into the depth of any sector in the economy.

That is why when the overall vision was put together, a parallel master plan was also made for ICT. The ICT Sector Strategic Plan became the foundation stone for digital transformation of our country.

The expectations for me and RISA were to deliver concrete steps toward the vision and the master plan: to continue the implementation of the national ICT agenda toward a knowledge-based economy. For example, we had transitioned from the early infrastructure and technology to focusing on the citizen-centered services. The expectation was to use whatever technology or tools to serve the needs of people effectively and efficiently.

What Was the State of Digital Government in Rwanda?

RISA was set up when the digital transformation in Rwanda had achieved very commendable progress already. As I mentioned earlier, there was a twenty-year national ICT masterplan that was broken down into four- or five-year plans, or subplans, for National Information Communication Infrastructure (NICI). In 2017, we were right in the middle of the last of such plans.

The first NICI plan had been about the institutional setup, putting in place the policies and procedures, basically, the laws and other strategies to create the enabling environment. NICI 2 was about laying the foundational infrastructure like fiber backbone and 4G networks. NICI 3 was starting to focus on the digitization of services. We had started to roll out digital services and other government digitization efforts, such as a national portal for citizens to access services, called *Irembo*; national cybersecurity programs; and public key infrastructure.

So, the digital infrastructure of the government was largely in place and the next phase of the plan, which was called the Smart Rwanda Masterplan, was to take it further to integrate and continue the efforts with the rest of government services.

What Was the Aim behind the Creation of RISA?

The primary responsibility of RISA is to implement all ICT activities in the public sector and second to support innovation and growth in the private sector. In terms of the institutional setup, we have a ministry in charge of ICT and innovation that coordinates the entire ICT sector in terms of policies, strategies, and procedures.

Therefore, RISA does the implementation—of course, in conjunction with other stakeholders from both the public sector institutions and private sector—to aim for synergies and efficiencies.

For example, under the leadership of the Ministry of ICT and Innovation, we have worked with the Ministry of Finance to ensure harmonization of acquisition of ICT goods and services starting from planning, budgeting, through what we call framework contracts. This has a couple of benefits. First, it reduces the costs to the government because we are able to consolidate similar needs and negotiate from economies of scale. Second, it enables us to avoid duplication, when one organization would be doing something that another organization has already done.

What Did You Set Yourself as a Concrete Objective When Starting the Job?

Expectations were very, very high from all our stakeholders for RISA. Now that the organization was in place, everybody expected RISA to be able to provide the technical support to solve any ICT challenge or to provide any guidance on anything they wanted to do that was digital. Yet, the team we had was very, very small, and they could not be able to respond to every need. The team also needed to be empowered from the skills point of view, through upgrade of tools and platforms.

Even with expectations very high, the recruiting of people, putting them in place, training them, getting them to levels at which they are able to offer services is not something that you can do overnight.

That is why we first had to do recruitment. It was a three-year plan of formation of the organization and building up its capabilities. This included having the right teams in place, really setting up the organization and enabling it to deliver.

What Were the First Steps You Took from the Three-Year Plan?

The very first thing was to have a team. The second thing was to have some sort of best practices and standards worked out and published—the ICT directives.

We inherited a team of about twenty staff members, right now we have a hundred-person organization. Recruiting and training was necessary, including to align them to the vision and to understand what we were trying to do. After showing them the big picture of where the country was heading, the next thing was to really make sure that the work they would be doing would be meaningful to them and to the whole country at large. To really demonstrate to the team that what they were doing has had a transformational effect within the society.

Once the team was in place and being trained, we started hammering it home that the critical thing was delivery. This is still a work in progress. The teams are going through on-the-job training programs, being introduced to new ways of working, and we have started to see the benefits. For instance, in the middle of COVID-19 lockdowns, the teams were stretched too thin, but we managed to support the staff across government to continue to work from home.

As You Started a New Way of Work for the Government, What Methods Have You Used for Steering Agencies in Your Intended Direction?

Continuous engagement and consultation are very important. The enables you to explain the idea to your stakeholders and provides the opportunity to get feedback from them as well.

The second approach that we are exploring is to be piloting some of the projects. This is based on the proof-of-concept (PoC) strategy that we have as a country more widely. The PoC strategy invites entrepreneurs who have good ideas to come and try them out in Rwanda. The focus areas are fintech, medtech, and agritech so far. So, we are working on this idea so that in the same manner we could implement some of the projects in digital government. This will lead to a "show-and-tell" kind of approach, which starts from a small team of our people focusing on trying something out. When they have finished something, they show it to their colleagues and peers. Showing them that this works, how it was done. It is something that we believe will create a bit of buzz in the team and people will like it. We intend to extend it and spread it wide across the entire public sector.

Our objective with this method is to address two things. First, it enables us to start small and then grow widely in capacity by getting people to an understanding of how to do something. Second, it also enables doing incremental improvements in terms of delivery. Even if it fails, the failure is not that big; it is contained.

Sometimes, such piloting has been and can be hard. The challenge is often how to convert a successful pilot into a live service, in cases where we are working with an external partner and the service would need to be contracted. This has led us to look into what we call procurement for innovation. We are working with our national public procurement authority to create an environment that will enable us to go into a pilot mode and then later smoothly transition into a live commercial or a contracted project within the same procurement.

Another approach we have tried to implement, and it is still in its infancy stage, is that we are building a sort of central help desk environment for the public sector. We are trying to set up an internal orchestration team, where every request or every need that comes into RISA is orchestrated to the most appropriate team in RISA to solve it. This will help to demarcate between the "firefighters" and the teams that are focused strategically on one particular item. It will help to use our resources in an efficient manner.

Just very recently the government did a major IT function reorganization that will improve the delivery a lot. The IT teams in sectors have been consolidated into a chief digital office headed by a chief digital officer (CDO) who we help to select and coordinate from RISA. Sectors are the ministerial responsibility areas, such as agriculture with the relevant ministry and its affiliated agencies, education with that ministry and its affiliated agencies, and so on. This new structure will help in terms of pooling resources together, both financial and human. It will also help in terms of exchanging skills across functions and sectors and managing the projects for faster and better delivery.

You Emphasized That You Really Started from Building Up a Team. How Did You Find Suitable People?

Oh, boy! That is the most difficult part of this job. This is even more difficult in the public sector because we cannot compete with the private sector in terms of remuneration.

However, one interesting observation is that we have noticed that people are not necessarily attracted by money. When they get a chance to understand the country's digitization vision and ambitions, they get excited because they are able to see the big picture and the greater impact to the development of Rwanda. This is something that they are excited to come and be part of.

This is how we all were able to attract the good team were at RISA and the ministry, all the new CDOs and business analysts in sectors that have been appointed. The work now is on how to keep on improving their skills and providing them with the required tools.

You Have Mentioned That as You Bring People Onboard, You Do a Lot of Training—How?

The best training is just getting these people jump into the action. Classroom-type of training does not cut it. While they are going through implementation, the necessary concepts are explained, and they carry on with the project. So, as they work through a piece of technology or deliver a project, they take time and see the bigger picture to appreciate it and see the work in the right light.

Another approach is assigning someone a project and asking them to follow it up until completion, with a specific purpose of learning some area or competence—we explain that purpose clearly to them. In these cases, we see that people get really excited and hungry;

they put in a lot of effort then, actually. This sort of coaching has been very, very instrumental for us.

One useful thing I have noticed is to get some people to focus vertically. There are those people who will always continue to work across fields. A good network engineer is going to be a network engineer irrespective of the sector in which they operate. But if you are a business analyst, you want them to get the nuts and bolts of a particular business or service. A good business analyst with experience from the health sector might struggle if you take them to the education sector, because the working dynamics are different. That is why they are encouraged to focus. If you are a business analyst or digitization lead, take one or two sectors, but do not take too many.

What Routines Have Been Useful for You as the Manager to Steer RISA's Team and Culture?

I have an open and collaborative style and approach. We use open office approach also for this reason. In the building where we work, I try to take a day then and again to walk around and through all the departments. Talk to all the engineers, all the staff, to encourage them and loosen them up so that they are able to relate and understand. Or to challenge them on what they are working on, creating a cooperation environment.

The idea is that whenever someone in the team faces a challenge, they would not shy from reaching out or approaching you. It has created a bond within the organization.

The other thing is to have a check-in period every now and then. Of course, we have the standard management meetings and executive meetings every other week. Every quarter we have a general staff meeting, when we give the team an update on where we are and where are we going. We try to hammer home the vision, strategy, culture, what we expect from them, and what they should expect from us. This sort of collaborative, open style has helped in getting the organization together and have the team understanding clearly what the leadership would like to see them do.

We have also started going to sports events together, such as football [soccer] matches. We do workshops where we get a team to present a project they are working on or also external workshops together with the industry.

What Routines Have You Employed to Be an Effective Leader?

As a leader of an institution like the one I am heading, you need to keep abreast of what is happening outside your circle of operation. What is happening in the industry at large? What are the global events that are shaping your sector or your industry? If there is new technology coming, how do you prepare yourself to benefit from it, or not to be disrupted by it, and rather ride on the wave?

So, one of the things that I have tried to keep in my schedule is reading and trying to study. This includes trying to talk to colleagues out there on what are they doing and what keeps them busy. How have they overcome the challenges that I might be facing? Of course, getting people's time like that is not an easy feat. It is not that they do not want to share but their sheer volume of activities makes them busy.

I take this as homework: if you do not read, you do not lead! If I do not read and see what is happening, then I will lose track of it and I am not able to lead the organization I lead. Our partners look up to me to have a team that advises them and does it correctly.

What Has Been Effective for Managing the Relationships with Outside Stakeholders?

Again, I like to count myself as lucky to be leading RISA because our country has a leadership whose vision is very clear in terms of transformation. This sets the momentum and agenda for all the activities and ensures collaboration, because our government is very driven by cooperation. The approach in the government is that if there is an institution in charge of a certain area, everybody else follows their lead.

This helps the effort, but you also have to really make it easy for others to respond to what you would want them to respond to. That is why we have been engaging others in government from time to time in sector meetings such as sector working groups, when we present what we are working on.

We need to keep engaging these stakeholders so that they understand where we are coming from, what our responsibilities are, and, most importantly, the value that we can bring into whatever they are doing right now.

We still sometimes argue with the other agencies, mostly about finding the budget to do things, how best to do them. This is good because it enables us to learn.

You Mentioned That You Set Out to Create a Certain Culture from the Start. What Are Your Mottos or Principles That You Have Tried to Install in the Team?

One principle that I am right now trying to tell everybody is to land one plane at a time, because you cannot land two planes at the same time. Just like in an air control operating tower, each controller is landing one plane or taking one plane off the ground at a time, even if there are several planes ready for takeoff and others ready to land. It means that you may have several projects currently at hand but do make sure that at any particular moment you are focusing on one only—making sure that you deliver it and deliver well.

Do less but do it well. The other thing is that do it fast and make sure that it has the impact. If you take on five different things and you do not do any of them well, then it kills the whole thing.

That is why, again, the CDOs are going to be very key for enabling us to deliver more. If we have fifteen of them, one in each ministry and each takes on one thing, then in a year we will have fifteen things delivered. In RISA, if each person in the team takes on one thing, we will have twenty or thirty different activities delivered.

The one thing that I keep on hammering on is the execution. To develop this "killer" instinct of "get something, finish it."

One thing that has proven to be difficult in this direction, and we have to keep pushing, is how to learn to say no to things that are either not aligned well to what we are trying to achieve or are not going to bring us immediate impact. We need to keep focus on critical aspects and works. That is why we are trying to set up the orchestration team that I mentioned who will receive all the incoming requests and then sift through and direct them to action appropriately. We might be able to easier push the issues that are as we want them to be or not really responding to our critical objectives behind in the queue.

Of course, it is sometimes very difficult to say no to these very high-profile institutions or people because they are coming to ask for help not for the sake of it, but out of a need. The way we try to handle it is to throw it back and ask, "How is it part of your strategy?" That creates a safer way of saying no if it has not been on the table before, when we reviewed things during the planning process. Another option is to steer them and yourself to put it on next year's plan if it truly might become critical.

What Do You Think You Have Achieved in RISA So Far?

One thing that I am really happy to see happening is that RISA as an organization and ICT, in general, have lived up to providing solutions to some of the challenges. A good example is the current COVID-19 situation when every organization has been calling RISA to help do the work to go through the pandemic. It has been really good to see this demonstration that ICT can and indeed does provide a solution.

Second, a good achievement is to have structured the RISA team in a way that we are all interlinked, able to work together and deliver.

Third, now people in different organizations are starting to understand that we cannot just jump into buying a system—you need to first understand what services you are offering. You first need to do business analysis to really understand the need and then go and develop or purchase a system.

You Brought Up That More Requests Came Your Way with COVID-19—How Did This Affect Your Delivery and How Did You Handle Them?

COVID-19 came in and disrupted a lot of our plans, so we had to adjust. We needed to jump quickly, and we rolled out quite a number of services. For example, a majority of government work now can be conducted online, students have been able to continue attending classes, and so on.

We tapped into the tools that were available from previous work to support the fight against the spread of COVID-19. For instance, some of the government agencies were able to use drones that had been piloted to deliver blood and medicines across the country by a local start-up called Zipline, and some other companies. Now, in COVID-19 time these drones were used to fly around different cities and tell people to stay at home, to look for lockdown violations, or the like. Another example was that robots were brought in to facilitate temperature checks or ensure that masks are worn at hospitals.

Have You Had Any Failures or Things That You Regret?

I would not say they are failures, but we have not been able to achieve several projects in the time that we envisaged. For example, we have been working on an enterprise service bus for the last two or three years but do not have it successfully completed as we intended. This is due to some limits we have had in technical and financial resources.

We also wanted to be further ahead with digital skills training for citizens. That has been hampered by COVID-19. We aimed at getting two to three million people trained on digital skills but have not even reached a million.

Sometimes we have had the issue of partnership when service providers have not come across and delivered as expected. We do want to promote the private sector through our work because they are the engine of economic growth. However, now we are trying to structure such collaborations in a way so as to less reinvent the wheel and rather borrow the wheels that have been done somewhere. Also, balance it better with doing some things on our own, in RISA, or in the government.

What Are the Next Challenges for You and for the Digital Government in Rwanda?

Now that we have restructured and reorganized our approach with the CDOs and are working very hard with the leadership of our minister to get the right funding, I believe that the next two or three years are going to be very critical. I view them as another pivotal moment in the digitization journey of our country because we will be laying foundational ground for the next ten or twenty years.

For example, service delivery requires having certain things in place. First, you need to automate the services more—we intend to embark on a massive service digitization campaign for services that are still manual. Second, what good are the digital services if citizens do not know how to use them? That is why digital literacy is going to be a cornerstone of what we will be doing in the next years. Third, even with digital services and skills in place, people need tools to use the services—whether smartphones, tablets, or what have you. Then the next thing is how can services be reached? 4G mobile connectivity is there all over the country, but the coverage in my neighborhood is useless if I am not able to access it in my home or office.

All that said, if we do not have an entrepreneur ecosystem that enables innovation to create different products and services, we will have a handicap to growth. We need to enable entrepreneurs so that they can innovate with different tools and drive the growth of the economy.

Finally, there are lots and lots of emerging technologies. To understand them and to be able to make use of them, we need to create a crowd of experts in these areas. Be it robotics, machine learning, AI, quantum computing, you name it.

So, our challenges at RISA are wider than just digital government, given our mandate. To achieve it all, we need to start speeding up the delivery. CDOs in the ministries will help a lot and ICT can in this way truly become a driving force for economic development of the country through all these different sectors.

What Steps Have You Taken to Make Sure That What You Have Been Starting Will Last?

We have a collaborative approach: we make sure that at least a couple of people are working on something—or anything—together. One person may take the lead and the other or others support in the work. This ensures that there is knowledge sharing and continuity through it.

The other strategy is coaching, of course. We are building a framework where everyone from senior team members coach junior team members and pass their knowledge around.

What Do You Think You Have Learned the Most in This Role?

I wish that someone had told me to put the technology hat aside early and focus on the public services and other aspects, but not technology. I spend more than half of my time on things that are nontechnical. I deal with procurement, with finance, with human resources, with legal. I do all these other things that are actually not at all my core competence.

If someone had told me this before, I would have asked for some time to get some knowledge and a picture of what these things are and how to do them. Right now, it has been a bit like fixing an engine of the plane mid-air. But all in all, it has a been great learning experience for me. Like a great MBA course of sorts!

What Other Skills or Knowledge Is Useful to Do This Sort of Job Well?

People management is key. You need to be really, really good at managing and engaging the team, and also at stakeholder management.

However, it has to be substantiated by the technical know-how. That is because even if you are good at managing stakeholders and engaging your peers, if you are shallow on the substance, it is not going to help. Good people skills can get you in through the door, but not keep you there. You need to at least understand the engineering part, the systems, the solutions while also ensuring that you are good at people and stakeholder management.

The third part would be to learn to understand the mechanics of how public service operates—the business processes. Then you will be able to succeed.

What Would Be Your Three Recommendations to a Colleague on How to Be an Effective Digital Government Leader?

Understand the "currency" of the country, the social capital. Then you will be able to succeed. What gets things moving? What really motivates people? How can you engage that? As I said before, you need to manage your stakeholders down, up, and also horizontally to be successful in digitizing the public sector.

Understand the business, the industry. If you picked me up and put me in the medical field, I would struggle.

In this role, I have come to realize that the private sector partners and solution providers are a double-edged sword. You need to have them on your side, you need to have the good ones because you cannot do everything on your own. However, you need to be ready so that they do not take you for a ride. You need to have your internal skills and capabilities to ask the right questions, to challenge them, so that they deliver what you want them to deliver. In addition, you also need to balance out what you give them and what you do internally. This is a function of the resources within the country, from finances to the technical know-how, available to you.

CHAPTER 11

José Clastornik

Uruguay

José Clastornik is an international consultant in digital transformation and has previously held different executive positions in public and private institutions.

During the fourteen years in which José performed as national CIO and Executive Director of AGESIC (the Information Society and e-Government Agency) in Uruguay, his country rose to leadership positions in the region in areas of digital and open government, digital rights, cybersecurity, and ICT industry development.

José has been a member of the board in different national and international organizations, including chaired the Network of Electronic Government Leaders of Latin America and the Caribbean (RedGEALC), and the Digital Agenda for Latin America and the Caribbean (eLAC).

He was recognized by Apolitical as one of the twenty most influential leaders in digital government worldwide and received the lifetime achievement award from LACNIC for his contribution to the development of the internet in Latin American and Caribbean countries.

José is in many ways the grandfather, or at least the godfather, of the digital government family in all of Latin America. First, he is considered synonymous with his native Uruguay rising in digital society and government sphere to lead the pack, as he built up from scratch and led for fifteen years AGESIC. The agency is one of the world's premier digital government institutions, with a unique setup and operational model of an "umbrella" organization for all works related to digital society.

Besides this demanding job, José has been engaged all across the continent sharing his wisdom, experience, and ideas about the future. Whenever colleagues from other governments ask, he has been willing to lend a shoulder and his thoughts. I have witnessed how much he is loved and respected by peers and the digital government community in the whole Latin American region (and beyond).

In many ways, José is the philosopher-type of a leader. Perhaps that is why he is one of the few digital government leaders in the world who found strength and motivation to stay beyond just one term in the role—always reinventing himself, the work, restructuring the agency, taking the country to new heights.

By the way, he calls the practices and thinking of people the "art of cooking." The next pages will reveal some of José's recipes and his art of cooking the digital government excellence.

—SIIM

How Did Your Digital Government Leadership Story Start in Uruguay?

After years at IBM, and some time in a start-up at the times of the dot-com bubble, I moved to work in ANTEL, the largest and government-owned telecom company in Uruguay.

They were setting up an internet company, and my first job as its CEO was to steer their strategy in the area. We decided to focus on IT and internet projects for the government. So, we specialized in developing projects like connectivity for public institutions such as schools and the creation of government portals and digital services.

About the same time, the Uruguayan government started compiling the first national digital agenda, and I became part of the discussions, actively involved in its work and debates.

In 2005, a new government came to office after the elections, led by President Tabaré Vázquez. In his first year, the new president created an advisory group for coming up with a digital strategy for the government.

The group suggested three big initiatives to launch. One was to set up and steer the digital agenda—for advancing digital development at large. Another one was related to the transformation of government, of the public sector. The third one was related to governance of ICT.

The recommendation was to sustain and strengthen these initiatives, making them something that could last and live longer than just a period. The initiatives had to be grounded in a specialized organization with the required capabilities and legal mandates. That is why the cornerstone of the suggestions was to set up what became AGESIC, the national agency for e-Government and Information Society.[1]

AGESIC was tasked to lead the three initiatives. The institution was to have a board of five directors. One of them would serve as the executive director, effectively leading the agency. I was then invited to come and join as the executive director and tasked to develop the institution.

Why Were You Approached or Selected to Join the Board and Take the Lead Role?

I think that my job at the time and the matter experience I had led to the offer. I was working on these topics domestically as well as internationally through the World Summit on the Information Society (WSIS) community and process.

As a service provider, we were working on some projects on access and digital transformation of government, projects that were part of the existing digital agenda, such as connectivity in schools, public internet points of access, and digital services delivery.

Maybe my experience with both the private and the public institutions also helped.

Did You Hesitate to Join and Take the Role? What Was Your Motivation to Join AGESIC?

It was not a "yes" immediately. The proposal was both motivating, and at the same time there were factors against it. My motivation was related to the real and positive impact we could deliver. We dreamed of building a digital nation.

I had been working with the public sector most of the time as a service provider, very close but still looking from the outside at those initiatives. This was the opportunity to go inside and do it, to change things that in my view could be done very differently.

My fears were related to knowing the reality of the political and bureaucratic environment. If you really want to change things, you will touch some interests, especially if you have high objectives and goals.

In the end, having a big challenge was also part of my motivation.

What Was Lacking in the Digital Government Area in Uruguay Back in 2005?

Everything was lacking! We had advances in the ICT industry and connectivity, but there were no foundations in things such as digital identity, cybersecurity, interoperability, digital privacy and data protection, access to public information, ICT standards and platforms, and so on.

We needed strong foundations for everything to be digital.

What Was the Mandate of AGESIC to Change the Scene?

When they first wrote it, it was about delivering the mentioned three initiatives. Their scope was not explicitly stated out initially. We could do various things under their headings, so to speak. Especially because the digital agenda initiative was about a nationwide digital policy, which can include most of the things we did.

AGESIC was purposefully created to be a kind of a wide umbrella. For example, once it was decided that the country must have a cybersecurity unit, it could naturally become placed in AGESIC and in reference to the digital agenda.

There was no political will to create new agencies, because each new agency has its own administrative costs. That is why AGESIC ended up being the roof or umbrella for the governance of cybersecurity, privacy, digital identity, access to public information, infrastructure for spatial data, some initiatives on national electronic medical records, and so on. Many of these initiatives had their own boards and governance structures as part of the overall AGESIC structure and governance.

In many ways, AGESIC was like an incubator for a lot of projects or more concrete initiatives. In some cases, we managed to move the initiatives and projects out afterwards; in some cases not.

What Led You to the Incubator Approach?

We came to the job with the mindset of incubation. We wanted to have the incubator logic in AGESIC in order not to own all the projects and forever.

Otherwise, our institution would be an operative institution, and we would never have time for new projects. If you run an operative institution, the scope of transformation you can start in the government is limited to the volume of operations you can deliver.

But if you only incubate something, this allows you to have impact in many more places.

What Were the Carrots or Sticks That AGESIC Had toward Other Agencies to Execute Its Mandate?

The way we liked to get things done for enforcing our policies is more with a carrot than a stick. Show yourself as a problem solver for others, so that whatever the problem they have, they can count on you. It is an attitude thing in the end. We believe this is more effective than inspection and sanctions, although we know that you must have them, too.

To give the carrots, you must have some capacities for doing operative things. The help can be in very practical form such as financing or technical know-how.

In general, institutions like AGESIC always have a dilemma between the logic of a directorate doing the regulative work and the operational delivery of making things happen. You can be one or the other.

I think you can mix them, too. We never wanted to make all the projects. We never wanted to have a big operations area in AGESIC. But this does not mean that you cannot do things.

For example, if you want to enforce interoperability, you need the rules or standards, but you also need a platform and a team that helps institutions to bring interoperability to their systems. A SWAT team helping the institution to deliver can be more effective than writing a regulatory decree on those things without taking into consideration the means to execute them.

What Was Your Own Role in AGESIC as the Executive Director? How Would You Describe It?

The interesting thing is that the title executive director was nonexistent in the regular units of the public administration in Uruguay. My first problem was for others to accept the legal definition. The national civil service organization wanted to change it. They were right, in a way, because the term is more related to private sector practices, to start-ups, and there you have a different context. This setup helps a lot if you want to have alignment of board and operatives in the field in a quick and flexible way.

My job was to look at the broad picture, articulating it with different actors inside and outside AGESIC, and managing the agency at the same time.

The job was really much about communication. Usually, in similar institutions the president of the board has a more external presence, and the general manager works more with the insides of the institution and for the delivery to happen. Having two roles in one meant that in AGESIC I was the one representing the institution abroad, the one going to the parliament to explain issues, but I was also the one who managed all the managers of each department to advance with the plans. So, communication in all directions was a huge part of the work.

What Were Your First Steps as Executive Director of AGESIC? What Did You Start Working On?

At the beginning, the main problem was that a broader vision and strategy was missing. What I immediately did was to get the ecosystem to work with us on these. In 2006, I had only a small team in AGESIC.

We started eight groups on different themes or work areas to start developing the plans. There was an Inter-American Development Bank (IDB) operation going on in parallel, and we lent some consultants from them.[2] We also contacted some external people representing different public and private institutions and asked them to join the groups.

The groups had the task of defining the action plans, starting from problems and immediate needs. In three months, they were to hand over three pages each on what we must do. One group was on interoperability, one on cybersecurity, one on privacy and data protection, one on digital economy (that changed to digital ID), and so on.

The time frame for planning was three years. We had put in place in 2007 a one-year digital agenda, a temporary plan. The groups came up with proposals for 2008–2010. Once the proposals were done, we had the road clear ahead of us. For example, in cybersecurity they had defined that we needed a national CERT, which meant we needed the legal framework and the financing for it. This was the way of making explicit the things we needed to work on.

We were able to involve the academic community in helping us out. In this context, you also need a bit of luck. For example, there were academics who had already done advanced work on issues such as access to public information, digital ID, privacy. When I called them for advice on how to write the relevant policies or regulations, they did not have to start researching. They only had to write down what they had been discussing for years.

They were able to deliver inputs for us in the matter of a few weeks. What was even better, their work came in with endorsement of the academia, and the legal framework got approved in parliament with wide consensus.

How Did You Work with the Wider Ecosystem after the Initial Strategy Making?

We worked with and relied heavily on the ecosystem collaboration in the beginning, also later.

The different initiatives defined its own governance, usually with a board, one or more councils, and working groups. Most of the people who worked in the initial strategy making worked afterwards in one or another group.

With the building of the new digital agenda and action plans, we had the opportunity to integrate more people and institutions into the ecosystem as more items were discussed. Action plans were more specific, for example, in open government and open data. Also important were the advances in cocreation and collaboration with the LAB, the Laboratory of Social Innovation in Digital Government.

Emerging technologies opened other windows or collaborations, for example, in artificial intelligence adoption. We can count also our work with the international networks as part of ecosystem engagement; we were purposefully active participants there.

You Worked in AGESIC for Nearly Fifteen Years. What Were the Key Initiatives or Strategic Periods across the Years?

In Uruguay, we have five-year presidencies. Fifteen years in government meant three presidency terms. This meant three digital strategy periods for Uruguay and for AGESIC. Their focuses still were derived from the initial founding initiatives.

So, our first strategy period in 2008–2010 was focused on the enabling framework. Second phase or period in 2011–2015 was for digitalization in government. The last in 2016–2020 was centered on the wider digital transformation agenda.

In the first period, the priority was the basic framework—legal and institutional base, technological platforms and infrastructure, digital inclusion, and capability building. The main objective was to create all these foundations.

During this period, we also started the whole incubation approach. We financed pilot projects, managed them for some time, then gave them to institutions to sustain. We did some hundred projects over the years; it was a nice mechanism of helping institutions with a carrot-style approach.

Across the years there were a lot of initiatives in the different agendas, for example, in document management, digital services, one-stop-shop portals, national digital medical records, interoperability, and more. Most of our initiatives had a three-step approach, in a way mapping the general strategy for our digital agendas. The first step went to building the solution infrastructure, the second was about expanding it out, and the third was for starting on real digital transformation.

Consider document management as an example. First you bring the digital solution in, including the standards for classification, digital signature, and interoperability. Then you need the different agencies to adopt it. At this phase, you are doing digitalization at most, not digital transformation, changing papers for digital files. You continue to change the processes next, and afterward you work on a true transformation stage when you are changing the relationship with the ecosystem and with citizens or providers.

With Eleven Boards and a Full Agency to Manage, Plus a Handful of Things in Strategy—How Did You Choose Your Priorities?

It is very easy to lose sight. You must know how to say no. I said no to many projects, although it sometimes gave me problems afterwards. And I said yes to things that I should have said no to.

Having a team with whom discuss the alternatives helps a lot.

How Did You Align the Setup of AGESIC to the Delivery of Initiatives?

In general, doing changes in the setup of organizations is not easy in the public sector, although we managed to do it in the first years.

For the first two to three years, we worked from the initial strategy setup. Then we realigned our approach according to our customers: one stream for citizens, one for government institutions, one for the ICT ecosystem, the last one for the target groups of our regulation.

The evolution of the structure was from groups formed for processes to markets, and later to areas, along with the strategy changes we had in those times.

When a change in our strategy was mature enough to be explained, then it was immediate for me that the structure would be changed to fit the new strategy. The organization had to be in line with how we were thinking about our work.

Related specifically to the delivery, I think that there were two important things that helped: a culture related to project management and delivery and a strong project management office working on it.

How Did You Build the AGESIC Team?

The very big problem we had with the standard way of getting people in was that public servants do not have competitive salaries. In some roles, the market paid two or three times more than we were able to.

If we look at it differently, then we must have had success in raising other motivations among people—because we were retaining many people in AGESIC, even if their salaries were not fine. By the way, human resources was of strategic importance for us. That is why we put the human resources department in the planning area, together with all other strategic functions such as the project management office or the communications team.

We used a range of arguments to motivate people to join, emphasizing the value of being part of continuous government innovation initiatives. We also told people that they would have a chance to mix with technicians and experts from all over the world and take part in staff rotation.

We also highlighted that they would get very good competences working with us, for example, a very good project management aptitude. Working in AGESIC was like getting a project management certificate. The same was later with cybersecurity, architecture, digital rights.

Funding some of the work with the help of international institutions gave us some salary flexibility. For example, we were able to bring some people in on contracts under the IDB operations.

The most critical people to get and retain were the technical guys, especially the ones looking into future topics: the architects, data specialists, cybersecurity people. Sometimes we had to train the specialists pool in the first place. For example, we designed a special operation with IDB only for the cybersecurity area to generate hundreds of specialists for the country, including for government and industry—also aiming to export the knowledge after.

What Were the Principles or Working Routines You Tried to Have and Take Root in Your Team?

Related to our mission, our mantra was "transformation with equity," and this defined our work.

Our organization KPIs were related to three things: being a reference in our areas of expertise; excel in delivering; and to be always innovating. All the initiatives were analyzed and measured in relation to these three axes, and we tried to make sure they took root in our team.

Some of our main working methods I already mentioned: incubation and outsourcing as much as possible for focus and innovation, the carrot before the stick, collaboration and teamwork, and empowerment for the team based on the defined strategies.

What Do You Think Were Your Greatest Achievements in Your Fifteen Years in AGESIC?

It was not one project, but the set of projects and initiatives, the results, the institutional framework. All combined and reflected in the international indicators that showed us making significant advances toward becoming a digital nation.

The most visible projects of AGESIC were the work to get 100 percent of services online, the building of the different platforms including gub.uy, the national electronical medical records system we launched: things that at least regionally became a reference on their own.

In a holistic sense, our greatest achievements were the vision we laid out and its realization. To me, leadership is about taking people from one place to another; it is about movement and change. I think this is what we managed to do in our country and with our team.

What Were Your Biggest Failures, in Your View?

My candidate for biggest failure concerns institutional communications. I have question marks; I do not know if it is a failure necessarily. We have done reasonably good work outside the country on showing what was AGESIC and what we had done in Uruguay. Inside the country, though, we did not communicate much at all.

We did campaigns of substance, such as the ones on security, digital rights, and campaigns for privacy awareness, but we chose to have a very low profile locally and show ourselves more as a technical unit. It was the adequate decision for an institution dealing with some regulations that would have political ramifications.

Yet, it resulted in fewer people in Uruguay knowing the full scope of the things we were doing. Most people had only a partial view about AGESIC, based on what they happened to encounter. We were sometimes surprised how little decision-makers or politicians knew about us.

Technical people knew us better, of course. But perhaps we should have changed the communications strategy at some point in time, to be more present and visible. This could have helped to increase our participation and enforcement capacities, which was going to be—or will be—needed at some point.

After Three Periods and Three Governments, What Made You Leave Finally?

I did not expect to continue for more than the first government period, when I first started. I stayed for the second period because I knew that AGESIC was not strong yet. My idea then was to stay only until the initiatives had their own life strength.

The three governments were from the same political party. For the third period, it was President Vázquez coming back for his second term. I really had plans to leave, plans to start new things, to deal with new challenges. However, it was very difficult to say no to the president, and there were still things left to deliver from the original initiatives, such as getting 100% of the executive branch services digital, and the national electronic medical records. I finally left after the last elections.

What Are the Next or Remaining Challenges Going to Be for a Digital Government in Uruguay?

There will always be places for innovation. With digital transformation, you have a lot of places to do it: you can go on and on. There is also always something new in technology.

One of the things I liked more to do was working on the things to come and the changes these might bring. I do not like delivering based on buzzwords, but we should still investigate the advancement they stand for. If you take something like blockchain, for example, it can potentially change the work of a lot of institutions in government, especially ones working on registration and record keeping. This represents a major challenge in redefining the institution; in some cases, it can even be a constitutional challenge.

Same for other technologies such as AI. The challenge—and opportunity—is that some basic parts of government should be revived institutionally with these technological changes around us.

How Did You Ensure That What You Started Lasts?

In a way, we worked on this every day. We were aiming to initiate a lot of changes of different kinds that should last. One of the ways was to have the instruments and the commitments institutionalized, working them into the legal frameworks—for example, specifying the things AGESIC had to do into a concrete definition of them in the law.

Second thing is related to the success of your work. If you have things that are working, things that are adopted in a significative way, then people are inclined to keep them.

The third way was to have longer-term operations ongoing with institutions like IDB or the World Bank. Within them, the government has a legal and financial obligation to keep the promises. If someone wants to change things there, it is possible but difficult. And usually, they will get an external justification for the reasons and best practices of the operation.

What you cannot avoid is when new authorities try to downgrade the institution: to give it less money, to downsize it. Also, you can downgrade the institution if you do not retain your best people. Other than that, any fundamental change will take a lot of time and effort, if it has been institutionalized and delivery has been your strength.

Looking Back, Is There Something You Wish You Had Known When You Started the Job?

Not much. I think the magic is in discovering the things as you are working with them. If you have the answers ready, there is not so much creativity. The creativity is finding the strategic and tactical moves; it is in understanding the new theory and applying it. If you are young with the experience of the old, this creativity is something you will miss, especially because there are no clear silver bullets in these matters.

Would You Recommend the Job to a Friend?

Absolutely. I think that when you are in a place like AGESIC, you are making transformation happen. Already by definition of your duty, you are working on digital transformation—you are transforming with technology.

The impact of this kind of work affects all people, all the community. This impact not only gives you satisfaction related technically to your profession. Because you do not just work on digital stuff, you are actually on a social mission—you will create social value. It is motivating that you have the power to make significant changes in your community, to leave something important behind.

I remember telling one friend from the World Bank back in the day that I had accepted the executive director position and planned to stay for one year. He told me to take care and to take into account that this kind of job is addictive, that I would be tempted to stay for longer. He knew it well!

What Would Be Your Recommendations for Being Effective in Such a Role?

I have been often asked what the recipe for success is. I am always saying four things—although these are not all there is to it, of course.

One, have a clear vision, like we had about digital transformation with equity. This defined the three governments I served and our work. Second, define a clear path and build institutions that can lead to the vision. Third, align the ecosystem to help along. Fourth, excel in execution.

And for all this to be possible, get the best people in your team.

Notes

1. AGESIC is the acronym from the name of the agency in Spanish—*Agencia de Gobierno Electrónico y Sociedad de la Información y del Conocimiento.*
2. IDB lends the countries in Latin America and the Caribbean money to fund infrastructure investments, social and economic development programs, and, increasingly, also public sector modernization and institutional capacity-building efforts. An IDB operation is usually a concrete lending and reform program with specific goals and deliverables, a limited term, earmarked funding, outside advisors bringing technical assistance along with funds, and so on.

CHAPTER 12

Lars Frelle-Petersen

Denmark

L ars Frelle-Petersen has served as the Permanent Secretary of Denmark's Ministry of Climate, Energy and Utilities since 2020.

In 2012–2017, Lars was the Director General at the Danish Agency for Digitisation (DIGST) under the Ministry of Finance, responsible for the Danish e-government strategy and its implementation across the public sector. He then led the digital transformation area at the Confederation of Danish Industries (DI), Denmark's largest business organization, as its Deputy Director General in 2018–2020.

Prior to DIGST, Lars worked for twelve years in various roles of growing responsibility in the Ministry of Finance in Denmark on large-scale initiatives and strategy for digitization and public sector efficiency. He has a master of science degree in public administration.

Lars was one of the first digital government leaders I met from outside of my own country. I had just entered the field in Estonia and made my first foreign trip destination to be Denmark as soon as I could to go see and learn from what they were up to there.

Denmark was already known for the level of digital maturity in their public sector. Starting in 2011, they were making new waves internationally. DIGST, the agency had just been set up and it captivated everyone, because Denmark had decided to make the digital channels mandatory for citizens and companies to use. The fact that such a strong step was doable in the very considerate and consensus-oriented culture in Denmark encouraged reformers elsewhere.

Lars was there at the lead of this and many other digital government efforts, also at helm of the strategy work and coordinating for digital delivery for seventeen years in the Danish government. He is a living example that effective digital (government) leaders do not have to—or sometimes even better if they do not—come from technology quarters only.

His very Nordic style of mild-mannered but relentless and patient stewarding was instrumental to being able to lead the Danish government in taking the next steps forward in its digital journey—to the absolute top of this league globally.

—SIIM

How Did You Get Involved in the Digital Government Field in Denmark?

I do not have a university degree in anything related to technology. I have a political science background and after university I started working in a very small council offering various advice to the Danish parliament.

About 2000, I ran into a guy who had been very active as permanent secretary many years ago and was now working in the financial sector. He came up with an idea to study why large IT projects always went wrong in the public sector, because we had just had a lot of scandals. We made the report together with a group of experts, and it became a pillar for the understanding of what were the problems concerning IT in the public sector, what were the learnings from some larger projects going wrong, and what should be done about it. That was my entry to the field.

At the same time, there was an understanding in the Danish public sector that if we wanted to modernize our public sector, we had to do more with IT. We had to find solutions on how to get more citizens to use IT solutions online. As a small country, you also have to be more agile than larger countries. One way of doing that is to use the IT right and bring down the costs for the public sector. We were already quite advanced in comparison with other countries: our citizens had personal registration numbers, land and business registers were there, and so on. We could build on top of that data infrastructure to get more of the public service offering online.

Based on the report, it was decided to create a joint task force composed of municipality, regional and state levels. They called together twenty-five young people—I was one of them—who came in to join the task force with my understanding of the large IT projects. The task force was put into the Ministry of Finance, and it was a very different kind of unit compared to the rest of the place. We were the first to have laptops, some mobile phones, we were sitting in open area offices together, and worked in a project manner as opposed to everlasting processes.

I was hired by the Ministry of Finance as a project leader and actually only for three years at first. But I ended up spending seventeen years in the ministry!

Was the Task Force Successful?

In 2001, people thought that within three years it would be all solved, and digitization would be a natural backbone of all we do. We realized very soon that this was not going to be the case. It was going to be a long journey to convince public institutions, in particular, but also the citizens to use this infrastructure. We did not even have the necessary infrastructure to make things work.

It was clear that institutions were too small to build by themselves the larger infrastructure they needed, such as a digital signature. So, the first years really went to making digitalization known and starting the journey. We built up the first digital signature, which was not too successful because it was too complicated to use and people did not really have anything to use it for and because the citizen-oriented solutions were not in place. We learned that perhaps even the public sector as a whole is sometimes too small in itself. The second-generation digital ID and signatures came together with the banks.

Thus, we learned to create those public-private partnerships. We first had tried to invent infrastructure for the public sector but could perhaps rather had others specify the needs and then share the solutions. We could also open up our solutions. For instance, we built up an EasyAccount or (in Danish) the NemKonto solution. It is a single register of people's bank accounts to make it easy to pay citizens money and not have every agency build their own systems and process for it. As a lot of private companies struggled with it, too, and we opened it up for them to pay their customers.

Municipalities were in the beginning quite hesitant to take their services online because they said there was nobody who would use them and no digital signature. A chicken-and-egg problem. With citizens, we had the problem of habits. It was very easy to go to citizen service centers in municipalities all over Denmark. That is why we took the bold and controversial approach to start making things mandatory to be used online.

The first thing we chose to make mandatory was digital invoicing in 2005. For the 20 percent of companies who had problems with it, we offered at the start an alternative channel where we converted their paper invoice to digital form. This led to the 2012 move where the government decided to start making all kinds of interactions digital-only between the citizens and the public sector, also between the public sector and businesses.

From the Task Force, What Led to Setting Up the Agency of Digitisation Quite a Few Years Later?

It was a stage-by-stage journey forward that had started from digital cooperation and digital communication as the task force focus. Every three years we made a new strategy, built new solutions, and then took the next step, building on top of previous work.

First, it was decided to institutionalize the task force after four years and turn it into an integrated unit within the Ministry of Finance. I continued there and became the head of the unit. The second strategy in 2004 was focused on payments, as said. In the 2007 strategy, we recognized the need for more shared digital infrastructure, such as second-generation digital ID, portals for citizens and businesses.

In 2011, again a new digital government strategy was prepared, and we proposed the target that 80 percent of all communication with the public sector should be done digitally. This was a task that required more employees, more effort, and it was decided to form a separate agency as part of the Ministry of Finance to carry out the task. The new Agency for Digitisation (DIGST) was given a role to lead the transformation of the whole public sector and cooperate close with the municipalities and regions.

What Made You Stay in the Field, and Then Step into a Leadership Role in DIGST?

What kept me in this journey was exactly that it was a journey. We had this sense of spearheading the transformation of the public sector; we saw ourselves as change agents. We saw the public sector taking on these different solutions and changes.

For me it was also a journey of getting more responsibility personally, seeing things grow, and succeed. It took me to a lot of different areas of the public sector. I worked with digitalization of our schools, health care, tax, and others to push the digital agenda forward.

Becoming the director general of the new agency was the crown of being part of the journey. When they formed the agency, I first became the deputy as a more experienced director general was brought in to start. After five months, she decided to step down and I applied.

Why Do You Think They Chose You?

A simple reason may be that I had led the work on the last two national strategies and had shown that I could make people work together. What has made public sector digitalization in Denmark successful has been that we succeeded in working together—importantly also between government levels.

The other was maybe that even if I was not the only one who had good ideas, I saw where we should head and how we could take the next step. Choosing a way where we did not try to eat the elephant in one piece, but did it piece by piece, getting closer to succeeding and being patient to do that.

I had this trust that I could combine the understanding of what technology and techniques we need and what is asked for by the political level. It is the connection between technology and politics that has to happen for digitalization of the public sector. I had perhaps the clearest idea of how it could be solved and how we could make the necessary decisions on the political level that could bring digitalization forward.

Did You Hesitate to Apply at All?

No, I had this idea from my previous work that this all would be possible. We had strong political backing early on to move forward with a digital push and also to make things mandatory.

As we were making the strategy in 2011, we had a minister of finance who was not much into digitalization. He would always tell me that he did not understand much about digitization—but it made sense to try to digitalize the public sector. I then went to him with the strategy we had worked on for a while, and his key interest was on the idea of making the use of digital solutions mandatory.

Very soon after, there was an election, and a new government came in place with new party leading it and they also took ownership of that strategy. The new government got behind the new agency creation, in particular. There was also very large ownership in the direction among the municipalities, which was quite surprising because it meant a tremendous change in how they offered their services.

Why Is the Ministry of Finance at the Helm of Digital Government Work in Denmark?

The Ministry of Finance has two main obligations in Denmark. Of course, one is to take care of the budget. Second, they are responsible for the modernization of the public sector. They have a task to improve the steering of public institutions.

They did not see digitalization first as a tool for real modernization. What happened between 2001 and 2011 was that two agendas got combined, especially with the state's financial troubles after the global crisis: the idea about efficiency and taking care of the money and the idea of modernization of the public sector became the key. How can we make public institutions more efficient, saving money to be used on other purposes, and how can we have a public sector that is modern, efficient, and trustworthy? Digitalization is the tool for this combination.

In the background, the successful companies in Denmark were becoming more global and more digital. They showed that to be successful, you must be digital. We could pinpoint to that and say that if the public sector is to keep the citizens' trust, we also have to be more advanced and digital. Otherwise, we would risk losing peoples' trust and willingness to pay taxes. We need to be with our services at the same level, as were the banks where you could get things done online. We needed to be seen as efficient as them.

In addition, the Ministry of Finance has the role to negotiate the budget every year. Part of the budget for the municipalities comes from the state level. This allowed for a big push for digitalization, because savings and investments became shared. If municipalities were more efficient and saved money through digitalization and invested into digital infrastructure with the state, they could keep some savings. For instance, when we introduced the digital post box for receiving official letters digitally, then the savings from not having to use stamps went to the state level but municipalities kept the savings from not having to handle the letters internally. It was actually a lot of money, so they had an incentive to work along with us. Through the years, we tried to become really good at finding such savings arrangements.

What Other Levers, Carrots, or Sticks Were at Your Disposal to Ensure Cooperation?

In addition to the money, we used legislation, of course. It had been a bold move when we introduced mandatory invoices first in 2005. We were quite afraid of using legislation more, until 2011. It was a big shift for the digital agenda that had not been very political until then; it had been mostly driven by civil servants only. From there on, it got more and more political.

Another lever was cooperation with the private sector. It was important, at least in Denmark, to convince the politicians that we could actually do it because there was a lot of mistrust to our ability to do IT projects. It meant a lot that we could show that the private sector was willing to cooperate with us and wanted to use the infrastructure that we developed. Things like real estate companies using the land and building registers and banks using the digital ID and signatures.

This is not a hard lever, but the sharing of success and helping out is very important to ensure cooperation. My aim was to make the agency capable of making others work with us. Because we had the stick tools of budget and legislation, it was not going to be true love. It was more a sense of respect for each other. We had to respect that other institutions had certain tasks and obligations. We had to convert that into something that we could work with and then have both of us succeed.

It was our underlining story as the agency: we make things work for different institutions. We did not steal things from them and run away with them, we did not send our minister out to say, "I did it." It was their minister that went out and said, "See what I have done." Once we started the projects, we made institutions part of the decision process; they had co-ownership and they put their money in, of course.

Many of the agencies, also municipalities, had the problem that they could not sell the ideas themselves. They needed us to help get going with the ideas they had. That is why many institutions were happy that we made a very bold strategy in 2011 because it gave them directions. It also meant that we had a shared sense of direction to start with.

What Became Your Own Strategy Going into to DIGST? What Did You Set Out to Be Your Objective There?

It was very important for me that the national strategy was also the agency strategy. We had the coordination for the national strategy across the board, including municipalities and regions. So, it was important for me to have the same vision and the goals widely shared within the agency and a shared view our role in it.

You Had Been There Already Before in the Agency, but What Was Your Hundred-Day Plan When You Started in the Director General Role?

The very first thing was to make operational this idea and target of 80 percent of transactions happening digitally. To have a plan how to get to the target by 2015.

The other thing was that it was a totally new agency, of course. It was formed of employees from two other agencies that were put together, and we did not perhaps share the same values, ideas, ownership of the agenda. My starting point together with my deputy at that time was to form a new culture. We set out to shift from being a traditional state agency to be a coordinating body for the digitalization agenda in the public sector working close together with other state agencies and regions and municipalities.

We did that by doing all kinds of things together as a whole agency at first. We were a small agency at the beginning, about one hundred twenty at the start. Before I left, we were about two hundred thirty and it continued to grow after I left.

We did a lot of joint planning of how to solve the path for the targets. It was a gift that we had been formed on one major specific goal and then left to work on it. Of course, more targets came our way later, but at the beginning there was mainly one target only. I reinforced the idea of cooperating because we would not succeed with the 80 percent mark by ourselves.

Then we had to work to get the agency to be known so that people would apply to work with us. We needed to attract some of the best to come to get the ambitious target done. It meant telling the story a lot about why were there and we what we needed to do.

As You Said, the Elephant Is Eaten Piece by Piece. How Did You Prioritize and Sequence the Steps? What Did the Road Map of Elephant Eating Look Like in Your Case?

I already knew that it would be important to start to do very early on something that could be successful. Even if it is small, start with something that you are sure that you can make: then you can work and build on that.

We obviously needed to review the infrastructure immediately to see where it could be scaled to the next level. We had to make sure we would have a digital postbox that works, for example—because all correspondence with the public sector would start to go there as opposed to your physical mailbox.

We then tried to identify low-hanging fruits toward the 80 percent target. We looked at what kinds of services were already used online, where the citizens were capable of using services online. We decided to pick out the services used by young people, of course, instead of retirement funds or such, where we would have interest groups against mandatory digitalization. For instance, we selected the service of young couples applying for maternity leave, where 50 percent or more of them were already doing it online.

We aimed to build confidence this way and use more time to develop out the more complicated ones. We needed to use this time to also remove blockers for next services. For example, one of the strongest lobbyists against mandatory online services were organizations for the elderly. We started seeking a dialogue for them, and they ended up starting to have elderly teach the elderly to use the solutions. It was a tremendous success, and they were prepared when the mandatory solutions finally reached them as the user group, too.

Did You Have Surprises along the Way?

We actually ended up seeing that the use of online services by the elderly was much higher than by young people. We had thought that it would be only natural for young ones to receive and read letters in the digital postbox, because they were already online. But it was the elderly who took it very seriously: they got educated, and they were very keen on using the digital postbox. Instead, the people between fifteen and twenty-five never opened the digital postbox because they did not think that they would get any important letters from the public authorities. They were in other messaging channels instead. We then had to work to get them to learn to find the right way to use the citizen portal and postbox there.

Another thing was that we all had thought that doing the digital postbox and services mandatorily would be more problematic with citizens than business. It turned out the other way around. Businesses can be very different from one another and the size can be very different, especially. Sending a pizza maker around the corner a note to the digital postbox is quite easy. Sending a postbox note to global logistics giants like Maersk or other Danish multinational companies is quite different. We solved a lot of these problems as we went along, but we had our ups and downs.

Did Politicians Stay behind the Strategy All the Way Through?

In the end, yes, but that was yet another reason for us to sequence it out how services would become mandatory.

I think at first not enough political people realized what we set out to do with the 2011 strategy and the 80 percent goal. Once the government realized that we would have to be going back to parliament every year with each new wave of services to make them mandatory, they got afraid that we could really make it happen.

Thus, we started by saying that we would first do only eight services mandatory by 2012, then next fourteen by 2013, then forty by 2014, and the rest in 2015. We made a promise to come back to the parliament every year to tell them how we have succeeded from the year before, and if it was good enough, then we were allowed to make the next legislation. This was a way to deal with some political hesitance and also to retain the buy-in by transparency.

Politicians often have that sense that when they have decided on something, it is already realized. However, if you made a decision today, you may see the solutions come live perhaps three or four years later. That normally will be after the next election. It can be difficult for politicians to accept why it can take so long, and too often us as public officials are too optimistic on how fast we can have new solutions in place. At least I can say that we have become more realistic and open that it is complicated. It has a lot to do with habits and culture; it is not just about introducing a new technology. You have to get an organization to work differently, and you have to convince the politicians on why it takes time to make it happen so.

That is why in my kind of role you have to work on a short and a long agenda. You have to think on a launch program where you can launch new things every year. At the same time, you have the possibility of taking a longer time on the things that require it, without getting a lot of questions about them. You have to have output; you have to deliver things. Small things are part of larger things; each one a step in the process. The waterfall model is often not a good idea when it comes to the political agenda.

How Did You Build Out Your Team to Achieve All of That?

I look for people who can make things happen in a very complex environment: getting skilled people around me who have different competences, who can bring things to the table, who have had different perspectives and experiences.

We could get a lot of people who wanted to work for us because we had these large technology projects, and we could show that we actually succeeded. If you want to work with the big tools, then you want to work with us. That was a good storyline.

I have to admit that DIGST team mainly came from the public sector. In more technology-based units, people could come from financial sector or anywhere. But what I discovered was that when you have people working in contact with other agencies or at the political level, I had more use of people who had the skills of working with the public sector already. They could either come from consultancies or from some other agency, where they had shown that they could actually make things happen.

On a management level, in particular, I looked for public employees who had shown that they could transform things, not just push papers around. They had to have what I was looking for in the willingness to cooperate. You can find a lot of people who have the habit of pushing others away so that they can show that they are the successful one. I looked for people who could make people work together and be successful together.

With the technical people, we had to protect them against red tape. We needed to attract certain people who just were not good at red tape. In the beginning, this was a bit complicated for us. A lot of people got scared because we made everyone write reports. We learned very fast that this was not a good idea. Some people are good at writing reports; others are not. We did not see at first that there should be the division of labor between teams focusing on building the infrastructure or deploying it, and other teams who took care of the political process.

At first, we were like a start-up company where everyone does everything but soon had the division of labor set up. We learned how to have all these different kinds of talents working together and have a shared agenda.

Who Was Your Most Valuable Hire through the Years?

I hired a very good deputy director general who succeeded me afterwards—Rikke Zeberg. She actually came from other parts of the public sector. We had been colleagues in the Ministry for Finance, then she had worked for the Danish radio for a while.

She was a very good public servant in comparison to me in a sense that she had control of the paperwork. This was necessary to build trust for our agency, that we were in control of what we were doing. She mainly handled the administration of the organization to begin with and from there developed the understanding of digitalization in general. We learnt a lot from each other. My role at that time was to have the ideas, the vision, and the leadership; she was very good in building up the organization to make things work. She made us very well organized in comparison to other agencies.

As we grew, we got more and more institutionalized, we started to have more and more maintenance of the solutions we built. I started to think about how we could stay innovative and not just renew the same infrastructure once again. What I tried from time to time was to put somebody else to lead such teams.

Say we needed to build a new generation of digital identity. The most obvious thing to do, in a way, would be to put the current manager in charge of the work. I found out that they would often just say that maybe we should build the same solution and do it slightly better; why reinvent the wheel? However, sometimes we do need to rethink the whole thing. Often, it was best to take somebody from the outside who had not worked with that technology to come in and ask the questions, and then maybe lead the things in a new direction. We needed to ask ourselves again the questions that we had stopped asking.

You Have Already Said a Bit about It, but What Was the Culture You Wanted the Team to Have?

I kept saying and wanted the people to really grasp that we were at a specific spot in the history. That they were there to change things and to make an impact. We were not there just to get paid. I told the story that we were part of something bigger. If we work together on this, we could succeed and bring the public sector to a new level.

Many of us who are hired by the public sector, we already think we are there for these reasons. At least we think that when we start. Sometimes we forget that after a while because we either get mixed up in red tape or institutionalized. That is why we have to be constantly retelling the story why we are here, why it matters, and where we are heading, how we should change that.

I have said it already: I also had to explain that we were not going to succeed with all of it by ourselves. We needed to cooperate with others. In fact, we were part of a lot of others. "Cooperate with others to make things work" was the mantra.

Because we were part of the Ministry of Finance, we were also very business-case driven. The DNA of the ministry is that if we wanted to come up with a good idea, it is not enough that the idea is good. It should also have a business case around it, either in an economic cost-benefit sense or it should be about a better service. Then the institutions who will deploy this solution will be willing to pay for it. Transformation will happen if we can get the cooperation of others and others also to pay for it.

That ended up being how we also prioritized our ideas internally, too. Every year we had a process in which everybody could come up with ideas for the work plan. Many, many good ideas came up, but many of them could never be brought to life because nobody would pay.

I emphasized the need for good infrastructure and wanted everyone to respect it the same way. We could find all kinds of solutions that could give us quick wins or have others pay for it, but if we did not have good infrastructure, we could not develop anything out.

What Are You Most Proud of Achieving as the Director General?

To see today that digitalization has become part of the solution of problems. We see it in Denmark as an integrated part of problem-solving in the public sector. Of course, digitalization has a lot of problems, such as surveillance, echo chambers, and things that are related to how we use the technology. But in general, using technology can be part of the solution.

Of course, I am also proud that a lot of technologies we built do make life easier and still do today. Our EasyID or (in Danish) NemID is used every day. We managed to go through COVID-19 by using technology in almost everything we have done. We have gotten to a level of maturity in the use of technology that makes all this possible. It all has been possible because we were able to build trust—in DIGST, in digitalization—by becoming more successful and doing what we promised.

What Is Something You Most Regret or You Think You Failed At?

I would have hoped to set up the next mission after the 80 percent target. I failed in the strategy we made afterwards that came out in 2016. It was very much about the maintenance of the shared infrastructure. I had hoped to set up new ambitious goals.

For instance, I had hoped that we could give citizens and businesses an expectation on how fast we would make decisions in the public sector when they handed in a form.

The problem was perhaps that we had had very big success by doing the strategies in cooperation with different layers of government. We had done the strategy work the same way four times by that time. For the fifth time we also tried the same way, but we should have realized that the political scene had changed. Suddenly dissociation was a problem, and the municipalities were afraid to set more goals together with us. We should have realized that people were scared that the next level after the 80 percent target was reached would mean that we might take away the decisions and the responsibility from the institutions, that we will centralize things even more, that we will close some municipalities down because we digitalized everything. They only reluctantly came along to make the next strategy, and the outcome was not that ambitious because of it.

The new strategy should have also had even more work in the direction of the private sector. We should have recognized that we cannot innovate everything ourselves; we should free up data and open the market up more. In utilities and especially with the climate agenda, in health care, in education. I did not fully understand the market while in the job; I had been groomed differently. I only first understood when I left the public sector in 2017 that if you want to have innovation also in the future, you have to feed the market and help the market to interact with you. Tendering makes it very difficult for the market to innovate. I am not sure that I fully understand it even today, but at least I can see now.

Another thing I regret is that we were underestimating the issues concerning security, all the way back to 2001. We came to this understanding through problems. We had a certain naive understanding that digitalization could only do good. Today we know it can do both, and no we have to work on that. Back then we did not see it coming.

What Made You Move on from DIGST in 2017?

Part of it was the feeling I had about the new digital strategy. I told myself that maybe it was time to hand over the keys and have somebody step in to rethink how we should make strategies. I had carried the stick to this level, and now the way we should do things from here should change.

Remember, I also had learned to ask myself who was the best to be put in front of any new project, and sometimes it was not the one who had led the former one. Maybe that is also the reason why I changed myself, because I had done the same thing now too many times.

I say I have never left the digitalization agenda, especially because I am back in government now. But you have to recognize when it is time that you have to give the sticks to someone else.

How Did You Make Sure That Things Will Last in DIGST and with the Agenda?

I hope that I made sure that when the time came for me to leave, it would not be important anymore if I was heading it. There was good staff in the organization who could continue our work. There also had been a generation shift and it has continued since then, because the agency is still very successful and doing a very good job. They are launching some of the technologies we decided on doing back in the strategy in 2016. For example, the next generation of digital signature just started being implemented in September 2021.

What Are the Skills Necessary to Be Effective in This Kind of Job?

You could go to this job from very different skills, but it would help to understand technology, of course. In addition, it is very hard to be a top manager of an agency without a very, very good understanding of how to interact at the political level and being part of the political process. This takes experience.

We have seen it when people come from private sector and have never worked within the public sector. It is just too difficult to navigate. In the private sector, you can make decisions by yourself. In an agency like DIGST, if you want to make large decisions, you have to convince others to be part of it, or they will more or less block you.

Of course, you need to be a skilled top manager to take on the role. You have to build up a very good toolbox, with experiences on how to cope with different situations. Otherwise, you will be like Bambi on the ice in the cartoon - falling flat all the time.

You need to recognize that institutions that have to change, have to build up the capability of transformation. There have been many cases of promises for digital transformation and then three years later scandals in Denmark. Why? Because in these cases, the institutions do not know what their capabilities are for transforming; they do not train or transform their organization.

If you play football, you practice for the tournament. If you are a doctor, you have to be skilled to do an operation. When it comes to digitalization, people often say that you can come in from the side and perform anything. Actually, you have to deal with culture, institutions, rules, long traditions, often with employees unwilling to transform. Technology itself cannot transform anything.

Institutions have to acknowledge that they need to have the people who transform the organization, step by step. Otherwise, these very rapid transformations of public institutions often fail or maybe succeed only for a short while, then they return to the old habits.

In Addition to the Skills, What Are Your Three Recommendations on How to Be Effective in This Role?

First and foremost, have clear goals. Where are you heading? What is your success? What have to be or can be the quick wins to show that you are on the right path?

You have to make things successful for the customer, for the citizen so that they can see a change. I think many public institutions do not think very much about the final customer; they are just there. There is no competition with others.

Another thing is that it is so important to be capable of cooperation, at least in my experience. I have said it many times: you cannot succeed by yourself. How can you make others part of your success? Either by stick or carrot, the right tools or making the right incentives.

The third point, maybe, is to build simple solutions. The private sector often has a better understanding of the end user. When we failed in creating very simple things, it brought hard work after.

CHAPTER 13

Luis Felipe Monteiro

Brazil

Luis Felipe Monteiro was the digital government secretary of Brazil from 2018 to 2021, with a duty to transform the public sector in the country. In 2020, he was nominated by the World Economic Forum and Apolitical as one of the world's fifty most influential people revolutionizing government and among the one hundred most influential in digital government in 2018.

Previously, Luis had introduced the culture for innovation in various public sector roles. He also worked for multinational companies, always involved in innovation and IT.

As a trained computer scientist, he holds a master's degree in information technology management, an MBA in information systems strategy from Fundação Getulio Vargas (FGV), and has completed executive programs from Georgetown and Harvard University in leadership, innovation, and digital transformation in government.

Nowadays, Luis is the CEO of Cateno, a payments technology company.

Each time I think about it, I cannot help but admire in awe. Brazil is a maze of governance complexity, bureaucracy at (sometimes) its worst at three (or more) levels of government. There is a population of 210+ million. Economic struggles. Doing digital transformation in a place like this . . . well, it takes guts. And some mad skills.

Obviously, Luis Felipe must have them because he did not fear the challenge and tackled it head on. As digital government secretary, he led the Brazilian federal government through a remarkable turnaround to a digital service building machine like no other. The speed of change of their delivery was beyond breakneck—launching several transformed services each day.

Everyone who has met Luis Felipe has seen the GOV.BR logo at back of his mobile phone cover. That logo is manifestation of how to—and that it is possible to—truly achieve digital transformation at scale.

The story of Luis Felipe and Brazil gives insights into how to reach that level of capability. It gives insights into how to build up a real strong central delivery capability and platforms, centered on the famous GOV.BR, both as a channel and as a movement.

—Siim

What Was Your Journey into the Digital Government Leadership Role in Brazil?

I am a computer science specialist by training. Since I was a kid, I was always very interested in computers and technology. I did my bachelor's in computer science, and after graduation created a company. Back at that time we did not call it a start-up, but it was a start-up creating websites and web platforms back in 1998–1999. After that I had an experience of working abroad in the United States through an international internship program through the organization AIESEC. I stayed a few months with SAP there.

When I came back to Brazil, I was hired by a consultancy company and stayed for eight years working with private sector and the financial industry mostly. I worked as developer, as software analyst and architect, then project manager. As my career started to be much more managerial than technical, I did an MBA with the area of management and IT. Then the opportunity opened to get into the government, and it was a time in my career when I was trying to settle what would be my future.

I started in government about eleven years ago, within an IT team under the Ministry of Planning and Budget. Within just a few months, I was selected to be the CIO for the Ministry of Communications. I had now all the IT infrastructure and services to manage within one ministry. What I saw was a huge gap inside the government between what IT infrastructure services was to what digital transformation should be. I led the team that created new services to communicate properly what we were doing. I then became the director for public management modernization, handling the goal to introduce an innovation culture into the public sector. From there I was invited to assume the post of CIO for the entire federal government as the Secretary for IT and Communication in 2018.[1] In 2019, I was shifted to the Ministry of Economy and became called digital government secretary.

So, my career moved me from IT specialist to the management field. The main insight that got me to my current position was that inside government there was a huge gap from technology to business.

When I first joined the government, I had to go through a selection process that took about six months of tests and rounds, then four more months of initial training. It means that the government in Brazil does select people thoroughly. Afterwards, once I had earned the respect of some executives, I usually followed or went with them as they moved to other ministries or higher roles.

What Was Your Motivation in Becoming the Secretary?

Every day during breakfast, when you turn on the TV, the government is in the headlights, and usually for bad news. In my view, the lack of quality in public services is something that citizens will never agree with. We have today the mechanisms to transform that, and to make it happen quickly. A rapid shift to a digital mindset is needed.

I had seen it first when I became in charge of IT in a government agency. Instead of building new data centers and doing some procurement, I decided to make a business transformation. That experience motivated me to continue.

Also, as the secretary I would be given the capacity to create a team around me that understood the vision: that the future of the government is a digital government. That the government will be a digital institution.

Did You Hesitate at All about the Challenge or the Role?

It is part of my personality to see the glass half full, always. In life, I usually see that there are many opportunities, in government as much as in other institutions. The government mainly needs highly skilled and highly motivated people to make that opportunity real.

When I started in the government eleven years ago, I looked at the position of secretary and decided that this was where my career should take me. Because I am both IT and a management specialist, the role fits. I would be who takes care of the entire government digital strategy. That is why I did not think twice.

What Was the Expectation Laid Out to You in the Role in Terms of What to Achieve or Fix?

In the public sector initially, I was meant to be a typical CIO with the aim of keeping operations running efficiently. As soon as I became the secretary, we set a digital transformation program that would be robust enough to make the transformation visual for every citizen. This was in the last six months of the previous president, Michel Temer, and my first year.

I had no political or personal contacts with the incoming next administration. From day one, they asked me what I thought should be done in Brazil within the IT and digital fields. Thus, we got the opportunity to pitch that program to the new Bolsonaro administration. They said that was exactly what we needed. The green light was given at the very first meeting—to let us make it happen.

Can You Give a Bit of Context about Where Was Brazil Standing in Digital Government Development in 2018?

I used to say that we were in the 1990s still. When I started, we had lots of technology inside the government, but it was used basically only within the public service itself. There were many administrative information systems, networks, and data centers, but almost no service to the citizens. The existing digital services were highly concentrated at the revenue agency only.

That was the huge business gap. I realized that the government did not understand exactly its goal back at that time. Today we do not spend a dollar more on technology than we spent three years ago, but we are doing much more for the citizens.

We also had a very decentralized IT structure and operation. I used to oversee the central government IT, but we have two hundred agencies with IT teams and their own budgets, systems, and goals—a digital labyrinth. We still have more than 160 data centers at the federal level. Well, the challenge was how to create synergy: how to make two hundred agencies move in the same direction and to create a unique digital platform?

What Was Your Vision and Proposed Strategy Then in More Detail?

The basis for my vision was that digital transformation in government could be done—like Estonia or the Brazilian revenue agency had managed to become digital. Second, the citizen is everywhere and interacts with multiple agencies and levels of government. We must transform the entire citizen journey to become really digital.

We had to learn from international experience. We asked the Organization of Economic Co-operation and Development (OECD) to do a peer review study on digital government in Brazil.[2] I also visited many countries in a short period; we got together all the strategies and lessons learned from the most advanced countries like Estonia, Denmark, the UK, South Korea, Uruguay, Portugal, and a few others. When I saw what they were doing, I thought what we could do to create or build the digital government in our country.

It was clear to me that the government should be a digital platform. As a platform, the government should provide products and services that are used to build policies and to transform services in a much, much easier and a standardized way.

There are major components in my vision of what gov.br should be—the digital government platform in Brazil.

First, we realized the need to consolidate the digital channels within the government. Previously we had more than 1,500 portals and 240 apps. Not even Google could help the citizen to find the official government digital channels in such a digital labyrinth. Gov.br consolidated all of that in a digital one-stop shopping for services, news, and government information.

Second was the need to create a seamless and secure form of citizen identification. We needed a digital ID so that citizens experience digital services instead of carrying a case of paper documents to prove who they are. Third, the data, not the citizen, should run from one agency to another. So, interoperability got also a major highlight in our strategy.

The next part was that we needed to consolidate and to optimize the government's IT infrastructure and expenditures within the public administration. Last, but not least, we had to streamline the business registration in Brazil. That was the one thing that was important for the president to reduce bureaucracy.

What Was the Time Frame for Your Vision and Strategy?

We planned it for four years, the exact period of the presidency and President Bolsonaro's mandate.

When I first showed it to the new administration, the executives asked, "Can we do that in one year?" I had to say, "Not really." "Two years?" Unfortunately, no. It was partly a technical negotiation to show them that the current situation was so bad that we should have to keep going in a very accelerated pace for all four years to make the digital switch.

How Did You Chart Out the Delivery Plan and How Hard Was It to Retain Delivery as Intended?

It was clear to me that we had to have deliverables from the very first week, in an agile way, in order to have feedback and renew the sponsorship on the program. Since the first week, there were new digital services available to Brazilians.

The first major step was in August 2019, when we launched the consolidated government portal gov.br. People had said that there was no way we could do a single portal for the Brazilian government: there were too many portals, and the control power of information was something rooted in the culture of the agencies. It was key to the success to get domain control. I stated, with the support of the presidency, that no one had the authority to create new websites outside gov.br.

For this to happen, I had to get very close to the communications agency by saying that if we create a platform like gov.br, the access for the end user would be much easier. Meaning, people would be moving around gov.br. It became clear that we would understand the citizen needs and would have metrics about the digital experience. Then President Bolsonaro stated by decree in April 2019 that from August 1, there would be no more multiple websites, and the government channel must be gov.br only. It meant that we had only three months to build the technical solution. On August 1, we launched gov.br.

We moved many of the steps in parallel. While we were creating gov.br, we had to make some quick wins, delivering services within the agencies. The goal given by my minister was that he wanted one thousand public services transformed in two years. It seemed impossible because the year before we had transformed a maximum of a hundred services.

In two years, we ended up transforming 1,100 services or 10 percent over the target. It means that at every business day, we were launching two new digital services. Things started to change fast and visibly.

Thus, the sequence for action was starting to transform the services with what you have at hand. In parallel, we were creating the platform stack. With a lot of services to transform, we went after those first that had the highest number of users. Second criterion was the development opportunity in Brazilian economy—would it be something that would scale into the economy? Things like international trade or social services perhaps were more scalable. The last priority criterion was cost reduction for the government side.

What Kind of an Organizational Setup Did You Build Up to Make Such a Rapid Delivery Possible?

I decided that my organization must be an internal service provider to the agencies, not just a regulator. We must help the agencies to make the transformation.

This way we would first create the platforms, then pilot the platforms with some agencies, then scale them up. Only at the end would we write any form of regulations. The agencies needed to see us as someone who was not there just to say how they should do something, but to deliver them services and resources to help the transformation happen. This way we got the buy-in from the technicians and executives at the ministries.

Within the digital secretary team, we had to have parallel teams. One team was for services transformation, including a relationships unit, a portfolio unit, a technical unit, and so on. Separately there were the platform and operations teams. I really had two velocities within the same organization. One team was small, agile, but not so deep diving. The other needed time to build up the digital platforms properly.

What Were Your Main Priorities within the First Hundred Days in the Secretary Role?

The first three months really went to setting up the services that were already in the pipeline or with higher impact. We wanted to showcase what we meant by digital transformation. It was not about simply making something handled by computers but to create a better experience for the citizens.

We did not have any deliverables in first three months on the platform side because that would take longer to create. Only in the second part of the first year did we make gov.br and digital ID available.

That is why I usually say: do not worry about creating new regulation or creating highly sophisticated technology, because tech is already there. Get your team to make quick wins and service delivery. Communicate those deliveries in a clear way for the end user. This way you will have the time and sponsorship to work on the highly technical and sophisticated platforms. You will get time, money, and the trust to implement any new regulations later.

The strategy is delivery! We learned that from international experience, especially from Government Digital Service in UK, and it worked very well in Brazil.

How Did You Manage to Retain the Focus on the Strategy Delivery, as You Went Along?

Personally, both my team and I have the skill to be disciplined and focus on what really needs to be done. As managers, our role is simple—set up the vision, get rid of the barriers, and keep the rhythm. That are the only things I do, nothing else.

As I mentioned before, we started from a blank page and decided which projects to handle first based on a few criteria. During the execution, there would be fires along the way and that is why I created a "firefighting" team, our "special forces." If something happened, I could send them to take care of it: to reduce the impact or to understand the issue there. They are a mixed team of operations, cybersecurity, and communications backgrounds. How we talk about the troubles to the public needs to be part of the package.

What Were Your Methods to Really Get Agencies On Board for Such an Aggressive Transformation Program?

We had an internal "sales team." Usually, public servants do not know how to sell anything; they usually do not do it. I had to recruit and train a team to sell what we were offering to agencies all over the government.

Data science was another important direction. Without the data, no one would take notice. When I could say that digital services were 97 percent cheaper than a physical service for the government to operate, I got their attention. We started to measure each transformation. We started doing the sales, marketing, and communications based on those result metrics.

On the one hand, we increased our reliability by delivering digital platforms to the agencies. On the other hand, we established a stronger central command over them. The OECD peer review listed some recommendations for the Brazilian government to do. One was that we should establish a digital champion role at the highest level with leadership and structure to make the digital transformation happen across agencies, a role responsible for policy and vision. We decided it so that the digital government secretary became the role holder with support of the presidency.

The important word here is *trust*. As a digital government leader, you do not just have to get the trust from your own teams, but mainly from other teams. If you deliver good services, then they will trust you, too. A part of the strategy was not to showcase us. The Digital Government Secretariat in that sense was a support unit; the ministries were who were publicly showing the results. We were just levers for them. In partnership, they received all the claps and recognition for services they built.

You Already Spoke about Adding Some Specific Skills to the Team, but How Did You Build Out the Team Overall?

In the beginning I had with me about a hundred people from the former secretary of IT, plus we had about three hundred fifty more professionals working decentralized at the agencies.

The initial team that I took along were IT infrastructure and software development specialists. I had to upgrade that team with more soft skills people.

When I left the Secretariat, I had about eight hundred people: two hundred with me directly and others spread to agencies. The six hundred people in agencies reported both to me and to the agency CIO at the same time.

The budget came by delivering our promises at the first year. I first had to show that the team was capable of delivering, and then I got the right to ask for more money from the second year onwards.

We also brought the previously outlying public-owned IT companies under the Secretariat's supervision. We have two public IT enterprises at the federal level in Brazil delivering the IT operational and software development work for the government. These companies became linked to the same digital strategy, because I was assigned to be their counselor in my role. This was how we got the capacity and the technology needed for transformation, without expanding the internal team too much in the beginning.

Where Did You Find the Skills and Talent From, and How Did You Lure Them Over to Work with You?

Brazil has some six hundred thousand public servants at the federal level, most selected rigorously like I was. Our internal opportunities to recruit people was huge. There were many professionals hidden somewhere inside the public sector with very important and interesting skills to add to our team. So, communications and the results became the way to attract them.

When we highlighted our results and deliverables, people wanted to work with us. When they saw us working, they knew that we had a different culture. The innovation and the digital transformation we delivered was our recruitment benefit, so to speak.

Public servants did not earn more to work for us. In fact, they worked harder while with us. However, they mostly enjoyed doing it because they could see the results. Usually at standard agencies in the federal level the citizen impact is much more abstract.

Who Were Your Most Valuable Hires?

One was my sales manager. He used to be an entrepreneur himself, and he was able to multiply his skills inside the team. Once he left, the sales team he had the ability to run things on their own.

The second one was our user experience director. He made the user-centric perspective work for us.

Third one was the platform director: a highly skilled chief engineer with a doctoral degree. He was able to create a very cohesive team that built and runs the operation of gov.br, digital ID, and many other central services.

What Routines Did You Use to Manage the Team?

Every Monday morning, we had what we called a flagship meeting. My entire managerial team, fifteen to twenty people, came together for one hour. We highlighted the things we need to take care of, updated the status of project teams, went through administrative things.

After COVID-19 hit and we started a remote work mode, I decided to start the day with a stand-up meeting with my cabinet team. Usually, these daily meetings were with the chief of staff, chief advisor, chief of communications, the portfolio director, and the deputy secretary. It was when we set up the things to be done. We went through all the agenda conflicts or priorities that we had to handle on a daily basis.

In my meetings, I was usually very quick to make decisions. I think that the worst decision is the one you do not make. I always try to understand the possible scenarios and then take care of the tough decisions.

I also took time for lots of calls from partners at other ministries, agency secretaries, representatives from IT companies. I did these as the daily routine, even if only to stay in touch and say, "Hello, how are you doing?" I kept these slots in my agenda to catch a breath and think whom I should call.

Did You Also Have Some Regular Routines with Outside Stakeholders?

I did have monthly meetings in digital strategy governance bodies of ministries. We formalized it so that every ministry must have a digital transformation plan, which has to correspond to the overall national digital government strategy we set. I was part of governance bodies for those plans, and in these meetings, we went through the portfolio of projects under each ministry.

The plans were structured in a way that they all have four main pillars: transformation of public services, consolidation of channels, data interoperability, cybersecurity and data privacy. We split the deliverables on these pillars for every quarter. At the ministerial boards and with my portfolio teams, I kept myself updated and oversaw the entire digital strategy.

One useful routine was to hold a weekly meeting with my peers at the Secretariat of Management and the Secretariat of Human Resources for the government. The three of us used to get together to discuss things such as how the logistics of the government would work in the future. Based on how the technology is involving, what capacities must we create within the public services? Which agencies should have the approval to recruit more people? For example, if an agency was not digital enough and came to ask for more people, the secretary for human resources would come to us and ask our team to step in and steer digital transformation there first. Or when COVID-19 came, the three of us proposed and led the switch of three hundred thousand civil servants to work from home.

Every month I also met with the special Secretariat team above me to go through our monthly performance measurement. Our key performance indicators were reported and discussed every month.

What Were Your Principles of Leadership? What Slogans or Sayings Did You Repeat to the Team?

Usually, I would say that we should be user-focused and citizen-centered. We must "be the citizen in the room," in any room we go to! We must take and play the role of the citizen. We did spend a lot of energy guaranteeing the quality that the user expects and that the user should receive.

Second, any decision we make has to be based on available data, not on guessing.

Third, we must push the boundaries to create a transformation in government. My team was quite unusual from standard public servants in the sense that they were always pushing the boundary and trying to make things that others thought were impossible. This made them highly motivated, but it also created a kind of stress for urgency.

Trust was a big word for us. Not only to trust ourselves, but to create trust within our ecosystem.

We were also very results driven. We did not sit over anything. We did not necessarily need to move fast, but we needed to be continuously moving. We were in a marathon, not a hundred meter run. Thus, I tried not to let people be idle or stuck in something.

How Did You Build These Principles into a Team Culture?

I used to work in internal communications and on team building myself.

Every quarter, we had a major event for the entire team. We refreshed our priorities; we shared the results from last quarter. I usually did some team-building activities with the team to create a new vision or to make the current vision clear for them. We awarded the people who excelled the most in the previous time period with travel tickets to some partner country that had digital government experiences.

Because the team grew very fast, it was important to establish straight communication channels. I asked my direct reports and managers to establish communication lines also with their teams.

At the end of every week, I sent a message to the entire organization. I did a small viderecording with the overview of what had we done and who were the people behind the results. I did that every Friday night, also to sort of say, "Enjoy the weekend," and that next Monday we would be together again to transform the government.

This was even more important in COVID-19 time. Ninety percent of my team was remote. Some of them did not know me in person, because we had grown fast. So, it was important to be at least face-to-face hearing directly from me. Their feedback was very positive on this.

What Was the Hardest Part of Your Job?

I am not passionate about the solution; I am passionate about problems myself. There might be many solutions, but the team should have the passion for the problems.

Fighting for the budget priority is tough. Resources are always limited, especially during a global health crisis. We had to prove ourselves and the strategic value proposition.

It was frustrating to wake up every morning and watch the news with citizens stuck to get a service delivered. I used to say to my team that there are two approaches we can take. One is to keep the broken process because this is "how the government works." Or we can take the other way and take the issues as an opportunity to fix, to improve people's lives. The hard part is to keep motivating the staff to take the second approach.

Citizen needs will change, technology evolves, problems will be always there. Digital transformation is a fascinating and an endless job.

In Your Time on the Job, What Do You Think Were Your Failures?

I do not regret anything, but I would certainly do some things differently now.

Mainly, delivery should be even faster. For example, we should have delivered the digital ID faster than we accomplished. We have a complex institutional environment, with many participants with decision power from the executive branch, the judicial branch, and the private sector. I had the duty to make this arrangement work. We had the correct vision; we succeeded in the public sector so far. It is harder to scale for the whole country, as I had hoped.

Looking back, I could have been clearer at start about the team and budget needs to make the transformation happen. But as I said, I set out to deliver with what I had.

What Do You Consider Your Achievements in the Role?

Gov.br platform is our main achievement. It was created from scratch, as a technology product, a government program, and as a strong community of supporters. I am very proud to reach more than 120 million Brazilians every month. It is a success; there is no rollback for gov.br.

With gov.br, we started a community of intrapreneurs inside government. We also turned gov.br into a brand, which people are proud of. Gov.br is a high-tech product that people enjoy using. And it is also a mission, a strategic program with clear goals and metrics.

We consolidated a design system to support the spread of gov.br branding. We see gov.br presence in every social media, on phones and laptop stickers—the logo is everywhere.

Gov.br is successful as a product, too. We have 120 million Brazilians using it every month. We have made 72 percent of federal government public services digital. We saved more than 180 million hours from bureaucracy. Nine out of ten Brazilians recognize gov.br, with no traditional propaganda done at all.

I am very proud that Brazil was just recently ranked seventh on the World Bank list assessing the current state of digital transformation in public service across the world in the GovTech Maturity Index 2020.[3] Brazil is the only country among the top ten nations with a population of more than hundred million people.

I am very happy with all we managed to do. I had a huge support from the executive team; President Bolsonaro; the Minister of Economy, Paulo Guedes; and Caio Paes de Andrade, the Special Secretary of State. The entire team made it possible.

What Is Still Left on the Table as Next Challenges for Brazilian Digital Government?

Digital ID use in the private sector is still in the backlog.

We also aim to make the government personalized for each citizen. We have now the platform, the data, and AI capability to make it possible. The team is still working on technology and privacy standards to make sure we can offer a more effective government.

So far, gov.br is still a reactive platform—you must go to it and request something. It will become a data platform that understands the customer and predicts their needs.

The other direction I wanted to foster is what I call the "anywhere government." It means that the provisioning of services should not be only at official government channels. We must share our APIs to publish public services within the entire digital ecosystem, such as a banking app, an e-commerce marketplace, or any other company. With a reliable interoperability platform, citizens could get government transactions done from anywhere.

What Made You Move On from the Job in Autumn 2021?

I have to say that was a hard decision. I was completely satisfied as the digital government secretary, with entire support from my team and from higher-level executives. But opportunities come and go, and most of what I planned back in 2018 was achieved in the last three years. Gov.br is a reality and will not roll back—checked. Brazil has one of most mature digital governments in the world—checked.

2022 will be the year to define a new digital strategy for the country. There are many other digital champions that can lead Brazil to another level.

That is why I decided to start a new professional journey. I moved to the private sector, working as the CEO for a payments company.

What Did You Do to Make Your Initiatives and the Change Last?

First, through international commitments. We signed some international partnerships with the UK, Denmark, Inter-American Development Bank, OECD, and the World Bank. These arrangements are hard to get rid of and help the continuity of the program, especially if there is donor funding involved.

Second, we built up strong support from institutions around government, such as Congress, the Court of Accounts, and the private sector.

Third and most important, it is done through delivering better services, reachable to every citizen. We have achieved getting more than half of the Brazilian population to use gov.br. There is no way back from this.

To Sum Up, What Do You Think Are the Skills Necessary to Do This Kind of Job Well?

You must be business- and citizen-focused. It is about people.

You must understand that digital is not IT. It is *with* IT, but not IT.

You should be open-minded and have open discussions to be able to influence people positively with your vision. You must be able to communicate very well with the stakeholders: the society, the media, with your own team members and government executives.

Finally, you must be tireless in solving problems.

Some skills you learn, others should be part of you.

What Are Your Key Takeaways from Your Time as the Digital Government Leader? Your Three Recommendations to Any Peer Doing the Same Job?

Do not start if you do not have the mandate. Be the digital champion; get the role for yourself.

Be bold but humble in that position. You need partners, not opponents.

Deliver from day one to your last. Deliver, communicate, learn, and keep walking.

Meet digital leaders from all around the world. There are not many people like us out there. Know your peers and share.

Make friends and have fun!

Notes

1. Secretary is the equivalent to a deputy permanent secretary or a deputy secretary-general level or similar in the Brazilian ministerial hierarchy—the key civil servant policymaker and manager responsible for a particular field of work.
2. See OECD. (2018). *Digital government review of Brazil: Towards the digital transformation of the public sector*. OECD Digital Government Studies, OECD Publishing,
3. See Dener, C., Nii-Aponsah, H., Ghunney, L. E., & Johns, K. D. (2021). Govtech maturity index: The state of public sector digital transformation. *International development in focus*. World Bank.

CHAPTER 14

Mike Bracken

United Kingdom

M ike Bracken is a founding partner of Public Digital, a global digital transformation consultancy helping governments and large organizations thrive and survive in the internet era. Together with colleagues at Public Digital, he coauthored the book *Digital Transformation at Scale: Why The Strategy Is Delivery.*

Mike was appointed Executive Director of Digital of the UK government in 2011 and its Chief Data Officer in 2014, where he created and led the Government Digital Service (GDS). After government, he sat on the board of the Co-operative Group as Chief Digital Officer.

Before joining the civil service, Mike was the Digital Development Director at Guardian News & Media. In his executive career, he has grown several technology companies and occupied C-suite roles in a variety of sectors in more than a dozen countries.

His nonexecutive portfolio includes Lloyds of London, the world's leading insurance market, and the Omidyar Network, a philanthropic investment firm. Mike also advises the Inter-American Development Bank and is the Honorary Professor at the Institute for Innovation and Public Purpose at University College London. He was named UK Chief Digital Officer of the year in 2014 and awarded a CBE.

Mike Bracken is a living legend in the digital government circles. Everyone knows him or knows about him for the work he and the splendid people around him did in setting up the Government Digital Service in the UK. They have defined what good looks like in this practice globally perhaps the most. Not to mention the earthquake they caused in Her Majesty's government, even if for too short of a while due to politics.

He is like the Obi-Wan Kenobi in this field—I dare not say Yoda, as Mike does not seem to be aging—spreading deep thoughts and "war stories" each time he speaks. Mike indeed has done deep, deep thinking about digital services, about the machinery of government, the culture and institutions of it.

He seems the mildest of lads, even soft-spoken at first—until he really starts speaking his mind and you realize from his words that this man has a fire inside him. This fire is the deep-rooted personal drive for truly improving government and going to battle with its worst manifestations, to truly make lives of people around us better even a bit.

I am still amazed that Mike is talking to me at all! By a complete address mishap, I stood him up when I was due to meet him the very first time at what was the initial rollercoaster of early GDS days, when getting to his schedule was very hard to near impossible. He must have waited for the rookie from Estonia for close to an hour, and this sort of a stunt on my end could have easily ended the mateship before it even had a chance to start. Instead, this too-short chat from way back in Whitehall led to many more whenever our tours have collided around the world.

—*Siim*

How Did You Become a Digital Government Leader in the UK?

The short answer is because a group of people more wise and worldly than me thought it would be a good idea.

I have a long background in civic tech and internet advocacy from outside of government, helping organizations like mySociety[1] and advising the government on the possibilities of the internet. At the same time, I had a long private sector career. I had mixed results at a wide number of roles: product manager, a COO, technologist, and a lot of senior leadership roles. I had worked in fifteen countries and had had a lot of business responsibility—far too much—at a young age as I was one of the first of my generation to understand what the internet meant. I was at the stage of my life where I was getting into board-level positions. I was in my early forties, so probably approaching the zenith of my career in terms of having twenty-five years of internet-era experience.

Through the 1990s and 2000s, there were a series of very-high-profile failures of enterprise, waterfall-style technology programs in the UK public system. A political space was opened up by a bunch of people including Tom Steinberg and Rohan Silva around the center of government, and they started to quietly lobby for a different way of doing things. It was given a lot of stimulus by Martha Lane Fox, who was the government's advisor on internet matters and the most stalwart supporter one could wish for. A truly amazing woman who became a great friend to many of us. She wrote a report that we helped to draft, in which she called for a radical change or revolution in leadership and the way of doing digital things in government.[2]

Most credit goes to Francis Maude, who became the minister for the Cabinet Office and backed the radical new way of working. Government Digital Service (GDS) is his legacy, and the UK reputation for digital government belongs to him. Tom Loosemore, my colleague and the intellectual founder of digital government in the UK, lead the way by starting up a team of fifteen or so people doing a small alpha version of what GOV.UK and a government service could look like. That enabled the government to talk to me about what the changed digital leadership role could look like. Then my own government offered me this role and I thought, "I have to do this, because I will not get a chance again."

Ian Watmore, who had run the first e-government unit in 2004 and who went on to serve as the civil service commissioner, recruited me. He was staunch in his support and helped me through the Whitehall minefield with great aplomb.[3] My predecessor Chris Chant was so skillful in guiding me around the elephant traps for a year and did so much to set the scene for necessary reforms to come. Kathy Settle and Tony Singleton were Whitehall insiders who sustained the nascent GDS and gave us the necessary antibodies to survive. Some of the civil service leadership quietly prepared the ground for digital leadership. Melanie Dawes helpfully secured our domains from the reach of powerful departments before we even arrived. Jeremy Heywood, the cabinet secretary, eased my path to the top tables.

There were many more. Leadership in that system needs support and toleration. Being asked to be the leader of the group of people I respected the most was such an honor.

In Addition to Honor, What Was Your Motivation or the Reason behind Such a Thought?

Professionally I believed that our system of government and the behavior of the state at its center had lost its way. The opportunities provided by the internet, namely its capability to improve the performance of our government in a digital era, had been almost completely ignored by our political and civil service class for decades. There was such a large prize on offer, and it was clear inside and outside the system that change needed to happen. Also, the reforms were largely nonpolitical. Everyone likes better services, at less cost, with happier users.

My motivation was also a very personal one. I am a survivor of one of the largest miscarriages of justice in our country, the Hillsborough disaster.[4] I spent decades coming to terms with how the institutions of the state, including the media, police, and judiciary, colluded to protect corrupt officials from truth and justice. A culture that allows that to happen must need reform.

My motivation was intensely personal because I wanted to improve the state and extremely opportunistic professionally because of the skills I have. My skill, if I have one, is to use the internet at scale to change institutions. Now I was suddenly presented with an opportunity to do that at the heart of government. If my motivation had been only professional, I would not have taken the job because the chances of successful reform of this system were very, very slim.

Why So and What Were Your Hesitations?

When one is trying to change an institution, whose leadership is both set against the change that you are bringing and is also hugely adept at repelling any change—that is a very hard ask. The organization should want to change, but it did not.

It did not understand the opportunity, nor did it experience the worst outcomes of the status quo. A remarkable number of our political and civil service class are not required to use the services and policies for which they are responsible. Either because they do not need to, in the case of claiming benefits, or because they can use intermediaries like accountants and solicitors, in cases like paying tax. That lack of accountability and empathy with users is a toxic mix, and present in the center mainly. Most government employees work with people to deliver services, usually in low to medium paid roles and outside of Whitehall.

In short, my hesitation was that although I had no doubt that the machinery of government could be rapidly improved by internet-era reforms, I was less certain that the Whitehall hothouse would tolerate such reforms. In 2011, it was nearly twenty years since the browser was invented and thirty years since the internet, yet the government organization still maintained that the networking culture of the digital area was not worthy of its attention.

That was the stance of people who wanted to retain a power structure. If you set yourself up to change any power structure, you know you are in for a hell of a fight, regardless of what support you have.

You Came in Knowing the Hardships; What Were Your Conditions for Taking the Job?

In a soft but consistent way, I made sure we had very hard powers. We were the advocate of the user. We had veto powers over spending, we had powers to close things down, like contracts. We had powers of reporting to Parliament on delivery. In some cases, we could take critical national infrastructure and run it if we felt it could be done better.

More prosaically, our powers included some ability to hire outside of traditional job roles and salary bands, to communicate openly not via the political communication system, and to engage directly with users. We were of the center of government, and we and others in the Efficiency and Reform Group made that a powerful center in ways which had never existed.[5] This was one of Francis Maude's great reforms.

We never wrote down a list of our powers. Had I done so, no one would ever have granted them to me. So, the minister, cabinet secretary and the Efficiency and Reform Group (ERG) made sure the powers were either manifested in other ministers' power or the financial power, or that we had veto power over their decisions. I started off with very few and somewhat ambiguous powers if you looked from public view.

That is why our team was tolerated and patronized for two years within the civil service. Only once we started delivery at scale and change happened far too often and quickly for the incumbents to deal with it, the pushback started. By that time, I was the head of the technology profession, the chief data officer of the UK government, and the head of its digital services. So, I had an awful lot of powers, but with power comes great responsibility. One of my responsibilities was to fend off the leaders of a system that wanted to remove those powers, often explicitly.

What Task or Expectation Did Politicians Give You for the Role?

The expectation of the new administration of British politicians was, I think, that we cannot continue to be so "un-internet." After thirteen years of Labour government, the coalition politicians had grown up in opposition using the tools of the open internet, just like any member of the public. They expected Gmail and Wi-Fi. When they saw government IT of the time, they simply refused to use it. Only a system with that appalling quality of internal technology could continually fail to deliver digital and technology services to the country.

So, there was a huge desire for change, and this made managing expectations difficult. Although politicians were largely happy to resist the critical voices in their departments because GOV.UK was raising the bar for the whole of government, many of them wanted us to make an app or fulfil a policy for them. Numerous times I was asked to widen the GDS mandate into National Health Service (NHS) or fix an already broken IT system like the universal credit in 2013, when the sensible thing to do would have been to recognize it as a failure and start again.

Sometimes we recognized the need and stepped in. The chancellor was most demanding in 2014 when he needed a multichannel advice service launched in support of his new pensions policy.[6] Sadly, he was invisible later when his Treasury rejected funding for GDS and government-as-a-platform in the budget review of 2015, which led directly to my departure and the stalling of the digital government reforms overall more importantly.

Making these big calls, selecting winning projects, and avoiding obvious routes to failure became a sixth sense. But it did mean on occasion speaking truth to power, telling ministers that their much hoped-for policy was actually in tatters, and showing them that the message from their own department or agency was often inaccurate.

There certainly was no expectation that GDS would turn into a success story. There was also no expectation that GDS and the Efficiency and Reform Group would take on the incumbent technology suppliers and end up taking £4 billion out of the IT supply chain as taxpayer savings. People's expectation was initially probably that we might make some pretty poor websites somewhat nicer.

If That Was the Case, What Sort of Ambition or Objective Did You Set for Yourself?

Tom and I were extraordinarily clear with each other that we were there to change the functioning of the machinery of government. And by doing that we aimed to change its culture. We understood fully that if we change some of the operating models or some structures, they would simply be changed back the moment we left. What we had to do was to change the operating cultures, because it is cultures and people that change institutions.

I do not really care to this day what was the size or shape of GDS, or even its mandate. The size and budget argument just prevails the internal Whitehall culture of winners and losers. Although the country wants better and joined-up services, much of Whitehall spends time arguing about power dynamics and which part of a bureaucracy should do x or y. The political legitimacy of this model, presided over by the Treasury, must surely be questionable at best. A civil service reform bill must be one of the necessary actions of a future administration.

What I care about is the eight thousand or so people whom we trained and developed to show and demonstrate that they could deliver services in a different way. They are never going to go back to signing five-year contracts with outsourcing it all to suppliers and then sitting there writing policy papers.

Did You Set Yourself Any Concrete Objectives, Too?

I did and then changed them halfway through.

In the UK, we do not have a tradition of fixed election periods. When we started, there was a coalition government, which was very unusual. This government also for the very first time had implemented a fixed-term election cycle in order to maintain the coalition. It meant that for the first time, ministers could now make long-term decisions because they knew they would be in the position for a long time unless they messed it up. That gave us a runway.

With this context, we set out to do some long-term change. We said we would go after making digital services great with GOV.UK as the single point of access to government services, with transformation program of twenty-five major transactional services, and building an institution out of GDS. Then we would start to take on some of the incumbent and legacy stuff, opening the culture a bit, and an awful lot of IT reform.

The aim in the second parliament became to take on what you would call the middleware of government, the platform stuff. This way a simple truth would emerge that you just do not need very large government departments to operate the services that they do, pushing paper around to operate government.

I Know You Have Considered the First Hundred Days to Be Crucial When You Start in a Leadership Role Because That Is When You Will Be the Fastest. What Was Your Plan for Your Hundred Days?

Tom and I had been thinking about all this for twenty years. mySociety was an organization starting to think outside-in about what government services could look like in a quite benign way. I also had spent most of my life with institutions that were struggling to adapt to the internet era whether it be in retail, finance, communications, or media. And then finding ways to hack around bureaucracies so that cultures could grow. After Hillsborough, I had spent an awful lot of time thinking about the structure and the operation of institutions and how cultures could go so bad as they had been in the UK.

So, yes, in the first hundred days, we made a lot of decisions and made them very quickly. Things like to create a series of digital leaders across government as a mechanism for making decisions outside of parliamentary authority. That is strategically a very interesting thing.

For instance, when we started, people would say, "Well, to do all that stuff, you are going to have to deal with the CIOs. I would be like, "Why? Why do CIOs make the decision of the boards?"

The departments and agencies had two power centers. First the IT one led by CIO, usually in thrall to big IT vendors and system integrators. Second was policy and communications people who like to control the message, the narrative, and write stuff and basically are control people.

Both of them had governance structures of their own across government. In the digital space we closed down both. Establishing overall communications and design team, led by Ben Terrett, Emer Coleman, and Russell Davies, with talent from different disciplines was a hugely important first-hundred-days move. I also started not turning up to meetings and not submitting papers, but instead communicating in blog posts, YouTube videos, and so on. We essentially started communicating to public sector workers all over the system rather than having internal, endless discussions in Whitehall.

We got the cabinet secretary to write to every head of department, whom I then went to see in their own board meeting and told them what we were going to do in GDS and how they would be included. Some permanent secretaries collaborated, several objected, most were disinterested. One even wrote holiday postcards throughout my presentation.

Nonetheless, they were told their part in it and asked them to nominate within thirty days a director or director-general who would be the digital leader and gave them a role description for that person. This elicited two sorts of responses. Some of the smaller departments saw the wisdom in that and that at last something would get done. One said something like, "Oh, just tolerate them; they are just kids in jeans, just making websites." A decision he regretted sometime later when pleading for help with his flagship policy.

Setting this governance model up was the first thing. Plus getting hold of common design, getting hold of the domain and finding out what on earth we had as a baseline. Some very basic things like counting the number of services on offer, getting some data about the transactions. In an organization without a functioning delivery center, no one had done that before.

Another one was starting to work on an efficiency report very quickly, to start to look at what was the financial size of the prize on offer in IT reform. Andrew Greenway and Richard Sargeant did the deeply unsexy work of validating the service data and creating the efficiency modeling so we could estimate the size of the prize.

All these things were the fundamental building blocks for the future power structures that we created. We got away with it because this was time toward the end of the first year of a new coalition government. Everyone was still looking at where the politicians were going. We paid absolutely no attention to politics, we were just getting on with reforms and we had a minister who had our back.

What Were the Priorities of Your Work from Then Onwards?

We selected probably ten to twelve individual things that we would kick off at once, and it was a period of intense work. I have never worked so hard.

It was the governance, the creation of GOV.UK, the common design principles, setting up the GDS, cutting through the preexisting IT contracts, bringing in spending controls. I could go on. Many people were not interested in the machinery of government, but we were deeply interested in it.

I went to Francis (Maude) after thirty days and said if this is going to work, I need to be in your office every week minimum. I was not going to write a digital strategy, although we ended up writing one at the end of 2012. Tom wrote it, and I am very proud of the strategy because it was full of hard targets. We had by then confidence to show our hand.

But at the start, I said to Francis that if I write down what we are really thinking, we would be out of government in five minutes. What we would do was follow a strategy of radical change of machinery of government by delivery of services and working practices that would create a new coalition between government and users. We explained that if we stopped and asked the leaders of the system for permission, then we would get pushback and delay. So, we were just going to get on with it. We called this "The Strategy is Delivery." The minister was delighted.

Although we would have conversations repeatedly where we would show a better service by literally showing a video of a happy user using a better service or showing a better financial outcome, and the senior people would ask, "Yeah, but what about the department?"

I would asked, "What about it?" "Well, this means a change for us." The point is that we had to literally demonstrate to them that we would be delivering better public services than they were currently. It was so clear that the desire to protect the perceived sovereignty of the department was more important than the needs of the user. When Francis Maude stood up in Parliament and said that future reforms would recognize this and put the needs of the user first, I knew our mandate was secure, and we had won his trust.

Did the Departmental CIOs Ever Stick Around?

In the UK, the model of outsourced, multiyear deals to a small number of vendors was so prevalent that the role of the CIO was often synonymous with someone whose core skill was contractual relations. We had to change that model, and that meant bringing in people who could change the model, who understood technology, and who could grow and sustain digital teams.

For every progressive, technocratic CIO, or similar, the government had many who were two years from retiring, did not know anything about internet-era technology, liked to go and watch a rugby or cricket match with an IT supplier, and wanted to sign a ten-year deal. They were just a different decade and they had to go. Anyone who was any good at technology would not come into government before because they could not get anything done technologically. The reason is that suppliers owned the market, defined the rules.

Changing the technology leadership groups was painstaking work. In 2013, we took on veto powers for hiring, as we had to stem the tide of CIOs and technology leaders looking for end-of-career sinecures. Many left in this period, and the work that Liam Maxwell and his team, plus the work on spend controls and the wider ERG group on contract negotiations, meant that we were changing the cozy relationships among CIOs, government procurement, and the supplier landscape.

These reforms were truly fundamental to improving government technology and efficiency, and it is an indictment of the previous technology culture in government that Parliament's scientific group back in 2011 wrote a paper about the central government IT supply chain and titled it "A Recipe for Rip-Offs."

How Did You Change the Supplier Scene?

This was so difficult, and GDS was only a small part of the story. To change from one way of working we had to demonstrate what good looked like, to show why the change was necessary. That was the role of GDS, which was one part of the ERG setting, Francis Maude's reforming team in the middle of the Cabinet Office. The wider ERG was tasked with helping departments spend more efficiently to achieve better outcomes, and its remit included property, commercial negotiation, fraud, technology, and digital, plus procurement reform.

At this point 84 percent of government IT spending was going to seven organizations. It is called an oligopoly and it is one step short of a cartel situation, with companies writing their own procurements. We started looking at those contracts. I sent a nineteen-year-old to one department meeting in Swansea to ask the supplier and the CIO three questions. The CIO actually commented that "they have sent someone who knows what they are doing."

The Parliament had set us the moral ground for radical change, and we started doing it. It was a team effort: with Liam Maxwell leading in GDS, plus ERG boss Stephen Kelly, and commercial lead Bill Crothers all tackling vendors head on about the current contractual arrangements. We started breaking up the contracts, making new ones, brought in spending controls, built the marketplace for a new type of supplier. We started to show people how to do it differently. We had a real breakthrough as the CIOs were departing and some of the younger people in their departments were ready to do things a little differently, getting proper infrastructure agreements in.

The supply market at first looked whether we would actually be sticking to our guns. Then you saw some of them change, but some of them decided to take the government on and that was a mistake. We had companies lobbying that I and others should lose our jobs. But we had the backing of a resolute minister, even when the companies were lobbying other ministers. The subsequent reforms including the digital marketplace brought thousands of SMEs into the government's supply chain and fatally weakened the multiyear, enterprise IT arrangement.

How Did You Build Your Team?

The team built the team.

Tom was there before me. He set up the GOV.UK alpha version team in December 2010. I went to see them and that is when I agreed to go in for the government role. I joined in May 2011. I spent at least half of my time that year sitting in a nice restaurant on the South Bank[7] and talking to people I had known for twenty to thirty years who would really care for the government. Persuading them to take pay cuts and come do this thing in government.

I had key roles in mind for GDS. I then went and got people who I knew I could depend on. People who had done this, who had been around the block.

The second thing happened, too, which is that we started working in the open. People were looking at the interesting things we were doing like GOV.UK and GDS as an institution, and for the first time, talent started to run at us.

I really did not want to bring too many people into government, I needed only some people who would do it right. People like Mike Beaven, who went on to lead the digital transformation of the twenty-five biggest public services from 2013 to 2015, I doubt would have ever been given the opportunity to demonstrate their change credentials at such scale. Once I got to a position of being able to look in the eyes of twenty people, I then knew we were going to be alright and even with the full force of pushback from departments starting at that point.

My God, we got some talent, and they were self-organizing. My job was to be the shield to the things we kicked off, to do the firefighting. I had utter confidence in Tom and everyone's ability to set them up in teams that delivered and only occasionally had to step in. I made several mistakes in the operational setup, until Stephen Foreshew-Cain came in as COO and professionalized and managed the entire operation. That is a testament to the talent we had: that I had the confidence to focus outwards rather than at the internal design of GDS.

How Did You Convince People to Join You?

Because the mission was to fix the government, to improve the government. How many times in life do you get a chance to do that? Not in the American sort of way of saluting the leader and going on a "tour of duty." More in the very British way that things are dysfunctional, and we should do something about it.

The open communication, building communities of practice, working on stuff that matters; all of this convinced people more than I ever could. A couple of people we persuaded to join, notably Leisa Reichelt, after they came to our attention for being constructively critical of some of our ways of working. In Leisa's case, she did not think we were doing user research as well as we should have been. She was right, so we asked her to join us in fixing it. Which she then did with aplomb.

What Kind of Culture Were You Trying to Have in the Team?

The culture I wanted was a combination of civic tech and the open internet culture that I grew up on.

I was an internet researcher before the web existed. I had seen early the emergent culture of the internet that was an engineering culture and how networked it was, how supportive it was of each other, how focused it could be on societal or governmental outcomes. I am a child of that internet, not the platform internet of Google or Facebook.

However, I also came from the political background where the government policy of the day toward our community at Merseyside was called "managed decline"; can you believe it?[8] So there was great unemployment, great social unrest, and high levels of community engagement, high levels of self-support. I had that culture, too. I still do, I hope.

Now, put these two things together. I wanted a sort of nascent internet culture for the government outcomes. To some degree, this culture had always been in part of the public service as a subculture with some nonconformist public servants. I wanted a lot more of that.

What Slogans or Mottos Did You Push for the Team Again and Again in This Regard?

I said things like "look sideways" to get people to work together and collaborate. These were simple statements to implore people to work collaboratively for the good. Also, to focus on delivery—that was "strategy is delivery."

Tom rightly pointed out that we needed to industrialize all that in a communication system. Ben Terrett, Russell Davis, Emer Coleman, and others came in with a combination of communication, design, also visual design skills to amplify and deliver the messaging.

What Were the Other Ways You Reinforced the Culture?

At monthly or quarterly events, we would get the teams together, and they were quite sizeable teams after a while. Every team had to get on stage and present what it was up to in five or ten minutes. There is no hiding in the open, and judgment of delivery in this way was no hierarchical exercise. It was not about what Mike thinks—the team had to stand up in front of peers and prove to each other if stuff was or was not delivered. That is the sideways pressure I wanted, which leads to peer support and asking for help. I did not want any hierarchical culture at all. I needed to be a visible leader, but I did not want this to mean another one of the crazy structures like the other departments.

Another thing I wanted people to do was to move around from team to team. I did not want any of the teams going native and literally have people sitting together. Of course, this brings some frictions but by and large these frictions are better than having silos.

I was doing a weekly video or doing events like Sprint, where we annually brought the government together to push the messages and show the work.

As much of the work that I, Kathy Settle, Mike Beaven, and others were doing was out in the departments and managing pushback across the Whitehall, I was very keen that there were visible moments when the teams saw that they had top cover. One came early on when visiting department leaders came to GDS on a tour in the run up to departmental sites moving to GOV .UK. The representative from the all-powerful (in Whitehall terms) Ministry of Defence asked to know when we would be sorting out her conflicting legacy IT issues, only to be informed that this was her job, not the people creating the services for the future. This form of visible leadership was so necessary in the early days of giving the organization confidence and support.

What Steps Did You Take to Empower This Awesome Team to Deliver at Its Best?

I did not want people to waste time. I was in a hurry to change things; I knew I could go any day. I did not want to read reports, so I rarely asked people to write them. If I wanted to know what a team was doing, I took a look at the actual services they were working on or in the blog. Or walk up and say, "Can I have a minute? How are you doing?" Government does need its bureaucratic reporting for admin and governance. We had that done in the backend and it was very, very small.

The formal mechanisms we put in place were really supportive even if teams did not recognize them as such. This included the service standard, the manuals, the spend controls. These stopped our teams of really talented delivery people having to do the hand-to-hand combat with departments that actually did not want to change. From such meetings and works I or others were able to go in later and clear out the issues with the department executives. It meant that the team was able to get on with the delivery at the same time.

How Did the Political Relationships Work Out for You?

Francis Maude is a remarkable man for his ability to manage me. I am not easy. I do have, understandably, profound mistrust of institutions. He realized that, and he also recognized very early that conventional management of officials was not going to work on me—with me submitting a paper every month, to be read by another official and there might be ministerial comments on the margin. I was in his office several times a week and we chatted. He invited me to meetings with colleagues to expose me in a protected way to the wider political system.

I remember wondering to myself if he was really into our mission, because he was going to have some difficult meetings with IT suppliers, many of whom probably were politically aligned to his party. He never flinched. He did more to uphold the value for money of public service in the UK than any minister I have ever seen, inside government or outside.

It helped because we were delivering. Other governments even were walking up to our ministers on international visits and saying what UK was doing digitally was amazing. And you know, if you are a top-level politician in a country like ours, all you get is criticism usually. Suddenly, even at constituency meetings people were coming in to say "thank you for making digital services easier and simple." All the optics had changed.

What Were Your Failures or Things You Regret?

I think I burned people out. I held people to a standard of personal engagement and effort that I held myself to, which was unreasonable. Often, we had quite young people, and some of the behavior I overlooked in the name of the achievements they were making was unsupportable.

I dread to think, but I suspect there might be some individuals who had a tough time, and I could have done more to help them. I was too keen to look at the greater good for everyone than to dive into those individual issues.

Could You Have Avoided Your Own Exhaustion?

I could have taken my foot off the gas, become a permanent secretary, be part of the evolution, part of the club. It is not in my makeup; I cannot change that. So, it was a conscious decision to not take the foot off. Also, this would have meant complacency. This sort of unwillingness to look at difficult problems and not take responsibility is the very thin end of a long wedge.

Do You Think You Managed to Instill Some Culture Change in Civil Service At-Large, Like You Set Out to Do?

I did not set out to change the whole thing; it is too big. What I set out to do was to allow some people a bit like me to see government as a place where they, too, could do anything. I am delighted when I see government departments today hiring service designers on their boards. People like Janet Hughes now running huge change agendas in agriculture and Tom Read running the GDS itself.

There is a whole new category of roles in government for service design, content design, user research, all shades of technology roles from front end to DevOps and architecture. Hundreds and hundreds of different types of people now get a go at running our government, even in small ways.

We did not break the caste system of the policy group who are self-selecting and do or look a bit like the politicians, the group who have been running the space. But it is inevitable in the very long term that if your system has enough people in it, who come from a different background, some of them are going to end up running the show. That is my hope. Even if the jury's still out on that.

If you look at COVID-19 times now, take a look at what worked and what did not work in government. It is the doers that worked. The people who know how to get stuff done.

You Said That You Knew from the Start There Was Going to Be Pushback and Struggles Ahead. Did You Start Doing Something Very Consciously to Make Sure That What You Are Starting Would Last?

We did a number of things. We had to create the conditions where people—in the media, the system, and in the user cohorts—would be vocally unhappy about the status quo, as many of them had given up hope of ever seeing change.

I have a reputation of being too openly critical or challenging, which might be part of my character. I was always very careful not to criticize the individual. Whitehall has many great characters, and most people are trying to do a hard job in tough circumstances. What I criticized was the monoculture, the homogeneous nature of the institution, in ways that I hoped would lead to positive change.

Actually, we had to do something loud to point out how broken things were. This way it became very hard to go back to old ways of working. We were extremely explicit for quite a long time very loudly about how lousy the things had been.

We also showed a different outcome, credibly. In the world of public policy, there is a dominant economic model or view that says public servants should not back winners or invest in any risk. Let the market provide. In the UK, we had left to the market the health, tax, borders, benefits, and pension systems. We paid billions and left the market to it and our services were scandalously inefficient and mostly did not work in the internet era. People and businesses up and down the country paid for that with their time and money, and the millions of failures to receive services undermined trust in our democratic and political system. Now, a small number of focused people with a real and knowledgeable grasp of the internet did a better job for a fraction of the price. It is hard to take that away.

Several of our works were aimed to be timeless, too. If you go back to our blog posts and read them, they were written to not degrade easily. We used the tools of the open internet to make stuff last. We were writing manuals for public servants for how to do their jobs. We were writing service standards that baked in those ways of working into the common practices. These were designed to last, and they have lasted very well. Those artifacts are more important than any policy papers because they exist today, and they exist in the open. Even when the mandarins remove them, as they are doing now, there remains a historical record of what good looks like.

What Was the Push That Made You Leave after All?

I was unfortunate with the political circumstances and the succession to Francis Maude when he had decided to leave. We knew there would be an election in 2015. The pushback to our reforms got worse at the start of 2014, and it was becoming clear to me I was not going to do a second parliament, as the support from the new civil service leadership and the new minister was just not there. I just could not sustain the cover for all these reforms.

Some top people at Treasury and key critics in departments whose failure to deliver flagship policy had become obvious decided that these reforms threatened their power base, and they were going to push back despite the obvious benefits the work brought. There was no coalition of politicians willing to spend political energy on the reform of civil service, and the chancellor and Number 10, the power base at the heart of the system, were otherwise engaged when it came to ensuring our funding and powers.[9] It would have taken an hour's conversation, or less, from the chancellor to discuss, but his officials stuck to the line that he was not supportive. A line which Number 10 reversed immediately after I resigned.

Also, we had planned the second parliament term to be about government platforms and the ministers were simply not attentive to the issue. Downing Street and the chancellor did not get involved to support the platform play. So, I left but in a high-profile way to shame the government into supporting the business plan, budget, and strategy that it turned down weeks before. They had just spent a lot of time telling everyone how brilliant we were digitally, and then the head of digital goes and walks out and says they are not backing it anymore.

Nonetheless, GDS was in great shape. Stephen Foreshew-Cain was bringing a more managerial and balanced style after years of frantic remedial work. My exit had magically made funding appear for the platform program, and GDS and other departments were maturing their digital talent teams.

I would have preferred to have left in a quieter and more managed way. I felt I did not get chance to say how honored I had been to provide leadership, and how supported I had been in the role by so many.

Would You Ever Take This Job Again?

A decade later, I would not take it now. I had two children whilst doing this job and have small kids now. When I left the role, all aspects of my life were exhausted.

What Are the Skills Necessary to Do This Sort of Job Well?

One needs to have failed. A lot. You need that experience, and I had a lot of it. One needs to have experience at delivering digitally, at scale, to users in their millions, and one has to have complete trust in, and honesty about, the capacity of your teams.

The other thing is that you need to have an astonishingly thick skin and trust your own intuition. And you must be part of a team with the same goals. Reform is a team sport.

What Are Your Bottom-Line Three Recommendations from a Leadership Point of View for Anyone Doing a Similar Job? What Does It Take to Achieve Excellence in Something Like the GDS and Your Work?

It always depends on the context, but I would say that governments are a manifestation of the culture of a nation. With Public Digital, we have helped thirty-six different countries with their digital transformation so far. We see the same patterns everywhere, but that does not mean there are one-size-fits-all answers, the generic "solutions" that get peddled by so many consultancies.

The first recommendation is that whatever culture you leave behind, it should look more like the culture that you would like your country to have. Along the way, you may win or lose or have some success or some failures on the rollouts of a system or a service. Yet, the long-term win is making your government more open, accountable, transparent, democratic, and a bit like you.

Second, everything is about the team. The most important team is the team around you, inside and outside of work. Do not neglect either of those. The friends, the family, the people whose voices and experiences made you the person who took this role are just as equally important as the officials and politicians and suppliers whom you will deal with during the working day. So, do not lose touch with yourself when you go into these big institutions.

Third, get out before you become too tired or when you do not achieve much. It is OK, that is life, move on, do something else. Do not hang around. If you are someone who wants to genuinely improve stuff and it is not improving, then go find something else to do. But be easy on yourself—not everything is going to be improved. If the line of improvement is gradually rising, that is OK.

Notes

1. mySociety is a not-for-profit social enterprise from the UK building and sharing digital technologies that help people be active citizens.
2. The report was called "Directgov 2010 and Beyond: Revolution Not Evolution," published in November 2010.
3. Whitehall is the street in central London where there are many central government offices, including the prime minister's and all the key ministries. That is why Whitehall has also become the colloquial name for whole British government, especially within the government circle itself.
4. Hillsborough disaster was a crush with 97 fatalities during a football match at Hillsborough Stadium in Sheffield, England on April 15, 1989, later found to be caused by negligence and misconduct by police and other services, but no one has been found guilty despite several trials.
5. Efficiency and Reform Group was a unit of the Cabinet Office in the UK, which worked in partnership with the Treasury (i.e., Ministry of Finance) and other departments on initiatives for delivering efficiencies, savings, and reforms across the public sector.
6. Chancellor is short for the Chancellor of the Exchequer—a traditional name for a minister of finance in the British government, in charge of Her Majesty's Treasury department.
7. South Bank is a commercial and entertainment district in central London, right across the Thames River from Westminster, the heart of national government in London. The restaurant was Skylon, a name derived from a famous architectural installation from the 1951 Festival of Britain, as a nod to the first post-war era of technological reform in the UK.
8. A policy view suggested in 1980s on UK national level for how to handle socioeconomic development and resulting civil unrest in the Liverpool area by reducing public funding so that people would choose to relocate to better-off regions.
9. Number 10 or Downing Street refers to the British prime minister, after the address of his/her official residence and office at Downing Street 10 in central London.

CHAPTER 15

Pedro Silva Dias

Portugal

Since 2019 Pedro Silva Dias has been the Group Head of Compliance at Millennium bcp, a leading retail bank in Portugal, with operations in Europe, Africa, and Asia.

Between 2015 and 2019 he was the CEO of AMA—Administrative Modernization Agency, the Portuguese public institution that is responsible for digital public services and digital government solutions.

Before 2015, he held several senior management roles in banking and in the health care industry in Portugal. He started his career as a management consultant at the Boston Consulting Group.

Pedro is a computer science engineer by training, with an MSc from Instituto Superior Técnico in Lisbon. He is also a master in business administration from INSEAD, and has completed executive education in Harvard Business School.

Pedro is a true Portuguese, at least according to my very subjective impression of a Portuguese style—which has been greatly informed by him and his team, for sure.

Pedro's style of work is very formal and informal at the same time. Very methodological, yet very relaxed at once. He is always joyous, but always also very serious. Serious about the "business" of making government better through digital means and about making lives of people better.

So, these traits are not all contradictory. The fact that they can be complementary perhaps shows that national cultures (or at least the stereotypes) do not matter in digital government; they do not determine excellence in this field. But good managers and leaders do, and Pedro is one of them.

He is clearly a man of delivery, and a man of good service delivery, especially. His challenge in Portugal was to take over the program and agency that had done great strides but gotten stuck somehow. He is another example of having a strong private sector experience under the belly can be of great benefit to make change happen in the public sector, too, and at an accelerated pace.

—SIIM

How Did You Enter the Digital Government Leadership Role in Portugal?

The story began in 2014. In Portugal, we were at the time under external aid or financial support from the International Monetary Fund and the European Union (EU). The government was pursuing a new strategy for deploying public services with a focus on optimizing the network of physical service outlets, while improving digital adoption and digital offering of services. It brought more attention to customer experience, and back then no one was really used to the expression "customer experience" in the public sector.

I was invited by the government to bring in some of the experience that I had from a Portuguese leading bank on streamlining and optimizing service delivery models, at the same time increasing the customer satisfaction with the services provided. I became responsible for a special task force working for nine months with Minister Miguel Poiares Maduro, within the Council of Ministers.

This minister was also politically responsible for the Administrative Modernization Agency (AMA), and wanted to further enhance the role of this agency in the area of public service delivery. He asked me to lead it from the beginning of 2015.

Did You Have Any Hesitations for Joining the Government?

For sure! I had about fifteen years of professional experience from the private sector. I had been a management consultant: I had worked in health care, I had worked in banking. But I had no experience with the public sector or with political affairs.

It was something that I had to think very thoroughly through. It was not a very clear decision from the beginning, and I had back-and-forth thoughts. It took me three or four months before finally accepting the invitation and deciding it would be good—for both Portugal and me.

What convinced me in the end, I think, were the conversations with the minister about his vision and objectives. That led me to an understanding on what was doable and what not, how to make the challenge of changing the public sector more achievable.

Did You Have Any Conditions for Taking the Role?

There were a couple of them to make me confident and empowered to take on the role.

First, I did not have any political experience, but I had some friends in managerial roles in the public sector, and I asked for their advice. They suggested to ask for a very strong mandate from the prime minister. The legislative piece launching our task force, a resolution from the Council of Ministers, got personally signed and promoted by the then Prime Minister Pedro Passos Coelho, as a sign that it should be taken seriously.

Another condition was the staffing and resources for the task force at first and then AMA. This is what took probably the most time: to come up with a common position in the beginning. I did get the opportunity to hire people as technical consultants, management consultants, recruiting them from public agencies and from private companies as well.

Another important thing was the ability to have a project management office, or PMO, set up as professional consultants who would monitor the delivery of the program and the key objectives.

You Said That the Minister's Vision Was Key—What Was the Objective He Set for You and Expected You to Deliver?

He had three concerns to solve or three objectives for me.

The first one was to help them create a doable vision and strategy. Of course, they had a political agenda already, quite clear in public speeches and keynotes. But they also really needed someone who could come up with a strategy that was doable, implementable, and that could be tracked quarter after quarter. This was what I most worked on in the first six months. We ended up with a robust plan from vision down to the follow-up metrics.

Second objective, and probably the one that we less successfully achieved I am afraid, was to promote more cooperation between the public services. Worldwide and surely in Portugal, there are a lot of silos in the public administration. There were fights, contests, enmity between leaders and managers of different agencies, entrenched in their positions that sometimes they held for twenty or more years in office. I was expected to be a fresh face, someone with no political affiliations or agendas, no legacy of any kind—someone who could build bridges. We got some of that done, but overall, less than on other objectives.

The third one was a very practical objective of improving the work and output of AMA. AMA in Portugal is quite a big agency, with two hundred fifty fixed staff members and a rolling set of hundred or hundred-fifty external consultants and service providers. Overall, you have some four hundred people working at the agency. It is also very much at the center of government, has a lot of power in terms of approving ICT expenditures and funding from EU Structural Funds. So, it is important that this agency works well, smoothly, and that its services are delivered on time without significant claims from other agencies or political parties.

What Was the Digital Government Situation Like Otherwise at That Time in Portugal?

Very many pillars and building blocks were already there, built up in years before. The citizen card as our digital identity; an interoperability platform, even if not perfect but working; open data portal and open data agenda were in place. "Only once" services and protocols were already starting to be implemented. All the key core components and building blocks of good digital services were working, though they all could be improved.

The problem was that the use of these services and platforms by the public sector agencies was very low. It is like you have the roadways, but you do not have cars going back and forth. So, the most pressing challenge was that we have the infrastructure, let us use it. Let us produce content, let us produce services. Then let us in parallel also work on the adoption side—let us incentivize citizens to use the services.

What Milestones Did You Set Yourself at the Beginning in Your Role?

To be honest, my initial thinking was that I really needed to learn, and to learn fast. As I had not worked in the public sector before; I did not have the personal connections, the network, the professional credibility of implemented projects yet.

My initial objective was in thirty days or sixty days to grasp the most important details of all the ongoing projects that were delayed and not working properly. Next, I needed to be able to contribute to a solution, to prove myself useful.

Of course, this was a very short-term objective. As I got comfortable with the projects, with the teams, with my direct reports, I rapidly shifted to what were the three higher objectives of the political managers and my minister. That is why I very rapidly started working on the strategy.

I also immediately adopted new management procedures. That was relatively easy for me because I had been the leader of an operational transformation unit at my previous job in banking. We were responsible for changing the processes and for improving work within the bank.

Another aim was to build up my network within the Portuguese public administration, to very rapidly get to know the most important stakeholders. It was necessary to get a very easy-going and effective cooperation, to be able to convince them to deliver and to deploy digital services using our platforms.

What Was Your Method for Learning Really Fast, as You Set Out to Do This as the Very First Thing?

I was privileged because we had a large set of very senior and experienced people in AMA, both in terms of technical skills as well as tenure. We had people who had worked at AMA since its inception. People who really knew all the stages and phases that the agency had gone through in its maturing process. We had even some previous cabinet members for ministers and secretaries of state: very well-connected people with a very solid knowledge of all the ecosystem that was fundamental to our job.

So, I tried learning from them all during my initial period. Talking to people a lot, picking their brain. This could have been difficult because as you talk to different people, you get different perspectives and if you are new, you do not know which version to go with. However, the predominant case was that all these people were very, very helpful in getting me up to speed.

I have always been a very detailed person, with a very hands-on approach—I go into details. I like to read the technical stuff; I am a computer science engineer by training. So, I took deep dives on the projects, on the business requirements, the technical solutions, and protocols. That helped me a lot as a I moved along.

What Was Your Method for Rapidly Building Up the Relationships?

I would say I had both a collective and an individual approach.

I am a fan of individual approaches. I had a lot of breakfasts, a lot of lunches with people. Not because of their importance or their title like CEO or CIO, but because they had something to share from my point of view. I prioritized access to information rather than seniority. I was looking much more to talking to people who had knowledge about projects, about past experiences, about why some stuff had not worked properly.

Of course, we also used a lot of events and even informal sessions to bring people from different angles and different agencies together. That is the collective part. As AMA is the central government agency that screens ICT expenditures and approves EU funded projects, we did workshops and even brainstorming sessions with the agencies that applied for funds or approval. I had a lot of opportunities to be part of several meetings with very diverse people from all sides of government, including local government structures as well.

What Did the Strategy You Came Up With Look Like? What Was Its Time Horizon?

I am not sure we ever put up a strict deadline on our vision and our objectives. More than three years is infinity in this field of ours, with the pace that new technologies are developed and the adoption of new tech. Planning for five years or more just did not make sense. That is why our plan was based on performance metrics, and none of them exceeded the next three to four years.

The strategy ended up having four pillars. The first one was more on the managerial side, on the digital service offering side. The aim was to increase the range of digital services available in new channels. We had a lot of legacy services and standard means such as web portals. But we lacked innovative approaches, especially for mobile platforms.

Second was the demand side. We were lagging behind the EU average in digital service uptake. This had a lot to do with the aging of our population, also with the digital literacy of the population. We had a lot to do there so that we could later increase the adoption of digital services.

The third pillar was interoperability, and this had a lot to do with efficiency. We needed to get data reused between the services, to make services better for people and not oblige them to use things in silos.

The fourth and final pillar was to improve the content that government provides to citizens—the way we presented information, the real customer experience.

This Is a Wide Agenda—How Did You Choose Where to Focus or What to Prioritize? How Did You Sequence the Actions?

Surely we had to prioritize or sequence. Sometimes we had to put some initiatives on hold, if resources were contested. However, a lot of these actions were perfectly doable in parallel, as they had different teams behind them.

We did not have to do it all by ourselves. For example, digital literacy and digital adoption work got a lot of support from local government structures. We only had to steer their engagement and their digital literacy programs for the local populations, as opposed to the interoperability stream, which was much more reliant on our own efforts and projects within AMA. There we not only developed the strategy but also we owned the infrastructure, and we had to build and grow the platform ourselves.

When it comes to the building blocks, we sometimes had to take several months to convince a specific agency to use the platforms. This certainly delayed rollout of some other work or services. But some of these building blocks are so important, and in my personal opinion we were not wasting time—we were investing time. The effort usually proved to be beneficial later on.

We were very effective in joining up the initiatives and actions from all parts of society. This was mainly done through comprehensive big programs such as the Simplex program, already in the government of Prime Minister António Costa, which was a mass collection of concrete projects to simplify and modernize the public services (and not only digitally). It was a lot of work to compile the program, because we gathered initiatives and ideas from all different kind of companies, labor structures, other agencies, cabinet members, even individual citizens. We did a lot of cocreation with them, too. In some years, we had two hundred or more different implementable initiatives in the Simplex plan. It showed the momentum that we had managed to instill and the umbrella we provided, because we did not deliver all or most of them ourselves at all.

Another interesting program that we leveraged was called Govtech, launched by then Secretary of State Graça Fonseca, where we challenged entrepreneurs and start-ups to come up with tech projects designed to improve public services. We joined with several sponsors and partners to fund those projects.

How Easy Was It to Retain Focus through the Delivery Years? How Much Did Your Priorities Change?

The most important deliverables stayed the same, even with the change of governments. This was probably not the case with most of our colleagues in other agencies. Surely some priorities did change within the bigger plan.

For example, in first years we worked quite a bit engaging the companies and coming up with public and private partnerships for a better service experience. When governments changed, there was more appetite for government-led work instead. Flagship projects such as Simplex and Participative Budgets rapidly became more of a priority. It meant that we had to adjust to a new political context, refocus a bit the course of action—but the overall goals and line stayed the same.

What Were the Tools in AMA's Disposal to Ensure Delivery and Get Other Agencies to Come Along?

One is pretty straightforward and that is formal power. We were within the center of government; we were directly reporting to the minister in charge of the Council of Ministers, Mrs. Maria Manuel Leitão Marques.[1] It meant we had a voice to positively influence the legislative agenda and push through government decrees for digital service adoption in agencies. It also helped that we had incredible and supportive government members, such as Minister Marques and then Secretary of State Graça Fonseca—very powerful government leaders, very knowledgeable, and very goal oriented.

The second level was the existence of the most important building blocks. Even if they were not widely used back in 2014 or 2015, they were working and that made us credible within the public administration.

The third and most important instrument has been already mentioned. AMA had the power of vetting and approving both the use of EU Structural Funds and ICT expenditures for every entity (with some very few exceptions, such as the tax authority). Everyone had to come to AMA to get funding for new ICT or digital projects, explain their motivation, their goals. We were able to attach strategic conditions to the disbursement of money and get agencies on board for things such as using the common authentication platform or feeding data to the national open data portal.

You Mentioned That You Started Changing the Management Procedures. What Was Your Management Style Like?

People have always told me, and especially within AMA, that in comparison to some of the predecessors I was a very talkative and a hands-on manager. We had a lot of people thirty to forty years old. They found the traditional leaders very distant, very formal, very hierarchical, and I am nothing of the sort.

I used to walk along the corridors, enter their rooms, jump into discussions. I am not a cabinet person. I do not sit in my office and call people to come in and explain things to me. I like to walk around and sit down with people, discuss with them. I love whiteboards, or blackboards even; I like to sketch things. This is from my background and formal training. As a computer science engineer, I studied software architecture a lot and I love to draw building blocks, protocols, layers, and so on. I love to discuss this all with the team.

People felt this was what they needed. I do believe it helped to create a cohesive team and very strong bonding within the agency.

I must be sincere that this style does have a drawback, of course. I like to know details, such as why are we going to use a certain protocol on these web servers or why is there a different certificate now for that authentication protocol. It is great for me, but sometimes it is an unnecessary burden on teams when things are already a bit delayed or when stress is mounting. I understand that it is not actually my job to be into details, and so I tried to limit it more as we went along. However, it does work great for making people close to you and have them take you as one of them.

How Did You Change the Team in AMA?

It changed quite a bit.

Some people were of the legacy type that you always have in public administration, at least in Portugal. During my tenure, a lot of them gradually left, although I never explicitly pushed anyone out. It happened as the environment changed, the daily priorities changed, the management structure evolved.

In a broad sense, there was in the end a higher mix of people with technical backgrounds and from outside the public administration, with no previous links to government. I brought in people from very different backgrounds, on purpose. I had the opportunity to hire lawyers who were experienced in innovation matters such as cocreation or partnerships with private sector. Before we had only had legal experts for public procurement or similar.

In the beginning, I also brought in people to the design side—the creative side of digital. They worked to design good interfaces, to simplify the language and communication with citizens, to improve usability.

In addition, I strengthened the team in business management and controlling functions. One of the issues in public administration, and AMA in particular, was that there was a lack of managerial control or a PMO way of doing things. I got some people from other agencies for this line, but also three or four private sector people who were specialists in managerial monitoring practices.

What Was Your Selling Pitch to Convince People to Join?

It was not easy. There were several cases when I lost the argument and did not get people to jump onboard.

The most convincing argument usually was to use my own experience; I was repeating that over and over. I was quite a young guy, back then: thirty-six, thirty-seven. I kept telling people that I myself had not had experience in the public sector, I had come from private companies. That it showed that it was possible to do things differently and to make a contribution coming from the private sector. There were plenty of opportunities for you to grow, to become CEOs or take other senior managerial roles with this experience to show for.

I also was able to convince them because I had no political affiliation. I was credible in this sense.

This all convinced specifically people in the age range, say, between twenty-six and thirty-two. That is the age when people usually have an ambition to grow, but they often are at some point stuck in their current careers. They see the change as an opportunity to do a different thing.

Another pitch was again from my own previous experience. I had come from the biggest private bank in Portugal, with more than 2.5 million customers. But then you come to the public sector and you really have the entire country to serve. If you come to AMA, you will have the freedom to propose and to innovate, to experiment or test new services for the entire country. Everybody on the street will have your product and use it.

Who Was Your Most Valuable Hire?

During my tenure I was privileged to be able to hire a lot valuable people.

But I could maybe single out an external consultant with AMA who knew us well, and whom AMA knew very well as well. He came into a new role we created. In rough translation, he became the manager for digital adoption.

He had a small team, but a very broad area of everything that had an impact on digital adoption. It might begin with digital literacy programs and trainings, involve usability of specific systems or creating incentives for citizens to adopt some services. Essentially, his work was to identify opportunities for rapidly increasing the digital adoption of all systems. But he had to prioritize in that sense. Thus, he had to understand where we would reap the most rapid rewards.

He was not an engineer, not a tech guy in terms of formal background; his training was in management. As such, he brought what the team lacked—the view of cost-benefit analysis. Where would we have smaller costs for the larger benefits? That became quite useful.

What Kind of Culture Did You Try to Build in AMA?

I tried to build it by managing by example, to set the example.

First, to make it clear that we were there to explore and to innovate. We will have quality controls at some point along the way; we will test stuff before production—so do not worry about failing! You will not crash the country. By the way, we ended up having some scares every now and then but it is part of the journey.

I did not love agencies that were just comfortable doing the same stuff over and over again. I wanted people to always find something to change in the way we were doing things, even if these were very tiny details. This comes from my professional background, as in the beginning of my career, I worked a lot with lean and Six Sigma methodologies. These give you the mentality that you are always on a journey, you never reach your destination. There is always room for improvement, for identifying waste. Already on recruiting I was trying to make sure that the new people coming onboard would have this motivation and drive in them to always do things differently.

The second aspect of the culture I tried to foster is another part of my personality and something that I understood was lacking in AMA. It was teamwork. There were a lot of silos within AMA, at first, with a lot of line managers who had formed their alliances. I had to force it in the beginning, even if a bit artificially, before it soon became more natural. I started several programs and initiatives to join people together and create cross-functional teams, making people talk to each other. Simple things like significantly increasing the number of social events and gatherings. I even hired a specialized consultant on human resources management and team building. He came up with formal diagnostics and designed a series of steps to promote more mingling and team melting. It did not always work out. Even after four years, some of my direct reports still had issues in working together—a little bittersweet aftertaste for me.

One thing we tried was putting people up for short-term project work in our political cabinet. We sent them for a few days or a week to help the state secretary to cocreate some new initiatives, for example. When you are in contact with people at that level, you have to become more cooperative. We selected such engagements and people for them strategically.

What Were Your Sound Bites or Slogans You Kept Repeating to the Team?

There were three words that we put in our slides each time, even if these were not officially our motto: "Simplify. Innovate. Cooperate."

I also have a personal motto that everyone knew. I oftentimes showed it when I was making presentations. It is from James Cameron, the famous film director, and it goes, "Hope is not a strategy. Luck is not a factor. Fear is not an option." You have to work, and you have to plan ahead. You cannot sit back and hope that everything turns out for the best. You need to prepare. Then you do not need luck. You also cannot be fearful to innovate, explore, test different things. As I used it so much, I guess it translated a little bit into the culture at AMA.

What Routines or Rituals Did You Use to Manage the Team?

I tried to balance some very formal approaches with very informal daily habits. You need both.

As an engineer, I know that stuff either works or not. It is binary, true or false. Therefore, I believe in formal approaches to that end.

Our every new system had to have a project charter, including a clear identification of resources needed. It needed to have a really strict and detailed time plan, structured and formal monitoring of all the activities in the plan. If there was a delay or higher-than-expected consumption of resources, we had to explain why and explain the deviation. I am a believer in this approach because of the motto from James Cameron. You need to work to guarantee that work brings results. Hope is not a strategy.

However, being excessively formal will risk making people very distant, very uncooperative, very ironical. That is why I always try to balance these formal approaches with very informal and easygoing interactions. Picked up a cup of coffee or even some cookies and went to talk to people working on the project, joining the flow.

The balance is to keep a formal frequency of meetings and follow-ups, but on daily basis be close to people and have their confidence. Even if you are the boss, your job is to help them find solutions to things.

Are There Things You Regret Not Doing in AMA or Things You Think You Failed At?

I would not call them failures, or at least complete failures. But there are results that I did not achieve as I wanted.

The first one is more an institutional matter, linked with the changing political agenda. My belief is that citizens do not distinguish or do not want to distinguish between private and public services, as long as their needs are taken care of. I never bought this distinction between the sectors. That is why, in my perspective, we should have done more to increase the number of partnerships and interoperable services between public agencies and private companies. Yet, this was not a political priority after the government changed during my tenure.

The second thing is about my ability to manage AMA for delivery. We had asymmetrical improvements. We had a couple of strong successes in some areas. Everything related to digital ID such as the use of citizen cards or the flagship project of Digital Mobile Key, for example.[2] At the same time, we were not successful beyond some small stuff in use of open data and reuse of data. I believe that we could have done more if I had more time. We did work a lot, given the resources we had, and the team did a great job. But as we had to prioritize sometimes; digital ID work was always much more important.

The third one is more on a personal level, and this is the one that bothers me the most. I feel I was unable to reach out enough to some of the most important stakeholders in our public administration. Although I developed some very strong friendship bonds with some core stakeholders and we still keep in touch down the road now, there were a few whom I was not able to bring onboard. It might have to do with incompatibility of priorities, characters, or conflicts of agency agendas. If I could go back and improve something, I would dedicate more time to anticipate such resistances and devise specific engagement actions.

What Are You Most Proud of Achieving?

We did several good flagship projects and meaningful changes in our society. In terms of specific solutions, I would emphasize the impact of ID platforms that are being used widely now—they exploded into use. In particular, the new ways for authentication in mobile phones. The Digital Mobile Key is a widespread success in Portugal; every private service is keen on using it. Banking and other sectors can this way get citizen data from public registries to serve people better.

As I am a people's person and a guy from the field, I found the success of Citizen Spots truly gratifying. It is a digital kiosk or a physical front office, where they teach how to use digital services and increase digital literacy. These are available nationwide, including in rural areas. The concept existed already before I joined AMA, with a great incentive from Minister Miguel Poiares Maduro, and his team of state secretaries, Joaquim Pedro Cardoso da Costa and António Leitão Amaro. We were able to take it to a completely new level, significantly enlarging the number of digital services that were available through them and, especially, the size and density of the network. There were thirty spots in Portugal when I joined, six hundred when I left. They truly made a difference in bringing digital services to people who previously were not able to use them.

Another success was on the delivery and usability of digital services from other agencies. We designed a customer experience and usability toolkit, especially for smaller public agencies. It came with a lot of snippets and reusable code that they could use. It helped many agencies to upgrade and revamp their web platforms, along with the available funding from the EU Structural Funds.

Yet another great outcome was the way we got people engaged in our diverse programs. It was important for the quality of the initiatives. Merit of their outcome goes not to us but to people who spent time to participate in these cocreation sessions all over the country—for

Simplex, for Govtech, for others—digitally, too, through our social media channels or dedicated websites we created to gather ideas and suggestions.

The more rural or remote the area, the more people were starving to be listened to. So, whenever you engage with them and show that their voice counts, they show up. In cities, it is a little bit harder. You need to show them that you will really walk the talk and do things. Success breeds success. It became easier once we showed how we had taken the ideas from last year and implemented them. It shows that you are accountable and not there for just the politics.

Why Did You Decide to Move from AMA and Back to Private Sector?

It was a combination of two factors that coincided.

On the one hand, there was a cycle coming to an end. My then Secretary of State, Graça Fonseca, was promoted to minister of culture. The minister herself, Maria Manuel Leitão Marques, got elected to the European Parliament, and a new cycle was about to begin. I could have stayed, sure, there was a lot to be done still.

But about the same time, I was invited to a very interesting and senior position in the bank that I had previously worked at. I was called to become the chief compliance officer and general director at the group level. This was professionally challenging and appealing to me.

Portugal had made great progress in many ways. Our entry to Digital Nations group was a testament to that and in some ways encouraged me to move on.[3] I had learned a lot and developed myself as a person and as a manager.

What Did You Learn the Most in Your Time in AMA?

It is a completely different frame of mind to constantly need to seduce, engage, energize, motivate, convince others to work with you—like you have to do in a public agency and as a leader of the national digital services agenda. You need to have partners everywhere. If you are a very senior manager or board member of a big private company, you compete with other companies, you do not necessarily rely that much on external partners although you do hire them. The importance of working within a network of people as a leader of a public agency—it really puts you out of your comfort zone. That was surely one of the things that I developed most in myself.

Another area of development was my ability to be a general manager. I had managed teams of several dozen people before AMA. In my previous bank job, I was managing a sizable team of some eighty people. But it is quite different from managing an entire organization of three or four hundred people. You are the ultimate guy setting the strategy and approving stuff there. You do not go any higher up, you need to take the shots. That makes you grow up quite rapidly.

Do You Feel You Ever Got Used to the Public Sector?

I do, at least to the extent that it allowed me to steer AMA forward and to create a productive organization that has very competent and professional people. As said, the scale and number of interactions you need to conduct to get anything done or approved is far more "particular" in the public sector than private sector.

When you are dealing with innovation and digital creation, you cannot cope with standard administrative processes that take you six months to approve projects and several dozen interactions with all relevant stakeholders. That is the reason why you have to invest your first hundred days in understanding all the processes, all the obstacles, and requirements. Then you can later use them as efficiently as possible. Otherwise, innovation will always stay on paper or stuck in bureaucracy and red tape.

What Were the Remaining and Next Challenges Ahead for AMA and Digital Government in Portugal?

I believe that I left AMA with a new and more robust team culture, with new optimized internal processes, and especially with more thorough and business-oriented management practices. AMA had gotten a team unity, cohesion, and a pride that the agency lacked before.

Moving forward I guess the agency had to prepare for a much faster innovation cycle on digital services provisioning. As I said, people just want to have fast, efficient, and easy services to satisfy their needs, no matter who is providing them. The digital readiness of the Portuguese population will make it easier for the adoption of digital services, but it will definitely make it much more demanding in terms of customer satisfaction and user experience expectations. I know the agency was well-prepared in terms of skillful and experienced people, but the financial resources are always an issue.

What Steps Did You Take to Make Sure That What You Started Would Last?

It is all about people and the culture instilled in the organization. Of course, we had a lot of formal changes and new processes being written and designed. Yet, all that can be easily replaced or changed. What matters most is what people want, how motivated they are, and what they believe in. As I left the agency, my strong conviction is that all senior managers would keep improving AMA and make it much better. The "sense of belonging" was truly high. As such, the agency was prepared to endure the new challenges and to even start a new growth stage.

What Are Your Three Key Recommendations to Fellow Digital Government Leaders on How to Be Effective in This Role?

The first one is to really have an ambitious, but doable, strategy and action plan. It is important that you understand where you want to arrive in an achievable time frame. Not to project out ten-year future scenarios, but concrete and observable three- or four-year objectives. You do need a good and objective strategy plan.

Second, it is a people business. You really do need to be surrounded by committed, knowledgeable, and innovative people. You cannot make it in this field if you are not in a team of engaged and innovative people. Invest a lot in people, in enhancing your own team, and in empowering them.

Third, a digital government leader is a central figure in an ecosystem. Therefore, you should understand and steer that ecosystem. It is very important to identify and manage all the traditional stakeholders: promoters, detractors, adopters, and so on. Leading change requires cooperation, partnerships, and even alliances with them. To be an effective leader in the building and adoption of new and transformative policies and digital solutions, it is fundamental that you understand, manage, and steer all the different players who are part of your digital government environment.

Notes

1. Maria Manuel Leitão Marques was the minister of the presidency and of administrative modernisation in Portugal in 2015–2019.
2. Digital Mobile Key is called *Chave Móvel Digital* in Portuguese.
3. Digital Nations is an international forum of some of the leading digital governments. Founded in 2014, it had 10 member countries in 2021, including Portugal since 2018.

CHAPTER 16

Randall Brugeaud

Australia

R andall Brugeaud has spent in total more than thirty years working in a range of public and private sector roles, with a major focus on transformation.

Randall was appointed head of the Simplified Trade System Implementation Task-force on July 1, 2021, a reform to simplify Australia's cross-border trade system. Prior to that role, Randall spent three years as the CEO of the Digital Transformation Agency (DTA). In April 2020, Randall was also appointed as the inaugural head of the Australian Public Service (APS) Digital Profession to raise the digital capability of the APS workforce.

Before the DTA, Randall was the deputy Australian statistician and chief operating officer at the Australian Bureau of Statistics. Prior to that, he was the CIO at both the former Department of Immigration and Border Protection and the Australian Customs and Border Protection Service. He previously spent more than a decade working with the Boston Consulting Group and a private IT consulting firm, which he founded and operated.

Randall holds a master of business administration degree, a graduate diploma in applied computing, and a bachelor of education degree. He is also a senior executive fellow of the Harvard Kennedy School.

What happens when you mix together a technologist, a business consultant, a top civil servant, a skillful communicator, and a network operator, adding a touch of the nicest personality, and a heavy dose of steady discipline? You get Randall.

He brought a breadth of experience and expertise to the job of kick-starting digital government work at Australia's federal level. If Randall would not have succeeded in making visible change happen and stick after several prior stuck attempts—then no one could.

Well, he did succeed splendidly in moving the DTA as an agency and all the government digital work from shambles to a level of astounding strength. Under his watch, Australia became one of the governments that truly put the crisis of COVID-19 pandemic to good use for accelerating digital services in the country.

Randall's story is fascinating also for his focus on the whole of government mechanisms and work, and the results he achieved there—considering Australia's federation and Westminster model of governance, in particular. This chapter offers food for thought on how to skillfully operate across silos and change that game, hopefully for good.

—Siim

What Is Your Background Story—How Did You End Up in a Digital Government Leadership Role in Australia?

I did not start off thinking that I was going to be a digital professional. Having grown up in mining towns, I was originally leaning toward being a mining engineer. I had a change of heart just as I was about to commence my university studies. While mining towns were great places to grow up as a kid, I was keen to spread my wings a bit and give the "big smoke" [a large city] a try.

About a month before I was due to start my first semester, I switched to a teaching degree. Needing to study topics like philosophy, psychology, and sociology had me asking myself if I had made a big mistake. The humanities were extremely challenging for a person who had focused almost exclusively on science and mathematics for their schooling life. In hindsight, it was a very good thing though. It activated my creative side; it helped me to deal with ambiguity, build arguments, and communicate and engage with people.

As I was approaching the end of my third year as an undergraduate, I came to realize that teaching was a profession that focused much more on seniority than it did on performance and the potential in terms of progression. It dawned on me that my progression through the ranks would be limited by the speed with which the more senior teachers either resigned, retired, or passed away. Given my background in science and mathematics, I decided to reskill early. That took me to enroll in a post-graduate IT course in applied computing, which I doubled up in my last semester of my teaching degree. It was an incredibly demanding load, but it introduced me to IT and led me to discover the digital government area.

As part of my major study, I developed an expert system that I was ultimately able to sell to the Australian government. My interest in working in government started there. I applied for and won a graduate role with the Australian Taxation Office. I started as a developer and worked through almost every ICT role you could imagine. After seven years, I reached a point where I wanted to apply my skills and experience more broadly, rather than just spending my time in one agency. I branched out into consulting, and I set up my own consulting firm, which I operated for more than a decade. During this time, I worked across a wide range of government agencies and agendas.

Although the work was incredibly rewarding, I experienced what many digital professionals encounter at some point in their career, particularly as they become more senior: a certain stigma associated with being a technical professional rather than a generalist. Rather than just accepting this perception, I decided to undertake an MBA degree. This provided an excellent learning opportunity for me, but also provided a credential that I had the skills and knowledge to operate as a general business leader, not just a technology leader.

After completing my MBA, I joined the Boston Consulting Group (BCG) as a consultant. This provided yet another learning opportunity in an environment where I was able to work with an amazing and diverse group of people in solving complex problems. I spent just over two years with BCG. I then returned to the public sector because I had a strong desire to be directly responsible for major impactful change rather than just advising on it. I wanted to be able to make a difference at scale. I was able to be involved in solving a range of wicked problems, starting with immigration and border protection, through to financial services, customs, and then assisting in the integration of the immigration and customs functions into what is now known as the home affairs.

I then moved in the role of chief operating officer at the Australian Bureau of Statistics. I had responsibility for their transformation program, technology functions, as well as ministerial and parliamentary services, human resource management, communications, media, and the methodologies the statisticians used. After I had been at the Bureau for about year, I was asked to take on the CEO role in the Digital Transformation Agency (DTA). Despite the job being large and complex, I saw it as an opportunity too good to pass up. Not everyone saw it the same way though, with some people suggesting that it was a hospital pass!

Why Did You Take the DTA Role and Why Were You Approached?

I saw the role as an opportunity to be able to have real impact at scale. I was motivated by the potential to have a lasting impact, one that was deeper than simply expanding my résumé. The role provided me with a set of accountabilities that allowed me to lead a set of structural reforms that could be made enduring. This is why I had rejoined the public service before.

The prospect of being directly responsible for the way the Australian Government approached digital to enable transformation was incredibly exciting. It brought together all my previous skills and experience and tested all of them. It allowed me to apply my experience in solving some of the most difficult problems at a time when governments globally were becoming more and more reliant on digital to conduct their business.

How I found my way into the DTA role is quite interesting, at least I think so. When I applied for my previous role as COO at the Australia Bureau of Statistics, the then DTA CEO, Gavin Slater, was on the selection panel. I ended up winning the role, and Gavin and I kept in touch. We caught up a few times to share our experiences and we talked a lot about whole of government transformation. About twelve months later I got a call from Gavin that he was planning to undertake some executive training in the US for a few months. We caught up in the following week and I ended up agreeing to act in the DTA CEO role for a few months.

It was basically a short-term consultancy. I spent a lot of time thinking about what they were doing and how they were doing it. I produced a ten-page summary deck that I presented back to Gavin on his return. The key points were my assessment of the current environment and a set of recommendations for things that should be done right away, things that should be done in the next three months, and things that should be done in the next year. It was an action plan for the DTA and for the whole-of-government digital more broadly.

I then returned to the Australian Bureau of Statistics and planned to continue the job I had left a few months earlier. It did not quite work out that way though, because soon after his return from the US, Gavin decided to move back into the private sector. Several people were considered for the role. It needed a very specific set of skills and experience as it was a very high profile, and a very complex job. Following a series of interviews, I was very pleased to be offered the role. I was appointed in June 2018 and started as the new DTA CEO the next month.

What Was the Expectation or the Mission Given to You with the Job?

The government's commitment to a more integrated approach to digital and to service delivery was crystal clear. I was expected to build support and navigate the complexities of government in a way that was both strategic and tactical. There was a need to build trust and confidence through rapid delivery, but also a need to build confidence that we had a strategic vision for the future.

The challenge in these types of roles is to be effective at a whole-of-government level where there are such a broad range of stakeholders and interests. The fact that you typically do not have direct control over all the levers you might need and the expectations being very high takes it to a whole other level. It is a very challenging place to be. It requires skillful navigation of the public service. It requires strong relationships, and it requires focus. I observed dozens and dozens of key priorities when I acted in the CEO role, when there should have only been six or seven.

So, the task was a matter of sifting and sorting through the work and building coalitions and support, while at the same time delivering incremental value and creating a strategy for the organization and government more broadly to move forward.

Did You Have Any Asks or Conditions Going into the Job?

One of the most critical asks was related to support. Having strong support and regular access to key public service leaders and the minister was fundamental to being able to have the required impact. I spent the first few weeks in the role making sure that I was clear on the minister's priorities and the expectations of government and key leaders across the public service.

If I was unable to get the support required or could not demonstrate the value that gave people confidence, there was a real risk that the DTA would cease to exist. Remember that I was CEO number five for the DTA in a span of just three years. There was a real risk that if we did not get this right, DTA would not be given another chance.

Tell a Bit More on the Context You Had to Start From—What Was the State of Digital Government in Australia, Also What Was Going on with DTA?

As with most countries, Australia was a long-term user of technology in government. I would argue that this was more of the "traditional" way of thinking about ICT, though. Many saw it as a back-office function, or a line item on the balance sheet rather than a strategic, differentiating capability. Transformation programs were invariably large, multiyear affairs that continually asked for more and more money and never actually delivered value to users or government.

Although this was the context in which we were operating, it was broadly understood that organizations, including government, were becoming more and more reliant on ICT and digital. They needed to do something differently. It was not sustainable to continue to increase budgets to deal with increasing volumes or complexity. Nor was it sustainable to respond to failures by investing in monolithic transformation programs focused on a particular platform, service, or silo of government. This could never achieve the outcomes the government was looking for. It was going to be critical for us as a nation to take a more coordinated approach.

The DTA was the most recent evolution in this path. It had followed a decade or more of central, whole-of-government policy functions that ultimately resulted in the creation of the Digital Transformation Office (DTO). The DTO sat within the government's communications portfolio and was tasked with looking at how to take a more user-focused, integrated approach to digital in the government. Communications was a relatively small portfolio, but it had the strong support of government through the then Prime Minister Malcolm Turnbull.

An interim CEO was appointed while a global recruitment campaign was undertaken. Paul Shetler was recruited as the DTO's first permanent CEO. Paul came with experience from the UK, including time with the Government Digital Service there. He came in with a bang. He made a lot of noise and people most definitely noticed he had arrived. I was working as the CIO of the Department of Immigration and Border Protection at the time and was involved in a few briefings with Paul and his team. Although Paul ruffled quite a few feathers, he showed people the potential of digital. He led several exemplars and started to build the foundations for a number of the whole of government digital platforms we have today. He also led the organization through a move to the prime minister's portfolio and a rebranding to the Digital Transformation Agency (DTA).

The agenda stalled though, with exemplars hitting dead ends and whole of government platforms struggling to gain traction. Government responded by changing the leadership. Paul was replaced by a very experienced public service leader as interim CEO while the hunt for a new CEO was undertaken. Gavin Slater was selected as the new DTA CEO. He brought lots of private sector experience in business, digital, and customer service, but he was new to the public service. Gavin created more order and structure, but it took time for him to learn how things get done in government. He did not initially understand the conventions or processes and worked hard at building the networks he needed to effectively deliver at scale. Gavin still did help to drive forward the whole of government digital agenda.

What Was the Team Feeling with All These Shuffles? What Sort of Team Did You Take Over?

The DTA team that I inherited included a range of skilled technical professionals who were passionate about digital. There was a mix of people with experience from both within and outside government.

We had lots of people who had just joined government, who injected skills and experience from their time in the private sector. We also had a number of experienced public servants who understood how government worked and had a range of connections on which we could build. Then between these two groups we had people who had some government expertise and either digital or nondigital professional backgrounds from the private sector. It was a diverse, high potential workforce.

The reactions I received from DTA staff as the new CEO were highly varied. Some people saw me as a "bureaucrat" who had been brought in to add process, stifle creativity, and slow things down. Others welcomed my skills, experience, my networks, and saw this as a real opportunity to move the DTA and the whole of government digital to the next level.

The two months I had been acting in the role helped me to hit the ground running. I was able to launch into the role and connect with staff. The advice I had provided to Gavin formed my playbook, which allowed me to massively accelerate my transition and implement the required changes. By the end of the first month, I had already been able to reset and refocus our priorities, plus adjust our operating model to deliver.

I also brought in some new people and made some adjustments to my executive team. I assembled people in a way that created a more logical alignment with what the government and the public service needed us to do.

What Was the Mandate for DTA When You Started? What Were the Agency's Levers to Do the Whole-Of-Government Job?

At the highest level, the role of DTA was to provide whole-of-government leadership for digital and ICT. We had policy and strategy functions along with the delivery, administrative, and governance functions. Our mandate was very broad. That is what made the CEO role so interesting and so challenging at the same time.

On the delivery side, we had people building lots of things. We built design systems, whole-of-government platforms, we did lots of journey mapping, and we provided support for agencies. We also assisted in the coordination of programs that allowed us to work across multiple departments and agencies.

We also had investment advisory and assurance functions, but these were relatively immature. We would capture information on performance of programs and provide advice to agencies on how they might be able to improve delivery where we saw issues. We could also coordinate their work, where we saw issues forming across programs. Our capacity to directly influence and direct was not there though. This meant that agencies could choose to ignore our recommendations or advice without consequence.

As part of a machinery of government change just prior to my start, the DTA had taken on a series of administrative functions from the Department of Finance. Things like digital procurement or sourcing and industry engagement came over to us. We were also responsible for the capability and skills function to steer that work across the government.

One of my biggest challenges was effectively navigating the gap between our mandate and our (low) level of direct control. Most of what the DTA was able to achieve was enabled through influence rather than hard controls. Checks and balances in procurement and budget processes and whole-of-government digital strategy mandates helped to a point. But in some cases, the other organizations were able to argue alignment at a high level, and we needed to trust that they would follow through. As I mentioned, this was an issue with our project assurance activities as well, where we provided advice rather than direction and this led to suboptimal delivery outcomes.

What Did You Set Yourself as the Objective When You Started in DTA—What Was to Be Your Concrete Mission?

Given its history, the DTA was sitting on very unstable foundations. Understanding the DTA's mandate, its capabilities and creating focus were my initial objectives. Proving that whole-of-government digital was worth doing was my macro-objective. This was a game of survival, with the existence of the DTA being at risk if we did not do a good job.

This meant that we needed to drive a strong focus on the user in all our thinking. We needed to set the strategic vision and strategy, we needed to establish the governance and the foundations that underpinned them. We needed to orchestrate the delivery of user-focused transformation.

Our strategy looked forward to 2025, and we built a plan that delivered outcomes every few months. We were able to provide a high-fidelity plan a year ahead, with less detailed plans supported by principles and direction statements beyond that.

We moved forward quickly with things like myGov,[1] digital identity, cloud services, skills, and so on. Proving our value through delivery was critical.

What Were Your First Steps in the Role? You Changed the Whole Operating Model in the First Sixty Days?

There were a few things I needed to do very quickly. I spoke about understanding the DTA's mandate, its capabilities and creating focus, but reconnecting the DTA into the public service was also critical.

Several public service secretaries had a major interest in the work of the DTA, so I prioritized engagement with them. I wanted to understand their past experiences with the DTA and get their advice on what needed to be done to make us more effective. I also took the opportunity to get their feedback on some of my initial hypotheses, particularly where I saw the need to bring the expectation and reality of what the DTA needed to do closer together.

In parallel with the external engagements, I needed to make sure that I had the right executive team in place and that we were organized to deliver. I needed to quickly establish formal governance. This needed to be sufficient, but not overbearing. We started with weekly meetings of our executive board to ensure that we were all aligned on our key priorities. I also created the capacity to formally communicate and engage with my minister and government through briefings, inquiries, hearings, and so on.

Last, but by no means least, I engaged my support network. Although these people had no direct interest in my work, they wanted me to do well and I respected and appreciated their sage advice. I also met with a range of industry executives because their engagement and support was critical to the effectiveness of the DTA.

Where Did You Get the Ideas from for the New Operational Model?

I had experience in operating model design from my time in consulting. I helped to design and refine operating models for all different types of organizations, with many patterns being relevant in the context of whole of government digital.

I looked first at the administrative order that established the DTA. I also looked at the charter for our minister. Interestingly, many people in the DTA, particularly those new to working in government, had never read the administrative order or even knew where to find it. These were critical foundation documents that described the strategic intent. Our operating model translated this into operational capabilities, or how we assembled resources to get things done.

Some things were not broken, so they did not need to change. But there were quite a few areas where our organizational accountabilities were getting in the way of delivery. The focus on users was already built into the DNA of the organization, as was a commitment to incremental and agile delivery. We had many of the right tools in place (such as journey maps), and rituals such as showcases and retrospectives were all retained. These elements just needed a bit of mindset shift to "can do" and "can connect."

I then made sure that our key internal and external stakeholders understood how the DTA was changing and what this meant for them.

What Sort of Coordination or Governance Did You Set Up with Other Government Stakeholders?

This was hard. The DTO and DTA had had several attempts at establishing the right governance, but they never quite got it right in my view. I was involved as a practitioner in a few of these iterations, including the digital leadership forum, which consisted of deputy secretaries from across nineteen departments and agencies. This was way too many for a top-level governance body. The members often sent their delegates and this lack of direct engagement indicated that it was not working. There was also no direct connection to secretaries for digital and ICT matters.

It took us two years to design and implement our ultimate target state governance model, but I believe we ended up in the right place. We did experience headwinds, including the fact that the public service was in the process of simplifying its governance. There were about a dozen forums that drew together secretaries throughout the year and this needed to be rationalized. Establishing a new governance body ran counter to the simplification objective. We were saying, "Although we know that you want fewer governance bodies rather than more, we think that digital is important enough to justify creating a new body." We were very fortunate that some very senior secretaries got behind this, and they supported the establishment of the Secretaries Digital Committee.

Today, this committee meets on a regular basis to discuss major issues, to set and support the strategic direction, and to assist in resolving significant whole of government issues. This is one of the things that I am most proud of for transforming in the governance of digital and ICT. As you would expect, the first few meetings were about establishment and information sharing. It quite quickly transformed into an important strategic forum though, providing leadership and advice for digital and ICT transformation as we aligned the meeting agendas with decision points that required broad support or spanned multiple portfolios. It is now at the point where contributions are often made by the secretaries themselves, with the DTA supporting discussions and providing insights from a whole-of-government perspective.

I should add that the Secretaries Digital Committee was and still is supported by a Digital Leadership Group, which is made up of senior digital leaders from across the public service. They support secretaries by discussing key digital and ICT issues and stewarding the whole-of-government transformation agenda.

How Did You Cement the Standing of the DTA?

I would have never been able to cement the standing of the DTA by simply shouting it from rooftops. We needed to demonstrate the value of the work we were doing. As we proved our value, then our stakeholders also started telling the rest of government about the impact we were having.

It required finesse though. We needed to engage more deeply with agencies on their delivery programs without encroaching on their accountabilities. We needed to support agency programs by sharing both our people and our facilities as well. These efforts added real value and became a force multiplier in terms of support.

We worked hard at bringing industry players "into the tent" as well. We would hold regular industry roundtables to share our strategic plans, and we would participate in industry events to help to improve their understanding of what we needed to do and the support we needed from them.

What Were Your Methods or Routines for Managing the Relationship with Political Masters?

This varied considerably depending on the minister.

My first minister was not a digital professional. He relied very heavily on me and DTA to provide advice and leadership for the digital agenda. His interventions were focused on the strategic policy problems that the government needed us to help solve and providing support when we needed it.

My second minister had a very strong technical background. He was very actively engaged in the detail and regularly provided input and direction in solution designs, delivery, and support. The conversations were very different. I would meet with the minister three or four times every week when the parliament was sitting, and often a few times when they were not. Many of the sessions were deep dives that involved us stepping through a particular priority or program and getting feedback from the minister on direction, relative priorities, and delivery.

The most important part of these engagements was ensuring the minister had confidence that the DTA could deliver and that we had the right relationships in place to be successful.

How Did the Institutional Setting or Cover Change for DTA during the Years? Who Was the Boss?

When I first started, the DTA was situated within the prime minister's portfolio. Following a set of ministerial changes, a Government Services Ministry was created and the DTA moved into the portfolio, which hosted social services. This move was made to allow the DTA to sit closer to the natural center of service delivery in government. The social services portfolio contained the big welfare and health support services' delivery machine for the government. We were situated in that portfolio for about eighteen months.

Just prior to my departure from the DTA, the agency was moved back into the center of government within the prime minister's portfolio. The move was preceded by a formal, independent review of digital in government. The review recommended that the DTA be moved back in the center of the government to be able to operate with greater independence and have the greatest impact at a whole of government level.

You Have Emphasized a Few Times That You Had to Remake the Team. How Did You Build the Team Out?

I did not need to remake the entire team. I was fortunate to have been able to inherit a team of skilled and passionate people. As we reviewed and updated our operating model and organizational design, I needed to make some changes to my executive team, but beyond that it was about filling specific capability gaps.

Given the level of competition for digital and ICT skills, I needed to pull every string and leverage every network I had to attract the right people to fill our gaps. Good leadership and successful delivery are strong draw cards though, so we ended up having a lot of great people who wanted to join the organization.

In hindsight, I think we should have put more weight on cultural alignment. The people we selected almost always had the technical skills and experience we needed, but they did not always have a good cultural fit. This left us with a few square pegs in round holes and it sometimes took a lot of time and effort to correct this.

Who Was Your Most Valuable Hire or Appointment?

It took me a while to get around to this—too long with the benefit of hindsight, but the appointment of a deputy CEO was probably the most important staffing change I made. Prior to that

I had five direct reports and I provided each with an opportunity to act in the CEO role when I was on leave or overseas.

Bringing in one deputy provided much greater clarity as to who was second in charge and it also allowed us to manage workflows much more effectively. After appointing a deputy, it was always clear as to who would act for me, who would represent me on governance bodies, whom I most needed to back brief, or who would clear the materials if I was away.

You Did Bring Up a Cultural Fit Issue about Team Building. What Sort of Culture Did You Want to Have in DTA?

The culture we were trying to build was inclusive, collaborative, and optimistic. We needed a mindset that we could solve any problem if it is worth solving.

We cocreated a set of values that encapsulated our culture. In a nutshell, it was a culture of focusing on end users, on working well together and sharing information, on being pragmatic and on having an impact. Given that fact that we operated in an uncertain and high-pressure environment, maintaining perspective and a sense of humor was also significant to us.

The team was just wonderful in maintaining our culture. After we codesigned our values, the executive team and I made our expectations clear and we demonstrated, or lived, the values. Our people were driven to share by default and respect and support one another regardless of their social and ethnic backgrounds, gender, and orientation.

Culture is what we made it and it is something we needed to continually work on. We also needed to call each other out if we felt that people were not living the values. People were not afraid to hold each other to account either, even me as the CEO. I recall that after one of our all-staff meetings at the height of COVID-19, one of my staff members told me that everyone was stressed and tired. They said that with all the pressure, I had become very transactional, and it would be nice to hear about my weekend, my family, or anything that was not work related. I needed to be reminded to maintain perspective to allow others to do the same. That brave intervention from one of the team helped me to remember the importance of maintaining perspective even when the pressure is on.

What Were Your Own Days and Routines Like as a Team Leader?

My days have always been quite structured. I am a very early starter. I get up at about 5:30 am each day and head to the gym. I eat breakfast when I get home and take some time to read the press clips and reviewing the emails I received overnight. I then head into the office, often doing a few calls from the car when I am driving in.

I have started the day with a thirty-minute stand-up for many years. I find this to be an important morning ritual where we can share what has happened over the last day, any blockers, and the key things coming up. We do this even when people are traveling.

As far as regular meetings are concerned, I set an hour aside every week for an executive alignment session and I did weekly one-on-ones with all my direct reports. I set aside time to think and plan, often on Friday afternoons. I used this time to think about what we have achieved, what we need to do, and whom we need to engage with to get things done or gain support. I shared this thinking broadly across the organization as part of my weekly newsletter that I sent to all staff members.

The rest of my week was packed with meetings, which were rarely more than thirty minutes. People have found it surprising, but every day I always have "clearing time" with my direct team: my executive officer and my executive assistant. We work through all the things that we have on our plate, which is incredibly helpful in keeping us all lined up.

I try and keep my evenings as clear as possible so I can spend time with my family and friends. The same goes for weekends, accepting that there will be times when I need to break out the laptop or get on the phone when things get really busy.

About once a month I would do "skip" meetings, where I meet one-on-one with the people who report to my direct reports. I do deep dives with my teams to hear about what they have been doing and provide any guidance they might need.

If You Do Look a Bit Back Now, What Do You See as Your Greatest Achievements in the Job?

I think it must be the fact that we managed to move the DTA from being on its knees and unsure of its future to a position of a respected and trusted advisor that is hard-wired into the most important governance bodies in government.

I am proud that the concept of more human-centered, coordinated digital practice and a different way of operating have become accepted. The DTA is also no longer subject to a sunset clause or end date that its initial mandate had. We were able to extinguish it just before I left the organization.

From a delivery viewpoint, our performance leading up to and during COVID-19 was exceptional. I could not be prouder of the way we came together to deliver during such an incredibly stressful time. The DTA, like the rest of the public service, came together and did exceptional things. There was no friction, no boundaries, no parochial behavior, just pure focused and coordinated delivery. The pandemic brought out everything good in the public service and the nation more broadly.

I am incredibly proud of our work on the digital profession as well, kick-starting systemic work on advancing the digital skills within the public sector. I am pleased to have been asked to remain the head of the profession even after leaving DTA. We have been able to build some incredible foundations that will support the profession for many years to come.

These things combined have really put Australia back on the global digital stage.

Tell a Bit More on How COVID-19 Changed the Way You Operated—How Did You Reshuffle Your Work in DTA?

I do not think there is any question that COVID-19 made every organization in the world reorganize their priorities. In the DTA, we had very good teams working on a range of very important issues before the pandemic hit. We were building big business cases for government. We were doing prototyping work for platforms like the future myGov. We were investing in significant procurement activities.

When COVID-19 hit though, we rapidly diverted our top people to support the government's response. We leveraged every available capability to accelerate delivery. It was good fortune that we had been working on our digital marketplace, which allowed the public service to buy infrastructure and capabilities from industry at a speed that would have otherwise been impossible. We used our hardware marketplace to quickly buy thousands of laptops to support the urgent move to home-based work across the government. We were asked by the prime minister to establish a whole-of-government COVID-19 information website. We had this up and running within twenty-four hours by leveraging the myGov prototype we had just developed, and we hosted it on a repurposed australia.gov.au website. The site brought in a new type of rapid content governance across a dozen departments and offices. This also allowed us to create a new WhatsApp information channel with the strong support of the technology community in less than a day.

Our existing relationships helped immensely as well, with Singapore, for example, providing us with access to their BlueTrace source code for what became the COVIDSafe app less than a month later.

Do You Think You Had Any Failures or Things You Regret?

I have had quite a number of failures throughout my career. I think this is entirely normal and part of how you learn and grow. If you think you have not failed in some way, you are either not pushing yourself or you are not paying attention.

One of the areas where I know I need to do better is dealing with politics. I am not talking about big P politics, it is more about the small p politics for me. There have been a number of occasions in my career when I have not focused enough on understanding motivations and relationships or what makes people feel secure or insecure. This has meant that I have either missed signals I should have seen or I failed to gain the support I needed to exert influence or get things done.

Some people are naturally good at this, but I have really needed to work at it. Part of my challenge is adjusting how I am wired. I am wired to be a very trusting person, for example. I put this down to having grown up in small country town where you know everyone, and it is clear whom you can trust and who you cannot. This is not the way it works in complex, multistakeholder environments though. You need to think and operate differently.

Although I am not claiming victory yet, I feel much better equipped now to be able to deal with the politics we face every day. I am much more aware of my surroundings and have the skills I need to be able to navigate complex issues and environments.

Would You Ever Consider Doing the Same Job Again?

I have a lot to do in my new role leading the Simplified Trade System Implementation Taskforce. But I would definitely consider another stint leading Australia's whole of government digital agency.

I seem to be attracted to wicked problems and the DTA has many wicked problems still to solve. The only caveat would be that I would try and drive a closer alignment between the mandate and the expectations of the organization than my first time in the role.

But What Make You Pack Up and Leave DTA in 2021 Then?

I thoroughly enjoyed the challenge, but after three years in the role it was time to move on. I came to the point in where I felt I had done the job that I set out to do. Because DTA was transitioning from a period of pioneering and transforming to a period of operating and maintaining, it was a time for a different person to take the reins.

I am pleased that I was able to make a clean exit and move seamlessly into my new role helping to simplify Australia's cross-border trade environment—a wicked problem by any measure. I left the DTA in a strong and sustainable position and they are now much better positioned to be able to drive the whole-of-government digital agenda in Australia than they were when I arrived. This was enabled by our constant work in creating the foundations required for enduring change: our internal and external relationships, whole-of-government strategies and policies, integrated governance models, and, very importantly, a culture that supported collaboration and inspired a transformation mindset.

What Were or Are the Remaining Challenges for DTA and the Digital Government in Australia?

How to resource whole-of-government capability is a major issue that is still to be resolved. We cannot continue to "pass the hat around" on capabilities of national significance, such as digital identity. How do we plan and resource at a national level for coordinated capability? That is the question.

The optimal mix of centralization versus decentralization still needs to be decided as well. I do not think we are ever going to achieve the full potential of whole-of-government digital in Australia until we see higher levels of centralization than we see today.

There is also the simple conceptual challenge of having people cooperate across government. This is very hard in practice, of course. The Australian public service (APS) is driving hard on the APS Enterprise concept, which is excellent. The concept is about driving the public service to think in terms of the whole rather than the individual parts; it is helping to break down the silos that limit our capacity to come together. This way of thinking and operating is fundamental to any initiative that crosses organizational boundaries.

You Said You Were Tapped into the DTA Leadership for Your Background and Expertise. What Would Be Your Main Recommendations for a New Peer or Colleague to Excel in This Type of Job?

First and foremost, it is the importance of maintaining and leveraging their networks. The broader, the better. This includes ministers and their offices, their peers, industry, international partners and friends and mentors they have built up during their careers. I wish someone gave me this advice earlier in my career.

Second, I would suggest they get out into their business, whatever and wherever that might be. I have learnt more from spending time working in the business operations of my various organizations than I ever have working from my office. This might be taking calls on a help desk, helping to clear passengers in an airport, or assisting with a survey collection in the Bureau of Statistics.

Third, creating focus is important. Being able to sift and sort the things you could do every day to just the things that you must do every day is critical.

Fourth, no matter how hard things get, maintain perspective. It helps to keep you grounded and not lose sleep when you should not lose it. There are a whole lot of things in life that are important. At the end of the day, you need to work out what is the most important to you. Remember that there are always people doing tougher than you.

And finally, back yourself and take a "hospital pass" every now and again. Although it is hard, there is no better way to find out what you are capable of than taking some well-informed risks. Do not be the person who never tries new things or holds themselves back because they are not entirely sure they can do it. Sometimes you just need to take a deep breath and jump!

Note

1. myGov is a platform to securely access government services online in one place—see my.gov.au.

CHAPTER 17

Shai-Lee Spiegelman

Israel

S hai-Lee Spiegelman last served until the end of 2021 as director-general of the Ministry of Innovation, Science and Technology in government of Israel, leading the formulation of long-term science, tech, and innovation strategy.

In her previous role as head of the Israeli National Digital initiative (Digital Israel), Shai-Lee led the formulation of the government's National Digital Plan, and its implementation in collaboration with various government ministries.

She first joined Digital Israel in 2014 as vice president for planning and external relations, after extensive experience in the high-tech world. Before government, she served last as VP of marketing at Microsoft's R&D Center in Israel and previously also as director of regulation and corporate affairs in Microsoft Israel.

Shai-Lee has a Bachelor's degree in Law from Tel Aviv University, and a Master's degree in Public Policy from Harvard University in the United States.

I probably have to use the prefix of "super" a lot now to try and describe Shai-Lee. She simply is a Superwoman in many ways.

She is super-energetic. Talks fast, decides fast, delivers fast. Shai-Lee seems to get energized from fighting bureaucracy, which Israel and governments anywhere have a lot of, and which usually is tiresome instead. Because Israel is a "start-up nation," Shai-Lee truly managed to bring a start-up spirit to the government and perhaps helped to "break things" that had to be broken to unleash the digital government in Israel.

Shai-Lee is super-effective and super-practical. She can handle dealing with a dozen things, communication lines, workstreams at once. At the same time, every meeting with her has to have a concrete outcome, a concrete follow-up. I guess if you are raising four children and managing a super-busy digital agency on a super-big mission at the same time—like Shai-Lee was doing at the time of Digital Israel. She has no other option than to be super-effective and super-practical.

Shai-Lee is super-strong to have lasted through the political cycles—or even cyclones—that Israel has been through in the last years and all the while keep growing the team, keep doing the delivery of their digital agenda. Stamina is her thing, and her word.

—SIIM

How Did You Rise to the Role of a Digital Government Leader in Israel?

I had worked in the high-tech industry in Israel and then reached a point where I decided that if I am working so hard, I might as well do it for greater good or impact. It happened that at the same time the government started building up Digital Israel and they were looking for people. I met with Prime Minister's Office staff who were leading this work, and they thought I would be a great candidate and asked me to apply. Myself, I felt the Digital Israel opportunity was the right combination between technology and policy and impact.

So I did apply and became number two in the agency. When Yair Schindel, the first head of Digital Israel left the government for the private sector, I was appointed to succeed him and served as CEO for more than four years.

Did You Hesitate at All When Taking the Job?

I did not hesitate at that point, although I had a lot of questions about how to succeed with such a big challenge and what should be the right first steps. But I loved the position; it was exactly what I wanted to do. Working for Microsoft, I had built up relations with people in the government. I had the expertise. It was just the right setup.

How and Why Was the Digital Israel Initiative Born?

Back in 2013 or 2014, we had people in Prime Minister's Office, led by the Director General Harel Locker and the Deputy Director General Yossi Katribas, who thought that making Israel more digital had to be one of core strategic priorities of the new government. They did not call the initiative Digital Israel then yet. They understood that we had a very difficult bureaucracy, that the government ministries were not very digitized. We did not use data in a meaningful way; we did not work with citizens in the center. They were also concerned about the gap between the Israeli successful start-up industry and the Israeli public sector.

Then they started doing global research on how other countries have managed to do it, met with the UK government and others, and the concept was born. At end of 2013, a government resolution was passed to establish a unit called Digital Israel under the Prime Minister's Office. The initial aim was to bring in people from the private sector and with an initial budget for six or so people to design and structure out what this entity would do.

What Was Your Role at First?

We started with only some very high goals given to us to help government services and small- and middle-sized enterprises (SMEs) in digitization. One of our first jobs was to build out the national digital strategy. Nobody knew ahead what exactly the Digital Israel project or team would have to be.

Fast-forward five years and we had a team of seventy people and budget of $US200 million a year. Back then it was all open: do we go for health care or education or smart cities? It was our luxury and an opportunity to design it all the way it should be. But where do you start, if digitization is going everywhere and everything needs work? Also, do you start with infrastructure, which might take three years of work before anyone sees any results, or start with quick wins and low-hanging fruits that are not as impactful, but people will see the results? What is the right combination of things?

Bringing this strategy together was my duty, role, and privilege.

What Was the State of Digital Government in Israel at the Time More Precisely?

Israel as a country was and had always been quite advanced in technology in general. We are known as a start-up nation, after all.[1] Government was used to working very well with start-ups, so the high-tech relationships were there. The country was also already well connected in terms of the internet; almost every house had access to broadband and mobile penetration was high.

Yet, the government services were lagging behind and were not citizen-centric. A lot of the services you could start online, but it was not end-to-end—at some point you had to print, fill, fax, or deliver something in person. Some ministries were more advanced, such as the Ministry of Health with health records and data. Many were lagging behind, and our development level overall was medium to low perhaps. Not as advanced as it should have been, given our overall tech scene.

The digital gap between the government and the private sector was unbelievable. The government and the prime minister understood that this gap is unbearable and made it a priority to change it to have the public sector meet the expectations of the people and meet the DNA of the start-up nation.

What Was the Concrete Expectation for You to Deliver?

To build the strategy, to build the national plan, and to do so in the next six to twelve months.

Also, we were put in charge of some priority projects that had started before but needed delivery. For example, there was a project to build an e-commerce platform for SMEs—for mom-and-pop shops to sell their products, especially from remote or conflict areas. Another one was to get more people to training, for which we realized early that e-learning had to be the way. So we started building a national e-learning platform based on Open edX called CampusIL.

What Did You Set Out to Achieve as Your Own Ambition or Objective Then?

I came from a very digitally advanced organizational environment and was surprised by the amount of work to be done on digital front within the government. My ambition became how to overcome these hurdles, to make this change happen. Many people inside government were initially suspicious. They thought that the politicians were simply saying some nice words, that it was another government resolution, but nothing would happen.

My ambition was to make this new unit the best, to bring in the knowledge from the private sector, and to actually change the government. This drives me all the way to today.

How Did the National Digital Strategy Then Come Together—and What Became the Strategy?

It took us more than six months, almost a year or so. On the one hand, you want to come up with a very wide and comprehensive strategy that will last for three to five years. On the other hand, you want to include a lot of ministries, and they all have unique perspectives and interests. We did not have mandate yet; we had to convince others to partner with us and take us onboard. This partnering, convincing, building of trust took more time.

Today you can go to any ministry and digital and technology innovation is among their main objectives, no need to argue about it anymore. Back in 2014, a lot of director-generals thought that digital is something that IT people could handle, what the CIO would do. Digital transformation was not understood the way it is a common phrase today, and we had to build this understanding up one-by-one with each executive. We had to show examples of opportunities, and it was a tiring process of bringing everyone onboard.

However, it was important because when we would go with the strategy to the government, it would not then be just us making the case. A ten-person unit alone cannot make all Israel digital. You need to have the whole government behind that or at least some of the major ministries.

We worked with ministries to understand their strategies, their priorities, their challenges to propose ways how we and digitization can help them. The aim was for every ministry to have their own digital strategy, as part of ministerial strategy. I made a presentation to each ministry with inspiring demonstrations based on my own ideas, other country examples, other sector examples on how their challenges could be met through digital tools or data. Then we proposed quick pilots to try some of it out in practice.

As the next step with overall strategy, we had to figure out how to prioritize and what would be the right time frame for the strategy, anyway. Three years? Five years? What would either allow to achieve?

I must say that back then there were not many good examples internationally to look at either, because we were trying to come up with a comprehensive digital strategy for the whole government. Most other countries focused just on changing the delivery of frontline services, but we wanted to go after the core government value delivery like health care or the educational system, too.

We ended up with three goals in the strategy: promoting economic growth, narrowing socioeconomic gaps, and making the government smarter and friendlier. The last is about better services, data-based decision-making, putting citizens in the center, managing privacy issues, and so on. For economic growth, we had initiatives to work on digitization of SMEs. We also brought to focus the govtech sector, to help this industry emerge and thrive. For the socioeconomic gap reduction, we focused on education and digital inclusion. Each goal had three or four more concrete objectives, then various projects underneath. It could have been projects from any ministry under any goal, and it worked as a matrix in that sense with ministerial strategies.

How Did You Set Out to Deliver the Strategy and to Sequence the Various Initiatives, Which Had Been a Puzzle First?

We built the strategy a bit like a working paper, to be updated regularly—say, every two to three years. For each year, we put together an annual plan and a budget based on the strategy. Each year we had about a hundred different initiatives and projects going. Each of these lined up to a high-level objective or goal, forming a map of sorts.

We had to keep things flexible and agile. Initially, we did not mention artificial intelligence (AI), for example. When we were refreshing the strategy more widely in 2019, AI was a big thing and there was no way to do a strategy without some focus on it and data. So, regular updates enabled us to add or change directions.

Within the strategy, we sought for a balance between a few long-term infrastructure projects like CampusIL, our online learning initiative and platform. Today, it is *the* online learning platform in Israel with a million learners and hundreds of courses, but it took us four or five years to make it happen. Or another bigger initiative was to build the data infrastructure for all health care data, adding each hospital one by one.

Next to these we had to deliver quick wins in order to get and keep legitimacy, plus have the ministerial support. Ministers need quick wins and political gains. Nobody will otherwise give you the budget you need for longer-term stuff, too. The quick deliveries were things like a website and e-commerce platform for SMEs, or digitizing the process of getting new medical doctors approved for their practicing license. The last one was a three-to-six-month manual process before, while these talented people had to wait idle in unemployment after medical school before they were allowed to start practicing. By digitizing the applications, we brought the bureaucracy down to a week, and the impact was amazing.

How Did You End Up in the CEO Role of Digital Israel after Two Years in the Team?

Digital Israel started as a unit under the Prime Minister's Office but then with the next elections we were moved under the Ministry of Social Equality. The current government is finally building a new digital authority—bringing Digital Israel there together with ICT Authority, aka the central technology agency for government, in charge of technology platforms.

With the move happening back in 2016, Yair decided to leave. I was willing to take over because of the ambition I had to change the government, as explained. The team was also worried that everything we had set out to work on would be gone. I wanted to step in to ensure the path we had started on. I thought it was really important at that point to have someone from inside take the lead, someone who knows the organization's DNA. Otherwise, it would be hard to continue delivering on the Digital Israel strategy.

My request was that we would be allowed to continue working as a separate unit with our own identity and DNA, even a separate office in Tel Aviv, close to the high-tech industry and talent.

What Was the Expectation or Task Given to You as You Became the CEO?

The main one was: deliver, deliver, deliver.

Second, we were expected to support the minister's policy agenda, even if we remained at arm's length to be as autonomous as possible. As a team, we had previously been quite free to do what we saw fit. With the minister for social equality, Gita Galmiel, we now had for the first time a political leader with their own agenda, too. That is why we started to work more on smart cities and with municipalities, also on the equality initiatives like digital literacy for minorities. It was useful in my view, because in Israel eventually the citizens meet the municipality much more than they meet the central government. Thus, if we do not work enough with municipalities, the digital gap will remain in experience.

Given the Horizontal or Matrix Nature of Governmental Strategy, How Did You Build Up the Collaboration with Ministries to Ensure the Delivery on Their End?

Indeed, maybe only 20 or 30 percent of annual projects were managed directly by our team and the rest by all different ministries.

The key for being on the same page was that the ministry and Digital Israel together appointed chief digital officers (CDO) to each ministry, who would lead their digital strategy making and delivery. We then worked with these people hand-in-hand each year on the annual plan, on the budget, and so on.

A lot of our influence also came from our budget. We were able to go to the ministries and say, "let's work together; here are our terms." The ministries had to appoint CDOs as part of their management, we would choose them together, and then in return we would match their budget for digital initiatives. Half of the money would come from Digital Israel, half from the ministry. This joint investment ability was also a great way to leverage the funds we had gotten for Digital Israel—we could double them for eventual strategy delivery.

The terms also included commitments on practices or how projects were to be carried out. For example, that customer journeys had to be done or data used. This was a way to bring the new practices to ministries real fast.

Very importantly, we also made an effort to raise the knowledge and skills and create a community of senior executives on digitization. We took some forty managers every year into a digital leaders program. We took them to weeklong custom-made digital leadership courses at world's top business schools; each month made them learning days on good service design and other new know-how. After four or five cohorts like this, we had some two hundred people from ministries who were our ambassadors and talked the language necessary for digital change. This way we could achieve way more than just with own people in our team.

Was There Ever Pushback from Some Ministries?

We were very lucky because a lot of the ministries wanted to work with us. First, there are not a lot managers who will say, "No, I do not need the funds; I have funds on my own." Second, we also brought a lot of experience of good private sector methodologies, new ways of doing things. Our team was very talented and young, not like typical government or civil servants whom you do not want to work with. Third, if things were a success, they got credit for it.

Thus, we actually had more demand than we could actually supply for. In addition, we were ambitious and impatient. As a new or young entity, we wanted to make sure we were recognized and that people understood our value and direction. That forced us to be a bit everywhere. At some point we had to start saying that we could work with five or six ministries only at a time. We had to start to focus.

How Did You Manage to Ensure the Delivery of the Plans? How Did You Help Ministries along the Journey?

It was quite chaotic at times.

People did not first really understand what we do and how to do their part. Transforming government services is about more than making citizens go to a website. Making personalized services is not easy.

Plus, when you are introducing new jargon and practices to the government about customer journey or user interface (UI) or data and these are things that people did not know before, it does not come naturally immediately. Everyone will approach it a bit differently, unless steered or supervised.

As Digital Israel, we wanted to make sure that all digital projects are done in the right way. Therefore, it was important to be there in all the projects, at least in some meetings or initial meetings, to explain how things should be done. We brought in the practice of customer needs or journey workshops to get the direction right for transformation. Say, you want to open a pizza store (or get any business license)—you would have to deal with then different regulators. We would then bring all these agencies together and map it out so you see the customer nightmare clearly. From that we could then apply the different hats of digital transformation to make it better.

We adopted the concept that digital transformation has five different hats or lenses to look at. One is user need and user experience (UX), another is data, another is UI, then process management, also technology itself. In the middle of it all stands the product approach. In the government, nobody knew the product manager's role or concept before. We started to bring this role into agencies.

To help the ministries deliver quick on the transformation plans and sessions, we did a big tender to facilitate the outsourcing of work and bring in practical digital capability in larger quantity. It was a centralized procurement for all different ministries to make available to them a pool of necessary competences to build their solutions out in the new way. They could get product management or design or other experience this way fast.

In addition, I already mentioned how we were educating and skilling the leaders. We also started doing online trainings on CampusIL platform to support the spread of good practices, and extended the efforts to bottom levels of government, not just managers. At the end of the day, it is these people who do the work of transformation.

With the strategy review in 2019, human capital efforts really rose to the core of our work and plans.

One of the Keys to Make It All Happen Was to Build Out a Great Team. What Was Your Approach in This Area? How Did You Bring Your Team Together?

The key was in three critical special exemptions, which we were granted as a government entity.

The first was the location. Government sits in Jerusalem, but if we were to be based in Jerusalem, the right talent may not come. They are in Tel Aviv, in high-tech offices there. Also, we needed to be in touch with the tech community for collaborations.

Another thing was that we managed to convince the Civil Services Authority to give us exemptions from the usual hiring process. The standard process of government hiring is a long one. First, you have to have an internal call for the positions, taking probably three months. Only then you can go outside and have a public competition, then you have to have the candidates pass exams, and so on. It can be eight to ten months of bureaucracy to bring someone in. We needed to attract people from industries where offers are made within forty-eight hours! So, to be able to hire right talent, we needed a different kind of recruitment track. We managed to bring the process down to a month or six weeks by going straight public with calls for applications.

The third exemption we got was on salary. Most of our staff were not on civil servant but special expert salary grade. This still forced us to offer pay at some thirty percent below market value, but not significantly below the market value that product managers or design or tech experts would have gotten on civil service pay otherwise.

We also were getting a good publicity buzz, so we had dozens or sometimes a few hundred résumés for each position—this was amazing. We did build this brand consciously, too. We had our own people bring their friends in a start-up company fashion. We made a point to be present at every conference in the high-tech industry for marketing who we are and what we do.

Seventy percent of the team was from private industry background, from start-ups to sectors like banking, which had experience with practical digital transformation. We also hired for some roles from inside the government because we also needed people who understood government. Fundamentally, we were looking for entrepreneurial people who can do their own job. As we had to work so much with other ministries, we also needed people who knew how to work with other people and convince other people into partnering.

What Did You Do to Keep the Good People?

We made a point to build a culture and DNA of a small start-up.

We also really tried to get people to attach to Digital Israel and the team. We had a lot of events, like Thursday[2] happy hours or celebrating holidays together with spouses as a big group.

One of my biggest prides is that while I was the manager for four years, almost no one left the team on their own volition (some I had asked to leave). Ultimately, what kept them was a chance to build things with impact and feel the impact.

Can You Tell a Bit More on the Culture You Were Building for the Team?

As said, we were going for the start-up DNA. We were building the bridge between the country's start-up nation identity and the government, reshaping the start-up nation spirit into the government practices.

But we also emphasized the need to have impact, to focus on delivery, to build partnerships and have less ego. We understood that we had to work very closely with all other ministries. If we would have taken credit or had behaved in a political way with powerplays to them, nobody would want to work with us. People even told us that we were not marketing our achievements enough, that people did not hear enough about our projects. I said that was fine. If the ministry's manager is getting the credit, and they are happy working with us, that was fine!

What Were Your Guiding Principles as a Leader?

We were working really hard so that everybody in the team would feel significant and important. In our biweekly team meeting, every time someone would present one of his or her leading projects. We gave credit and recognition by giving out stars every week and we mentioned what the person got the star for. This was important because there was so much work to be done.

Each employee was managing a lot of projects in other ministries and a lot of it had to be based on good relations. We did not have a forcing power over the ministries. Our impact came from our professionalism. Every one of us had to be on top of our game. Each time they had a meeting with someone, the team members were representing us all. If they did not perform—say, did not come to the meeting prepared, this would have affected our brand. This also meant that people had to be confident in themselves, and that is why giving recognition exactly mattered.

I always said I had the best job in the government. I truly felt this way because the team was the best in government. Because our unit was the best place to work in.

In addition, I am not a very hierarchical and formal person. With our team, as we were working together, we were developing together and attached to each other. For example, with my management team—my five or six "right hands"—we are still really good friends to date.

What Were Your Most Effective Management Routines?

There were the whole-team biweekly meetings that I mentioned, for recognizing and over-viewing the work across the whole team and for informal knowledge transfer in the team.

With my management team, we had a weekly meet-up and it was always a very in-depth meeting. For two hours, we would bring issues and discussions to the table on what we needed to do. It was not about sharing information on what each of us does and then going our separate ways. Instead, we debated and decided together.

It was very important to have people involved in the annual planning because this ensures delivery. It was a bottom-up process with everyone involved from day one, starting from the lowest employee until the management. Each person would submit in their own project proposals, then team managers approved them, and then it went to the management for discussion and debate. Then we would present the whole plan to the whole team so that everybody could see all the projects.

We also very openly did the quarterly review of the annual plan's delivery. Each person reported what was done, what was late, what was going on, what were the barriers, what was working or not. We would sit each quarter for half a day with the management team and review each line of work, giving guidance as necessary. An efficient project management software was an essential part of making all this transparency and involvement possible.

Probably some 20 to 30 percent of my time went to managing up. It involved taking time to introduce to the minister or my director-general all the projects we were doing, explaining to them what digital is about. We spent time especially on preparing them for every conference or public speaking event, because they did not know our area themselves. Obviously, we had to also work with the minister on getting government resolutions put together and passed if we needed them.

Each quarter I did a one-on-one with all director-generals of ministries to review delivery and plan ahead for the next stages.

Looking Back, What Do You See as Your Biggest Achievements in the Job?

First, I am proud that I managed to build and get approved the national digital strategy for a first time in Israel, and also to update it a few years later. This is now a document that every-body knows.

I also think I did manage to influence the culture of the government in terms of digi-tal transformation. Everybody in the government speaks about it now. Ministries have their CDOs, everyone understands the importance of data and digital, everybody wants to do it.

Everybody also wants to partner with Digital Israel, and that is an achievement in itself. This step from six people whom nobody knew who they were or what were they going to do, from start-up to a sustainable organization—this is what I am extremely proud of. It is not easy with a growing headcount and budget, changing strategy, changing ministries and ministers, and so on.

If I look at the product-level things I worked with, I would say CampusIL is definitely the achievement. It was my baby, my idea. We managed to build the platform, agree to have global leading institutions offer their courses in Hebrew on it, get our own universities to offer online courses, too. It has brought real impact, whether in form of low-income families having free access to exam preparation courses for their kids, or by enabling the move to distant learning during the recent COVID-19 pandemic. We made it take off ground with a few courses that were very popular—to get the platform known and people on it. At the core, CampusIL success came from an amazing product team who did not give up even if hurdles emerged.

Are There Things You Regret or Things You Think You Failed At?

Focus is one—we were trying to be everywhere. We could have probably gotten more done by being more focused. It also made my managerial job harder.

We also did have problems telling our story, selling the strategy at first. It did not help that we were doing so many things at once, with all the ministries and so on. Being not focused enough made the mission harder to capture into an explanation for others.

When 2020 Came, You Decided to Move On—Why Did You Make This Decision?

I had been at Digital Israel for six years, four as the manager. I thought perhaps that is enough time and to have someone else take the lead. At the time, there was also another election and the new minister of science and technology, Yizhar Shai, offered me a director-general position in that ministry. He was from high-tech industry himself and was looking for someone with combined tech and government background. It is a very small group. I was very happy to accept his offer and to work with him.

What Were the Remaining or Next Challenges for Digital Israel as You Left?

Data is the challenge. We had started work on data strategy, but it was near the end of my term. I am talking about how can government really utilize and leverage the data in the right way? For making better decisions or providing access to data for academia and industry for building companies. There is also lots of work ahead to get data sharing going between different ministries' silos and agencies, to get the data governance right.

Second, we had only started work on AI and how to get government more accept the new technologies. For example, how to support with regulation the introduction of self-driving cars or build sandboxes for new technologies like cryptocurrency and blockchain. Inserting cutting-edge new tech into government is a big-big-big challenge.

How Did You Make Sure That What You Started Would Stick and Last?

I believe everyone is expendable in the end. My hope was that I had such a great team, who was sure to manage it without me. The management team were all strong managers, all my deputies.

We were also in constant touch with them for the first few months. Every time they had a question, they could come to me and we talked it through.

It was also very important for me that someone from my deputies would get the CEO position when I left. In fact, I had three deputies who were fully capable and wanting to take the role and put in the application. Succession is much easier in this manner.

Looking Back Now, What Were Your Biggest Learnings in This Job—Anything You Wish You Had Known at Start Already?

Obviously, a big learning for me coming from outside was that government is such a plane carrier. It is real heavy and massive; turning it takes a long time. When people ask me about the work in government, I say it is like moving walls. I had days when I was frustrated, and angry, struggling with this terrible bureaucracy. How patient you have to be, willing to again and again explain the same thing, meet the same challenges—that I did not know in advance.

However, when you succeed, there is magic in it. In its impact—like getting a tens of thousands of students to get free online preparation courses for university matriculation. It is the best thing ever when they tell you that because of your platform, they got a higher score getting into the university than they would have gotten before. There is nothing compared to that in any job that I have done before, and I was in the best companies, really.

Looking back, I knew some of it. I knew to believe in what you do and be passionate about it. I knew that I needed to have the stamina.

Did You Ever Learn How to Fix Bureaucracy, as You Had Initially Set Out to Change Government Ways?

No, I never managed to fix bureaucracy. After six years in government, I knew how to work better with it. I knew now where you can go around. I knew how to explain to the bureaucracy what I was doing. I knew what were bureaucrats' interests and how to talk to these interests to make things happen.

Today I can challenge the bureaucracy more by saying that I did this or that three years ago and it is possible. Before I did not have this to show for.

Fundamental issues have remained. In the private sector, if you have a good project, you can have the budgets, you get a green light from your boss and just run. But in the government you may have the budget, you may have a good project, you may even have a go from your bosses, and then it takes still a year to convince everyone because there are a lot of gatekeepers and procedures like tenders.

If Despite It Being Hard, Someone Still Wants to Do This Kind of Job, What Skills Are Necessary for It?

You have to aim high and be strategic. If you want to make the government more digital, it is never about this or that project. It is about national initiatives, vision, strategy. You have to learn to prioritize what to do and what not to do. Also, how to promote why you are doing this—why is it important?

You have to be willing to listen to others to convince them, also be patient not to get upset and understand that people have other perspectives. They are used to doing things in some way; you want to change that. You are moving the cheese for them, as the saying goes.

You also have to learn to think in the digital transformation hats: about UX and UI, about customer journey, about products.

These things mostly can be learned by practice only. I am not sure if maybe twenty years ago I would have known how to do the things that I am doing today. However, you still can have or learn the initial capability of empathy, working with people, being coherent and clear on what you are saying or want to do.

What Are Your Three Summary Takeaways from Your Digital Government Leadership Role, as Recommendations to Any Peer on How to Be Effective in This Job?

As said before, be strategic.

Be very professional. Otherwise, people will not listen to you.

Doing digital is a puzzle to solve. You have to understand what it takes and its parts. It is not enough to be a good manager: you have to be a great leader, understand innovation, understand tech, understand the moves, understand how digital can affect products and services.

Notes

1. Israel has become globally known and marketed as the Start-up Nation to highlight that it has a sizable high-tech industry and large number of tech start-ups despite its small size, with an ecosystem for them to thrive in.
2. Thursday is the end of work week in Israel, with the work week starting on Sunday.

CHAPTER 18

Taavi Kotka

Estonia

Taavi Kotka is an entrepreneur and former Estonian Government CIO. He has been honored as the European CIO of the Year in 2014, and Estonia's E&Y Entrepreneur of the Year in 2011.

Taavi served as the GCIO in Republic of Estonia from 2013 to 2017, during which time he cofounded Estonia's e-Residency program and led its delivery. Prior, he worked in the private sector. He started his career as a programmer, rising to be a CEO of the largest software development company in the region—Webmedia (now Nortal). Taavi also served as president of the Estonian Association of Information Technology and Telecommunications from 2009 to 2013.

Since leaving the government, Taavi has been back in private sector, helping his start-ups and consulting large enterprises and governments on digital transformation. Besides his own company Proud Engineers, he has been the CEO of Jio Research Center in Estonia since 2018 (a subsidiary of Indian telecom giant Reliance/Jio).

It is quite certain that I would not have become the Government CIO for Estonia if it had not been for Taavi to fill those shoes as my predecessor. We joined the digital government work around the same time, both part of wider political effort to restart the digital innovation engine for the country and government.

To wake up an engine once the battery is a bit flat, you need to jumpstart it. That is what Taavi is so awesome at. With his professional credentials and ice-cold logic, personal charisma, and even if sometimes a forceful style, he can inspire people and get delivery out of them. He has bold ideas and a wide vision. Most of all, he is not one who fears to bang some heads. Tanks do not have fears.

I was the digital policy advisor to the prime minister, when Taavi joined as the GCIO. We quickly formed a tandem of sorts—with me trying to help out at policy level, but mostly learning by tagging along. He was my mentor through these four years, even if we never called it that.

He was an entrepreneur-turned-GCIO, but always remained an entrepreneur in spirit—or an engineer, he would prefer to say himself. He was conscious that he was not going to last in government for long, but decided to make the most of it and ended up staying longer. That was enough to get the engine started for the "second wave" of digital society in Estonia, as Taavi himself calls it.

—SIIM

How Did You Enter Public Sector and the Government CIO Role in Estonia?

I am an IT engineer and an entrepreneur. Until 2012, I was part of the team that built one of the largest software engineering companies in Estonia and our region, called Nortal by now. Once I sold my shares when exiting the company, I had this non-competition clause that said I could not work in the private sector doing ICT for two years.

It was noticed by the then minister of economic affairs to whom the Government CIO position in Estonia reports. The secretary general of the ministry made the first move by asking me if I would like to become the deputy secretary general for ICT, which corresponds to the Government CIO in our country. It is a nonpolitical position, and this is very important because I clearly stated that I was not willing to play any political games. Policy—yes, politics—no.

Obviously, in the first meeting I declined the offer. As the joke goes, you do not work in government if you are truly free and healthy. I had just won the Estonia's Entrepreneur of the Year award in 2011, issued by E&Y, and a government career was not an option that I was considering. But then I asked for two things.

First, I asked to have full political support, for however crazy the ideas were. I asked for politicians not to interfere if we were to create something extraordinary. Second, I asked for a parking position for a car behind the ministry building as the place was in Old Town in Tallinn. It was harder to get the second thing done!

I also saw an opportunity to get more money for ICT development. It was the year 2013, the exact time for the planning of next period of European Union Structural Funds until 2020.[1] With extra funds, we could influence how and what digital innovation was doing in the government. When you want to execute something, you need a good idea, a great team, but you also need assets or money. So, if I could get more money for investments, then we could continue talking about me joining.

What Was Your Main Motivation Still to Take the Role—Besides the "Golden Handcuffs" from the Exit?

Part of it is from my upbringing. The thing was that I could not do military service in my youth, but I had been always taught to be a patriot and that you have to do something for your country. The Government CIO role was a chance for me to give back to Estonia. I planned to be in government for only two years, but it became extremely interesting, and I stayed twice as long.

Also, there I had a certain amount of enthusiasm to try and prove that coming from the private sector I could show government officials that not everything has to take time and that you can move fast, too. Like any private sector employee, I had a wrong understanding on how government works, but that epiphany came later.

I think the most important motivation was the fact that even if people know me as a leader or an entrepreneur, I am deep down still an engineer. I actually like doing stuff, so I saw an opportunity to solve some larger challenges than you can get to solve in the private sector. There, the challenges are far simpler, mostly on silo basis, repeating from client to client, bringing impact to a limited number of users. This was a chance for me to get to do something new, and as an engineer, you always go after the challenge. In software engineering, a bigger challenge means a more complex system to work on. Government has some of the biggest systems in any country.

Plus, the challenge in government is also bigger because normal innovation stimulus like money does not work in there. You have to find a different way to push through your ideas; you have to find other ways to motivate people. Options or bonuses do not exist, you also cannot hire the best people from the market due to budget limits. You have to deal with the limits you have. These look like small things, but actually they make every step more complicated. For an engineer, the bigger the challenge, the bigger the opportunity.

What Made the Minister or Secretary General Choose You, and What Were You Called In to Do or Deliver?

The Government CIO position had existed already on paper for years, but the secretary general could not find a proper person for the job. In this role, you need somebody there who has respect from the market and who is knowledgeable in the field.

I had been the president of the IT Association in Estonia. This is a role where other companies had selected me, and I had their respect. Having operated in the ICT market for more than fifteen years, I also knew what the market lacked and what were the holes in the digital society ecosystem. The secretary general hired me without giving me any agenda or topics— she trusted me to know what needs to be done. Same with the minister.

What Were the Things That Needed to Be Done? What Was the State of Play in Digital Government in Estonia in 2013?

Estonia has had two significant waves of digital innovation in Estonia within the last twenty-five years.

The first was in 1990s, when we started to think about simple core questions like who is behind the device? How can I connect the people? That led to our national digital identity, to X-Road,[2] to a significant usage of digital services by the people in Estonia. The basic tools were there and worked. The issue was how to get the ministries and agencies that operated in silos to understand who the customer is, how to motivate government officials to improve the services and to continuously improve their software, and so on. These were the questions that were still unsolved.

Many of the ICT systems were old and tired, having been built during the first wave of digitizing Estonia. So, we had to set the ground for the second wave; we needed to make the change happen.

What Was the Institutional Setup Like—Including the Mandate for Your Role?

The job of deputy secretary general for ICT is to make sure that the whole sector can flourish and to take a look at what needs to be done for that. For example, I focused on a lot on ICT education because we were starved with the lack of engineers. But it meant that I was forced to explain a lot why the Ministry of Economic Affairs was now dealing with education suddenly. The CIO in a company needs to think how to grow the whole business. It is the same thing in government—you have to think about the whole digital society and its development in the Government CIO role.

The role was placed in the Ministry of Economic Affairs and Communications in Estonia, but that does not matter at all in the big picture of things. What matters instead of what is the department is how much executing power and mandate you get for the role. For us, we got our biggest opportunity and mandate to push things when we were able to get the control of basically all ICT investments in the government. It meant that we had more than just words to support our direction.

For example, we started demanding that all ministries come up with departmental ICT strategies and defend these in front of us, if they wanted to get investment funding for new services or software development. This ICT strategy process pushed the silo ministries to think better about where to invest and in which order, to actually plan their work ahead, to consider how many applications they had to rewrite and when. This way we could start influencing their priorities and what sort of innovation they were doing, but also how they would do it—the IT management and service development methods.

So, you as the Government CIO can be under the Prime Minister's Office, but it does not matter without the levers. The silos will be the kingdoms; you cannot fix it without the proper levers. You cannot replace them or tell them how they should organize their work, unless you have strong ways to motivate them. Like in our case: if you do not meet the cybersecurity requirements or follow the policies, you do not get funded.

What Did You Set Yourself as Some Concrete Objectives to Achieve?

In the bigger picture, I wanted to see the ICT exports and the sector growing, start-ups to flourish. I wanted to see more positions opened up for tech talent training in the universities.

In government, I saw a big opportunity in using technology to solve some very complicated problems. Issues like tax fraud, which led to our work on the value-added tax (VAT) reform. We made it mandatory for all companies to digitally report data about any significant transactions to the tax agency for automated control work, and this brought a sharp increase in budget revenue and fall in the fraud.

Or the problem to fix the reporting that companies have to do to meet government requirements. The reports do not add any value for companies' products or services. Government forces the companies to spend some money to get data from them, but what if companies opened their data to government so that agencies could read it at any moment without additional costs? Things like this could benefit 90 percent of the economy.

What Were Your First Steps or Actions in the Role?

As I said before, you need ideas, you need a team and money to make stuff happen.

With ideas, I put them on a big mind map with some of the initial team members. The ideas were gathered this way: you first see a problem or a challenge, meaning what you want to influence. Then you think about how you can influence that. The mind map helped to understand in one canvas all what we needed to influence and where to focus. It was clear that we definitely had more ideas than there was capability to deliver. Plus, as time goes on, new ideas would emerge—like e-Residency did.[3]

Once the ideas were clear and we knew there would be more along the way, I had to look who was on my team. I inherited a twenty-five-person team. I fired at least half of them along the way for misfit, brought some new people in. I saw that we could drive the change the most through other departments and teams, by changing how they saw ICT development. Since Estonia has a decentralized government setup, they were to be in charge of their field anyway and planning for delivery.

You have to remember that I was still a newbie to the government, so I had to learn things like how laws were generated or what is the paper trail you always have to have behind your work. I did know how to push things through, in general. But I had to learn how the cogwheels work in government, whom to push the things with there. I have studied different disciplines in my life, and the pattern is always the same. It takes four to six months to understand how the discipline works. It takes time to get to know the governance model, to know the processes inside. That is what I had to do when going into the government.

I directed my biggest focus to the money. I chased money. I spent my days in different meetings that might have had a slightest connection to funding; went to all relevant briefings, made the case for investment into IT in any meeting. We ended up getting some 200 million euros for IT investments from EU funds for seven years. It was four times the money that there had been before in our field. It was more money than we first had ideas for back then.

How Were You Able to Deliver on Your Objectives from There On, Also Given the Small Size of the Team?

I am a chess player also, and in chess you always play with what you have in your hands. It means that if some of my resources or people are so busy and cannot be used, I do not bother them with new ideas or new stuff. I look for a different step that can be done.

The different step in this case was to go outside the immediate team often. I always see the whole ecosystem as my team, not just the people hired into the ministry or into the agency under me. The team was everybody who was interested and open and motivated to work along, even if it was not me paying their salary. That is exactly how we got things like the VAT reform or e-Residency done.

It was possible because I was already known in the market. I could go and open any door as necessary, whether the headmasters of universities or CEOs of large enterprises. I was continuously working with the wider sector, getting feedback and input to my work, doing this huge amount of communication with them and aligning work.

How Did You Influence Other Government Departments to Get Onboard the Initiatives?

First, people want their work to be meaningful. It is extremely important to give them a clear understanding of how their effort will make the world and the country better. They need to see the path, and government officials quite often miss that in their everyday work.

Second, charisma and reputation. If people know you are the person who executes, the guy who delivers and actually does interesting stuff, they want to join you. They want to be part of success. You are then providing them an opportunity to play along in a huge change that will impact on the society.

If we can help to make something good happen, then as humans we want to be part of it. People want to do interesting and really cool stuff. Through charisma, you can motivate them in this direction.

Sometimes it needs for you to help the leaders of other departments to understand what is important. That is how we got the Ministry of Culture, which usually is not the most tech-savvy, to be a frontrunner in Estonia in ICT planning and some big projects.

Charisma works at least in the beginning, until the work hits some hard brick wall. Then most people pull away, which is human as well. In the government, people continue to be afraid to fail because they fear it will affect their career. In the private sector, things also do not go as planned but you try again and again. For me it is so that if you have a solution that will solve some problems and if you do not push it until the last moment, you are actually failing then.

I did hit some walls, too. I am allergic to stupidity. I want to have things done, and if I get stuck with somebody who is not even trying to understand, I use the tank method. It basically means very aggressively using journalism or political support to go over the people and to not care if they are against things. If you have some public profile in the society, your word has more weight. The example is with e-Residency. We needed to have Ministry of Finance make some changes in the law, and it was not happening. It took one critical article in the newspaper with my quotes to get it going.

The best impact we had was through support to some noticeable innovations in different areas. A lot what we did was not to get others onboard, but to enable others with our help—if their initiatives served our KPIs. Like when we needed to have more cybersecurity specialists in the country. TalTech (university) was willing to invest in there, so let us do it! Let us make it happen together. It will be their baby, but we will also shine together with them, and the country moves forward.

Can the Tank Method Also Backfire?

Surely some reforms were stuck even with or because of it. But we also had a great team with you being at the Prime Minister's Office at the time. There was a loud and noisy CIO—me, and then somebody—Siim—who was more reasonable and went to smooth it out with a deal.

If you are noisy, you certainly get attention to the issue at the very least. This opens up a chance to get some outcome or step forward. If you just keep waiting and explaining again, again, again—it is not going to end up in a decision soon enough.

The need to be persuading all the time meant that everything came the hard way. That is because as I said, the normal motivational ways like profit, money, bonuses—nothing like that can be used in government. There are only two incentives: public fame or public shame. I was aggressive because I did not have time to wait. I was thinking all this time that I had only two or three years in the role.

With the Usual Incentives Not Available, How Did You Motivate Your Own Team to Deliver?

There are three things that people need or want, according to Daniel Pink, and I fully agree.[4]

What people want is autonomy. They also want mastery—they want to get better; they want to get new skills. Doing some new reforms motivates because it lets us try things out, to learn from this experience.

The third thing is to have a truly great challenge. People need to be part of something big, to have a mission that gives meaning to their everyday tasks. For example, if you work on ICT policy administration daily, you do it because the country's economy actually starts to grow from it. Nobody goes to work for the sake of working only. They have to find a cause in it.

Of course, we all also need a certain amount of money. The base pay has to be a reasonable amount, not a laughable one. If you are chasing something bigger, you are also willing to accept a lower salary for some time. Like me: I did not know my salary and I was shamed by the national business newspaper for it. But I truly did not care. I just had said to pay me as much as the ministry paid the other deputy secretary generals. So, you need to receive enough pay to take the money issue away from the table and then the other motivation factors take over.

How Did You Choose the People to Your Team? What Was the Factor You Looked For?

I have done so many employee interviews in my life to be able to basically look into the eyes of a person and can tell if we can match or not. The key is: can the person deliver?

But again—you are not able to bring extreme talent to the government. Changes can take years, talent is not willing to wait that long. I also think we have to find better ways in governments to share success with the teams. Not in the style of the US presidential press conference, where the team stands behind when the president talking. If I was a prime minister, I would do a scheme whereby if an independent commission terms a reform a success, the team behind it would get a share of the value generated or savings made to the budget. Like a bonus system. If the value is in millions, you could even get millions.

Who Was Your Most Valuable Hire?

I got myself a right hand without whom I would not have survived even two years. Aet Rahe came to be the head of our ICT policy department, which was my core team. We acted as a tandem team, not in a chain of command. We told the same messages, pushed the same things, did not matter which one was at the table. She ensured delivery from the team, because you do not mess with Aet! She has amazing execution capabilities. It allowed me to focus more to work with everyone else around us in the ecosystem to multiply our impact.

How Did You Advance the Culture in the Team?

Most of the cultural change came from changing more than half of the team.

One thing I wanted the remaining people to change was their approach to work. We could not solve all the problems, so we needed to narrow our focus. The core team was capable of delivering two or three important major changes in a year. The rest was just small things that needed to be addressed. Previously, everyone was trying to do all the things at once all the time, and not much was getting done.

The team needed to start making a difference between what mattered and what was noise. Things like getting investment funding distributed in a proper way through the ICT strategy process, with proper strings attached. That might seem a small thing to set up, but not if you realize the impact it was going to have on changing the mindset and practices of other ministries.

But I knew my time in the GCIO universe would be short, which means that there was no point for me to focus on building up in full my type of culture. Just some things that had to become natural.

Besides focus, we valued delivery and success. We brought in the tradition of highlighting our work plan and the key planned initiatives visibly on the wall in the office. We painted up the image of an apple tree. At the beginning of a year, all the planned stuff was marked with paper apple tree blossoms; while in works, we changed them to yellow fruits; once completed, the red ones. Some apples also went to rot, if stuff did not get delivered. Each apple had a person's name on it. So, you could visibly every day see the progress of everybody on their key deliverables. There was a routine made to regularly jointly update the tree, especially by doing the "harvest" together with celebration at the end of the year.

By the way, I am actually very bad with people! I am extremely demanding for outcomes, for results. Like, if I go to a restaurant and I get the food that I know that I can cook better, I cannot tolerate this. The same thing is if I ask staff to deliver a strategy proposal and they deliver me a first version that is so lousy that I as a non-expert can do better—then I am irritated. In these ways, I was hard with my team.

What Were Your Routines to Ensure That Delivery Was Happening?

I had Aet! It was mostly about simply going through people's KPIs and their progress against them regularly. Face-to-face, on a weekly basis, keeping this review cycle steady.

Also, we annually held some big events. An annual international big conference, for example, or a seminar retreat for top civil servants. These were the places where the team had to show developments and achievements. So, these were useful to push them to deliver. You had to show your stuff there.

But still, our success did mostly come through the success of other ministries and pushing and helping them.

What Were the Things You Kept Saying to the Team Again and Again?

Prioritize! Often in government documents, everything is in Times New Roman style, twelve-point-sized font long text—no priority or focus. But you need to figure out how to sequence things, how to go step by step and go after the big barriers. If you cannot get past the big barrier, solving the three small things on the side does not matter.

Fail fast. If you hit the brick wall and cannot smash it with a tank, get there fast. Then try it differently. For example, we did not get all the ministries necessarily onboard with the ICT strategy work or to do it properly. My approach was "Forget it, let us move on with those who are willing to learn." We should not be stuck and waiting for the sun to come down with those ministries who were resisting to do proper ICT planning; we could get to them later.

What Are the Things You Regret from Your Time in Office, or Things You Failed At?

We operated as well as we could. Of course, if I were to start again today with the knowledge I have now, we would do things differently. Some things we might not have even started, which ended up hitting a brick wall—but still. You cannot change the past.

We failed with the service concept, with bringing the concept of service ownership and management to the public sector in Estonia. A lot of countries focus on life event services for more integrated experience, for example. We did that for a short time but realized that it was more important first that every silo should understand what their most impactful services were and focus on making these the absolute best in the world in their agency. So that you would not bother the citizen, that you would not bother the enterprises with unnecessary bureaucracy. We were not fully able to teach that to the silos.

We tried several ways. We did policy work to push the idea, with white and green books and stuff. Yet, top civil servants just could not understand what a service is. The state secretary asked, "Is the policeman on the street a service?" with a laugh. I could not understand the question! Of course, he is! So, our job in digital service development is actually not about bringing in ICT. It is about improving the services, and ICT might be an element of it.

Governments and officials are not naturally used to serving the country but commanding the country. That needs to change. I had too limited time in the end. Such a mindset change needs more than ten years of steady work.

What Do You Consider Your Biggest Achievements While in Office? Did You Manage to Make Any Difference?

At the end of the day, knowing the resource we had or the team or time we had, we did a lot. I like to say that we were the authors of the second wave of digital innovation in Estonia!

We did solve some complex problems like VAT tax fraud together with the Tax and Customs Board. This meant changing the culture and mindset of some agencies, and that is big. Some ministries started significant change, using technology and right investments we gave them through the ICT strategy work.

Estonia is the best tax collector in the OECD. We have the best in education in PISA tests.[5] These impacts have come, partially, through using technology properly. These happened when the investment, the technology, the understanding, the motivation, the responsibility was put in place. This all led to a second wave of Estonian digital society development.

It was not the job of one person, and it happened through a decade, but I am glad that we were able to contribute to it with my team. Or push and support others to do it.

What Made You Stay in Government Longer Than Planned, and What Made You Leave after Four Years after All?

The key initiatives still needed my work. I understood that e-Residency program, as one of our key reforms, would not fly unless I stayed longer. VAT reform was still in action, the law had just been accepted. New national digital strategy and investment plans were all still fresh and needed putting to action; the departmental ICT strategy push had just started. The course was set, but not steady.

I left when I was sure the course would continue, that it would not radically be altered overnight—when you came in as the successor. Also, I lost Aet as my deputy and strong right hand when she left.

I ended up having some serious health issues, because of the stress I got from the job. I started to understand that the society and the government were taking advantage of the fact that I was willing to be the CIO, without giving recognition back. Government officers like to say that it is an honor to serve the country, like you should do it with no condition. Yes, that is all it takes if you do not have other choices! If you do have other choices also in the private sector, it has to be a two-sided road. It is an honor that you trust me to be the CIO, but also do salute the talent and the work. I know it sounds arrogant, but this is the reason why it is hard to attract from private sector some real good leaders to work in government.

The sad part is that if somebody, a good friend, asked me now if I would suggest working for the government—I would say probably "no." One thing is that you do have to give back to the country, and it is important that you should try. But having spent four years there, I saw that the returns you get or how quickly you are forgotten or the negativism you get from the society or media while in the job—it may not be worth it. You have to be extremely strong mentally to handle the pressures, and there are other more rewarding ways to influence your country. Earn money and be a sponsor to the parties, for example. You have to have a huge self-motivation to last in an actual public office, like my inner engineer was fascinated by the chance to solve some big problems. Yet, this lasts only so long.

How Did You Make Sure That Your Work Would Last?

Well, I chose the successor!

But I also knew that as the processes we managed to create had required hard work to put in place, they would be also hard to change overnight or drop them overnight. The way we distributed ICT investment for impact was going to be in place for some time, the principle that each silo should be responsible and improving their services was going to still there, and so on.

We did put in place reasonable things that had not been in place before. And it is hard to drop reasonable things just like that.

Knowing What You Now Know, Is There Anything You Wish You Had Known When You Started?

How to operate in the public sector. It is something that is very easy for government officials to understand, and very hard for entrepreneurs. Every time I argue with people from the private sector about why this or that change is not happening and fast enough, they do not get it. "It makes sense, why do they not just do it in government?" they ask.

Because the reasonable everyday motivations you are used to using in the private sector just do not work in government. In the private sector you never have to ask a question like "Do you not want to do a reasonable thing?" Of course, you do! In government, there is an upside-down logic sometimes instead. There are all these excuses. People have strong positions, but their meaning in life is to survive, and for that reason they do not do anything. You also cannot offer them an incentive. Even if the change would be reasonable.

Is There Any Skill That Can Be Learned to Be Ready to Take Such a Job?

I never start anything if I do not have proper vision, proper team, proper money. These three elements always need to be in place and you have to learn that. This is a skill to understand if you have them or not.

First of all, you have to have ideas that are worth believing in. Then you have to have people who actually believe in them. Then you have to have money to support that crusade. Then you also have to have operational skills to keep it going, and charisma to remove the obstacles and get the political support (or any support you need). That is the formula, and you can learn it through experience.

Your words also have to have weight. It is a skill; it is something you have to consciously build out earlier. I started building my public profile in 2007. If I had just been a CEO of an enterprise coming to government CIO role without no profile, I would not have been able to start have impact immediately.

What Are the Key Things to Do to Be Effective as a Government CIO or in a Similar Role?

You need to figure out the dilemma if are you the CIO for the country or the government. If you are just in charge of the government, you are responsible that the services in the government are up and running, working properly so that the services are delivered to the people. Or are you the CIO that changes the way the whole country operates? Figure out where you want to operate.

Then you have to know your limits. These will determine what you can achieve and what can be your big goals or the change you can actually make. Choose the goals according to the team and the budget ability you have. Money is not always the issue, though. I think we have proven that in Estonia, looking at what budgets we have had here to build a digital society and what some other countries have had with not much result to show for. But you need some money, at least.

Finally, lead through others. If you operate through other ministries and stakeholders, you multiply your ability to inflict change. If you just change your own field and just with your own team, you affect just one silo. If you change the mindset in ten ministries, you multiply your execution power by ten times.

Notes

1. EU Structural Funds are a major source of budgetary investment funds in many countries in European Union, aimed at raising and evening the socioeconomic development level across the EU. Each country can decide together with the European Commission on where and how their share of funds will be used in each seven-year funding cycle.
2. X-Road is the data exchange and interoperability platform used for government-wide secure data sharing.
3. Estonia became under Taavi's steering the first country in the world to offer e-Residency—a chance for people from anywhere in the world to apply for Estonia's state-issued national digital identity and thereby start using the digital services available in Estonia, without needing to be ever physically present in the country necessarily.
4. Taavi is referring to the theory on how to motivate people from Daniel Pink's book *Drive*.
5. PISA, or Program for International Student Assessment is a well-known comparative assessment of learning outcomes of students worldwide, organized by OECD.

CHAPTER 19

Tim Occleshaw

New Zealand

As the government chief technology officer and deputy government chief digital officer, Tim Occleshaw led the New Zealand public sector's digital government team from its inception in 2012 until stepping down in late 2019. During Tim's term, New Zealand became to be hailed as a standout digital nation and was a founding member of the Digital Nations Group.

Prior to his digital government role, Tim was deputy commissioner at Inland Revenue, responsible for information, design, and systems, and before that, CIO at the Ministry of Social Development. He was recognized as New Zealand CIO of the Year in 2008. Tim has also worked in the financial services sector in both Australia and New Zealand in various executive roles.

Outside of his digital leadership roles, Tim is also a professional musician and published author (under the pen name William Henshaw). Tim currently is semi-retired, and a part-time consultant in digital governance.

One of the first times Tim and I properly talked was in a place called Hell. Not to worry—it was only a cellar bar in the medieval old town in Tallinn, Estonia, when Tim was in town for one of the very first Digital Nations meetings. So, Tim and I started from Hell.

This became a series of conversations that continued across several continents, and quite a few craft beers. We picked each other's brains on whichever practical digital government steering questions either of us was pondering about. Tim has always been conscious of having an active life outside of work and outside of government. Therefore, a lot of our chats wandered to areas way beyond the digital government matters, too.

Tim came to the leading role in the New Zealand digital government scene at a time when the task was to elevate the game to the next level and across the whole government: from setting the strategy to daily routines of coordinating delivery or assisting the exploration of new directions (like in the Services Lab).

The work that Tim, Colin (his boss), and their team did to build up strong coordination and governance mechanisms to steer the rather autonomous players to step in the same rhythm is inspiring, in particular.

—*Siim*

How Did You Enter the Digital Government Leadership Role in New Zealand?

A lot of my career path has been accidental—I have just seen opportunities and gone for them. I had been working for the New Zealand government for about eight years as the CIO for the social welfare department, and then deputy commissioner of taxation (responsible for information, technology business, and service development), when this opportunity arose.

Across the government, I could see a lot of fragmentation, a lot of waste, and opportunities to improve the experience of citizens that were not being taken. I had come from the private sector, where I was the CIO for one of the big Australian and New Zealand banks. There everything is competitive and about commercial advantage; you cannot share anything. I went to government with an expectation that it should be possible to share stuff and learn from each other. And there was not much of that happening! It seemed like an opportunity. When the job was created to actually do something about it, I went for it and was lucky enough to get it.

I joined to lead the newly created GCIO team as the Government CTO, also titled as Deputy Government CIO (later Chief Digital Officer or GCDO). This was New Zealand's digital government team, and I was excited by the prospect of delivering the government's digital strategy—our first challenge! This strategy, and its accompanying action plan, included information, technology, digital services, and agency leadership.

What Was Your Motivation to Apply?

There was a lot to do! Having worked within two of New Zealand's largest agencies, developing their technology and digital services, the next logical step was to endeavor to leverage that as much as possible across government, working with every delivery agency. Plus, I am a tinkerer by nature. I know that I need new challenges, or I might start to tinker with things that are already humming along nicely. I thrive on change, so I seek out challenges that I can apply myself to.

What Was the Institutional Context of Digital Government Steering in New Zealand at the Time?

New Zealand had set up a special "e-government" team, like the private sector had done at least ten years earlier. But it was getting to a time when people started to realize that a separate team was not really the best way to do things. Business *is* digital; you cannot separate them, nor have a digital team that is not connected to the rest of your services and technology organization.

That is why, back in 2012, New Zealand had decided to establish more formally the function of a government CIO. We would build a team around the GCIO that would drive digital in a dedicated manner across the public sector: to come up with a consistent and common set of standards and a digital agenda, leveraging ideas and assets for the whole of government. GCIO was designated as one of the roles of Colin MacDonald, the chief executive of the Department of Internal Affairs—one of his many jobs! So, my role supporting him was the most senior role purely dedicated to digital government. In my view, the creation of my role and the new digital government team in 2012, to develop and drive New Zealand's digital government strategy, was when the government really got serious about digital.

Less than a year later, the government started reconsidering whether the Department of Internal Affairs was the right place for the GCDO work, because many other countries had created discrete digital organizations. My view has always been that having the function as part of a large delivery agency is important. We recommended against creating a separate GCDO organization in New Zealand. Some people thought I was mad. But I had by then seen the real benefit in having the GCIO as part of a big operational organization with a strong delivery track record. Digital teams in other nations have been accused of not having to deliver anything, for not being on the field of play with frontline service delivery agencies. In our setup, we were always on the field of play. We were true peers of those service agencies.

Did You Hesitate at All about Whether to Apply For, or to Take the Job?

I knew that there was a huge amount to do. I knew that from looking into government from the outside, as a customer. Digital government across New Zealand was just about nonexistent. We needed to really ramp up the effort. We would have to get government agencies to cooperate in ways that they had not really done before, and it was not going to be easy. The only thing to do was to jump right in. It was exciting.

I think coming from both a private and a public sector background was helpful. Coming from the customer delivery side, rather than being a technologist, was helpful also.

Did You Have Any Conditions Going in or Asks for the Role?

I remember thinking at the time about what would be the key factors for success, and if I did need to negotiate anything special in that space. I had known Colin for a while and knew I would have from him the support I needed. So, in the end, the only thing that I asked for was the ability to build my own team in my own way. It was a pretty good match to Colin's thinking, because as I said previously, being GCIO was one of his many complex jobs and he needed someone to drive the digital work for him.

What Was the Expectation to You, or the Ambition Laid Out for You to Achieve?

The expectations were about the same: establish the team, build a strategy, get on with delivering. Building the strategy was the very first challenge. We had three or four months to build a digital strategy for the whole government and have everybody agree to it.

Ministers were thinking operationally: they wanted delivery of a concrete action plan with the strategy, and they wanted to be able to tick off the actions so that the public could see real progress within the first year. The action plan contained more than a hundred deliverables, and I am proud to say that we managed to deliver more than 80 percent of those within the first year.

For me personally, I think my greatest ambition at that time was to get government agencies to join up. We needed to get them to operate as a coherent ecosystem, rather than silo agencies having their own approaches; replicating or rebuilding what had been built by others; not sharing; squabbling with each other; being competitive. I believed we could do better than this in New Zealand, being small and agile as a country. Every agency I had to work with was a ten-minute walk down the road. Having the necessary conversations was not difficult, and I could look people in the eye when I needed to.

My belief was that New Zealand could be a leading digital government in the space of three or four years. I think we got there sooner than I had hoped, when we were spotted by Liam Maxwell of the UK, and invited to join the initial group of Digital Nations.[1]

What Was Your Team's Mandate and the Mechanisms or Levers to Achieve These Aims?

The scope of the mandate officially was all agencies in the public service, plus five crown entities (such as the New Zealand Transport Agency, Tertiary Education Commission, and Accident Compensation Commission). Having that scope allowed us to work across all sectors.

Our job was to work with those organizations and influence them. We also had some limited powers of compulsion. For example, they were required to use a couple of shared capabilities, such as infrastructure-as-a-service or desktop-as-a-service offerings provided by vendors on contracts that we negotiated centrally. We did not provide these services, just brokered the deal and kept it all standardized. These mandatory offerings saved the government a significant amount of money.

Going beyond the official mandate, we were sometimes called to work with other government agencies unofficially. If any agency had a "digital" problem, there might be a ministerial conversation asking for our help. We would then roll up our sleeves and jump in to work alongside them, even if they were outside our mandate. We got involved with some local government organizations in this manner, too. We were always happy to help because that enabled us to build broader relationships and help a much larger cross-section of the New Zealand community.

Our mandate also included providing guidance and standards to agencies, which was helpful. Many of those standards did not actually exist at the time we were established, so we had to build them. We often achieved that by leveraging some very good work done by other Digital Nations. Digital.govt.nz leveraged work done by the UK and later enhanced by Israel. New Zealand's Digital Service Standard leveraged work done by the Canadian government's digital team based on UK standard. I am a great believer in leverage and reuse. Not everything needs to be built from scratch, and we had so much to do we did not do things that were not necessary.

In 2018, the then-new minister of finance, the Honorable Grant Robertson, took a real interest in what we were doing. He wanted to ensure that the government was getting the best bang for the buck with its digital and ICT investments. We proposed that the GCDO would need to be involved in reviewing all major investments with a large technology component, or any digital service component, and had to provide ministers advice on them. That strengthened the mandate for the GCDO team, as now we needed to endorse any big plans. Through that process change we were able to glean that there were more than a dozen discrete initiatives in the pipeline proposing to build an authentication or login system. Our strengthened mandate gave us a lever to compel agencies to use the government's official identity and authentication system—RealMe.

What Was Your Initial Plan or Essential Steps in the First Three Months of the Job?

I took over an organization that was going through a significant change and had had a temporary leader (reporting to a temporary chief executive) for some months. Job satisfaction and morale were pretty low; the digital team did not have any kind of plan. It had grown in an ad hoc way; thus, its structure was not optimal.

One of the first things I had to do was to build a new organization. That meant some new people but also restructuring—putting people in the right places. The team had been more about policy than anything else, so I focused on our new areas of accountability and structured the team on those. That needed to be done quite quickly, including giving people as clear as possible job descriptions and objectives. The lack of clarity had been a big factor in the poor satisfaction and engagement for them.

At the same time, we had been given a small budget to get the team's deliverables underway. That allocation of funds had been granted several months before I joined, yet there was no plan for its use. In my first six weeks, we built that plan and got it approved. That guided our first year's work.

Of course, the big activity in the first hundred days was the government digital strategy. I joined in December; the strategy had a target deliverable date of April to gain cabinet approval. Before the cabinet, we needed to get all the agencies to agree to the yet-to-be-developed strategy. It was tight. Part of the way through this period, the government added investment assurance and oversight to our mandate, which made it somewhat more complicated even. Ultimately, the strategy was signed off by all parties in June, so we got it done in a hundred fifty days.

During that period, I tried to do everything in a way that got buy-in across all the other agencies. Even when hiring senior people, I established interview panels that were all made up of me, plus two of my peers from other agencies. These were people I wanted to build relationships with, plus they had the right sort of skills and backgrounds, and graciously gave their time. When we built the first digital strategy, we set up a task force of about sixty senior people from across all the agencies to make sure we had the buy-in from all the big technology "investors."

What Was the Time Frame for Your Strategy?

We chose a four-year time frame for the strategy. We knew that during that period new processes and technologies would come about, there would be restructures in government, all that sort of stuff. So, the strategy needed to be looking out a bit further over the horizon than just a shorter-term transactional perspective. Yet, we also did not want to go too far into the future so that it became nebulous.

Even with a four-year time frame for the strategy, we said that we would do a full review of the strategy halfway through it, and to change it whenever it needed to be adapted. We also planned for a full review of all of the actions every twelve months and to get ministers to sign off on those.

What Was the Gist of the New Strategy?

The underlying aim was to lift New Zealand from being rather fragmented in digital efforts to a nation that would be, at worst, in the "front half of the pack" globally.

A more concrete objective was to ensure that New Zealanders were able to engage with government digitally, on their terms, and not have to navigate many different ways of engaging with government. Another area was the information space: aiming to ensure appropriate security and privacy of people's information. This included creating the government chief privacy officer role.

We also had an objective focused on investment leverage. One of the pieces of our work was an inventory of all the big technology projects that had some sort of digital service implication.

This was eye-opening. We got to see that there were way too many agencies trying to build their own authentication systems, as I said already before as an example.

The practical part of the strategy was the action plan—the list of things agencies were going to deliver. That is the part the ministers liked the most. This is pretty standard stuff, but, very importantly, it was where agencies were spending their ICT budgets. We made sure that we included big transformational projects already underway, plus some new ones. The action plan was our vehicle for the GCIO to have oversight of those projects and be able to provide input to agencies and to the ministers about their investment decisions.

In terms of transactional services, we set ourselves a target of having 80 percent of the most common citizen transactions with government online. To do that, we had to identify a list of top twenty or so transactions by volume, then negotiate with the agencies that owned and delivered those transactions or services to citizens, and then persuade them to be part of the plan. We also had to ensure that the target was defined appropriately. Simply being able to find information and download a form does not count! The target time frame was two years. When we started, there was less than 30 percent of these common transactions online. We got to the 80 percent target about two months after the deadline; at target date the stats showed us sitting at about 78 percent. So, we were a bit disappointed by that—but still New Zealanders got a significant benefit.

What Were the Mechanisms Foreseen in the Strategy for Ensuring Its Delivery?

The strategy had an activity stream on leadership across the system.

We knew that we had a cohort of chief executives and operational leaders in the public sector who were very capable, but many did not know much about digital or IT. They would not admit it, but a few might have been daunted by technology. Many pushed the ICT or digital decisions down their organization; they would not let digital stuff come to the top table.

We needed to change that because we needed to get top executives to buy in. So, we started the program of expert workshops for the executives. We brought people in from MIT and from industry. CTOs and CEOs of very large organizations. That was very successful; we managed to get chief executives involved in conversations and in our governance and collaboration framework, called the Digital Government Partnership.

We also kicked off the digital graduate intake program. This targeted bringing in qualified and digitally savvy new entrants into the public service, ensuring that they got a coordinated set of experiences and training across multiple agencies who had agreed to be part of the program. We cycled those new people through a structured rotation of three to four different organizations in their two-year tenure in the program. It built up a cohort that is now something like seventy or more people who are out there working in agencies, but also part of GCDO team as well in spirit.

What Else Did You Employ for Ensuring the Strategy's Delivery and Especially across the Government?

Collaboration is an absolutely critical thing. We knew that we did not have a big stick to hit people with. I have always been a believer that the big stick does not work anyway. You need to demonstrate leadership, to "walk the talk," and you need to make people want to go along with you on your journey. I think you need to demonstrate that you are doing what you want others to do. Anybody with children knows that! They do not do what you tell them; they do what you *do*.

Without buy-in, without agencies believing in what we were seeking to achieve, we could not have succeeded. Influence was always the biggest lever that we had. Creating the governance and sharing framework that I mentioned previously—the Digital Government Partnership—was critical. This included almost sixty senior-executive-level people from across the government. If we had not done that, we would not have been able to convince ministers to set up a ministerial group to drive digital government. Ministers agreed to this in 2018, after chief executives supported us in advising their ministers to join.

You Had Planned for a Mid-Term Review of Strategy after the First Two Years—How Much Did You Change the Plan Then?

At the mid-term review, the strategy did not change significantly, although the action plan did. There were numerous new projects underway and, as a system, we had got better at working together.

Very soon after that mid-term review, we commenced work on the new digital strategy that would replace the first one at its conclusion in 2017. The new strategy was very different. We wanted to ensure that not only did it deliver for government and citizens but also that it had more relevance for the private sector. After all, the private sector is not just a key part of government's supply chain, but increasingly a part of government's service delivery.

The new strategy would still encompass government broadly from both the state sector and local government. At the time of the first strategy's end, New Zealand had a change of government when the Right Honorable Jacinda Ardern became prime minister. This government created the first formal ministerial role for digital government at the end of 2017. That signaled a shift in focus for us, narrowing or sharpening our focus to the public sector. The new strategy, my last major task in the role, was launched as the Strategy for a Digital Public Sector. I also decided then that it was time for somebody else to take the reins from me in the role.

With Changing Politics and Otherwise Things Happening in Life How Did You Manage to Keep the Delivery of Strategy in the Intended Line and Your Focus on the Strategy as Opposed to Current Events?

It is always hard. The agencies were constantly trying to get their projects over the line. Every agency in New Zealand would tell you the same story: that there was not enough money to deliver all the things that they had to deliver. They would tell you that building something that could be reusable by somebody else was not really palatable for them. "I do not have enough money to do it; I do not have enough time to do it." Or their minister might say publicly that, of course, they were interested in the best thing for New Zealanders and to do the right thing by building stuff that will get plenty of reuse, but then privately say to the chief executive they wanted their quicker (and cheaper) delivery. Delivering things in a way that other agencies might benefit from them was merely a nice-to-have.

Quick delivery, particularly in the final year of a government's three-year term, is quite a challenge when you are trying to get agencies to think longer term. The reality is that you really only have eighteen months, or two years at best, to get big stuff done in any government. The rest of the time you are either helping to brief in new ministers, or the government is working in more of a caretaker mode with an eye toward the next election, and not making big or risky decisions that would not bring a delivery for them within the current term.

For me personally, I always think about the future, and I have got a fairly strategic brain. That is sometimes a problem because I am not great on routines, details, and processes! But I am always able to kind of lift myself out of the day-to-day and think forward. Perhaps thinking about what I need to put in place now in order to deliver the big thing in two or three years' time.

Some years ago, an old friend quoted a phrase that stuck in my mind. He said, "You have to be in the dance, but you have to also be on the balcony." He meant that you have to roll up your sleeves and get on with delivering now, being hands-on with activities and focused with people. But you also have to continuously keep the vision, the big picture, the strategy firmly in your mind, and be looking in from the outside. Stopping to take a breath, particularly during even a high-stress situation, is a very valuable thing. Get up and go out for a fifteen-minute walk. Have a beer and conversation with someone who faces similar challenges. I find that those sorts of things can help the answer you are seeking to arrive in your mind sometimes.

I have always tried to have a space allocated in my diary that my assistant knew not to offer out without talking to me first, for going around and talking to people, or just thinking about stuff. I tried to ensure that every week I would spend at least half an hour just thinking about what it was that I would have to get done in the next five days. Then I tried to make sure that those tasks had either some of my time set aside for them, or that I had very clearly assigned them to somebody whom I could trust to get them done. I had to keep this routine and structure because it does not necessarily come naturally.

Your Title Changed Half-Way through Your Time in the Office—Why?

Yes, I became the deputy chief digital officer instead of CTO and deputy CIO.

It was a step change that signaled a bigger mandate and role given to us. It came with a small budget increase, which helped me to get some more people to do some more things on the digital front.

But I was also trying to ensure the role and our work made sense to outsiders. The private sector partners who had an understanding what was happening in other countries in the digital space, and the people from banks especially, were asking why is there no chief transformation officer or chief digital officer in the government in New Zealand? Within the government, we all understood what our office did, but it was not always clear to outsiders.

We used the change to clarify our mandate, to better explain outside government what it was we did, and also to build the consistency with other nations. We also understood how the New Zealand public service works. That the state services are a cohort of separate organizations with common purpose and common principles, but very little in the way of common work programs and common strategies. We were trying to swim against the tide of that and the title change helped by adding further clarity.

How Did You Build Your Team? What Key Roles or Competences Did You Look For?

The initial team was, in my view, too introspective. They focused internally on trying to develop useful standards and policies to give to government agencies, then crossing their fingers and hoping that these would be taken up. We had some incredibly smart analysts, and there were a few strong leaders within the group, but many were not as great at engaging people. We needed an ability to convert deep strategic thinking into a vision that people can actually understand and buy into. We needed to shift focus there, starting with the leadership.

We also had commercial people primarily focused on government sourcing contracts, like trying to secure a whole-of-government Microsoft deal. Some of the global corporations we dealt with are much larger financially than the New Zealand government technology spend, so we had very little leverage. In fact, we needed to work with the supply chain in a very different way. I brought in a former senior executive from one of those multinational tech corporations, who was able to engage the big suppliers building serious partnerships with them. This meant working out ways that these suppliers could leverage stuff they developed or tested in New Zealand into other parts of the world. They could showcase their good stuff with our help and our endorsement.

In addition, I needed to establish an agency relationship function because we did not have that initially at all. We hired people from across the system, some of them former CIOs of agencies, to manage the agency relationships and spend time with key decision-makers and leaders. Having that credibility as CIOs was extremely helpful.

Finally, I had to make sure I had enough people who were project delivery specialists and who would drive the delivery results. We had plenty of good thinkers, but we needed more operational delivery people. So, we brought some of them in as well.

What Was Your Selling Argument to Convince People to Join You?

I think my "sales pitch" to most was that we had a clear and strong vision. I certainly had a clear vision of where I wanted to go with New Zealand's digital government offering, and I could see a way to execute a reasonably good chunk of it, and to get New Zealand to stand out.

I was very enthusiastic about the vision I had, and that probably helped me sell it. I am not a natural salesman, mind you. It also helped that I had "been around"—in a big bank, CIO of New Zealand's largest government organization (social development), in the tax department. All of this gave me a reasonably solid network, and Wellington is a small city in a small country.

What Was the Culture Fit You Were Aiming For in This Team?

I wanted an organization that understood its job was about building a better digital world in the big sense.

Everything we did had to be about making things better. First, better for our citizens in New Zealand, better for government agencies, for New Zealand to set a better example for the rest of the world. But I also wanted an organization that saw itself as part of something huge—that it was a global movement. So, second, we were making government better for the citizens of the world.

Every time I stood up in front of people, whether it was an internal event, or at a conference, or a media interview, I tried hard to make sure that I was talking about the vision: where we were going, what I saw the future looking like. I unashamedly took every opportunity to promote that vision for the future. I learned this years ago in a technology role at one of the major banks—always talking in terms of customer's experience as opposed to the technology encouraged others to change their language and thinking.

Sometimes the legacy problem is not the technology; it is the thinking! Having a clear future vision helps people move away from the past, even if they invented that past.

As a Leader of the Team, What Were Your Principles or Mottos You Kept Infusing?

There was one thing that became a slogan. I do not remember whether I was the first person to say it or whether it was our media lead who worked closely with us. When talking about who we were and how we had to deliver our job, we had a simple mantra: "centrally led, collaboratively delivered."

That was our way of reminding the whole system and ourselves that we were in the center and leading the digital agenda. But the delivery was actually being done across the whole system in every agency. It reminded agencies that there was central leadership, and they did have to do some things our way. But it also reminded everybody that the delivery was in their hands The agencies were the ones with the money, with the big systems, with the big projects. This mantra was even on the back of our business cards, and it stuck with us.

A big part of my approach to leadership is, of course, to bring in the best people I can find in terms of skills, experience, and intelligence. But just as important, I always seek to bring in people who have the right kind of cultural and personality fit, whom I could trust to get all this work done. After that, I think a big part of the leader's role is to give people clarity about what they have to deliver and then get out of their way.

It is really important to make sure your people really understand their accountabilities and goals, so there is no ambiguity. I believe people want to do a good job and be acknowledged for that. In my experience, if you have someone who is not doing a good job, it might be because they are not clear on what the job is. They may not see it the same way that you see it.

Second, I tried to make sure the people feel confident, empowered, and supported to get on with their job. Stay out of their way and do not look over their shoulder. Let them succeed.

What Were Your Routines to Handle Relationships with Peers or Stakeholders in the Government?

We had all the structured stuff I have mentioned—our Digital Government Partnership and its governance groups. Through those, we worked regularly with peers across all the agencies.

However, it was also important to maintain some much less formal relationships. We would go out for lunch or have a beer every few months with some senior people of other ministries; having an open, unstructured chat; maintaining the interpersonal relationships on casual level. This was in order to make sure that if one ever needed something from the other, we could just pick up the phone.

You Served under the Government CIO—Later GCDO—Colin MacDonald. How Did You Two Work Together?

Colin was the designated GCIO or GCDO, accountable for the overarching strategy and delivery at the end of the day. But he had a whole bunch of duties in his role in this wide department that Internal Affairs is—from local government and gambling policy to passport issuing. Much of his work, both policy and operational delivery, did not have much to do with digital government. Colin is a very capable leader, but, like many, he did not have much time to devote to detail. He could have only a few hours each week to be the GCIO. That is what my team and I were there for.

My role was to do the bulk of the work, but I could not have been successful without him. Colin was seen as a true peer by all the big agency chief executives because he was in charge of a large, pressured delivery organization. He could get the chief executive's attention if it became necessary. They listened to him.

We worked in a very integrated way with each other to ensure we got the best outcomes that we could. We were both together in the ministers' meetings because the minister expected to see the most senior person. But when Colin left the meeting, he often did not have the time to spend on debriefing it and explaining to me what needed to be done. He just needed me to get on and get it done.

Because Colin had distance from the day-to-day digital government work, he was often able to look at the work I was doing like the strategy and guide us for better outcome: some less detail here or more content there. His guidance was very much a part of our final strategies.

We had regular meetings of one-hour catch-up every fortnight, plus together in the governance groups. I always saw my role as ensuring that he was across the big issues, and particularly aware of any difficult agency relationship, in case a peer called him.

Looking back, I think our two roles were entirely complementary and neither could have succeeded without the other.

During Your Term, You Were Able to Raise More Funds for the Work—What Was the Trick to That?

It is not enough for an idea to just make good sense to get governments to invest. You have to prove the value.

The way we raised the budget for shared services—our common capabilities—was by setting ourselves the target of savings generated by the investment and proving we had met it. We commissioned one of the Big Four accounting firms to give us a framework and methodology through which to measure the savings. We also had them report on the results, which were then reviewed and confirmed by the Treasury. Being able to prove that your work had resulted in savings that exceeded your budget many times over was a hugely valuable exercise. We were also able to gain increased funding for investment review and assurance-related work because we had a proven track record in avoided costs across the system.

You Have Told Me at Some Point That It Is Important to Know When to Lead and When to Follow. How Did That Manifest in Your Work?

Sometimes the best strategy is not to break new ground but to be the first to follow. To take something that already exists. If it is good, just use it. If it is *nearly* what you need, tweak it. Even buy off-the-shelf. Then you can put your energy into something else.

That is why I always want to look for something that exists. A good case is the digital service standard. When we were starting the work on it, there were some people in the team who were quite determined that they would invent the New Zealand service standard from the ground up. They were saying that it had to be specific for our context. I ended up stopping it because I saw that there was a perfectly good service standard that originated in the UK and already had been tweaked by others, especially in Canada. If it worked for their First Nations,[2] it could possibly work for our Maori communities, for example. So, the team had to show me why it would not work for New Zealand, or we would go ahead and use it. We ended up adopting it with only minor localization. That is how the New Zealand's Digital Service Standard was born.

If You Sum Up Your Term in Office, What Are You Most Proud of as Your Achievements?

I would say that the delivery of the government's digital strategy was the single-most important thing. Well, two things as I ended up working on two strategies. They book-ended my seven years of leading the GCDO team. I started with developing the first digital strategy, getting it over the line and signed off by the whole system. Then six years later, I ended my time doing the same thing. We got the most recent digital government strategy signed off by the minister and published just before I finished up. Both strategies were important pieces of work. I suppose I am prouder of the first one because it was truly groundbreaking.

Another accomplishment would be the Digital Government Partnership governance model. There have been a number of people who have said to me over the years that it was a stroke of genius. I am here to tell you that it was just common sense, not genius at all! All I was trying to do was dismantle about a dozen completely fragmented and competing governance groups that were adding no value for anybody and create a new structure with a level of orchestration that gave us some control of the meeting agendas. The partnership model brought us agency buy-in to drive the delivery of the strategy, because we got a team of sixty senior executives across the public services involved.

Coupled to that is the achievement of getting the ministerial digital group together. This was by no means solely my success. Credit must go to Colin and the whole team, of course. This group was a great success though. Every two months the most senior ministers got together to discuss digital strategy and the work program for the whole public sector. Agencies had to report to them on what (and how) they were doing, while we listened. It meant that if they had not worked with us from the beginning to get our buy-in and support, the discussion might end badly for them, with ministers wanting to know why they had not engaged the GCDO.

Another thing is the common capabilities. I was very proud of having delivered those and saving a lot of money. I was once criticized by a peer from another country for negotiating a contract with a large multinational vendor described as "old school." I explained that it meant we now had a complete view of agencies spend with that particular company, and therefore a lever to manage it down. Those common capabilities, and common software contracts, definitely have an important place in our story.

Do You Think You Had Any Failures?

Yes, I do. My biggest regret of seven years is that I was not able to successfully challenge the decision to close our digital services lab.

In my opinion, the lab was a great success and run by an outstanding team of professionals. When it was established, we did not know if it was going to work or not. In the lab, agencies could try out things they did not yet fully understand, could figure out how the new technology might benefit them—or not. They could work together in a safe environment that did not have a government or agency brand on it. It was a place where government agencies could all get together and just try new technology. Like building out legislation-as-code as an experiment.

It had some great successes. One example was the housing rates rebate system, which benefited about fifty local government authorities. We built it once instead of all of them having to go off to build their own because it was mandated in legislation. We must have saved tens of millions of dollars for those organizations. Or when we set up a really intricate virtual reality system, just to see how it might benefit some work. It turned out to be possible to simulate for policy analysts and decision-makers someone being indoctrinated into the world of hate, and what it was like to be the subject of such a person's attacks. This helped focus some of the policy response after the terrorist attack in Christchurch in 2019.

The lab was funded by small financial contributions from agencies. The expenses were largely just people's salaries. It was not a huge amount of money burned if a project did not succeed in the lab. Far better than the consequences of a failure in the agencies' own environments.

But the decision was to shut the lab down, and I gave up in the end. We lost some really good people because the lab closed, some of them going back to private sector to do amazing things for other people. I still do not know what we could have done differently. I think part of the problem for ministers might simply be that failure is *never* palatable for them. Even though failure is part of any healthy development cycle, and even within an environment where it is safe and relatively low cost to fail.

Are There Any Other Regrets You Have?

I am not sure I always got the balance right between working outwardly with agencies and overseas and working closely with my team. In fact, probably I traveled too much in the last year or two. I did not see enough of my team; I became too disconnected. New Zealand is so far from everywhere that usually it was a long flight to get to wherever I was going, I would end up a week or two away from the office at a time. Possibly that played part in my failure to keep the lab open—I just was not there often enough.

You Already Touched Upon What Made You Move On—the Difference of Views Over the Scope of Strategy. Was That All?

I stayed in the job for seven years, which is longer than I have stayed in any other job in my career. Usually, I would do more like four years in a role. I stayed in the deputy GCDO role because I loved it. And I moved on because it was time to move on. Time for someone else to take over.

Besides the strategy viewpoint differences, I did have family reasons also because I needed to be with my elderly mother in Australia more. I felt, still feel, very proud to have played my part in building a very strong team, some significant and enduring foundations, and securing New Zealand's place as a leading digital nation.

Maybe I might have also started to undo the good things because, as I said, I am a tinkerer by nature. So that was part of my decision, too.

What Do You Think Were the Outlying Next Challenges for Digital Government in New Zealand?

I wanted to get into user-driven government, which had met some resistance during my last year of tenure there. To get from user-centered service design of ten years ago to user-driven experience. To get citizens much more involved in driving government strategy and policy.

I would have made the lab into a digital *government* lab, not just services. I could see the benefit of including policy work in there by bringing in people whose background is not so much technology but things like psychology, or sociology, or anthropology—to think very differently, very holistically about government. About how citizens and government need to engage in the now, in the medium- and longer-term future, which is not just about services. For people with a background in policy, this probably is horrifying. Some view policy as the sole domain of trained policy analysts, whereas I do not.

Here is an example I have often used: think about a scenario where you want to travel overseas. You might need to think about visas, or if you have paid your taxes or fines (if not, you might be stopped at the border). You are probably engaging with a travel company or website. What if, once you assert your identity safely, you could authorize the agent or bot to do all those things for you, Through APIs, the systems engage with government systems and figure it all out for you. Tell you if you need a visa, and you can there and then order it. Or renew your passport, pay your student debts, notify health or welfare services, whatever.

This frightens people, because that would mean government letting go of the control of the interface with the user. But the old way means you have to compel people to come to government *on our terms*. It means people have to navigate multiple access points and find a way to integrate them around their needs. Well, I do not agree with that. A government paid for by taxpayers should be supplying services *on citizens' terms*. That is another reason I wanted to take our strategy toward the private sector more.

How Did You Ensure What You Started Would Last?

Even though I did not get my "ideal" digital government strategy through, I did get a good one. This locks in the direction for the next few years, as much as one can in government.

Throughout my seven years of this journey, I was always aware that I was not the most important person in the agenda. The people who deliver day-to-day for the leaders of the teams, the people who do the work, deliver the outcomes. Those are the most important people. Always. So building an enduring structure, building job descriptions that have the right level of clarity of accountability and control and empowerment and so on and so forth, securing the budget for these things—that is how you make stuff endure.

That would always transcend my tenure in the role because I was inevitably going to leave at some point. I always had in my mind that I could be leaving next year, I could be leaving next month. One can never be sure. That is why I always tried to make sure that I had enduring structures in place, budgets in place, the right people in place.

Would You Take the Same Job Ever Again?

Now I know a lot more than I did back in 2012, when I just saw an opportunity and went for it. Now I would want to make sure that the job was going to be about those things that I talked about before: helping to ensure that citizens can engage government at all levels, including policy and strategy in a much more holistic way. It would mean letting go of tradition. So, if the job is going to be about that, yes, I would be interested.

What Do You See Are the Core Skills Necessary to Do This Job Well for Impact?

Resilience, perseverance. You have to be able take the occasional punch to the head. And there is so much to do. It is not a job for the fainthearted.

You have to be able to do a sort of "cat herding," to juggle things that might occasionally be on fire—something very, very difficult. Humans all think differently. You cannot come up with a brilliant strategy and just tell people that from next Monday, that is going to be their strategy. You have to be able to consistently articulate and repeat your compelling vision and get people to *want* to come with you.

You need to be able to hold your vision and your strategy firmly in your mind while you are negotiating the details with the people who will deliver and facing the people who are opposing. Sometimes you need to have a spare hand to put out one of those fires.

Finally, there is the key skill that my friend quoted to me many years ago: that thing about being able to be in the dance at the same time as being on the balcony. That is a core skill for anyone who is leading in digital government, because there are so many moving pieces moving at different speeds in different directions.

What Are Your Recommendations to a Good Peer from Another Country—Tim's Friendly Advice for How to Perform Digital Government Leadership Well?

That is a tough question! I would say first to remember that the main game is about heading toward a better digital world. Do not let anything distract you from that vision.

Second, it is about people. There has been a lot of talk about sticks and carrots. I believe you cannot direct people and organizations to go against the objectives that are set by their bosses or their ministers. You have to work with people by being on their side, supporting them to change their organization's objectives if these are out of date or just not right.

The last thing, question everything. I do not necessarily mean challenge or resistance; I just mean look critically at everything. I have seen lots of occasions when somebody is doing something because it has always been done that way, even though the context has changed significantly. I would say that these days some things do not need to be done at all in a digital world. Sometimes the legacy thinking is just wrong, out of place. Always have a cold critical look at something that you feel is not quite right. It probably *is* not quite right; maybe it was put in place in the analog world and is not even needed anymore.

Notes

1. Liam Maxwell was chief technology officer for Her Majesty's Government in the United Kingdom from 2012 to 2016. He led the founding of Digital Nations, an international forum of some of the leading digital governments—which was initially called Digital-5, when the United Kingdom, New Zealand, Estonia, Republic of Korea, and Israel set it up in 2014.
2. General term for (groups of) Canada's indigenous peoples.

CHAPTER 20

Yolanda Martínez

Mexico

Yolanda Martínez currently works as International Telecommunications Union (ITU) overall lead for GovStack Initiative, helping governments accelerate the digitalization of government services.

In the public sector, Yolanda led the national digital strategy of Mexico, the digital government unit at the federal level, and the Zapopan digital city program at the local level. She has led several digital transformation initiatives in the private sector while at Deloitte Consulting.

In the international arena, Yolanda led the Office of the Inter-American Development Bank (IDB) in Chile, has collaborated with United Nations agencies, and joined OECD as a peer reviewer for the digital government strategies of various Latin American countries.

Yolanda has been recognized by Apolitical as one of the twenty most influential people globally in digital government. She holds a PhD degree in information and knowledge society from the Open University of Catalonia (UOC).

Yolanda is like a shining sun. If she enters the room, it fills up with energy, with light, with positivism that she just cannot help but radiate. She is always "super active," as she would say herself, speaking very fast and through a wide smile.

You cannot lead a team that transforms a country of 130 million people, a federation with three levels of government, thousands of entities at all these levels, and almost no digital services at start, if you are not a walking (I should say, running) fusion reactor like Yolanda. I mean, the effort you have to make is just massive, especially if your time to do it is limited like hers was. Delivery had to be especially paced because the presidential terms are fixed.

GOB.MX and the national digital agenda behind it, together with the very strong central coordination they created, redefined how government works in Mexico. It has inspired digital and open government movements globally.

The reactor within Yolanda is called passion. Passion for technology, passion for designing well, passion for really making people's lives better, passion for her country, her team. Passion for life. She is Mexican, after all!

—SIIM

How Did You Enter the Field of Digital Government and Become the Leader in it in Mexico?

I was responsible for the city technology office in Zapopan, Mexico, before joining the federal government. I come from a background in information systems, plus I did my master's degree in public policy with a focus on ICT for development. I worked in Deloitte Consulting for a while after school, before joining the city government.

Work in Zapopan really allowed me to put into practice everything that I wanted to do about using ICT for development. It was very encouraging for me to be able to define and codesign a strategy together with the mayor, Hector Vielma, and a great team of colleagues. They really shared the vision that technology was a great enabler to have a city that is inclusive, sustainable, and designed to make the life of the people easy. It was the very first time that we set up a digital agenda in the municipality, as part of an overall development plan directly led by the mayor. We were able to redesign the experience of people in the city with digital, making it the main source of information and access to services.

When I was about to finish my term as the CIO of the city, I was invited to participate in a digital agenda event of one of the national presidential candidates, Enrique Peña Nieto. He was the only candidate making proposals about digital transformation. I was a speaker at the event. I presented in three minutes what we had done in Zapopan, and the challenges we had at the municipal level in Mexico with digitization. We have 2,445 municipalities in thirty-two states in our country. It is a very important level of government, and all three levels of government are independent.

The future president and his team led by Alejandra Lagunes were very interested in really understanding what the challenges were in implementing digital agendas. Alejandra invited me to join the presidential transition team once they won the elections.

The transition team was responsible for understanding the current state of different policies in the country. When the new president enters the office, the transition team already has done the work, knows what is going on, and then goes to take over the actual work. Alejandra was leading the team of digital transformation, and for me it was amazing to be part of it. It was like a dream to be able to become the chief of the digital government unit for my country. It was also the first time in Mexico that a National Digital Strategy Coordination (NDSC) Office was put in place at the presidential level.

Did You Hesitate at All about Joining the President's Team?

No, I was super happy. I was in Washington, DC, for a job interview with the Inter-American Development Bank, when I received the call from Alejandra. She said she wanted me on her team, and I thought for only like half a second and said, "This is amazing, I will be there." This was a Friday, and I started on Monday the next week.

Was There Any More Concrete Mission or Deliverable Set for You to Come and Take Care Of?

We did not get any concrete instruction, more a confirmation that digital transformation was extremely relevant and a priority for the president. He asked us to present him the way forward. He said he was convinced digital was the important policy to have, and us as his team should look at best practice and how to put it into practice.

I am very thankful that I had the freedom always to really propose things and see those things happening. That is why I think he was a great president in the sense that he recognized that digital has to be a priority but also recognized that his team should do the work to make it happen. We were not given a recipe; we did the work to design the recipe for what should be, in our humble vision, the best for Mexico.

For Background and Context, What Is the Institutional Setting of Digital Government in Mexico?

We have different ministries related to the area, including the Ministry of Communication and Transport, that are mainly focused on connectivity. We had before a digital government unit within the Ministry of Public Affairs, that already had a transversal mandate over ICT policy, digital government services, and the digitization strategies of other entities. Each of the 299 federal entities have their CIOs.

When we did the diagnosis of the current situation during the transition period, we discovered that there was a lot of work done in terms of connectivity and the digitization of services, but we saw a lot of asymmetries. Big entities like tax office or the state oil company had a lot of resources in terms of budgets they managed and the technical capacity in their teams. A lot of other entities did not have much of a budget, did not have the capacity or the skills to really keep up with the best practices on digital government.

So, we wanted to have a different setting with the purpose of somehow leveling the playing field for all government entities, including different levels of government. For this, we wanted to capitalize on everything that had been done in the country and that had given results and consolidate it into a coherent strategy. Putting in place coordination to leverage and put order into IT governance, IT procurement, building of reusable components. This would allow everyone in government to have access to the best equipment, the best tools for standardizing how government approached the citizens or how citizens approached government services.

That is why we moved the digital government unit reporting line to the NDSC at the president's office, and it got the execution role for the digital strategy efforts across the federal government and for collaboration with state and municipal authorities, with respect to their independence. The task was to have a nationwide digital agenda that was sound and made sense, and set the priorities in terms of connectivity, digitization of federal government services, open government, and citizen participation. As we had an agenda that was important to the president, the unit became very strong in terms of mandate.

With the new government, the Ministry of Public Affairs was about to disappear. We wanted to leverage all their normative efforts that they had done before, like the 2012 law of digital signature. We wanted to rescue such important efforts and to continue strengthening them, so the unit became our base.

The new digital government unit, reporting to the NDSC, was put in charge of public sector ICT policy management, procurement, and prioritization of projects and investments in order to be able to make the digital agenda actionable. The setup was an important innovation itself because it is not a matter of how much budget we have for the agenda but instead how well we align the budget available to what is a priority. In our case, it was GOB.MX, the single point of access to government services, to government information, to open data, and to participation.

The unit and its setup became a great enabler for major transformations in how the 299 federal government entities approached digital and put citizens at the center. This was possible with a very good governance based on such a strong mandate and because we were part of the president's office.

How Did the Decision Emerge That Very Strong Central Coordination Was Exactly What Was Needed?

In the transition team, we did a very in-depth analysis of best practices. We went into reading every single digital agenda that we found on the internet; we had a spreadsheet with all the countries and the link to the digital strategy that they had at the time. We wanted to really understand what the trends were, the best practices internationally.

Doing all this work allowed us to really make our case to the president on how important it was to first recognize all the prior improvements, no matter who had been ruling in the government. We were not starting from zero. We had 40 percent of connectivity around the country; we had a lot of data and government websites out there. For example, the Civil Registry Office had been doing the digitization of birth certificates for more than two decades, so we had them already digitized from 1930 onwards. All those efforts we wanted to recognize. We just needed to coordinate and unify the experience.

That is why the other important decision in our case indeed was the institutional arrangement for effective coordination. We suggested to the president that we needed an entity at the highest level, which could really sit down at the cabinet level and talk to other ministers peer-to-peer.

That is because digital government work was transversal to all the ministries. If we would be able to talk to other cabinet members as equals, we could show them how their ministry was doing in terms of compliance to the National Digital Strategy. Otherwise, we could run the risk of not being that relevant. But we wanted to be enablers of the main business of the government. We were aligning the agenda already during the transition time, so that the new government coming in would understand that digital was as important as the economic policy or health or education for the development.

In the digital era, all ministers needed to see digital as their best leverage to really meet the commitments of president's agenda and deliver their plans as ministers. I would say to them, "I am here to serve your objective." I think this made a total difference in how we could build our collaboration, because they could realize that we were there to help them meet *their* agendas.

How Easy Was the Transition from City to Federal Level for You?

At the city level, it had been quite different, because it was 100 percent operational in terms of providing services to people. Our team was responsible for everything that happened in the city and super hands on in fixing things. Very, very transactional.

In the city, we did not have much money to invest in technology. We did the best we could with what we had. At the federal level, I was extremely impressed by the amount of money that they managed and the technology they had. I thought, how can they have all this money available and none of the services were online? Even the major services sometimes lacked in digital, although some were good—I already mentioned the asymmetry we saw.

I remember that I had to take time to understand how the civil service worked when I first joined the city government. I was coming from Deloitte Consulting originally to government and it had been very different there. I remember going and asking where was our office of talent management? I needed someone to go and recruit students from the university to help us with our work in the city. They told me that we did not have such an office, and I had to go recruit the students myself if I wanted to have them. In city government, we had to do everything on our own. So, I did go to the universities; I enjoyed that.

When I went to the federal level, it was the other way around again. There we have a federal civil service function. I went to the human resource office and said I wanted to have an internship program to get kids from universities to come and join the unit. The only thing they asked me was how many I wanted! So, infrastructure like this makes a whole lot of difference in how you can deliver.

What Were Your First Steps During the First Months in Office?

In Mexico, when you join the federal government with a new presidential team, you have four months to design the National Development Plan. So, our first priority was to make sure that the digital agenda we had worked on during the transition, was going to get into the National Development Plan. This allowed me also to test the team that I had inherited from the Ministry of Public Affairs.

We went to a lot of meetings for this drafting, especially with Ministry of Finance, which was responsible for the development planning because the budget is associated with it. We transformed the initial agenda to a document that met the minimum requirements of the overall development plan.

We wanted to have the agenda as a "living" document—the challenge was how to integrate it to the fixed six-year overall development plan. How to have flexibility in adjusting our priority each year. We did manage to fit the major parts of the agenda to the plan. It had sixty-nine action lines for the 2013–2018 period for us, and these became a priority for the whole plan.

The method was that we would make those lines actionable later, as I and the unit also had some legal faculty ourselves to publish transversal regulatory frameworks like standards or policy documents, for example. So, the development plan included major action lines like "Digitizing all government services" to be enacted by the presidential decree, with the KPI of share of services digitally available. Based on this, I had the legal mandate to publish secondary legislation. Things like GOB.MX standards.

This type of legal arrangement was extremely important, I think, for providing certainty on how people could use digital as the channel to interact with government, and for allowing us the flexibility to test different approaches, especially with reusable components. Yet, it still gave us a very strong mandate from the National Development Plan, together with the budget assigned for its delivery.

How Did the Initial Agenda Become the Eventual Digital Strategy?

We had learned a lot in that transition period and that is why it was a very good use of our time. We studied the plans of the previous government, reviewed the indicators, reviewed the budget—besides the international best practices. When we took the actual office, we took some more time to validate the understanding we had reached from outside and to iterate the initial plan.

Interviewing my whole team and getting to know them, was one part of it. Since they were from the career civil service path, they had been long enough in the sector to really be able to provide a lot of knowledge on the history of the unit and the history of the policies that we would be promoting. It helped to really understand where we were standing.

Another thing that we had done during the transition time was that we interviewed literally everyone in the ecosystem: the IT chamber of commerce, the major digital civil rights organizations, the international organizations with presence in Mexico. So, when we took office, we were already known by the ecosystem. We were very outspoken that we really wanted to take the digital work to the highest level, and were very open to listen to suggestions, including through working in the open. This gave us trust from the ecosystem and support for different initiatives.

To cement the final plan, we made in 2013 a major event to with the president and Alejandra to present the National Digital Strategy. I still remember that day, because to me it felt like I could not have been in any place better than this. I felt the drive to do my best to make my country really leverage the digital era. I was so excited because of the event and having the president there meant that it was getting serious!

There we were, a small team that had now six years to really make a difference in our country, and to really contribute and to really honor what others had done as well. The President clearly pointed our way that ours was the team that was going to deliver the strategy. This proved useful as it facilitated the work we did for the rest of the of the presidential term.

What Was the Main Focus or Priority in the Strategy, and How Did You Set Out to Deliver It?

It was GOB.MX, the single point of access to government services, government information, open data, and participation. Through GOB.MX, all government entities were going to be equals in front of the citizen. It would not depend on whether you had a super big digital team or very small and modest IT capabilities. GOB.MX would be a shared service, providing same quality standard of service to the citizen, no matter the capability of the entities behind the service.

There were also some other ways for setting the conditions more equal to all government entities. We had price contracts for that to really democratize access to the best technology to all government entities and levels of government. We negotiated one fixed price, for example, for the software licenses and the same price was available for all entities, whatever the number of users. All of them were paid for by the Ministry of Finance.

But we really put our efforts to GOB.MX. We had a great team of developers, UX designers, legal advisors who worked together to have a very strong normative framework for it. We introduced a presidential decree that mandated GOB.MX as the single point of access to information services, to open data, to citizen participation mechanisms. This presidential decree allowed us to coordinate all these efforts to align the digital experience and really put the citizen needs at the front.

This allowed us to build an integrated team of great professionals. If we would have wanted to have the same level of team in all government entities and in all 2,445 municipalities, it would not have been simply possible. But if you have a great team at the center of government with strong political support with the best access to programming frameworks, UX techniques, user needs research, then that team becomes a shared service for the entire government.

How Did You Get the Other Entities Onboard with the GOB.MX Agenda?

It was not an option for the entities to follow the standard or not. In addition, we had enough capacity to mentor them and to make an accompanying change strategy with the entities to help them comply with the GOB.MX decree.

We set up an entire ecosystem to really convince our colleagues from the different areas that it was easier for citizens to go to one place to get their service done with the best quality than going to more than five thousand government websites that were not standardized, that did not share the same experience or security level. Doing it together avoided duplication of efforts and capacities, and the entities could now focus on really understanding the user needs to build the best digital service that would comply with the quality standards we set. The quality requirements included things like time to respond, accessibility for people with disabilities, communicating in a very easy and understandable way, and so on.

All that requires a lot of work, and we did a lot of training. I really enjoyed having the office full of public servants every day, taking different courses. We had workshops also together with the state-level and municipality-level governments that were voluntarily applying the federal government standard. It was a huge benefit for the citizen because the government people now started to understand that users did not care about the level of government responsible for the service. They just needed to get the service anywhere, anytime, on any device. We still had to make good cases in terms of the benefit for the citizen for state governments for them to voluntarily decide to align with our work, sign an agreement, and accept a joint national service standard.

We worked always in the open, very collaboratively. We always made our case as to why we were recommending to follow such and such things. But once we had them agreed and published, then everybody had to comply with that. Because that was the only way to scale up enough to really make an impact, especially in a huge government like Mexico.

How Did You Coordinate All These Other Governmental Stakeholders More Widely, Too?

We managed to do it by being open enough and inviting to collaborate, but also tough enough when we needed to ensure standards and the compliance to legal frameworks. We always codesigned all the standards, all our policies with government entities. But once the standard was set, then it was a legal matter to follow it. Just like I explained for GOB.MX. We involved entities in the discussion, but once the presidential decree was signed, it was not about if they wanted to follow it—they had to.

Besides GOB.MX, we had to set our focus on the budget as a priority. This comes from the logic of how the public sector works. Once you have priority in the national development plan, then you align the spending agendas with the help of Ministry of Finance. As all the entities in the federal government must comply with the national development plans, we got to work on aligning their ICT spending with the digital agenda. We had seen during the transition team that there was a lot of money in the entities for digital work. We mapped their spending priorities and realized they had all this money in technology like data centers, enterprise software, all that. They had less than 10 percent of the budget going for digital services.

We needed to reprioritize the spending across the government so that entities would not just spend on what they wanted. As part of it, we also mapped which agencies had some reusable components that could save us time and money in building transversal solutions like authentication, signature notification, citizen satisfaction surveys, and so on. Entities had to set a priority to the national digital plan, which was renewed each year. The first priority there was to make services digital, but it also included the need to open up the data or implement interoperability.

We had the mandate for our unit to validate if the proposed spending that entities had planned was aligned to the one or more of the sixty-nine action lines of the National Digital Strategy, or we would not approve their investment projects. Of course, many CIOs did not like this at all in the beginning. But we explained our work and showed them evidence of how much money was spent in total in the government and on similar things. It was the very first time they saw aggregated data, and that got many of them thinking. Nobody just had not taken the time to make an analysis of aggregated data.

We showed them the data at the meeting of the Interministerial Commission for the Development of eGovernment (CIDGE), a governance body engaging the federal entity CIOs on a regular basis. I said that budget and joint effort was going to be a discussion item every time we met from there on as we needed to align our priorities, join our forces, or we would be overspending.

How Did This Commission Work as Your Main Governance Body?

We used it as the key forum for codesigning the policy and standards, because all agencies needed to comply, and we also really wanted to share with them everything we were learning. When we sat down with our colleagues at first, I realized that they were busy managing their day-to-day operations in their agencies. Although we had learned so much from best practice research during the transition teamwork, they did not know or have time to look up these things themselves. We could build capacity together by sharing the learnings.

So, the forum was both for control and even more for communicating to our colleagues the learnings and reasoning. Even if we had the mandate to dictate policies and regulations, we always did ask feedback first on how to make the proposals better. They knew we had the mandate to push things, but they were also very eager to participate if given a chance.

I remember the very last session of the Interministerial Commission where we presented the final results of our term and the strategy's delivery. It was amazing to see in the aggregated view that we all had really made an impact in the life of people by digitizing almost 80 percent of federal government services. I told the council that it had been an honor to work together and to build our country, and these were the results. I saw it in their faces right then: "Oh, wow—we did achieve a lot by working together."

Besides the council, we held an end-of-the-year celebration event where we gave out GOB .MX trophies to recognize all the great teams and people from all around the government. The trophies represented a modest investment in financial terms but allowed us to give a huge recognition to digital teams that were making GOB.MX a reality for citizens every day. The trophies looked amazing because of our designers' effort, and it mattered most what they stood for. It was recognition of the effort and success that these digital teams from everywhere accomplished to make their services digital and to meet the standards we had set. We gave trophies for agencies with the highest satisfaction rating for their services, for technical teams that complied best with our requirements, and so on. We started inviting ministers there to receive the trophies on behalf of their agencies. The most important prize was the digital service excellence award, and it went to the service with the best evaluation from their users.

An event like this was very easy to organize, but it was our most important event of the year. There each of our own unit's teams and leadership presented what we had been doing and what we were planning for the next year, and we recognized the hard work of everyone during the year. It all helped greatly with government-wide team building.

Setting the Focus Is One Thing, Keeping It Another. How Hard Was It for You to Maintain the Focus on Your Approved Agenda?

In our case it was easy because we always prioritized GOB.MX as the main thing. I remember the discussions around whether to have a standard for different websites or build a single CMS and start migrating all the websites. You really need to have a very good case, because you present the idea and then a lot of phone calls are going to happen. Once we decided to go for a one-single-point of access and the reusable components for it, to have a team of developers doing it all, then you cannot lose your focus anymore. This was now our single priority.

Also, losing focus was hard because our KPI was also very simple—how many digital services were launched this month? That was the question in every meeting that I had with different government agencies every day. The target was clear: digitize all the government services, according to the standard and according to the user needs. Everything else was in place to serve that.

I actually went around plugging our agenda and work into high-level discussions or initiatives that were happening on other issues or crises—if it helped toward the target of 100 percent of services online. For example, one of the commitments in the national Open Government Partnership (OGP) action plan was to be fully transparent on the traceability of files under investigation. This can be a digital service; it can be built on a reusable component for traceability. Working with that team, we helped them solve a big sectoral problem for the country. It showed everyone how digital could help solve the policy problem in an easier way.

In Mexico's Digital Government Agenda, Open Government Was Always a Very Big Part. How Did That Come About, Because It Is Not Necessarily the Case Elsewhere?

In our case, we have a very active civil society—very active civil organizations. Mexico was one of the founder countries of the OGP. We had highlighted this already during our transition team review of Mexico's existing initiatives and international commitments. We wanted to follow that commitment based on the principle we had to build our agenda on top of what was already working.

You Have Talked Sometimes Quite a Bit about the Work on Making a Birth Certificate Standard Together with State Governments. What Was That About and Why Was It Important?

That one was a huge, huge victory for us to reach with digital also at the state and local levels.

As every state was independent, we had thirty-two different formats and thirty-two different procedures for something as extremely simple as requesting your birth certificate. It was not a technical challenge. It was about using the political weight and support of the president's office, and evidence how it made no sense at all to have people going to the place they were born to get a birth certificate—especially for, you know, the seventeen million Mexican people living in the US.

We achieved it near the end of the president's term in office because first we had to build up credibility toward our office in the way we worked and identifying what was the benefit of the way we proposed. By 2017, we had enough leverage, capability, and evidence as a team to sit down with governors and major city mayors and say that we were ready as a country to go to further standardize this one service.

Technology allows us to really collaborate more and to make seamless and integrated experience for citizens, based on a shared platform like GOB.MX, or the payment gateway, or others. All we needed to do in practice was a little adjustment in local regulations for registries, and we had a service whereby people could get their birth certificate in minutes.

How Did You Build the Team Out?

We did not change the initial team that joined from the Ministry of Public Affairs. I like to say we grew that team and our capacity to deliver.

Once we decided that we were going to go with GOB.MX and build it by ourselves, then we set out to grow the team with relevant technical expertise. We got developers, solution architects, UX designers, UX writers. We also went after expertise necessary for designing and developing the digital services, for example, for quality assurance before launching any service.

I really spent time at the beginning to interview the existing team and analyze what were their skills. I was also looking to understand their motivation because they knew a lot that was valuable. I also asked them, "This is the plan forward; who wants to change their activities?" I did find a lot of people saying what they preferred to take on the new arrangement. So, we set out to see how we could work as a team—and it worked! It required me to go to my colleagues in the human resource department and convince them to help me see these rearrangements through, because there usually are requirements and tests and so on to enter or move talent in the civil service.

Having the flexibility to hire people from outside was extremely important. We found a way to work through the national trust fund aimed at boosting connectivity in the country. We made a facility there to hire the technical expertise we needed and not necessarily have them come through the long civil service path. We put together terms of reference for the types of skills we needed at a time, according to how GOB.MX was being built up and to each year's digitalization priorities.

We also needed to have a team that was fully motivated to do what they were doing. Although I personally encourage work-and-life balance, the work we did was very exciting and so you ended up working a lot still! Also, in the president's office, work was happening Monday to Sunday and into the evenings. To work under such pressure, the team has to be motivated and not do it not because it is an obligation to go to work.

I tried to leverage all the resources available for the team to be good and to deliver. When people needed to go see a doctor or to the kids' festivals, I did not need to be told—just go and please enjoy! Because if people were happy at home, they were going to be happy in the office and we needed happy people building GOB.MX. The federal government also had a lot of ways to help them, like with family care or paying for people's studies. I always encouraged the team to use such means.

As You Were Expanding the Team, Who Was Your Most Valuable Hire or Addition?

I cannot think of just one. My whole leadership team was extremely important.

I put a lot of attention to who was going to be my head of legal, because we were the government, and we needed our work to have legal certainty. I needed a legal professional who understood that our role was to hack the government. Often in meetings, we would have other entities' lawyers say that something was not possible because the law said this or that. The role of our legal head was to say that yes, we knew the law, but we could change the law. And that we were going to start working on changing the law for it to meet the digital era, to make digital services that were easy to use and accessible to people.

The other important people were in the digital service team, responsible for digital service design and delivery. They had to really understand what we wanted to do with GOB.MX, to understand how important it was to manage all the digital teams in all the federal entities and beyond, to be able to make standards to meet a challenging digitization plan.

GOB.MX was the front end of digital government, but at the back end the crucial thing was to manage the budgets for technology. So, our team responsible for ICT policy was reviewing all requests for our funding approvals for ICT projects that agencies wanted to do. That was a lot of work, and it had to be done fast. We could not take a month to respond to authorize a budget expenditure—we had people waiting to use the money. We set ourselves an eight-day response deadline, and even this is a long time if you are in a hurry to buy something in technology. This team had to work together with agencies a lot on how they structured their ICT buying plans, how were the cases for funding made, and so on. It was important to have this team be a good one to meet the deadlines, because otherwise powerful agencies would go calling the president's office and claim that we were not responding. However, if the request was not okay, it was not authorized—I never hesitated to say no when I needed to as I trusted this team.

Another very important one was the design team. I had in them a team that really understood that design covers everything, all the way to a great look and feel. It was important how GOB.MX looked every day, to really improve the experience. Alejandra (Lagunes) came from Google, and she had a focus on design, which is why we encouraged and empowered this team. The design team said that they never had had a boss who paid so much attention to them as I did. I did indeed always worry if our design team had everything they needed to work correctly, and that they would feel as important as the legal team or policy team or the superstar programmers we had.

Building the team was my biggest challenge and something I enjoyed the most, because I met such great people. People who really believed in what we wanted to do, and really committed themselves. It takes so much to find the right profile, and to have them then commit the same way you are committing to a position. It is hard because the leadership team does not stay in government if the president changes. From the beginning they know that they have only a fixed term. This means uncertainty, and people have to be willing to deal with uncertainty and to commit. That is why I value the team I had, because they committed to doing our great work.

What you discover is that when you have a team that delivers, whom you empower and trust, they start spreading your values and principles. Then other entities start saying the same things or doing the same ways themselves. I enjoyed going to meetings in other agencies and seeing how their teams had taken on this digital culture or digital DNA of ours, giving our speech and being proud of making the services digital. It was very, very emotionally satisfying.

Once You Had the Team, What Were the Principles or Culture You Wanted Them to Follow?

"Let us put the citizen first." That was the most important thing. Each time somebody came to show me things, I always asked, "Who is the user and what would the user say about the product." This principle was also very powerful to break through the legal debates. That was the basis for saying it was not about what the law or federal procedure said, it was about what does make the life of people easier. Our job is to make the life of citizens easier, let us put the citizen first (and change the law if necessary). I told my team to always tell it like that to the other agencies.

I also told my team that we had a very cool job—we are making the life of citizens easier! We got paid to build great digital experiences for people. Take the legal team, for example. Their job was not to review legal documents. They were paid to build the experience of the people. This was an eye-opener for the otherwise super formal legal guys.

I was also always saying that we should work in the open and collaboratively. When anyone from the team presented me some work, I asked who else had reviewed it or participated in the design. Or when we were going to have a meeting with other entities to review this.

I tried to advance a culture of self-autonomy. I told the team what our goal was, and I trusted them to do it—especially the leadership team around me. I promised that if they would call me, I would be there. We had this challenging plan to accomplish and so I would not tell them what to do to deliver it, because I trusted them.

Another principle was that I always listened to my leadership team. I deeply enjoyed sitting together with them as a team to review our challenges, our priorities, the things that we were requested to do by the president's office, but which we did not have in the plan. I listened to all this team very carefully because we had this great joint responsibility. I had the pleasure to lead it but tomorrow it could be anyone of them doing it. So, we needed to work as a team and be honest with each other about the solutions or plans we were proposing to present.

I really enjoyed that our office was very different from traditional government offices: very open. I was always running from one meeting to another, but I always wanted to see what my team was doing. So, even if I was running by it was important for me to chat quick to the team members or look at their screen and give feedback. I wanted to be in touch with what everyone was doing. When we were about to release something, we always had like a town hall—everyone could come, the more people the better. "This is the new feature going live, what should we change?" We were trying to really produce teamwork, have the team be very open and enthusiastic.

If my team was staying late, I stayed late. I always had a lot of things to do. I remember when we were doing the testing for the birth certificate launch, the team was up for forty-eight hours or more. I was there, too. All of us, including all of leadership team, were doing the testing, reviewing the scripts, trying to find what was wrong, having a lot of tacos (we ate a lot of tacos!). That is how you build credibility in the team that you are there, and you work. You gain then a lot of respect that you are in this way coherent with what you are saying and what you are asking from the team.

Where There Any Routines You Used Regularly to Manage the Team?

We had daily leadership meetings; we kept that discipline well. Even if I was away, we were always connected. I used to travel a lot to different states as I wanted to support the digital teams at the local level, and Mexico is a very big country with thirty-two states. But there was no excuse that we could not connect and deliver.

Another important thing was that everyone knew the project plan for the year, what were the goals and the objectives. We were in an open space, so it was very easy to know what was happening in the office with everyone. That was important to me, given the open style. I also met for one-on-one with my team leaders every week.

We had the monthly meetings with the CIO council. Our team could always join them; we were open to them. They usually did not go and not because they did not want to, but because they were usually busy. Preparing for this monthly meeting meant that the entire team had to sit down and prepare the materials. This CIO council meeting was like the monthly checkpoint on how things were going.

And, of course, there was daily communication in Slack, in WhatsApp.

How Much Did You Spend Time Managing Up, Once the Presidency Was in Full Swing?

With Alejandra as my boss, we communicated every day. With the president, it was mostly when we saw each other in the office going out or coming in. I would always then say in a sentence or two what we were doing or launching right now—to ensure that work was going in the right direction. Only rarely did we have an actual meeting on specific issues.

I always remembered to have the freshest numbers in mind, so that if I saw the president around the office or any other minister, I would know our or their KPIs by heart. With ministers, I would then nicely also point out what they still needed to do. I made a point to always recognize their teams in such a quick chat. So, with three minutes in the hallway, I had to get a lot done. Such constant sync helped us to accomplish what we did accomplish, especially with very tight deadlines.

What Are the Things You Wish Could Have Worked Out Better During Your Time in Office, or Things You Would Do Differently?

It took us maybe four years to have GOB.MX mature enough to start going into federalizing the services. It was not a technical issue. It required a lot of negotiation with the governors and ministers of finance, just like with the birth certificate—which we learned a lot from about doing national standards while respecting independence of state- and municipal-level regulations.

If the presidential period had been a little bit longer, we could have done more of such services. We just ran out of time, but we had the recipe. Once you have the recipe and a shared service, you can scale.

For example, we also launched the common standard for professional certificates, which implied that we had to standardize the university degrees of nine thousand institutions. We did it by changing the law and managed to do the whole work in three months.

What Was for You the Hardest Part of the Job?

I think the hardest part of the job was trying to change things and investing my energy optimistically in some areas where it just was not worth it in this way.

That happened to me with the birth certificates, too. We defined at the beginning that it should not cost the citizen to get the certificate, as it was a constitutional right and as we had done all the work at federal level. So, there no cost in issuing at the state level. However, it was an important income for some states. So, I spent a lot of time for about a year in the meetings with several states and could not make them agree. Still today, the birth certificate issuing comes with a fee.

I was really affected by it because I thought it was total nonsense. I had a solid business case to try to convince them. After that year I said to myself, no more energy on this. I was not going to go to any more meetings, the service was running and sustainable. I decided to spend all this energy instead on working with the other ministries to accelerate the change in regulations so that the physical birth certificate would not be required, or asked, because there was a web service to check it. There would be no point in printing out a birth certificate if you could check it through interoperability. Then it does not matter if you charge for them, nobody is going to have to print it anymore.

In just three months of heavy work with government entities, we managed to change 155 sectoral regulations. I saw then the value of rather working with the people who wanted to change. I used to be very mad at the people in some states who were in favor of the fee. I am always super positive, and to me it was hard to be mad!

In 2017, You Actually Took the Wider Role and Replaced Alejandra Lagunes as the National Digital Strategy Coordinator—How Did That Come About?

In Mexico, there are a lot of changes at the cabinet level when you start the elections year. Alejandra was invited to help a candidate run for president. So, she left the NDSC role. I felt very honored when she proposed me to the president as the successor, because it is a presidentially appointed role and office.

It was the last year of our national strategy, and it was very important to really consolidate a lot of effort done over the past five years. I was ready but my biggest worry was that the team would start to look for other opportunities, as this is a common thing to do near the presidential term's finish. I remember talking to my leadership team in the digital government unit and saying that we had a commitment to the president, and Alejandra, to the people who trusted in us. I asked them for just one thing—to stay until the end of November 2018, if possible. It would be too much to bring onboard someone with a learning curve in the last year; it would not be worth to even try. "Let us finish this," was my plea.

We were so solid as a team that everyone stayed. We knew it was the last year, we knew that we had learned so much; we were willing to take risks and also push others until the end. Like we did with digitizing professional certificates, which we pushed through the legal department and the president to sign at the very last year.

I handed the digital government unit management over to the head of digital service team, but we were all still part of the same big leadership team.

What Was Your Trick or Recipe for Attracting Good People to Join Your Team?

People wanted to come because they wanted to give back to the country or they fell in love with the projects. We had quite a few people joining who wanted to make a difference because they had had personal experience with some service and wanted to improve them.

The people we recruited through the trust fund mechanisms rotated more. Sometimes they joined for just one project. The people who stayed in the civil service track, they keep the culture and the values, they have good memories from our work together. I used to tell them that they want to put GOB.MX in their résumé, so they should do our best on it and for everyone in the country.

You Had to Depart with the Rest of the Team When the President Changed after the Next Elections. Were There Any Steps You Took During Your Term Consciously to Make Your Initiatives and Reforms Last?

The most important thing for the lasting effect was that we built services that people used.

To be honest, when we were handing over our office, I was worried if the services and even GOB.MX would survive. We had put in a lot of work and effort in GOB.MX. But I then thought we had done our work and delivered something that really helped and facilitated the lives of people.

I guess that is exactly why GOB.MX is still running, even if not with the same design—but services are not undone. That is something that I feel proud about. Even today, I can get my birth certificate online, my professional license, I can open up a business in one day and be fully online. Eighty percent of federal services are digitally there. I can use all these services because we attended to people needs.

So, when you build something that is used massively, then this is the guarantee itself. You solved a need, and anyone who comes to office also wants to solve needs.

By the end of our presidential period, we put together a document with recommendations for the incoming government, telling them all that we had learned and also suggesting ways they could set up a different coordination arrangement, if they wanted to. To our surprise, they came and kept the coordination. Even if the new presidential team has different priorities, the national digital strategy office is still in place. They have a national digital agenda. The services are up and running and used by people. In the end, this is the most important thing because we built the services for the people to use. We managed to do our work!

If the Next President Comes Calling, Would You Work the Same Job Again?

Definitely! I love the work we managed to do.

If I were to go again, I could do it with more experiences as I have been advising other governments now, worked with Interamerican Development Bank, and so on. I am growing as a person.

If I would be called to serve my country, I would definitely do it. I love Mexico, and I love being a public servant. Anything I could do to make this country a better place, I would do it.

Is There Anything You Wish You Had Known When You Started the Job?

I would take more risk. I think I was very cautious at the beginning because I wanted to understand how the federal government worked. I had also a lot of legal responsibility, because I had to sign things and I always super-carefully reviewed everything. I wanted to make sure we complied with any type of normative that we needed to comply with.

This made my learning curve tough. I really wanted to have clarity on how we could lead the strategy and how to make a very radical change with GOB.MX, and I wanted to do it right from legal point of view. This took us a lot of time as a team to understand how we could make it all legally right: to collaborate with states to respect their independence, to manage so that even when brought to court trial all the documents would be valid.

GOB.MX is legally very strong now because people are still using it. We developed a lot of legal frameworks to give that certainty to users. This took time.

In 2018, when we were launching these federalized national services, I realized we did not have much time and we pushed ourselves more legally. So, I wish I had known earlier to work through the complexity of different levels of government to provide legal certainty in all digital services in a faster way. Now that I work with other governments, I tell them that they need to immediately start working on the legal framework to collaborate with different levels of government.

What Are the Core Skills to Be Successful in This Job?

I think empathy, first.

You also have to have the understanding to give the same importance to the technical things as well as the legal things, because you are in a government. You can have the best digital solution, but if it is not certain from the legal point of view, it will not last. You have to understand what it means to be digitally at the edge, as well as legally support it. That does not mean overregulation. Rather, be very creative in your legal terms to make every digital initiative certain but flexible to keep it up-to-date. Thus, you need to set up your team with these kinds of skills or have them yourself.

For a leader, the biggest skill is to know how to manage a multidisciplinary team: to enjoy leading a team of very different perspectives and understand the challenges of each of your teams when you ask them to deliver. That is something I really enjoyed the most. Whether it was sitting with my leadership team, listening to the different perspectives that were so specialized, and then having them come together. To me, every leadership team meeting was an opportunity to learn so much. To really understand that my role as a leader was to solve differences and provide for collaboration so that we can follow the plan we had ahead of us.

What Is Your Summary of What Does It Take to Be Effective in Such a Digital Government Leadership Role? What Would Be Your Recommendations, Concluding from Your Experience?

Be resourceful. Try to leverage everything, every resource that you have available to deliver. Starting from political support and trust, which gives you freedom to define a vision or for executing it the way you think is best. Your team, your budget, your collaboration with international ecosystem. Like we have in Red GEALC, where different Latin American and Caribbean countries learn about each other's best practices to solve issues very quickly, by sharing. Leveraging all these (and other) resources and managing them to the best of your knowledge really makes you deliver.

Be consistent. This is something that I am always very committed to. If you say you are going to do something, do it. If you say you are going to stay late with your team, do stay late with your team. Even though you may set goals that seem challenging, when your team sees you there, they are there.

Codesign things. In the digital government unit, we had such a fun and diverse group of people. You need to give them space to say what they think, and our deliverables could not have been instructed. They had to be codesigned to work, and we always codesigned—all our standards and policies. When your team codesigns, then your team starts sharing and building out the vision, and then it is unstoppable.

Really invest in your UX design team. I think these teams are something new in government. In our case, we encountered the challenge that most of our CIOs were still more dedicated to technical support. They had all this investment in back-office solutions. You should drive that they complement the skills in their teams with designers, focusing on how to advance the experience for the end user. A great head of design, great head of UX writing—for making the government and complex laws understandable. This is one of the most important rights for a person to have: the right to understand what the government is telling me. You have the obligation to make things simple for the citizens.

EPILOGUE
How to Lead a Government to Digital Excellence

You have now met with twenty remarkable digital government leaders in this book: reading about their achievements and the working methods and learnings that went into making their success happen.

They share plenty of tricks and good practices to copy from or use for inspiration. Having been in a digital government leader's shoes myself, I can confirm that each chapter is rich in detail about what works and what is needed to do similar work in any government or organization.

As such, synthesizing or summarizing any of these stories feels like I am committing an injustice to the individuals and their insights. Surely the details of practices will inevitably get lost. Regardless, I will attempt to generalize the overarching themes and most-common aspects that keep reappearing through the twenty leaders' journeys in leading a government to digital excellence.

The following pages will read a lot like the classic ABC of management or general leadership, public sector management, and reform wisdom. Or digital transformation best practices. This is to be expected, because digital government leadership is first and foremost leadership in its core, and only then about the digital and government specifics—the specific contexts in which the leadership wisdom and best practices have to be applied. But at the start and end of the day, digital government leadership is about—well, *leadership*.

Several insights can be considered trivial or common knowledge. However, the fact that digital progress varies so widely over time and across countries is enough reason to highlight the aspects that might seem trivial or obvious—because these are not necessarily applied or followed systematically.

To my eye, ten common themes stand out from the stories. They are by no means exhaustive and do not carry any pretense of complete conclusions. Perhaps, let us think about them as the ten most basic traits of what it takes to be an effective digital government leader. The concrete ways of how to apply them will always depend on the context of governance setup, digital maturity, culture, the wider ecosystem, and so on. But there are certain general roles or hats that leaders should adopt to be effective in their missions, whatever their context is in detail.

Deliver, Deliver, Deliver

Delivery is where all the remarkable digital government leaders have put their sharpest focus on and made the strongest efforts for, from their *very* first days in the office. Whether it is the policy changes or actual products and new digital services that they have set to deliver, the act of delivering is what matters the most in this (or any!) job.

The obvious reason is that your time in office can be—and often is—limited. If you do not start immediately, you will lose in potential impact you can make in sum during your time. The more unstable your role and the context you operate in, the better it is to run as fast as you can because you are running against time.

It can also be that the political masters expect quick results. Even if they have not explicitly said so, they do. Or at least they will like results if you can make the quick wins happen. If you deliver, you build credibility. This may be a prerequisite to be able to ask for levers or resources from higher-ups or build up soft power to ensure collaboration from other stakeholders—plus, get support from the public, too. These are preconditions to maintaining the momentum of change for the time when things will get harder (at some point they most probably will!) and also helps to speed up delivery in the next phase and to make changes stick for lasting effect.

Delivery is also the only thing that brings results and impact in terms of digital government development in the direction of the vision that likely brought you to office in the first place. Thus, you are most probably driven for delivery yourself. Without the taste of actual delivery, it is easy to lose confidence to keep going. Delivery gives you yourself assurance.

There are many ways you can organize and lead for delivery: through remaking or creating policy, strategy, organizational structure, processes, team, culture, values, your own routines. You have seen many such useful ideas and practices in the chapters before, each a bit special given their different contexts. Whatever works for you, just start *managing for delivery*, and keep doing it. This is fundamental because it will not be you doing the work, as you know well (or will find out immediately).

Something you see from the stories is that you must be present and follow through enough—then things will happen. It is not enough to initiate and sit back. You also need persistence because hardships most probably will come, too. That is exactly why you need to constantly be ready to reconfigure for delivery.

You should be the chief delivery officer if you want to be an effective digital government leader.

Strategy Is Your Job—and Your Opportunity

More often than not, political masters will not give you a concrete deliverable to reach. Their expectations are often quite generic or, completely at the other end of spectrum, narrowly operational. They want you to figure out what to do, as long as you "do the digital thing" and take the country forward. The best political masters also purposefully give such a freedom to their chosen people.

Think of it as a sweet spot, actually. This is where the remarkable digital government leaders thrive. They grasp the opportunity to carve out the vision and strategy to reach it and the action plan to put the strategy in effect. In many ways, strategy setting is a core role of top leaders in any organization. In digital government leaders' case, it is particularly important because they (you!) are essentially setting the strategy for the whole government (and country).

The chance to set the strategy is a sweet spot because a skillful strategist and leader can use it to build up the portfolio of activities and create a road map for lasting change. Wide-scale impact usually requires hard work on governance mechanisms, infrastructure, and platforms that cannot come as quick wins in a short time frame. But the work to build them has to commence early, accompanied by smartly chosen quick wins and constant delivery to sustain support and air cover for longer-term changes.

Setting a clear vision, an ambitious strategy, and an achievable action plan also can help to make delivery easier, because it can empower the team (if accompanied by a suitable management style and processes) or rally other stakeholders behind, especially if cocreation has been your way to craft the road map. Naturally, each and every strategy will be different in substance, depending on the core problem to solve, the resource conditions, and the existing state of digital affairs.

Note how several stories in this book speak about the need to be ready to revisit the plans as you go along and, in particular, if the context changes. COVID-19 affected the strategies and delivery of all the leaders in this book who were in office when the pandemic hit. Notably, they all seized the opportunity it provided to boost the digital progress journey they were trying to lead anyway—by mobilizing to make lasting impact.

A good strategy takes into account your limits, your resources, and is realistic in ambitions. However, you can also strategize to amplify your starting resources by leveraging the ecosystem and your surroundings; thus, you do not have to always be constrained by what you start with.

You should be the chief strategy officer or the chief planning officer if you want to be an effective digital government leader.

It Is Hard without Proper Political Support

Some of the remarkable digital government leaders in this book emphasize that a strong political support from highest-possible level in your country is the most fundamental precondition to any success in your role. They imply that if you do not have it, perhaps do not even try.

However, some others in the book have been a bit more risk-taking and dared to start the journey with less clear political backing. They have then moved at the first possible instance to carve out the support they needed to succeed.

Whether you have it from the start, or you request it as a precondition to taking the job, or you start with what you have and once you have proved delivery capability, you seek a political air cover then—you will need the political support one way or another to be effective.

Building up a digital government means transforming how government works and how public services are run. As with any change, this is bound to inevitably create some opposition. Bottlenecks will appear, if not in the direction you set out for, then in terms of speed and depth of delivery you can squeeze out of the "system" of public sector around you. If you want to deliver, you need backing to be able to smooth (or fight) your way through the bottlenecks.

The faster you have to deliver, the more backing you need. The more profound the changes you are starting, or the more legacy or even hostile the public sector is about the change you bring, the more backing you need. For example, if the government around you is not naturally geared for collaboration, you will need some enforcement levers to have them fall in line if the milder ways of influencing and negotiation do not work.

Effective political support does not just mean voicing out the rhetoric of recognition. Political masters need to take actual steps to give you the institutional levers for coordination and delivery across the government (the sticks) or through the power of their office put weight on stakeholders if you need them to.

If you do not have such hands-on readiness and champions from the start, start building the base for it. Even better, give it a thorough thought before you take the role and put in the asks. You will save a lot of time and energy later if you can carve it out at the earliest.

Note that you can never take the political support for granted. Delivering helps to keep it. But you also need to manage up or sideways, as necessary, to keep the political masters on the same page and in the loop with what you do. Yours is a political role in that sense, whether you like it or not. Best to embrace it like that. Mind you that in some jurisdictions, you would have a political role also by definition—if you are also a deputy minister or otherwise a political appointee, for example.

You should be the chief political officer if you want to be an effective digital government leader.

It Is a Networked Job and a Job of Networking

More than half of the people featured in this book highlight that your most important role—next to strategy and delivery—is stakeholder management. This is the *most* common thread through the bottom-line recommendations of each of the twenty people interviewed.

You should pay attention and devote ample time to this part of the role. It enables you to leverage beyond your own thin resources so that you do not get stuck. It can also ensure necessary collaboration for delivery, because in your whole-of-government role you need really the whole government to change and deliver.

Even with strongest political support and in less democratic contexts, it is hard (if not impossible) to coerce collaboration. That is why you see in this book so many "charm offensives," cocreation mechanisms, and "carrots before the sticks" approaches to build networks and partnerships for delivery.

You need to navigate your public service, but also the wider ecosystem around you. You need to figure out the win-win opportunities to build institutional arrangements for involving others in decisions and delivery, to make efforts to build personal relationships, and also to sustain them over busy calendars.

Many leaders in the book talk about the need and ways to make other people and agencies successful, supporting them in their hardships and aspirations, and also having them take the recognition. This indeed has often proven to be the best possible way to ensure alignment and collaboration from others around you, for the long run, too.

Networking and stakeholder management is not just about you as the leader. You need to gear your whole team toward it through culture and practices that support it. Most of the work gets done by others around you anyway, and relations can be broken or built at every step of that journey.

You should be the chief relationship officer or the chief networking officer if you want to be an effective digital government leader.

Good Communications Will Empower You

Among the self-manifested lessons learned or even regrets of the twenty digital government leaders, one special theme stands out. Several of them say that they would make more effort in public communications, in hindsight.

Similarly, several of the stories highlight how the leaders have excelled in communications outreach and how this has brought benefits in terms of strong public support, stakeholder buy-in, political backing, talent recruitment, and more.

The need to be an effective communicator through media, public relations, and marketing efforts only increases in time with the accelerating attention economy. As it becomes constantly harder and harder to gain attention, the more deliberate, systemic, and calibrated your communications effort must be in order to reach the groups you need for your successful delivery. It is a job you cannot just leave to the communications staff, because you are the main spokesperson for the work you do. Whether you like it or not, it comes within the package of your position.

You should be the chief communications officer if you want to be an effective digital government leader.

The Team Will Determine How Far and Fast You Can Run

This is truly common management knowledge but the key success factor for any leader is to build the best possible team around you. Finding the right talent is hard for everyone, as you see from the interviews in the book. However, the interviews perhaps also give you hope that it can be done after all. Your mission and you yourself will be the attraction factors, especially once people start seeing delivery and can see that change is indeed doable. Bright and hard-working people will come to join you if you are worth joining with.

You might have to be resourceful and a bit innovative in tapping into the talent pools already in your government. Most of the effective leaders have also been very visible, vocal, and constantly out there in the wider digital or technology community around them, sometimes even globally. That is another reason why an active communications effort (see previous lesson) is very valuable.

Once you start to have right folks in the team, there is quite a bit more to be done in order to get the most out of their potential. You can empower them with enabling management style and routines, instill a needed culture and values, watch out for their well-being, and so on.

You should be the chief recruitment officer or chief talent officer if you want to be an effective digital government leader.

Work for Lasting Change—Every Day

All effective digital government leaders know that on one good (or bad) day their time in office will be over. That is why they consciously pay attention and actively take steps to make the changes they start in their governments to have a chance of lasting. This is important because organizations (especially governments) can be quite resistant to long-term change and fall back to previous ways if the counterforces have not become strong enough.

Some of the leaders have had a very acute understanding of the need to lay the ground for enduring change if their working context is a hostile or unstable one, or if their terms have a natural limit because of their political masters. They are then even more carefully and actively taking care from day 1 in their office that the way they do things could continue without them there.

Most lasting change potential naturally stems from building up strong and mature teams that can keep going without prior leaders, from leaving behind a strategy for the next years, from building up a culture that is different from what was there before.

However, you can also take concrete steps to instill the change a bit more into the machinery of government. Policies, standards, laws, institutional arrangements, or international donor assistance deals: there are several ways to make it harder for successors to immediately uproot previous changes.

In addition to such defensive moves, there are also proactive ways to facilitate continuity. You can make the transition smoother by choosing your own successor or laying out the tracks for the successor to come in and have an easy time to just continue, for example, by properly handing things over in documentation and leaving behind recommendations. You can also invest into building the tools and platforms for digital services in a way that make it easy to continue iterating and maintaining them.

At the end of the day, the best way to ensure continuity and make the change last is delivery—creation of digital government solutions of a new quality that meet people's needs. If users get value from the services you built, if agencies get value from the platforms and tools you provided them, they will be the force behind keeping these services and platforms going. The better your delivery of actual results that improve lives, the more likely the results will be sustained. It does not make sense for rational successors to override policies that work well.

There is no special chief officer role for ensuring continuity; this is part of what any chief officer should do. Simply keep in mind that you will likely be leaving someday and manage for enduring change every day in your job to be an effective digital government leader.

The Job Is Hard—Be Ready for It

You have seen from the interviews that this job can be exhausting. The harder the context and the more backlash there is, the more it will squeeze you. Or you will feel lonely at times, especially at start of the journey. Everyone in the book has gone through some tough fights along the way. At the very least you will have some battle scars to show.

If you want to keep delivering and achieve any impact, you should watch out to keep your own stamina and a clear mind. These will keep you going through the hardships of building the team, or when political support wanes, or backlash from stakeholders arises. Keeping your mental and physical health, happy family and other relations outside work, a balance of work and life—all these have their important part in it. Make sure that you do not lose yourself in the work, especially as several leaders in this book do remind you that there is a life after the job, too.

You should be the chief wellness officer for yourself if you want to be an effective digital government leader.

Fix Your Sight on the Users—The Impact on Citizens and Businesses

In face of hardships, the effective digital government leaders maintain their perspective and the bigger picture by reminding themselves what it is that they are doing—the mission and vision. It means mostly keeping their sight on the users and the impact they make on their lives, for example, on how digital services can improve the life of citizens and businesses.

The reminders of purpose can serve as a powerful re-energizer for yourself and the team. It also gives you boldness to try things again or differently, again and again. That is why so many leaders have some of their mantras or team values framed around citizen-centricity and the user focus. One practical trick is to keep reminding yourself and the team that you are users and citizens, too. At the end of the day, you are doing things better for yourself, too.

Fixing the sight this way also ensures that you are actually delivering for impact, not just for the sake of delivering something. It often happens that you are the lone or main voice of people as users in the government—at least at first, if this has not been the practice before. This should empower and embolden you.

You should be the chief customer officer if you want to be an effective digital government leader.

Your Effectiveness Is in Your Own Hands

If all the previous recommendations make you doubt your own ability to do this kind of job, do not worry.

First, all these different "chief officer" roles highlighted in this epilogue, all the relevant know-how and skills, can be learned and gained. None of the twenty leaders had all of it innately. Be encouraged that effectiveness comes from nurture not nature mostly.

Remarkable leaders have learned the necessary things along their career and studies, mostly through practical exposure and experience. From both successes and failures, as always. Several of them have been keenly observing and picking up practices from peers from around the world. All of them say that they kept learning on this job itself and even speak about the importance to consciously keep learning. Entrepreneurs have to learn government ways. Technologists have to learn the management and networking ways.

The list of useful or even necessary skills can be long, because it is no easy job you have. But here you have twenty stories about how the job can still be done, and with incredible impact. Nobody was born ready for it.

There are a few necessary innate characteristics. For example, you should love or at least be able to handle challenges. If you fear them, you probably will not consider the role anyway. Similarly, you must be at least moderately a social person. If you fear or dislike work with people, there are other jobs out there.

Second, there is no one career or learning path to becoming an effective digital government leader. Even if many of the twenty people in this book have a technology background, this is not a requirement. Sure, you need the appreciation and understanding of what and how the digital tech effects transformation. This can be picked up along your way, if you are curious and willing.

Entrepreneurs with a deep private sector history can excel in a top government role, even if the adjustment does not come naturally at first and they need to learn the new operating conditions fast. Similarly, civil servants can be effective if they are entrepreneurial enough.

You also do not necessarily need to have decades of experience to be effective. However, the more relevant experience you have, the more effective you will be and faster. This is logical for any role.

Therefore, if you need to run very fast in this role or the context for your work will be a tough one, do build up the skills and experience for it as fast as you can. You will be able to be so much more impactful. But you do have in this book shining examples of how people with shorter levels of experience can excel just as well—with the right mindset, their overall ability and energy, plus some courage.

Therefore, it is mostly your mindset and your approach that makes all of the difference. Mindset and approach can be cultivated; these are in your own hands.

Adopt the examples, insights, and tips from this book into your mindset and approach, and you shall see how much quicker and stronger your government starts to excel digitally with you in the lead. Good luck to you on this learning and leading journey!

ABOUT THE AUTHOR

Siim Sikkut served as the Government Chief Information Officer (CIO) of the Republic of Estonia, also titled as Deputy Secretary-General for Digital Development in the Ministry of Economic Affairs and Communications, from 2017 to 2022.

Siim's role was to set the strategy and policies and to launch and steer strategic initiatives and regulation in areas of digital government, cybersecurity, and connectivity in Estonia. While in office, he successfully took on the double challenge of continuing the Estonian government's twenty years of digital progress by steering the next innovation cycle, while keeping the existing digital services up-to-date and running smoothly.

Siim has been a serial intrapreneur in the public sector and was one of the founders of Estonia's ground-breaking e-Residency program. He has been nominated as one of the world's TOP20 most influential people in digital government by Apolitical. Siim also chaired the OECD Working Party of Senior Digital Government Officials from 2019 to 2021.

Previously, he worked as the Digital Policy Advisor to three consecutive prime ministers in the Government Office of Estonia, coordinating the digital policy planning and execution across the government. Siim's prior experience also includes work in the Estonian public sector in areas of strategic foresight, national strategic planning, and public financial management.

Siim Sikkut graduated in 2005 from Princeton University in the US with a BA degree in public and international affairs, focusing on economic development and policy. He also holds a MSc degree in international management from the University of London, UK.

He currently advises governments and digital leaders on digital strategy, the leadership and governance for its delivery, digital service reforms, and public sector innovation. Siim is an in-demand keynote speaker around the globe on these topics, plus on how a digital society and government have been built in Estonia.

Siim resides in Tallinn, Estonia, with his wife and three daughters.

INDEX

Italic page numbers denote photographs.

Abadie, Daniel, *83*, 84–96
  background of, 84–85
  on context of Undersecretary job, 85, 87
  digital government leadership recommendations from, 95–96
  leadership style and practices of, 89–93
  on starting the Undersecretary job, 87
  on successes/failures as Undersecretary, 93
  on transition to/from Undersecretary role, 86, 93–95
  vision and strategy of, 85–89
Access to Information Portal, of Canada, 19
Achievements:
  Daniel Abadie on, 93
  Bolor-Erdene Battsengel on, 67
  Alex Benay on, 26
  Aisha Bin Bishr on, 12
  Randall Brugeaud on, 214
  Cheow Hoe Chan on, 80
  José Clastornik on, 142
  Lars Frelle-Petersen on, 156
  Hillary Hartley on, 118–119
  Anna-Maija Karjalainen on, 41
  Taavi Kotka on, 242
  Barry Lowry on, 55
  Luis Felipe Monteiro on, 169
  Innocent Bagamba Muhizi on, 131
  Tim Occleshaw on, 257
  Diego Piacentini on, 107
  Pedro Silva Dias on, 199–200
  Shai-Lee Spiegelman on, 228–229
Action plan, 248, 251, 281
Administrative Modernization Agency (AMA), Portugal, 191–202
AGESIC, *see* Information Society and e-Government Agency), Uruguay
AgID, *see* Digital Agency, of Italy
AI, *see* Artificial intelligence
AIESEC, 161
Alawadhi, Hamad, 10
All-department or all-hands meetings, 38, 117
Al Maktoum, Mohammed bin Rashid, 3–6, 11
AMA, *see* Administrative Modernization Agency, Portugal
Amazon.com, Inc., 98, 99, 103–105
Animal and Public Health Information System, of Northern Ireland 47
Annual planning, 8, 223, 228
ANTEL, 137
Anywhere government, 169
Apple Inc., 74, 99
APS, *see* Australian Public Service
APS Enterprise concept, 216

Ardern, Jacinda, 252
Argentina, Daniel Abadie's efforts in, *see* Abadie, Daniel
argentina.gob.ar, of Argentina, 87, 88
Artificial intelligence (AI), 27, 143, 223, 229
Australia, Randall Brugeaud's efforts in, *see* Brugeaud, Randall
Australian Bureau of Statistics, 205–206, 216
Australian Public Service (APS), 216
Australian Taxation Office, 205

Baltacioglu, Yaprak, 17, 28
Battsengel, Bolor-Erdene, *59*, 60–69
  background of, 60–62
  on context of CITA job, 62
  digital government leadership recommendations from, 69
  leadership style and practices of, 65–67
  on starting the CITA job, 64–65
  on successes/failures with CITA, 67–68
  on transition from CITA, 68–69
  vision and strategy of, 62–65
BCG, *see* Boston Consulting Group
Beaven, Mike, 181, 183
Benay, Alex, *15*, 16–29
  background of, 16–18
  on context of CIO job, 17–18
  digital government leadership recommendations from, 29
  leadership style and practices of, 22, 24–26
  on starting the CIO job, 20–21
  on successes/failures as CIO, 26–28
  on transition from CIO, 28–29
  vision and strategy of, 18–25
Bethlenfalvy, Peter, 113
Bezos, Jeff, 99, 106
Bill and Melinda Gates Foundation, 61
Bin Bishr, Aisha, *1*, 2–14
  background of, 2–3, 5–6
  on context of SDO job, 4–6
  digital government leadership recommendations from, 13–14
  leadership style and practices of, 9–12
  on starting the SDO job, 7
  on successes/failures with SDO, 12, 13
  on transition from SDO, 12–13
  vision and strategy of, 3–4, 6–8
Birth certificates, of Mexico, *see* Digital birth certificates, of Mexico
Blockchain, 8, 143
Blue Origin, 106, 108n1
Bolsonaro, Jair, 162–164, 169
Boston Consulting Group (BCG), 205

Bracken, Mike, 48, 117, *173*, 174–187
   background of, 174–176
   on context of GDS job, 176
   digital government leadership recommendations
      from, 186–187
   leadership style and practices of, 181–184
   on starting the GDS job, 178–179
   on successes/failures with GDS, 184
   on transition from GDS, 185–186
   vision and strategy of, 176–181
Brazil, Luis Felipe Monteiro's efforts in, *see* Monteiro,
   Luis Felipe
Brison, Scott, 17, 20, 28
Brugeaud, Randall, *203*, 204–217
   background of, 204–206
   on context of DTA job, 207–208
   digital government leadership recommendations
      from, 216–217
   leadership style and practices of, 210–214
   on starting the DTA job, 209–210
   on successes/failures with DTA, 214, 216
   on transition from DTA, 215–216
   vision and strategy of, 206–211, 214–215
Budget:
   Daniel Abadie on, 86, 89–91
   Aisha Bin Bishr on, 5
   Mike Bracken on, 179
   Lars Frelle-Petersen on, 152
   Taavi Kotka on, 244
   Barry Lowry on, 52
   Yolanda Martínez on, 265, 266, 268–269, 272
   Luis Felipe Monteiro on, 168
   Shai-Lee Spiegelman on, 225
Buenos Aires, Electronic Government of the City, 85–86, 89
buenosaires.gob.ar, 85
"Build culture," 79
Build to Share solution, of Ireland, 51–52
Bureaucracy, 183
   Bolor-Erdene Battsengel on, 62
   Cheow Hoe Chan on, 73, 79–80
   Shai-Lee Spiegelman on, 230
Business-case driven approach, 156

Cabinet Office, Ontario, 113, 115
Cabinet Office, United Kingdom, 61, 175, 181
Cabinet Secretariat, Mongolia, 61, 63, 65, 69n1
Cameron, James, 198
CampusIL platform, of Israel 222–224, 226, 229
Canada:
   Alex Benay's efforts in (*see* Benay, Alex)
   digital service standard in, 249, 256
   Hillary Hartley's efforts in (*see* Hartley, Hillary)
Cardoso da Costa, Joaquim Pedro, 199
Career paths, of digital government leaders, 285
Central coordination, 162, 216, 255, 265
Challenges, embracing, 5, 239, 285
Chan, Cheow Hoe, *71*, 72–82
   background of, 72–73
   on context of GovTech job, 73–74
   digital government leadership recommendations
      from, 81–82

   leadership style and practices of, 76–80
   on starting the GovTech job, 75
   on successes/failures at GovTech, 80–81
   on transition from GovTech, 81
   vision and strategy of, 74–78
Change resistance, *see* Resistance to change
Chant, Chris, 175
Chaos, embracing, 117
Charisma, 238–239
Chief officer role, effectiveness in, 285
Christchurch terrorist attack, 258
CI/CD process, 77, 82n3
CIDGE (Interministerial Commission for the
   Development of eGovernment), 269
CITA, *see* Communication and Information Technology
   Authority), Mongolia
Citizen-first approach. *See also* Customer-focused
   approach; User-focused approach
   in Argentina, 87
   in Italy, 103, 104
   in Mexico, 272–273
Citizen Spots, of Portugal, 199
City of Milan, 101, 107
Civil Registry Office, of Mexico, 265
Civil servants, as digital government leaders, 285
Civil Services Authority, of Israel, 226
Clastornik, José, *135*, 136–145
   background of, 136–138
   on context of AGESIC job, 138
   digital government leadership recommenda-
      tions from, 144
   leadership style and practices of, 141–142
   on starting the AGESIC job, 139–140
   on successes/failures with AGESIC, 142–143
   on transition from AGESIC, 143–144
   vision and strategy of, 138–141
Clearing time, 214
Cloud computing, 77
Cocco, Roberta, 107, 108n3
Cocreation, 57, 152, 277, 281
Code for America, 111
Coding, 48, 69
Coleman, Emer, 179, 182
Collaboration, 36, 129, 182
Communication, 282–283
   Bolor-Erdene Battsengel on, 64
   Alex Benay on, 21, 22
   Mike Bracken on, 179, 183
   Cheow Hoe Chan on, 78
   José Clastornik on, 142–143
   Anna-Maija Karjalainen on, 38
   Yolanda Martínez on, 269
   Luis Felipe Monteiro on, 164–165, 167, 168
   Diego Piacentini on, 108
   Shai-Lee Spiegelman on, 229
Communication and Information Technology Authority
   (CITA), Mongolia, 61–69
Congress, of Brazil, 170
Consistency, 277
Conte, Giuseppe, 106
Continuity, 283–284. *See also* Lasting change, creating

Continuous set of processes, 99, 102
Control, for DTA, 209
"Cool kids" factor, for Ontario Digital Service, 115, 116
Cooperation, 156, 158, 197–198. *See also* Inter-agency cooperation
Co-op placements, 118
Coordination, 36–37
Core skills of leaders:
    Daniel Abadie on, 95
    Bolor-Erdene Battsengel on, 69
    Alex Benay on, 29
    Aisha Bin Bishr on, 13–14
    Mike Bracken on, 186
    Cheow Hoe Chan on, 81
    Lars Frelle-Petersen on, 158
    Hillary Hartley on, 120
    Anna-Maija Karjalainen on, 42–43
    Taavi Kotka on, 243–244
    Yolanda Martínez on, 277
    Luis Felipe Monteiro on, 170
    Innocent Bagamba Muhizi on, 133
    Tim Occleshaw on, 259–260
    Shai-Lee Spiegelman on, 230–231
Corruption, 106
Costa, António, 194
Cost-cutting, 37
Council of Ministers, of Portugal, 191
Court of Accounts, of Brazil, 170
COVID-19 pandemic, xv, xix
    adjusting strategy and delivery in, 281
    Bolor-Erdene Battsengel on, 67
    Alex Benay on, 29
    Aisha Bin Bishr on, 9
    Randall Brugeaud on, 213–215
    Cheow Hoe Chan on, 78
    Lars Frelle-Petersen on, 156
    Hillary Hartley on, 117–119
    Anna-Maija Karjalainen on, 42
    Barry Lowry on, 51–52, 54–55
    Luis Felipe Monteiro on, 167, 168
    Innocent Bagamba Muhizi on, 131
COVID-19 Contact tracking app, of Ireland, 51
COVID-19 pass, of Italy, 107
COVID-19 self-assessment tool, of Ontario, 119
COVID-19 vaccination certificate, digital, 52, 55, 68, 90
COVIDSafe app, of Australia, 215
Creativity, 66–67
Credibility, 273
Crothers, Bill, 181
Culture, of government:
    Alex Benay on changing, 20
    Bolor-Erdene Battsengel on, 66
    Mike Bracken on changing, 177, 184
Culture, team and organizational:
    Daniel Abadie on, 91
    Bolor-Erdene Battsengel on, 66–69
    Alex Benay on, 23
    Aisha Bin Bishr on, 10–11
    Mike Bracken on, 177–178, 182–184, 186
    Randall Brugeaud on, 213

Cheow Hoe Chan on, 76, 79
    Lars Frelle-Petersen on, 153, 156
    Anna-Maija Karjalainen on, 39
    Taavi Kotka on, 240–241
    Barry Lowry on, 53–54
    Yolanda Martínez on, 272–273
    Luis Felipe Monteiro on, 168
    Innocent Bagamba Muhizi on, 129–131
    Tim Occleshaw on, 254, 255
    Diego Piacentini on, 103, 107
    Pedro Silva Dias on, 197–198
    Shai-Lee Spiegelman on, 227
Customer-focused approach. *See also* Citizen-first approach; User-focused approach
    in Denmark, 158
    in Finland, 39
    in Israel, 226
Cybersecurity, 140, 142

Daily leadership meetings, 273
Danish Agency for Digitisation (DIGST), 149–158
Data-driven approach, 103–104, 117, 167
Data Governance Board model, of Ireland, 51
Data Protection Authority, of Italy, 105
Data science, 165
Data strategy, of Israel, 229
Davies, Russell, 179, 182
Dawes, Melanie, 175
Decision making, quick:
    Mike Bracken on, 178–179
    Luis Felipe Monteiro on, 167
Delegation, 21, 116–117, 244
Deliverables:
    Alex Benay on, 19–20
    Randall Brugeaud on, 209
    Cheow Hoe Chan on, 74
    Yolanda Martínez on, 263–264
    Luis Felipe Monteiro on, 164
    Pedro Silva Dias on, 195
Delivery:
    Daniel Abadie on, 87–88, 96
    Bolor-Erdene Battsengel on, 64–65
    Aisha Bin Bishr on, 11–12
    Mike Bracken on, 182, 184
    Randall Brugeaud on, 211
    Cheow Hoe Chan on, 77–78
    José Clastornik on, 141
    Hillary Hartley on, 115, 116
    Anna-Maija Karjalainen on, 39
    Taavi Kotka on, 238, 240, 241
    managing for, 279–280
    Yolanda Martínez on, 267
    Luis Felipe Monteiro on, 163–165, 169
    Innocent Bagamba Muhizi on, 127, 131
    networks for, 282
    Tim Occleshaw on, 248, 251–253
    and political support, 281–282
    Pedro Silva Dias on, 195, 199
    Shai-Lee Spiegelman on, 223–226, 228
Deloitte Consulting, 263, 265–266

Denmark:
digital government of, as model for Brazil, 163
Lars Frelle-Petersen's efforts in
(see Frelle-Petersen, Lars)
international partnerships between Brazil and, 170
Departmental ICT strategies, of Estonia, 237
Department of Finance, Australia, 209
Department of Finance, Ireland, 48
Department of Health, Ireland, 47, 51
Department of Immigration and Border Protection,
Australia, 207–208
Department of Internal Affairs, New Zealand, 247–260
Department of Public Expenditure and Reform,
Ireland, 48
Deputy chief digital officer, of New Zealand 253
Deputy Ministers' Committee on Technology and
Transformation, of Ontario, 116
Design District, of Dubai, 7
Design process, commoditizing, 92
DevSecOps process, 77, 82n4
Digital Agency (AgID), of Italy, 100, 107
Digital birth certificates, of Mexico 265, 270–271,
273–275
Digital economy, in Mongolia, 61
Digital first service delivery, 19
Digital government excellence, 279–285
communication for, 282–283
creating lasting change, 283–284
delivery of, 279–280
mission and vision for, 284–285
networking for, 282
playbook for, xvi
political support for, 281–282
preparing for hard work of, 284
setting strategy for, 280–281
team management for, 283
Digital government leadership, xvi–xvii
Daniel Abadie on, 95–96
Bolor-Erdene Battsengel on, 69
Alex Benay on, 29
Aisha Bin Bishr on, 13–14
Mike Bracken on, 186–187
Randall Brugeaud on, 216–217
Cheow Hoe Chan on, 81–82
José Clastornik on, 144
Lars Frelle-Petersen on, 158
Hillary Hartley on, 120–121
Anna-Maija Karjalainen on, 42–43
Taavi Kotka on, 243–244
Barry Lowry on, 57–58
Yolanda Martínez on, 277–278
Luis Felipe Monteiro on, 170
Innocent Bagamba Muhizi on, 133
Tim Occleshaw on, 259–260
Diego Piacentini on, 108
Pedro Silva Dias on, 201
Shai-Lee Spiegelman on, 230–231
Digital Government Partnership, of New Zealand, 251,
252, 255, 257
Digital Government Secretariat, Brazil, 161–171
Digital graduate intake program, of New Zealan 251

Digital identity (ID), 101, 155–156, 163, 164, 169, 199
Digital Israel (Israeli National Digital Initia-
tive), 221–231
Digitalization Agency, Finland, 41, 42
Digital Leadership Group, 211
Digital literacy, 194, 224
Digital Mobile Key, of Portugal, 199
Digital Nation Expo, of Mongolia, 65
Digital Nations, 200, 202n3, 249
Digital Pathways project, of Mongolia, 61, 63
Digital Postbox, Denmark, 152–154
Digital services lab, of New Zealand, 257–259
Digital Service Standard, of New Zealand, 249, 256
Digital signatures, 149, 158
Digital skills training, of Rwanda, 131, 132
Digital Transformation Agency (DTA), Aus-
tralia, 204–217
Digital Transformation Office (DTO), Australia,
207–208, 210
DIGST, see Danish Agency for Digitisation
"Disagree and commit" principle, 104
Document management, 141
Driving licenses, digital, of Argentina, 92, 93, 96
Drones, 131
DTA, see Digital Transformation Agency), Australia
DTO, see Digital Transformation Office), Australia
Dubai, United Arab Emirates, Aisha Bin Bishr's efforts
in, see Bin Bishr, Aisha
Dubai Executive Office, 3–5, 8
Dubai International Financial Center, 3, 14n1
Dubai Internet City, 3, 14n1

EasyAccount (NemKonto), of Denmark, 149
EasyID (NemID), of Denmark, 156
Eaves, David, 120
E-commerce platform, of Israel, 222, 224
Efficiency and Reform Group (ERG), UK, 176–177,
180–181, 187n5
e-Government Office, Dubai, 6
18F agency, US, 111–112, 119, 121n2
18-step plan, of Ireland, 50–51, 55
Electronic Government of the City of Buenos
Aires, 85–86, 89
Electronic health records, 91–92, 142, 143
El Kaissi, Zeina, 10
e-Mongolia program, 61–68
Empathy, 95, 176
Empowerment, 53, 89–90, 183
Entrepreneurs, as digital government leaders, 285
e-Residency program, Estonia, 28, 237–239, 242, 244n3
ERG, see Efficiency and Reform Group (ERG), UK
Estonia:
e-Residency program, 28, 234, 237–239, 242, 244n3
Taavi Kotka's efforts in (see Kotka, Taavi)
as model digital government, 61, 162, 163
Value-Added Tax reform, 237, 238, 242
X-Road platform, 34–36, 40, 43n3, 236, 244n2
Estonian Association of Information Technology and
Telecommunications, 236
European Union Structural Funds:
in Estonia, 235, 238, 244n1

in Portugal, 191–193, 195, 199
Executive standups, 117
Exhaustion, avoiding, 184, 187
Expectations of political masters, 280
    Daniel Abadie on, 85, 95
    Bolor-Erdene Battsengel on, 62
    Aisha Bin Bishr on, 3–4
    Mike Bracken on, 177
    Randall Brugeaud on, 206–207
    Hillary Hartley on, 112
    Anna-Maija Karjalainen on, 33, 42
    Taavi Kotka on, 236
    Barry Lowry on, 48–49
    Luis Felipe Monteiro on, 162
    Innocent Bagamba Muhizi on, 125–126
    Tim Occleshaw on, 248–249
    Diego Piacentini on, 99
    Pedro Silva Dias on, 192
    Shai-Lee Spiegelman on, 222, 224

Failures:
    Daniel Abadie on, 93
    Alex Benay on, 22, 23, 27–28
    Mike Bracken on, 184, 186
    Randall Brugeaud on, 215
    José Clastornik on, 142–143
    Lars Frelle-Petersen on, 157
    Hillary Hartley on, 119
    Anna-Maija Karjalainen on, 41
    Taavi Kotka on, 241–242
    Barry Lowry on, 55, 58
    Luis Felipe Monteiro on, 168–169
    Innocent Bagamba Muhizi on, 131–132
    Tim Occleshaw on, 257–258
    Pedro Silva Dias on, 198–199
    Shai-Lee Spiegelman on, 229
Finland, Anna-Maija Karjalainen's efforts in,
    see Karjalainen, Anna-Maija
"Firefighting" teams, 165
Five whys method, 103
Flagship meetings, 166
Following through, 21
Fonseca, Graça, 195, 200
Foreshew-Cain, Stephen, 181, 186
Forums, idea exchange in, 101
Four-quadrant model for transformation, of Joe
    McDonagh, 57–58
Fox, Martha Lane, 175
Frelle-Petersen, Lars, 147, 148–158
    background of, 148–151
    on context of DIGST job, 150–152
    digital government leadership recommenda-
        tions from, 158
    leadership style and practices of, 155–156
    on starting the DIGST job, 153–154
    on successes/failures in digital government,
        149–150, 156–157
    on transition from DIGST, 157–158
    vision and strategy of, 152, 154
Fun, at work, 39
Funding, 119, 238, 256. See also Budget

Future Accelerator, of Dubai, 8
Future State Modernization Committee, of Ontario, 118
FWD50 conference, 21

Galmiel, Gita, 224
An Garda Síochána, Ireland, 51
GCIO, see Government chief information officer
GDS, see Government Digital Service, UK
Gentiloni, Paolo, 100
GitHub, 88, 101, 102
GOB.MX platform, of Mexico, 264, 266–272, 274–276
Google, Inc., 7, 74, 272
gov.br platform, of Brazil, 163–164, 169, 170
Governance model and arrangements for digital
        government coordination, 18-20, 29, 36, 50, 138,
        140, 167, 179, 209–211, 216, 238, 251, 255, 257,
        265, 269. See also Institutional setting, for digital
        government
Government-as-a-platform, 18, 177
Government chief information officer (GCIO):
    rebuilding setup of, 23–24
    recommendations for success in role of, 29, 43
Government Digital Service (GDS), UK, 25–26, 48, 111,
        121n3, 175–187, 207
Government digital strategy, for New Zealand,
        250–252, 257
Government services, digitalization of:
    in Argentina, 87
    in Brazil, 162–164
    in Denmark, 150–152
    in Israel, 222
    in Mexico, 264, 269, 270
    in Mongolia, 62–65
    in New Zealand, 251
    in Rwanda, 132
Government Services Ministry, Australia, 212
Government Technology Agency of Singapore
        (GovTech), 73–82
gov.ie platform, of Ireland, 56
GovTech (Government Technology Agency of Singa-
        pore), 73–82
GovTech Maturity Index, of World Bank, 169
Govtech program, of Portugal, 195
GOV.UK platform, 175, 177–179, 181, 183
Greenway, Andrew, 179
gub.uy platform, of Uruguay, 142
Guedes, Paulo, 169

Hands-on management style, 195–196
Happiness Agenda, of Dubai, 3–4, 7–8, 10
Hard work, 64, 69, 284
Hartley, Hillary, 109, 110–121
    background of, 110–112
    on context of CDDO job, 111–113
    digital government leadership recommendations
        from, 120–121
    leadership style and practices of, 116–118
    on starting the CDDO job, 114
    on successes/failures as CDDO, 118–119
    on transition from CDDO, 119–120
    vision and strategy of, 112–115

Health Service Executive, Ireland, 51
Helping others, 53–54
Her Majesty's Treasury department, UK, 177, 178, 185
Heywood, Jeremy, 175
Hillsborough disaster, 176, 178, 187n4
Hiring. *See also* Team building
  Daniel Abadie on, 90
  Aisha Bin Bishr on, 10
  Randall Brugeaud on, 212–213
  Cheow Hoe Chan on, 79
  Lars Frelle-Petersen on, 155–156
  Hillary Hartley on, 118
  Anna-Maija Karjalainen on, 40
  Taavi Kotka on, 240
  Yolanda Martínez on, 271–272
  Luis Felipe Monteiro on, 166
  Diego Piacentini on, 101–103
  Pedro Silva Dias on, 197
Holocracy model, 12, 14n2
Housing rates rebate system, of New Zealand, 257–258
Hughes, Janet, 184
Hürelsüh, Uhnaagijn, 61
Hybrid cloud data center, of Ireland, 52

see IBM, 137
ICT Authority, Israel, 224
ICT Sector Strategic Plan, of Rwanda, 126
IDA, *see* Infocomm Development Authority), Singapore
IDB, *see* Inter-American Development Bank
Identification documents, digital, 163, 164, 169, 199
Incentives, 239, 240
Incubation approach, 138, 140
Inflection points, managing through, 76
Infocomm Development Authority (IDA), Singapore, 73, 74
Information management law, of Finland, 36–37
Information Society and e-Government Agency
  (AGESIC), Uruguay, 137–144, 145n1
Infrastructure:
  building, 77, 101, 153
  increasing use of, 192
Infrastructure-as-a-service model, 77, 249
Innovation, 77, 105, 157, 201, 235–236
Institutional setting, for digital government. *See also*
  Governance model and arrangements for digital
  government coordination
  in Australia, 212
  in Estonia, 236–237
  in Finland, 34
  in Italy, 100
  in Mexico, 264–265
  in New Zealand, 247–248
  in Rwanda, 125
Inter-agency cooperation. *See also* Networks and net-
  working; Stakeholder management
  Daniel Abadie on, 92–93
  Bolor-Erdene Battsengel on, 63, 64
  Aisha Bin Bishr on, 4, 5, 9
  Randall Brugeaud on, 209–211, 216
  José Clastornik on, 138–139
  Lars Frelle-Petersen on, 152

  Anna-Maija Karjalainen on, 36–37
  Taavi Kotka on, 238–239
  Barry Lowry on, 52–54
  Yolanda Martínez on, 264, 267–268
  Luis Felipe Monteiro on, 165
  Tim Occleshaw on, 248–252, 254, 255
  Pedro Silva Dias on, 192, 194, 195, 199
  Shai-Lee Spiegelman on, 224–225
Inter-American Development Bank (IDB), 139, 142,
  144, 145n2, 170, 263
Interministerial Commission for the Development of
  eGovernment (CIDGE), Mexico, 269
International Civil Service Effectiveness Index, 61
International Monetary Fund, 191
Interoperability enforcement, 139
Invoicing, digital, of Denmark, 150
Ireland, Barry Lowry's efforts in, *see* Lowry, Barry
Irembo portal, of Rwanda, 126
Israel, 249. *See also* Spiegelman, Shai-Lee
Israeli National Digital Initiative, *see* Digital Israel
Italy, Diego Piacentini's efforts in, *see* Piacentini, Diego

Johnston, Jenny, 48

Kagame, Paul, 125
Kanban boards, 39
Karjalainen, Anna-Maija, *31*, 32–43
  background of, 32–34
  on context of GCIO job, 33–35
  digital government leadership recommendations
    from, 42–43
  leadership style and practices of, 38–40
  on starting the GCIO job, 37–38
  on successes/failures as GCIO, 41
  on transition from GCIO, 41–42
  vision and strategy of, 33, 35–37
Katribas, Yossi, 221
Kelly, Stephen, 181
Key performance indicators (KPIs), 3, 4, 142, 239, 241,
  266, 270, 274
Kotka, Taavi, *233*, 234–244
  background of, 234–236
  on context of GCIO job, 236
  digital government leadership recommendations
    from, 243–244
  leadership style and practices of, 238–241
  on starting the GCIO job, 237–238
  on successes/failures as GCIO, 241–242
  on transition from GCIO role, 242–243
  vision and strategy of, 236–238
KPIs, *see* Key performance indicators

Laboratory of Social Innovation in Digital Government
  (LAB), Uruguay, 140
Lagunes, Alejandra, 263, 272, 274, 275
Lasting change, creating, 283–284. *See also* Succession
  planning; Transitions, preparing for and making
  Daniel Abadie on, 94
  Bolor-Erdene Battsengel on, 67–69
  Alex Benay on, 28–29

Aisha Bin Bishr on, 13
Mike Bracken on, 185
Cheow Hoe Chan on, 81
José Clastornik on, 143–144
Lars Frelle-Petersen on, 157–158
Hillary Hartley on, 120
Anna-Maija Karjalainen on, 42
Taavi Kotka on, 243
Barry Lowry on, 57
Yolanda Martínez on, 276
Luis Felipe Monteiro on, 170
Innocent Bagamba Muhizi on, 132
Tim Occleshaw on, 259
Diego Piacentini on, 107
Pedro Silva Dias on, 201
Shai-Lee Spiegelman on, 229–230
Leadership style and practices. *See also* Digital
    government leadership
    of Daniel Abadie, 89–93
    of Bolor-Erdene Battsengel, 65–67
    of Alex Benay, 22, 24–26
    of Aisha Bin Bishr, 9–12
    of Mike Bracken, 181–184
    of Randall Brugeaud, 210–214
    of Cheow Hoe Chan, 76–80
    of José Clastornik, 141–142
    of Lars Frelle-Petersen, 155–156
    of Hillary Hartley, 116–118
    increasing effectiveness of, 285
    of Anna-Maija Karjalainen, 38–40
    of Taavi Kotka, 238–241
    of Barry Lowry, 52–54
    of Yolanda Martínez, 267–269, 271–275
    of Luis Felipe Monteiro, 165–168
    of Innocent Bagamba Muhizi, 127–131
    of Tim Occleshaw, 253–256
    of Diego Piacentini, 102–105
    of Pedro Silva Dias, 193, 195–198
    of Shai-Lee Spiegelman, 224–228
Lean methodology, 197
Learning, 80–81, 129, 193
Lee Hsien Loong, 76
Legal risk, 276–277
Legislation, 36–37, 65, 152
Leitão Amaro, António, 199
Leitão Marques, Maria Manuel, 195, 200, 202n1
Licensing systems, 81, 224
Listening, 29, 273
Locker, Harel, 221
Loosemore, Tom, 111, 175, 178, 180–182
Lowry, Barry, *45*, 46–58
    background of, 46–48
    on context of GCIO job, 48, 49
    digital government leadership recommendations
        from, 57–58
    leadership style and practices of, 52–54
    on starting the GCIO job, 49–50
    on successes/failures as GCIO, 54–55
    on transition from GCIO, 55–57
    vision and strategy of, 48–52

McCluggage, Bill, 47
McDonagh, Joe, 49, 57
MacDonald, Colin, 247–248, 255–257
McGrath, Michael, 47, 48
McGregor Theory X and Theory Y approach, 53, 57
Macri, Mauricio, 85, 87, 88, 92, 93
Madia, Marianna, 100
Maersk, 154
"Managed decline" policy, 182, 187
Management routines:of Aisha Bin Bishr, 11–12
    of Randall Brugeaud, 213–214
    of Cheow Hoe Chan, 77–78
    of José Clastornik, 142
    of Hillary Hartley, 117
    of Anna-Maija Karjalainen, 38
    of Taavi Kotka, 241
    of Barry Lowry, 58
    of Yolanda Martínez, 273–274
    of Luis Felipe Monteiro, 166–167
    of Innocent Bagamba Muhizi, 129
    of Diego Piacentini, 104
    of Pedro Silva Dias, 193, 198
    of Shai-Lee Spiegelman, 228
Managing by example, 197
Managing for delivery, 279–280
Managing up:
    Alex Benay on, 27
    Randall Brugeaud on, 211–212
    Cheow Hoe Chan, 76
    Yolanda Martínez on, 274
    Shai-Lee Spiegelman on, 228
Mandatory digitalization of services, of Denmark
    150–154, 237, 249
Martínez, Yolanda, *261*, 262–278
    background of, 262–263
    on context of digital transformation jobs, 264–265
    digital government leadership recommendations
        from, 277–278
    leadership style and practices of, 267–269, 271–275
    on starting NDP for Mexico, 266
    on successes/failures in digital transformation
        efforts, 274–275
    on transitions between digital transformation roles,
        265–266, 275–277
    vision and strategy of, 263–267, 269–271
Maude, Francis, 175, 176, 179–181, 183–185
Maxwell, Liam, 48, 180, 181, 249, 260n1
Medium, recruiting with, 102
Mental health, for leaders, 27–28
Metrics, developing, 4
Mexico, Yolanda Martínez's efforts in, *see* Mar-
    tínez, Yolanda
Microsoft, 221, 254
Mind mapping, 237
Ministerial digital group, of New Zealand, 257
Ministry of Communication and Transport, Mexico, 264
Ministry of Communications, Brazil, 161
Ministry of Culture, Estonia, 238
Ministry of Defence, United Kingdom, 183
Ministry of Digital Development, Mongolia, 63

Ministry of Economic Affairs and Communications, Estonia, 235–244
Ministry of Economy, Brazil, 161
Ministry of Finance, Denmark, 149–152, 155, 156
Ministry of Finance, Estonia, 239
Ministry of Finance, Finland, 33–43
Ministry of Finance, Italy, 105
Ministry of Finance, Mexico, 266–268
Ministry of Finance, Rwanda, 126
Ministry of Finance, Singapore, 79
Ministry of Government and Consumer Services, Ontario, 113
Ministry of Health, Israel, 222
Ministry of Health, Italy, 107
Ministry of ICT and Innovation, Rwanda, 126
Ministry of Interior, Finland, 34
Ministry of Labour, United Arab Emirates, 2
Ministry of Planning and Budget, Brazil, 161
Ministry of Public Affairs, Mexico, 264, 271
Ministry of Social Equality, Israel, 224
Mission, 284–285
    Bolor-Erdene Battsengel on, 63–64
    Alex Benay on, 18
    Randall Brugeaud on, 206–207, 209
    Cheow Hoe Chan on, 74
    José Clastornik on, 138
    Lars Frelle-Petersen on, 157
    Hillary Hartley on, 112
    Yolanda Martínez on, 263–264
    Innocent Bagamba Muhizi on, 126
    Diego Piacentini on, 99
Modernization, digitalization as tool for, 151–152, 194
Mongolia, Bolor-Erdene Battsengel's efforts in, see Battsengel, Bolor-Erdene
Monteiro, Luis Felipe, 159, 160–171
    background of, 160–161
    on context of secretary job, 162
    digital government leadership recommendations from, 170
    leadership style and practices of, 165–168
    on starting the secretary job, 164–165
    on successes/failures as secretary, 168–169
    on transition from secretary role, 169–170
    vision and strategy of, 162–165
Motivating others:
    Daniel Abadie on, 90–91
    Taavi Kotka on, 239–240, 243
    Yolanda Martínez on, 271
Muhizi, Innocent Bagamba, 123, 124–133
    background of, 124–125
    on context of RISA job, 126
    digital government leadership recommendations from, 133
    leadership style and practices of, 127–131
    on starting the RISA job, 127
    on successes/failures with RISA, 131–132
    on transition from RISA, 132–133
    vision and strategy of, 125–127, 131
MyArgentina platform, of Argentina 85, 87–90, 93, 94
MyGovID, of Ireland, 51, 55–57

myGov platform, of Australia, 209, 214, 215, 217n1
myResponder, of Singapore, 75
mySociety, 175, 178, 187n1

NASA, 106
National Development Plan, of Mexico, 266, 268
National digital strategy, of Israel, 222–223, 228
National Digital Strategy, of Mexico, 265–268
National Digital Strategy Coordination (NDSC) Office, 263–278
National Health Service (NHS), 177
National Information Communication Infrastructure (NICI), of Rwanda, 126
National resident population register, of Italy, 101
NDSC, see National Digital Strategy Coordination) Office
Neal, Olivia, 25–26
Negotiation, 69, 104
Nem ID (EasyID), of Denmark, 156
NemKonto (EasyAccount), of Denmark, 149
Network of Electronic Government Leaders of Latin America and the Caribbean (RedGEALC), 277
Networks and networking, 282. See also Inter-agency cooperation; Stakeholder management
    Randall Brugeaud on, 216
    Anna-Maija Karjalainen on, 37–38, 41, 43
    Pedro Silva Dias on, 193
New Zealand, 51. See also Occleshaw, Tim
NHS (National Health Service), UK 177
NICI (National Information Communication Infrastructure), Rwanda, 126
NIC Inc., 111
Nortal, 235
Northern Ireland Civil Service, 47
"No," saying, to projects, 86, 130

Obama, Barack, 111
Objectives:
    Bolor-Erdene Battsengel on, 63–64, 66
    Alex Benay on, 19–20
    Mike Bracken on, 177–178
    Randall Brugeaud on, 209
    Lars Frelle-Petersen on, 152, 158
    Hillary Hartley on, 113–114
    Anna-Maija Karjalainen on, 35
    Taavi Kotka on, 237
    Barry Lowry on, 48–50
    Innocent Bagamba Muhizi on, 126–127
    Pedro Silva Dias on, 192–193
    Shai-Lee Spiegelman on, 222
Occleshaw, Tim, 245, 246–260
    background of, 246–247
    on context of GDCO job, 247–248
    digital government leadership recommendations from, 259–260
    leadership style and practices of, 253–256
    on starting the GDCO job, 249–250
    on successes/failures as GDCO, 257–258
    on transition from GDCO role, 258–259
    vision and strategy of, 248–253

ODS, *see* Ontario Digital Service)
OECD, *see* Organisation of Economic Co-operation and Development
Office of Chief Digital and Data Officer, Ontario, 111–121
Office of Chief Information Officer of Canada, 17–29
Office of Government Chief Information Officer, Singapore, 74
Office of Government Commissioner for Digital Transformation, Italy, 99–108
Office of Secretary for IT and Communication, Brazil, 161
Office of the Government Chief Information Officer, Ireland, 47–58
Office of the President of the Republic of Rwanda, 125
Office of Undersecretary of Digital Government of Argentina, 85–96
Off-the-shelf solutions, using, 256
OGCIO, *see* Office of the Government Chief Information Officer, Ireland
OGP (Open Government Partnership) action plan, 270
Oligopoly, 181
Onboarding, 128–129
"Once only" principle, 50, 55, 58n1, 87
Ontario, Hillary Hartley's efforts in, *see* Hartley, Hillary
ontario.ca platform, of Ontario, 112–114
Ontario Digital Service (ODS), 111–121
Ontario Onward Acceleration Fund, 118, 119
Ontario Student Assistance Program calculator, 114
Open, working in the:
    Alex Benay on, 24
    Mike Bracken on, 181
    Hillary Hartley on, 117, 119
    Yolanda Martínez on, 267, 273
    Innocent Bagamba Muhizi, 129
Open-door policy, 24, 38, 89
Open government:
    Alex Benay on, 22, 24
    Yolanda Martínez on, 270, 273
Open Government Partnership (OGP) action plan, 270
Open-mindedness, 11, 13–14, 170
Open-source code, 119
Operational models, changing, 210
Organisation of Economic Co-operation and Development (OECD), 163, 165, 170, 242
Outsourcing, 73–74, 142, 180, 226
Oy Suomi Ab, 35, 43n4
Oyun-Erdene, Luvsannamsrain, 61–64

Paes de Andrade, Caio, 169
PagoPA platform, of Italy, 101
Parallel teams, 164
Parliament, Danish, 149, 154
Parliament, UK, 176, 178, 180, 181, 185–186
Participative Budgets program, of Portugal, 195
Partnerships, 76, 133, 200. *See also* Private sector, partnerships with
Passos Coelho, Pedro, 191, 192
Peer-to-peer learning, xv
Peña Nieto, Enrique, 263, 267, 270, 274

Phoenix system, of Canada, 17, 18, 22–23, 26, 27
Piacentini, Diego, 97, 98–108
    background of, 98–99
    on context of Commissioner job, 99–100
    digital government leadership recommendations from, 108
    leadership style and practices of, 102–105
    on starting the Government Commissioner job, 101–102
    on successes/failures as Commissioner, 105–108
    on transition from Commissioner, 106–108
    vision and strategy of, 98, 101, 102
Pilot programs, 127–128, 140, 164
Pink, Daniel, 239
Platform-as-a-service model, 77, 80, 81
PoC (proof-of-concept) strategy, 127–128
Poiares Maduro, Miguel, 191, 199
Policymaking, 25, 258–259
Political support, 281–282
    Daniel Abadie on, 92
    Bolor-Erdene Battsengel on, 62
    Alex Benay on, 20–21
    Aisha Bin Bishr on, 6–7
    Mike Bracken on, 179, 183–184
    Randall Brugeaud on, 207, 210, 215
    Cheow Hoe Chan on, 76
    José Clastornik on, 144
    Lars Frelle-Petersen on, 154, 157
    Hillary Hartley on, 115
    Anna-Maija Karjalainen on, 37
    Taavi Kotka on, 235, 239
    Barry Lowry on, 52
    Luis Felipe Monteiro on, 162
    Diego Piacentini on, 105
    Pedro Silva Dias on, 195
    Shai-Lee Spiegelman on, 224
Poncho design system, of Argentina, 92
Portugal, 163. *See also* Silva Dias, Pedro
PPARS, of Ireland, 49
Presentations, team, 182–183
Presidential Innovation Fellowship, of US, 111, 121n1
Priority setting:
    Daniel Abadie on, 86
    Bolor-Erdene Battsengel on, 64
    Mike Bracken on, 178–180
    Randall Brugeaud on, 209–210
    Cheow Hoe Chan on, 77
    José Clastornik on, 141
    Lars Frelle-Petersen on, 153, 156
    Hillary Hartley on, 114
    Anna-Maija Karjalainen on, 37, 39
    Taavi Kotka on, 237–238, 240, 241
    Barry Lowry on, 51
    Yolanda Martínez on, 267, 270
    Luis Felipe Monteiro on, 164–165
    Innocent Bagamba Muhizi on, 127
    Diego Piacentini on, 101–102
    Pedro Silva Dias on, 194–195

Private sector:
  digital gap between public and, 222
  digital transformation in, xv, xvi, 5, 99–100
  motivations in, 243
  partnerships with, 8, 131–133, 149, 152, 157, 195
Process building, 102
Procurement, 22–23, 106, 119
Professional certificates, standardization of, of
    Mexico, 274, 275
Project management, 102
Proof-of-concept (PoC) strategy, 127–128
Public Digital, 111–112, 120, 121n3, 186
Public Services Card, of Ireland, 55
Purpose, *see* Mission
Python Software Foundation, 103

Rahe, Aet, 240–242
Reach program, of Ireland, 49
Read, Tom, 184
RealMe system, of New Zealand, 249
Recognition, 242–243, 269
Recruitment, *see* Talent, attracting
RedGEALC (Network of Electronic Government
    Leaders of Latin America and the Caribbean), 277
Reference design and governance, 49
Reichelt, Leisa, 182
Relationship management:
  with new subordinates, 49
  with political masters, 67, 211–212
    (*See also* Managing up)
Renzi, Matteo, 99, 100
Resistance to change, 283
  Mike Bracken on, 175, 180, 183, 185
  Cheow Hoe Chan on, 76
  Lars Frelle-Petersen on, 153, 154
  Hillary Hartley on, 115
Resourcefulness, 277
Results-driven approach, 168
RISA, *see* Rwanda Information Society Authority)
Robertson, Grant, 249
Role clarification, 253
Rwanda, Innocent Bagamba Muhizi's efforts in,
    see Muhizi, Innocent Bagamba
Rwanda Information Society Authority (RISA),
    125–133

SADe program, of Finland, 34
SAP, 161
Sargeant, Richard, 179
Schindel, Yair, 221
Scorza, Guido, 100
SDO, *see* Smart Dubai Office
Secretariat of Human Resources, Brazil, 167
Secretariat of Management, Brazil, 167
Secretaries Digital Committee, Australia, 211
Sector meetings, 130
Self-autonomy, 273
Servant leadership, 116
Service ownership, 241–242
Settle, Kathy, 175, 183

Shetler, Paul, 207–208
Sikkut, Siim, 239
Silos, breaking down:
  Alex Benay on, 23
  Mike Bracken, 183
  Randall Brugeaud on, 216
  Taavi Kotka on, 237, 242
  Pedro Silva Dias on, 192, 197–198
Silva, Rohan, 175
Silva Dias, Pedro, *189*, 190–202
  background of, 190–191
  on context of AMA job, 191, 192
  digital government leadership recommenda-
    tions from, 201
  leadership style and practices of, 193, 195–198
  on starting the AMA job, 194–195
  on successes/failures with AMA, 198–200
  on transition from AMA, 200–201
  vision and strategy of, 191–195
Simpler, Faster, Better Services Act, of Ontario,
    115, 118
Simplex program, of Portugal, 194, 195, 200
Simplified Trade System Implementation Taskforce,
    Australia, 215
Singapore, 215. *See also* Chan, Cheow Hoe
Singapore Civil Defence Force, 75
Single-domain approach, 87–88
Singleton, Tony, 175
SingPass, of Singapore, 77
Six Sigma methodology, 197
Skip meetings, 214
Skunkworks projects, 21, 23–25
Skylon, 187n7
Slater, Gavin, 206, 208
Small- and middle-sized enterprises (SMEs), digitaliza-
    tion for, in Israel, 221, 222
Smart cities, 224
Smart City Expo, 9
Smart Dubai Office (SDO), 2–13
Smart Nation and Digital Government Office
    (SNDGO), 73–74
Smart Rwanda Masterplan, 126
SMEs (small- and middle-sized enterprises), digitaliza-
    tion for, in Israel, 221, 222
Smyth, Ossian, 48
SNDGO, *see* Smart Nation and Digital Govern-
    ment Office)
Social capital, 133
South Korea, 163
Spiegelman, Shai-Lee, *219*, 220–231
  background of, 220–221
  on context of Digital Israel job, 221, 222
  digital government leadership recommendations
    from, 230–231
  leadership style and practices of, 224–228
  on starting the Digital Israel job, 223–224
  on successes/failures with Digital Israel,
    228–229
  on transition from Digital Israel, 229–230
  vision and strategy of, 221–224

Spotify, 118
Stakeholder management, 282. *See also* Inter-agency
    cooperation; Networks and networking
    Alex Benay on, 26
    Randall Brugeaud on, 210–211
    Barry Lowry on, 54
    Yolanda Martínez on, 268–269
    Luis Felipe Monteiro on, 167
    Innocent Bagamba Muhizi on, 127–128, 130
    Tim Occleshaw on, 255
    Diego Piacentini on, 101–102, 105
Standard setting, 68, 249
Stand-up meetings, 167, 213
State Treasury of Finland, 33–34, 43
Steinberg, Tom, 175
Strategy adjustments:
    Aisha Bin Bishr on, 8–9
    Cheow Hoe Chan on, 78
    Lars Frelle-Petersen on, 157
    Barry Lowry on, 51–52
    Tim Occleshaw on, 252
Strategy for a Digital Public Sector, of New
    Zealand, 252
"The Strategy is Delivery", concept and slogan, 117,
    165, 180, 182,
Strategy setting, 280–281
    Daniel Abadie on, 85–89
    Bolor-Erdene Battsengel on, 62–65
    Alex Benay on, 18–25
    Aisha Bin Bishr on, 3–4, 6–8
    Mike Bracken on, 176–181
    Randall Brugeaud on, 206–211, 214–215
    Cheow Hoe Chan on, 74–78
    José Clastornik on, 138–141
    Lars Frelle-Petersen on, 152, 154
    Hillary Hartley on, 112–115
    Anna-Maija Karjalainen on, 33, 35–37
    Taavi Kotka on, 236–238
    Barry Lowry on, 48–52
    Yolanda Martínez on, 263–267, 269–271
    Luis Felipe Monteiro on, 162–165
    Innocent Bagamba Muhizi on, 125–127, 131
    Tim Occleshaw on, 248–253
    Diego Piacentini on, 101, 102
    Pedro Silva Dias on, 191–195
    Shai-Lee Spiegelman on, 221–224
Succession planning, 106–107, 229–230, 243.
    See also Lasting change, creating; Transitions,
    preparing for and making
suomi.fi services, of Finland, 35, 37
Suppliers, 119, 180–181, 254
Sustainability, 57

Talent, attracting:
    Daniel Abadie on, 90
    Bolor-Erdene Battsengel on, 65–66
    Aisha Bin Bishr on, 9–10
    Mike Bracken on, 182
    José Clastornik on, 142
    Hillary Hartley on, 117–118

    Barry Lowry on, 53
    Yolanda Martínez on, 275
    Luis Felipe Monteiro on, 166
    Innocent Bagamba Muhizi on, 128
    Tim Occleshaw on, 254
    Pedro Silva Dias on, 196–197
Talent Cloud, of Canada, 21, 24
Talent management, *see* Talent, attracting; also Team
    management
Tallinn University of Technology (TalTech), 239
Tank method, 239
Tax and Customs Board, Estonia, 242
Team, restructuring of, 249–250
Team building:
    Daniel Abadie on, 89–90
    Bolor-Erdene Battsengel on, 65–66
    Alex Benay on, 25–26
    Mike Bracken on, 181
    Randall Brugeaud on, 212
    Cheow Hoe Chan on, 75, 78–79, 81
    José Clastornik on, 141–142
    Lars Frelle-Petersen on, 153, 155
    Hillary Hartley on, 114, 116
    Anna-Maija Karjalainen on, 40
    Taavi Kotka on, 237, 240
    Barry Lowry on, 52–53
    Yolanda Martínez on, 271, 272
    Luis Felipe Monteiro on, 165–166
    Innocent Bagamba Muhizi on, 127, 128
    Tim Occleshaw on, 248, 253–254
    Diego Piacentini on, 102–103
    Pedro Silva Dias on, 191
    Shai-Lee Spiegelman on, 226
Team Digitale, Italy, 102, 106
Team management, 283. *See also* Management
    routines
    Daniel Abadie on, 88, 89
    Bolor-Erdene Battsengel on, 66–67
    Aisha Bin Bishr on, 11
    Mike Bracken on, 186
    Anna-Maija Karjalainen on, 38–40
    Barry Lowry on, 53–54
    Pedro Silva Dias on, 195–196
Team presentations, 182–183
Technology, promoting, 65
Technology leadership groups, UK, 180
Tel Aviv, Israel, 226
Temer, Michel, 162
Terrett, Ben, 179, 182
Theory X and Theory Y approach, 53, 57
Three-step approach to agenda setting, 141
Time frames, project:
    Bolor-Erdene Battsengel on, 64
    Cheow Hoe Chan on, 75–76
    José Clastornik on, 140
    Barry Lowry on, 50
    Luis Felipe Monteiro on, 163
    Tim Occleshaw on, 250
    Pedro Silva Dias on, 194
Toronto, Canada, 117–118

Transitions, preparing for and making. *See also* Lasting change, creating; Succession planning
  Daniel Abadie on, 86, 93–95
  Bolor-Erdene Battsengel on, 68–69
  Alex Benay on, 28–29
  Aisha Bin Bishr on, 12–13
  Mike Bracken on, 185–186
  Randall Brugeaud on, 215–216
  Cheow Hoe Chan on, 81
  José Clastornik on, 143–144
  Lars Frelle-Petersen on, 157–158
  Hillary Hartley on, 119–120
  Anna-Maija Karjalainen on, 41–42
  Taavi Kotka on, 242–243
  Barry Lowry on, 55–57
  Yolanda Martínez on, 265–266, 275–277
  Luis Felipe Monteiro on, 169–170
  Innocent Bagamba Muhizi on, 132–133
  Tim Occleshaw on, 258–259
  Diego Piacentini on, 106–108
  Pedro Silva Dias on, 200–201
  Shai-Lee Spiegelman on, 229–230
Transparency, 10–11, 20, 22, 24
Treasury, New Zealand, 256
Treasury Board, Ontario, 113
Treasury Board of Canada Secretariat, 17, 19, 20, 25
Tribe model management, 12, 14n2
Trust building:
  Daniel Abadie on, 90, 92
  Alex Benay on, 23
  Aisha Bin Bishr on, 10–11
  Lars Frelle-Petersen on, 156
  Hillary Harley on, 115
  Anna-Maija Karjalainen, 33, 36, 41
  Barry Lowry on, 53
  Luis Felipe Monteiro on, 165, 168
  Diego Piacentini on, 105
Turnbull, Malcolm, 207

United Arab Emirates (UAE), Aisha Bin Bishr's efforts in, *see* Bin Bishr, Aisha
United Kingdom:
  Mike Bracken's efforts in (*see* Bracken, Mike)
  digital service standard in, 256
  Government Digital Service of, 25–26, 48, 111, 121n3, 174–187, 207
  international partnerships between Brazil and, 170
  model digital government of, 163, 249
US Digital Service, 111
University of Oxford, 61

Unpopular decisions, making, 19–20
Uruguay, 163. *See also* Clastornik, José
User-focused approach. *See also* Citizen-first approach; Customer-focused approach
  in Brazil, 167
  in Canada, 114, 117
  in New Zealand, 258–259
  in United Kingdom, 180
UX design, 267, 278

Valtori, Finland, 34
Value-added tax (VAT) reform, of Estonia, 237, 238, 242
Values of team:
  Aisha Bin Bishr on, 10–12
  Randall Brugeaud on, 213
  Anna-Maija Karjalainen on, 39
  Barry Lowry on, 53–54
  Diego Piacentini on, 103–104
Vázquez, Tabaré, 137, 143
Vendor of record mechanism, of Ontario, 119
Veto power, 20–21, 50, 176
Vielma, Hector, 263
Virtual assistants, 86, 94–95, 259
Vision:
  Bolor-Erdene Battsengel on, 63
  Cheow Hoe Chan on, 74–75
  José Clastornik on, 142
  for digital government excellence, 281, 284–285
  Luis Felipe Monteiro on, 162–163
  Innocent Bagamba Muhizi on, 125, 130
  Tim Occleshaw on, 253, 254, 260
  Pedro Silva Dias on, 192
Vision 2020 plan, of Rwanda, 125–126

Waterfall model, 154, 175
Watmore, Ian, 175
Weekly business reviews, 104
Whitespace Fund, of Singapore 79
Winddown Fridays, 23
Work-life balance, 29, 271
Workshops, 36–37
World Bank, 61, 144, 169, 170
World Summit on the Information Society (WSIS), 137

X-Road platform, 34–36, 40, 43n3, 236, 244n2

Zapopan, Mexico, 263, 265–266
Zeberg, Rikke, 155
Zipline, 131